Family and Feuding at the Court of James I

Family and Feuding at the Court of James I

The Lake and Cecil Scandals

JOHANNA LUTHMAN

OXFORD
UNIVERSITY PRESS

OXFORD
UNIVERSITY PRESS

Great Clarendon Street, Oxford, OX2 6DP,
United Kingdom

Oxford University Press is a department of the University of Oxford.
It furthers the University's objective of excellence in research, scholarship,
and education by publishing worldwide. Oxford is a registered trade mark of
Oxford University Press in the UK and in certain other countries

Published in the United States of America by Oxford University Press
198 Madison Avenue, New York, NY 10016, United States of America

British Library Cataloguing in Publication Data
Data available

Library of Congress Control Number: 2023942277

ISBN 978-0-19-286578-6

DOI: 10.1093/oso/9780192865786.001.0001

Printed and bound in the UK by
Clays Ltd, Elcograf S.p.A.

To my parents, Jan and Margaretha Luthman, for instilling in me a love of books, learning, and dogs.

Acknowledgments

I completed this book despite the letter “H” trying to trip me up in the homestretch. For months, the “H” key on my laptop keyboard was giving me trouble: sticking, popping off, and getting lost. You do not realize how much you need the letter H until it becomes a struggle to produce it. After some months of bureaucratic delays over the summer, I received a new keyboard, triumphantly writing unlimited amounts of Hs. The triumph was short lived. Soon, the H on the new keyboard came loose again, until it finally broke and fell off altogether, impossible to fix. It was as if my laptop was bewitched, or perhaps just laughing at me. Determined to continue, I struggled on with just the little rubber stump underneath the key, until I finally received a brand-new laptop a few weeks before I turned in the manuscript. Whenever I look at this book in the future, I will forever feel that little rubber stump under my right index finger.

Unlike the troublesome H, others have been much more supportive. I have received assistance from my home institution, the University of North Georgia, in various ways. The UNG Presidential Semester Award allowed me one semester off from my teaching duties and provided funds for digital images of archival sources, books, and rights to publish images from the National Portrait Gallery. The Department of History, Anthropology, and Philosophy at UNG has also assisted with a timely course release, funds for images of archival sources and reproduction rights for images from British Museum and Royal Institute of British Architecture.

Many people have read my work and provided invaluable feedback. My colleagues in the Works in Progress writing group have provided helpful comments on a couple of particularly thorny chapters. I want to thank Thomas Greene especially for helping me with Latin translations. Audiences at several conferences over the years have asked pertinent questions and given helpful comments, allowing me to seek new angles and clarifying points. The anonymous readers of the book proposal, sample chapters, and the full manuscript provided insightful and expert comments, which helped me improve and clarify my arguments.

Thanks also to Jon Culverson, curator at Burghley House, for permission to include the portrait of what is believed to be little Georgi-Anna Cecil, and to the Church Monument Society and Michael Statham for the pictures of the tomb of Anne Lake.

The expert and professional editors at Oxford University Press make for a smooth publishing process and a better book. Any errors that remain are my own, of course.

My husband Marko Maunula—an accomplished historian, bright intellectual, brilliant cook, sharp-eyed editor, and irreplaceable companion—supports me in more ways than I can enumerate here. He reads everything I write and helps me improve it. He is my everything.

Contents

List of Illustrations

List of Abbreviations

APC	*Acts of the Privy Council*
BL	British Library
C	Court of Chancery
CSP	*Calendar of State Papers*
Downshire	Historical Manuscript Commission. Report on the manuscripts of the Marquess of Downshire
HPO	*History of Parliament Online*
ODNB	*Oxford Dictionary of National Biography*
PROB	Probate
SP	State Papers
STAC	Court of Star Chamber

Note on Dates and Spelling

The English used the Julian calendar (Old Style) until 1752. This calendar counted the new calendar year from March 25. Many other parts of Europe adopted the Gregorian calendar (New Style) in 1582, having January 1 as the first date of the new year. Corrections in the Gregorian calendar also led to a ten-day difference in dates between England and most continental Catholic countries. In this book, I refer to sources based on the New Style listing of years (new year begins on January 1), but use the original day and month as written in the source.

When quoting sources, I have mostly retained the original spelling. For greater ease of reading, I have changed the use of "u" for "v" when needed, and in some cases "i" for "j." In addition, seventeenth-century writers did not use standardized punctuation, so I have added commas and periods when warranted.

List of Persons

Thomas Cecil, earl of Exeter (1542–1623). The elderly patriarch of the Cecil family after the death of his half-brother Robert Cecil, earl of Salisbury. When his first wife died, he married Frances Brydges Smith, almost forty years his junior. His new wife became the target of Ladies Lake and Roos, who accused the countess of adultery with Lord Roos and attempting to poison Lady Roos. Exeter and his wife sued the Lakes and Lady Roos for slander in the Court of Star Chamber.

Frances Brydges Smith Cecil, countess of Exeter (1580–1663). After her first husband Sir Thomas Smith died in 1609, the beautiful twenty-nine-year-old widow remarried the elderly Thomas Cecil, earl of Exeter. She became the target of Lady Roos's accusations that she had an adulterous affair with the earl's grandson, Lord Roos, and that she had also tried to kill Lady Roos by poisoning her. She denied the charges and informed the king, who began investigations into the matter.

William Cecil, 2nd Lord Burghley (1566–1640). Eldest son of Thomas Cecil, earl of Exeter, from his first marriage. He was fourteen years older than his stepmother, the second countess of Exeter. His son, William Cecil, Lord Roos, married Sir Thomas Lake's daughter Anne in 1616, and when this marriage turned sour, Burghley was pulled into the developing feud between his son's in-laws and his father and stepmother, the earl and countess of Exeter.

William Cecil, Lord Roos (1591–1618). (Sometimes spelled Ros or Rosse.) Roos was the only son of William Cecil, 2nd Lord Burghley, eldest grandson of Thomas Cecil, earl of Exeter. Lord Roos was the heir to the vast Cecil estates. In his youth, he spent much time abroad in the Catholic countries of France, Spain, and Italy, places he clearly preferred to England. His failed marriage to Anne Lake became the impetus for the feud between the Lakes and Cecils and the resulting scandals.

Robert Cecil, earl of Salisbury (1563–1612). Robert Cecil was Thomas Cecil's younger half-brother. Robert Cecil was the most powerful adviser to King James, and the most powerful person in the Cecil clan until his death in 1612. He served as the king's Secretary of State. Young Lord Roos was beholden to his uncle for his friendly and honorable receptions in foreign courts.

Sir Thomas Lake (1561–1630). Sir Thomas Lake, father of Anne Lake, Lady Roos, was the patriarch of the newly rich and powerful Lake family. Of humble origins, he was very ambitious and rose to power through service at the court of Queen Elizabeth and then King James. By early 1616, he had finally achieved his goal of becoming one of two Secretaries of State. The feud with his daughter's in-laws, the Cecils, led to his downfall.

Mary Ryder Lake, Lady Lake (ca. 1575–1642). Sir Thomas Lake's wife, Lady Roos's mother. She was the daughter of a wealthy haberdasher in London, who served as alderman and Lord Mayor of the city. Like her husband, she was fiercely ambitious and wanted to advance her family. She was a driving force in the feud with the Cecils, as she believed her daughter was mistreated by Lord Roos and the countess of Exeter.

Anne Lake Cecil, Lady Roos (1599–1630). Daughter of Sir Thomas and Mary Lake, married to William Cecil, Lord Roos, the earl of Exeter's grandson in 1616. The breakdown of this marriage became the impetus for the feud between the Lakes and Cecils. The arguments began with property disputes but ended with intense personal attacks. Lady Roos accused the countess of Exeter of having an affair with her husband and of trying to poison her twice.

Sir Thomas Lake, Jr. (ca. 1595–1653). The eldest son of Sir Thomas and Mary Lake, Lady Roos's brother. He became involved in the feud between the families and served as the plaintiff on behalf of his sister in a slander suit against the earl and countess of Exeter and two of their servants.

Sir Arthur Lake (1598–1633). The second son of Sir Thomas and Mary Lake. He became directly involved in fights between the Lakes and the Cecils when he had a violent altercation with Lord Roos, who forcefully tried to remove his wife from the Lake estate Cannons outside of London. He was also one of the defendants in two later suits brought by the earl and countess of Exeter against Lady Roos and the Lakes.

Diego da Silva. Da Silva was a Spaniard who entered Lord Roos's service at some point during the young lord's foreign travels, probably around 1610. He became Roos's boon companion and followed Roos in his travels as well as his exile. He was also considered a crucial witness in the investigations and court proceedings between the Lakes and Cecils.

Sara Swarton. She served the Lake family, caring for their many children. When Anne Lake married William Cecil, Lord Roos, Swarton followed Anne into her new life as Lady Roos. Swarton became an important witness in the slander lawsuits, since she claimed to have been present when the countess of Exeter confessed her adultery and attempted poisoning to Lady Roos.

King James I of England and VI of Scotland (1566–1625, ruled in England 1603–25). King James arrived in England in 1603 and reigned until his death in 1625. He became personally involved in the Lake-Cecil feud, first by investigating and attempting to mediate and secondly as a judge in the Star Chamber slander suits between the two families.

George Villiers, Marquis of Buckingham (1592–1628). George Villiers became King James's last and most powerful favorite. He received ever loftier titles, finally becoming duke of Buckingham in 1623. His rise also meant the eventual downfall of the powerful Howard family (much through their own doing). Buckingham was very powerful, and the Lakes tried to use his influence to their advantage on several occasions, with limited success.

John Chamberlain (1554–1628). A leisured gentleman of London, who had friends and connections at court, like Sir Ralph Winwood. For years, he wrote biweekly newsletters to his friend Sir Dudley Carleton, who served as English ambassador in Venice and in The Hague. Chamberlain's letters are a central source for anyone dealing with the Jacobean court.

Sir Dudley Carleton (1573–1632). Carleton was an English diplomat who served as ambassador in Venice and in The Hague. Striving for a court appointment in England, Carleton was sure to keep up with the news at home, so that he could know if any positions became available. In addition to Chamberlain's regular missives, Carleton was also the recipient of letters from many others at or near the court. Because Carleton wanted to be Secretary of State, his friends made sure to tell him of all the different turns of Lake's troubles with the Cecils. If Lake fell, Carleton might be able to get the secretary post.

William Trumbull (ca. 1575–1635). The English agent in Brussels, acting on behalf of King James there. Trumbull was a skilled diplomat, creating a vast international network of people who could provide him with information. He was also the recipient of many letters from England, keeping him abreast of events at the English court. Letters to and from Trumbull form an important part of the source material for the Lake and Cecil feud.

Sir Ralph Winwood (ca. 1563–1617). James's secretary of state from 1614 to 1617, sharing that position with Sir Thomas Lake from 1616 to 1617. Winwood was responsible for the foreign correspondence and Lake for the domestic. Winwood had served in a variety of court positions before that and in diplomatic posts in France and The Hague. A staunch Protestant, Winwood was against alliances with Spain, and viewed the more Spain-friendly Lake with suspicion. The two were rivals at court. He befriended Lord Roos to Lake's great chagrin.

Prologue

> For my part I know not what to conjecture, but yt shold seeme that Sir Thomas Lake and his are falne into a laberinth, whence they know not how to get out, for yt behoves him to make goode proofes of so heinous imputation against a Lady of her sort [the countess of Exeter], and yt stands her upon likewise to cleere herself from so fowle scandalls of precontracts, adulterie, incest, murther, poison, and such like peccadillos.
>
> John Chamberlain to Sir Dudley Carleton, Feb. 28, 1618[1]

In early 1618, Anne Lake Cecil, Lady Roos, openly accused Frances Cecil, countess of Exeter—her husband's youthful step-grandmother—of having an adulterous affair with her husband, William Cecil, Lord Roos. With the help of the countess of Exeter, Lord Roos had fled England, his wife, and his family for exile in Italy. As if stealing the affections of her husband was not enough, Lady Roos also claimed that the covetous countess had already tried to murder her twice, once with a poisoned enema and a second time with a poisoned syrup of roses. Now, she was planning on giving it another try, set on silencing Lady Roos forever and perhaps also murdering Sir Thomas Lake, Lady Roos's doting father and King James's Secretary of State. When the countess of Exeter heard the accusations, she vehemently denied all of them, rushed to see the king, and begged him to help her defend her honor and clear her reputation against Lady Roos's malicious slanders. The countess asserted that Lady Roos and her parents had made up the tales as revenge against her, since she refused to help them cover up their own crimes and theft of Lord Roos's property.

Not surprisingly, the sensational accusations and the countess of Exeter's response caused quite a stir at the court of King James I. The "king and council, at this time, are troubled with no other business as much as the foul matter betwixt your good acquaintance, the Countess of Exeter, and the Lady Roos and her mother," Adam Newton informed his brother-in-law Sir Thomas Puckering in February 1618.[2] Soon servants, lawyers, foreign diplomats, ambitious career climbers, court observers, news writers, and others would get drawn into the maelstrom of the scandal.

The king ordered his Privy Council to investigate Lady Roos's accusations. After several months, James and the council found themselves at an impasse, unable to determine who was lying and failing to mediate between the Cecils and the Lakes to either side's satisfaction. Frustrated with the lack of progress, the king referred the matter to the courts of law. In April 1618, the earl and countess of Exeter sued Sir Thomas Lake, his wife Mary, their daughter Anne Lady Roos, son Sir Arthur Lake, and servant Sara Swarton for slander in the court of Star Chamber, the highest criminal court in England. The Lakes hit back with countersuits, accusing the earl and countess of Exeter and their servants of conspiring to accuse Lady Roos and the Lake family of libel and slander.

The lawsuits dragged on for months, with both sides and the court collecting witness statements and other evidence. Keenly aware of the case's political significance, ambitious courtiers and court observers tried to pick the winner, calculating their chances for any available positions or opportunities. The date of the trial was moved forward. King James decided that he was going to have a direct hand in the judgment after all: the king was going to sit with the judges in the court of Star Chamber and hear the case himself. In late January and early February of 1619, the case finally went to trial. The Lakes lost decisively. King James and the other judges found Lady Roos and the Lakes guilty of forgery, slander, and suborning witnesses. Furthermore, Sir Thomas Lake had abused the powers of his office as secretary and was promptly stripped of his position. The Lakes and Lady Roos were heavily fined and ordered to pay court costs and damages to the earl and countess of Exeter. They also had to cover the expenses of their own imprisonment in the Tower "at the king's pleasure" (meaning however long the king wanted to keep them there). The triumphant countess of Exeter was completely vindicated, looking forward to her enemies having to admit their faults and beg for her forgiveness in the public forum of Star Chamber.

Having researched and written about Elizabethan and Jacobean scandals aplenty throughout my career, I have perhaps become somewhat jaded and used to learning about outrageous behavior, or accusations thereof. Even so, when I first came across this episode, I found the sheer human drama of it very intriguing. The case raises many questions and piques one's curiosity. What would lead a person to invent such claims against another? Why would people go to such extreme lengths to defend a lie—or to defend against a lie, for that matter? Why would the king, court, and council get so involved in what appeared to be a particularly nasty family dispute? What was at stake for the people involved, and for their contemporaries?

To date, historians have only produced summaries of the scandal (of varying accuracy), included mostly in biographies on King James and in books and articles that deal with politics and court scandals at the Jacobean court (the Epilogue deals more extensively with the historiography of the case). However, no substantive account had been produced, which prompted me to start digging further into this Jacobean episode to find answers to my questions.

I quickly realized that the scandals which erupted in 1618 and concluded in the slander trial in 1619 were just the tip of the iceberg. Below the surface lurked escalating disputes between the Lake and Cecil families that went back several years, and which continued after the scandalous trials concluded in 1619. In addition, my research into the feud and the various family members took me into many different areas and corners of early modern England and Europe. One minute I was researching early modern medicine and ideas and practices regarding poisons, and the next I was looking at Jacobean foreign and religious policies in the 1610s. After that, I spent endless hours poring over court records from the court of Star Chamber, and later focused on the issues of gender so prominent in the accusations the Lakes and Cecils hurled at each other. I struggled with the complexities of property law and turned to the more familiar state papers and court politics. I had to learn more about the educational travels of Elizabethan and Jacobean gentlemen next, and the architecture of Tudor and Stuart manors and gardens. Each discovery made the case more perplexing and frustrating, pulling me in so many directions. What was this case *really* about? What did it mean? What was the main theme? As a historian, how could I make sense of it?

Eventually, it felt as if I was wrestling a large octopus, struggling to keep control of a wriggling mess of tentacles trying to free themselves. Every discovery pulled me toward something new, and one or two of those tentacles slipped out of my grasp, taunting me with the implication that I would inevitably leave out much if I narrowed my focus. And then it dawned on me: the family feud between the Lakes and the Cecils was the main story. The scandal was the outcome of the feud, and the varied impact of the protracted fights between the family members in turn allowed me to explore different areas of early Stuart politics, culture, and society that are so prominent in the feud. Putting the feud in the center allowed me to accommodate the many disparate strands in my research. I did not have to wrestle the octopus. The feud was the body, and once that was established, I could simply follow each tentacle where it would lead me. Finally, the beast grew still.

Answering the questions about the Lake and Cecil scandal requires a deep dive into the history, society, and culture of England during the reign of King James I (ruled 1603–25), as well as a fuller picture of the individuals and families involved. This book aims to do just that by providing the first full account of the festering feud between the Lakes and the Cecils, the scandals that grew out of it, and the consequences for the people involved in England and beyond in the early decades of the seventeenth century. These family disputes provide a window into the early Stuart world.

The Reign of James I: The Context

King James VI of the Scottish Stuart dynasty also became king of England, the first of that name there, after the 1603 death of the childless and unmarried Queen Elizabeth I, the last of the Tudors. Sir Robert Cecil, the earl of Exeter's half-brother, had been the main minister at Queen Elizabeth's later court. He supported and helped orchestrate the ascension of King James and the new king retained him as his most important advisor and minister until Cecil's death in 1612. The Cecil family, already important during the previous reign, established itself firmly in the upper echelons of Jacobean society as well.[3]

At first, the new king was popular. A male ruler seemed to usher in a new period of comforting normalcy for people living in a firmly patriarchal world. During the second half of the 1500s, England had been ruled by two sovereign queens, Mary and Elizabeth Tudor, for the first time in its history. While some thought female rule downright monstrous, most accepted it as something to be endured.[4] Neither Mary nor Elizabeth had any children, which caused consternation for the security of the succession. The English had not had a royal male heir since the time of Henry VIII in the 1530s and 1540s. In 1603, King James brought his wife and, even more importantly, his two sons and a daughter to England. A "complete" royal family thus promised greater political stability and continuity.

King James relished in the pomp and glittering entertainments of English court life, but he was also inordinately fond of retreating from the bustle of the capital to enjoy hunting and simpler living quarters in mostly male company. Sir Thomas Lake, Lady Roos's father, initially served as the king's Latin secretary. Lake often accompanied the king on these hunts, hoping that the king's favor and familiarity with him during the retreats would translate into higher political appointments and greater influence. For a time, Lake's efforts bore fruit and his influence grew.[5]

King James also seemed to bring greater security for the Protestant religious settlement in England. The Protestant reformation, a European-wide movement in the 1500s, had been a halting and messy affair in England. Begun under King Henry VIII in the 1530s, England lurched back and forth between Protestantism and Catholicism for decades, until the Anglican settlement under Elizabeth's early reign established a conservative form of Protestantism as the official Church of England. Catholicism became illegal. The English population was mostly Protestant by the time of James's ascension, but English Catholics, some living in exile outside of England, and some practicing in semi-obscurity within the borders of the kingdom, still hoped for a restoration of their faith, or, at the very least, for a more liberal policy toward practicing Catholics. Most of Europe had been wracked by decades of bloody religious warfare in the latter half of the sixteenth century.

Religious fights continued in the seventeenth century, intertwined with complex dynastic and territorial politics. This charged mixture of faith and politics ignited the massive European-wide Thirty Years War in 1618. King James wanted to keep England out of the bloody and expensive wars, but he also needed to find appropriate royal spouses for his children, as well as good political and financial alliances for himself and his country. Balancing political and religious goals made for precarious and difficult foreign and domestic policymaking in the early seventeenth century, something the Lakes and the Cecils also tried to negotiate for their benefits.[6]

Finding a wife for Prince Charles, heir to the English throne after the untimely death of his elder brother Henry in 1612, was an important part of foreign policy during the time of the Lake-Cecil feud. At the time, King James favored a marriage to a Spanish princess with a rich dowry, but the main sticking point in the on-again-off-again negotiations was religion. While James might be willing to allow a foreign princess to remain Catholic, he did not want her to become a beacon and source of succor for English Catholics. The Spanish, for whom the reconversion of England to Catholicism had long been a goal, utilized the marriage negotiations to seek other concessions for Catholics within England.[7] Although Sir Thomas Lake never formally converted, many viewed him as well disposed toward the cause of Spain and favoring more freedoms for English Catholics. As a result, Lake was able to get the support of the Spanish ambassador when the consequences of the Lake-Cecil feud got him into hot water with the king.[8] Lord Roos also had a very friendly relationship with the Spanish ambassador and favored visiting Catholic sites with his Catholic traveling companions. The religious politics in both Europe and England thus intruded in the Lake-Cecil feud.

Although married with children, James vastly preferred the company of men. His relationship with his wife, Queen Anna of Denmark, was cordial, but became more distant as time passed during his English reign. The couple had two more daughters born in England, but both died young in 1606 and 1607. After the death of the little princesses, James and Anna mostly kept separate courts, joining together at holiday celebrations and major ceremonies. When Prince Henry died in 1612, the royal couple grew even more distant, as James spent more and more time with his favorites.[9]

Both the Lakes and the Cecils tried to use connections to royal favorites to prevail in their feud. By the 1610s, court politics had become more dominated by the king's male favorites, specifically the very handsome Robert Carr, earl of Somerset, and even handsomer George Villiers, later duke of Buckingham. Since his days in Scotland, James had male favorites, with whom he had close and personal relationships and whom he rewarded with titles, riches, and power. He loved these men. Seventeenth-century people were not familiar with the term "homosexual" and would not have used it. Same-sex physical relationships between men were generally seen as a most terrible sin. Moreover, sodomy was a capital crime in sixteenth- and seventeenth-century England, although it was not very common to see men prosecuted or sentenced. It was certainly no secret that James preferred male companions and that he loved his male favorites. In 1617, the king informed a crowd of courtiers that he loved Buckingham "more than any other man, and more than all those who were here present." He continued to explain that those present "should not think of this as a defect in him," because "as Christ had his John, so he, James, had his George."[10] Few had the wherewithal to accuse their king of sodomy openly: those condemnations mostly occurred after the king was dead.[11]

Historians have debated whether James had sex with his male favorites, or if the relationships were platonic deep friendships.[12] However, nobody doubts the king's intense emotional attachments to his favorites. In letters to Buckingham, the king called him his "sweet heart" and "dear child," and signed himself off as Buckingham's "dear dad and husband." In one particularly affectionate letter, James poured out his love for Buckingham: "God so love me, as I desire only to live in this world for your sake, and that I had rather live banished in any part of the earth with you than live a sorrowful widow's life without you."[13]

Unlike his predecessor the single Queen Elizabeth who became furious when her male favorites married, James actively encouraged his male favorites to marry and have children. He displayed no jealousy toward the favorites' families, but rather viewed them as part of his family as well. Whatever may or may not have happened in the royal bedroom, the king never hid his love for his favorites. He was openly affectionate toward them in public, often kissing and embracing them, leaning on them when his bad legs required support, and so on. Jacobean courtiers understood the king's preferences enough to try to introduce new handsome young men at court as potential rivals to royal favorites deemed too have risen too far.[14] Royal favorites could garner much political and economic capital: Buckingham, the last and most powerful of the favorites, was astute enough to also establish his own network of patronage at court and beyond.

By the late 1610s, the time of the Lake-Cecil feud, repeated scandals at the king's court had taken some of the "new-king" shine away. It was an especially volatile period: several high officials in James's administration were removed because the king felt they encroached on royal powers, while others fell as a result of their involvement in criminal or otherwise problematic behavior. In the fall of 1619, John Chamberlain noted that some joked an alternate Privy Council meeting could be held in the Tower of London, since prisoners then included "a Lord Treasurer, a Lord Chamberlain, a captain of the pensioners and a secretary."[15] Around 1623, an anonymous writer penned a lengthy poem entitled "Fortune's Wheel," which outlined the rise and fall of the many Jacobean politicians and courtiers as "Fortune's wheele is quicklie turn'de aboute."[16] Criticism of royal courts as places of sin, vice, and backstabbing aggression and ambitions was a literary trope that had existed long before King James came to the throne. However, the scandals that rocked the Jacobean court in the 1610s did harm its reputation, making it appear particularly immoral and more open to criticism. As Alastair Bellany has aptly argued, the murder of Sir Thomas Overbury by the favorite Somerset and his wife was especially problematic, since the King's own favorite was implicated, also casting a shadow over the king himself. King James worked to stymie further scandals, but with limited success.[17]

King James strongly believed in the notion that kings were divinely ordained to rule their subjects and the limits to their power were few. The troubled court career of the lawyer Sir Edward Coke serves as an example of scandals ensuing as a result of questioning the king's powers. In 1616, Coke found himself in trouble after the king learned that his legal opinions seemed to question the royal prerogative. Coke had made it to the top, appointed to the high position of Justice of the King's Bench. After angering the king, he lived in uncertainty for a while, until the king decided to remove him from his position. Desperate to return to the king's favor and his legal career, Coke hoped that he might be restored if he were able to please the king's rising favorite Buckingham.

Buckingham came from relatively lowly beginnings and was busy ensuring that his family rose with him, searching for rich marriages for his kin. Coke decided to offer his young daughter Frances as a wealthy bride for Buckingham's brother, failing to ask his wife or daughter's thoughts on the matter. Coke's wife was Elizabeth Cecil, Lady Hatton, the earl of Exeter's daughter. Frances Coke was thus Lord Roos's first cousin: the many tentacles of the Cecil family were heavily involved in Jacobean court politics. Lady Hatton was a woman of strong opinions and she and her husband had already had great and public disputes, some of which had been mediated by the king and Privy Council.

When Coke attempted to marry off their daughter, Lady Hatton took her into hiding. Coke, outraged by what he interpreted as his wife's insolent actions, summoned up an armed posse, broke down doors, and dragged his daughter out of her hiding place. Lady Hatton summoned up her own men and followed them, until forced to abandon the chase. Lady Hatton tried to get the Privy Council to punish her husband for his violence. At first her appeals received some sympathetic ears, but then word came from the absent king that Coke had been within his right to take control of his own daughter. As a father he had the right to marry her to whomever he chose, the king insisted. This family drama played out during the summer of 1617 and the letter writers were busy reporting about the many scandalous twists and turns, taking sides and sniffing the political winds. Many believed that Coke had taken his paternal prerogative too far in his rough treatment of his daughter. In the end, though, Coke's daughter, supplied with a large dowry, did marry Buckingham's brother. Coke enjoyed a brief restoration at court, but he later lost his position again through his own stubborn insistence on legal opinions that rankled the king.[18]

The most famous of the 1610s court scandals involving outright criminal behavior was the murder of Sir Thomas Overbury by the royal favorite Robert Carr, earl of Somerset, and his wife, Frances Howard. Carr had risen like a comet at court after the king first became enamored with him in 1607. The celebrated court beauty Frances Howard, daughter of the earl of Suffolk, and Carr fell in love. Unfortunately, Frances was already married to the earl of Essex. In an infamous church court case that played out in 1613, Frances Howard argued that her marriage to Essex was null, since the couple had been unable to consummate it. King James, who favored the new match between Carr and Frances Howard, stacked the judges in the case in favor of annulment, gave Carr the noble title earl of Somerset, and threw the lovers a fabulous wedding at court after Frances's annulment had been approved.

Sir Thomas Overbury, Carr's friend and mentor, had opposed the relationship, finding it distasteful and politically problematic. In order to get rid of this annoying obstacle, Carr manipulated Overbury into openly refusing royal orders, which landed him in the Tower. While Overbury was imprisoned, the lovers plotted to have him poisoned. The poison was administered in medicines and sweets offered as special treats from concerned friends. The poisons did their work rather slowly, but Overbury eventually succumbed after suffering lengthy and painful digestive symptoms.

After Overbury's death, the new earl and countess of Somerset were secure in the king's favor for two years. By the fall of 1615, one of the king's secretaries learned of evidence that Overbury's death had been the result of poison rather than disease, as was first thought. He informed the king. James ordered an investigation, which snowballed until it reached the earl and countess of Somerset. The king began to distance himself from his favorite. In fact, the two had already begun to grow more distant even before the investigations began, as Somerset started to treat the king with disrespect and coldness. At first, the servants and associates who had procured and delivered the poison to Overbury were tried and found guilty. By the spring of 1616, the Somersets found themselves on trial for accessory to murder. The countess of Somerset quickly confessed and was found guilty. Somerset, the king's former favorite, stubbornly insisted on his innocence, but was nonetheless found guilty. Both were sentenced to death, but the king commuted their sentencing to imprisonment in the Tower. A few years later, the king pardoned and freed them from the Tower, and they lived out the rest of their lives in obscurity in the country.[19]

Sir Thomas Lake had first cultivated ties with Somerset, but his hopes that the favorite could help him advance in his court career were dashed when Somerset's scandal and conviction rendered him politically dead. The countess of Somerset's parents, Thomas and Katherine Howard, earl and countess of Suffolk, managed to survive the downfall of their daughter and son-in-law, so Lake began to work more closely with them. Suffolk served as the king's Lord Treasurer. Like Lake, the Suffolks were also friendly toward the idea of the Spanish match for Prince Charles and received annual payments from the Spanish ambassador. However, the Suffolks eventually fell victim to a scandal of their own. In 1618, after Lake's scandal had already erupted, the king learned that Suffolk and his wife had been involved in taking extraordinary bribes and otherwise profiteered from Suffolk's exalted position as Treasurer.

Suffolk lost his position as treasurer, and after a lengthy trial in the court of Star Chamber, the earl and countess were found guilty of corruption, and the couple were heavily fined and imprisoned for a time.[20] Trying to navigate the politics of the court during this volatile time was not for the faint of heart.

The Lake and Cecil Feud

Historians have already investigated many of the Jacobean court scandals, especially the Overbury murder and the fall of the Somersets. However, the Lake-Cecil feud has not received the same attention. When historians and other writers have mentioned the feud and its associated scandals, they have tended to interpret and make judgments about the case and the people involved with hindsight in mind, focusing more narrowly on the results of the slander case and its aftermath. In other words, since they knew that Lady Roos and her family were convicted of slander and forgery in the end, they conclude that they must have been the villains in the story all along. The retelling of the story has thus been influenced by that rather limiting perspective. In fact, the disputes and scandals were a great deal murkier than the court judgment suggests and the Cecils far from blameless.

Because of Lady Roos's accusation of poisoning, historians more familiar with the Overbury murder have tended to view the Lake-Cecil fights as a poorer copy—or as an echo—of the very real and fatal crime in the earlier Overbury scandal. However, Lady Roos's adultery and poisoning accusations were only the spectacular culmination of almost two years of escalating family disputes: it was far from the only crime the two sides claimed the others had committed. Contemporaries of the Lake and Cecil families largely did not see the scandals simply as a copy of the Overbury case, but understood it as different in nature, having followed the developments between the families for some time. Observers were aware of the complex web of property disputes and accusations of fraud, questions about the paternity of the countess of Exeter's youngest child, allegations of Lord Roos's impotence, physical brawls, a challenge to a duel, an illegal and secretive flight out of England, and so on. Rather than just focusing on the apex of the Lake-Cecil feud, we need to view it in its totality in order to fully understand its impact.

In comparison to other Jacobean court scandals, the Lake-Cecil feud also proved unique because of King James's direct involvement in it: he sat in the Court of Star Chamber and judged the case himself. The king and his Privy Council had mediated in disputes between major court figures and their families before, such as the case of Sir Edward Coke and Lady Hatton. James wanted an orderly and harmonious court: when important figures fought publicly, it reflected badly on them as well as the king's royal authority. However, he had never been so directly involved in lawsuits.

The king first tried to mediate between the Lakes and the earl and countess of Exeter, but after the case proved too problematic, he decided to let the case go through the official channels of the legal courts. In other scandals which had ended up in legal courts, like the Overbury murder and the Suffolk corruption case, the king did not get directly involved in the court process itself, preferring instead to stay away from it in order to maintain an appearance of impartiality. However, in the Lake v. Exeter case, King James exceptionally decided to be present at court and to sit in judgment over the trial.[21] James liked to present himself as the wise and just biblical King Solomon: he made the reference himself on multiple occasions, and others made it about him as well. The fighting between Ladies Roos and Lake on the one hand, and the countess of Exeter on the other, seemed to lend itself to the analogy of Solomon judging between the two women fighting over a baby (1 Kings 3:16–28). Both James and his contemporaries played on the analogy several times in the case. King James also liked to show off his logic and deductive reasoning skills by exposing frauds.[22] As we will see, the information he had gathered before the trial between the Lakes and the Cecils ensured that he believed this case would allow him to do both. The king wished his judgment to be final in the case, and to end the scandals, but in that he did not quite succeed.

The events of the feud played out at diverse places: the royal court, the courts of Star Chamber and Chancery, London town homes, luxurious country estates of the elite, ambassador's houses, as well as servants' quarters, roadside inns, London streets and parks, and wherever gossiping mouths met eager ears. Lord Roos, the alleged errant husband of Lady Roos, spent a large portion of his life travelling throughout Europe so we get to follow his itinerant tracks as well. He favored the Catholic countries of France, Italy, and Spain, where he visited courts, collected art, saw the sights, spent too much time with Catholic priests for his Protestant family's comfort, and wined, dined, and gambled the nights away with his companions. At one point, King James also appointed him to a diplomatic mission to Spain.

While the main persons involved in the feud were gentry and nobility, the investigation into the various accusations introduces us to persons from all walks of life: administrative workers, international couriers, barbers, jewelers, tutors, doctors, gentlewomen companions, maids, valets, falconers, laundresses, stable boys, and every other stripe of servant. Noble households like those of the earl and countess of Exeter were expansive and complex. The Lake-Cecil feud reveals the inner workings of these large households and the sometimes-fraught relationships between masters and mistresses and their employees. Elite men and women were rarely alone, almost always accompanied by servants to attend to their every need. As a result, servants had intimate knowledge about their employers, their actions, their speech, and their bodies. Because of the secretive nature of the alleged adultery and poisoning, most of the witnesses in the later court cases were servants, or family members and friends of servants, who had been privy to servants' tales about their employers. As we will see, servants could be pressured by their employers to provide testimony in their favor, but servants who had left their employ might find it easier to speak more freely, although they might be thought only to seek revenge against an unfair employer. The words and testimony of servants, and the questions about their loyalties and trustworthiness, became central issues in the court cases.

When historical persons behave badly, or are accused of behaving badly, it affords us intimate insights into the norms and values of the society that branded certain behavior as improper, sinful, or criminal. In the Lake-Cecil feud, both sides accused each other of several bad behaviors that were easily defined as both sins and crimes: attempted murder, adultery, incest, forgery, fraud, suborning witnesses, violent attacks, and illegal imprisonment. In addition, the Lakes and the Cecils also both argued that the other side were inherently bad people, not living up to the expectations for men and women of their specific positions.

Very often, these accusations and insinuations were couched in highly gendered terms. Lady Lake and Lady Roos argued that the countess of Exeter had compromised her sexual virtue and expressed disloyalty to her husband: she was a bad wife. The countess of Exeter (and others) argued that the fact that Lady Lake and Lady Roos had been able to even dream up the sordid accusations of adultery and murder against her, must mean that they were themselves entirely morally corrupted and evil. Furthermore, Lady Lake's assertive and domineering ways, and Lady Roos's impertinence and doggedness, made them altogether bad women in the eyes of many seventeenth-century people. On the other hand, Sir Thomas Lake was a bad man because he allowed himself to be too much influenced and ruled by his wife and daughter, both of whom he should control as the man of the house. The earl of Exeter, according to some, was an old fool, cuckolded by his much younger wife. Finally, Lord Roos, according to most, was a bad man because he was unable to control his wife, his finances, and his impulses and emotions. Investigating the Lake-Cecil feud thus also gives us an insight into sometimes competing ideas about gender, about how seventeenth-century people believed men and women should behave and how unfeminine and emasculating behavior could seriously damage a person's honor, reputation, credibility, power, and authority.

Since the story of the Lake-Cecil feud meanders through so many different places, the sources for this book are similarly varied. For the scandals engendered by the feud, I have mostly used newsletter collections, family correspondence, letters preserved in the state papers, diplomatic exchanges, and diaries. For the legal wrangling, I use court records from the equity court of Chancery, but most come from Star Chamber, a court that developed during the Tudor period but was abolished at the beginning of the Civil Wars of the 1640s. Unfortunately, the Star Chamber records are spotty and only portions of them survive. Luckily, because the main court case involving the Lakes and the Cecils became so famous, the formal court records can be augmented with other sources. People jostled to attend Star Chamber—a public court—and take notes of the proceedings, so they would be able to keep their friends and acquaintances up to date. As a result, we have quite detailed information about the main trials. In addition, Privy Council records help establish the formal orders of the king's council in the case, such as warrants and conditions of imprisonment and releases. Wills and recorded deeds, along with more court records, help to detangle the complex property disputes between the Lakes and the Cecils. Medical treatises and herbals highlight the medical practices behind the treatments Lady Roos received, which she claimed had poisoned her. Libel verses and other literary works show how seventeenth-century contemporaries perceived the feuding family members as well.

When the Lakes and the Cecils presented their versions of the arguments, their accounts varied widely. "Trials are imaginative recreations of past occurrences," as Barbara Shapiro has aptly put it.[23] Anyone who has seen a modern courtroom drama knows that witnesses to the same events can experience and understand them very differently, depending on their personal context, references, and motivations. If people are lying and manufacturing evidence and testimony, distinguishing between falsehoods and reality becomes even more difficult. The contemporaries of the Lakes and Cecils found the families' divergent tales confusing and were often unsure who to believe and how to establish what might have "really" happened. Speculations were common.

From a distance of four hundred years, it can be even more difficult to differentiate between lies and realities. Careful reading of the available sources can help us establish basic facts, but the truth of some arguments will necessarily remain elusive. However, that does not mean that we cannot learn much from the feud. In this book, I let the feuding men and women tell their own stories and explain their motivations. My focus is on understanding why the tales took very particular shapes, how people contextualized those stories, and why people reacted to them in the ways that they did.[24]

1
Meet the Families

> Since my being abroad I have received so much honour by your name, that I do not know how I may presume to use it to my profit.
>
> William Cecil, Lord Roos to his uncle Robert Cecil, earl of Salisbury, June 3, 1606[1]

> Sir Thomas Lake was bred (...) a States-man under Sir Francis Walsingham at Court, where such his dexterity and dispatch, that he would indite, write, and discourse at the same time, more exactly than most men could severally perform them, being then called the Swift-sure; such his celerity and solidity in all Affairs!
>
> David Lloyd, *The Statesmen and Favorites of England* (1670)[2]

The Lake-Exeter feud was a clash of powerful families, which is one of the reasons why so many contemporary observers found the details of the fighting and accusations endlessly fascinating, and why the consequences were so far-reaching. Some people relish the private and public failures of the powerful. In addition, the patriarchs of both families held important court positions, which also meant that their feuding, and potential fall, could open political and economic opportunities for others. Although both the Cecil and the Lake families were members of the elite, they were not equals in the deeply hierarchical Jacobean society. By the reign of King James, the Cecils had become a politically well-established and immensely rich noble family. By contrast, Sir Thomas Lake rose from humble origins and was the first in his family to reach the inner circle of royal power. The Lake-Cecil feud was thus a clash of an established noble family and an ambitious newcomer.

The Cecils

The Cecil family, while certainly distinguished, was not among the oldest English noble families. Nonetheless, by the time of the feud in the 1610s, they had been very prominent in England for over half a century and had a history

Family and Feuding at the Court of James I: The Lake and Cecil Scandals. Johanna Luthman, Oxford University Press.
 DOI: 10.1093/oso/9780192865786.003.0001

of royal service since the reign of Henry VII. Sir William Cecil (1520–98) was the first in the family to gain a significant position and reach the ranks of the peerage. Cecil's grandfather and father had served at early Tudor courts as Yeoman of the Chamber and Yeoman of the Wardrobe but had remained minor figures. William Cecil began his court service during Edward VI's minority, even serving as one of two Secretaries of State. He managed the difficult feat of surviving Queen Mary's reign, even though he had signed his support to the devise passing the crown to the Protestant Lady Jane Grey rather than Catholic Mary Tudor when young King Edward died. When Elizabeth Tudor became the next queen, Cecil's real rise to prominence began. He became the queen's most trusted and longest-serving adviser and Privy Councilor. He was first appointed Secretary of State, then became Lord High Treasurer and Lord Privy Seal. The queen ennobled him in 1571, when he became Lord Burghley.[3]

Lord Burghley married twice. His first marriage to Mary Cheke produced only one son, Thomas, born May 5, 1542, shortly before his young wife died. During his second marriage to Mildred Cooke, Burghley had three daughters and three sons. Only one of those sons, Robert, survived. Much later, Burghley's eldest son Thomas became the 1st earl of Exeter and one of the main characters in the story of the Lake-Cecil feud. Lord Burghley's first-born was a rather typical example of a son who enjoyed the privilege his father's position brought but demonstrated little interest in performing the necessary tedious and hard work that had enabled his father's rise.

The generations of Lord Burghley's male descendants traveled abroad in their youths, and this foreign experience became a crucial aspect of the Lake-Cecil feud. More noble and gentry families had begun to send their sons abroad to complete their education by the latter half of the 1500s. The travelers were expected to learn languages and become conversant with the customs and cultures of high societies in continental Europe. In addition, they were expected to create useful social networks and befriend important people. This knowledge and networks would enable them to serve the sovereign and the state—and themselves and their families—more ably, especially in matters involving foreign policy and diplomacy. In the late 1500s and early 1600s, educational travel had not yet formalized into the so-called Grand Tour, so the travel locations and experiences were more varied.[4]

The elder Burghley himself was not a well-traveled man. As he was establishing his position at the court of Queen Elizabeth, he wanted to ensure that his eldest son would be prepared to follow in his footsteps to serve the queen. Consequently, Thomas Cecil traveled first to France, and then onwards to the

Netherlands and Germany in 1561–62. Burghley soon began to complain that he was not receiving enough performance reports and that his son appeared to be spending too much money. Like other young educational travelers, Thomas was accompanied by a tutor who was supposed to oversee his travel arrangements, education, and behavior. The tasks of Thomas Windebank, young Thomas's tutor, proved difficult. At first apologetically, but soon exasperatedly, Windebank admitted to his employer that he was unable to control his charge. Burghley was aware of his son's faults: he slept late, was "negligent and rash in expenses, careless in his apparel, an immoderate lover of dice and cards, in study soon weary, in game never."[5] The father became increasingly disillusioned with his son and feared that the brilliant court career he wanted for him was not going to be possible. Dejected, he told Windebank that Thomas would "be meet only to keep a tennis court" once he returned from his travels.[6]

The situation deteriorated further. Windebank and Thomas hastily left Paris after Thomas apparently had seduced a woman there. Windebank thought the best course of action was to remove young Thomas from the situation before it escalated, because the young woman in question "is a maid, and her friends will hardly bear the violating of her."[7] Windebank may have failed in another of his tasks, as Burghley had specifically asked him to "have great regard that he [Thomas] may return with a chaste body."[8] They traveled on to the Netherlands, followed by Germany. Thomas was keen on going to Italy as well, and Cecil, having been informed of his son's more sober and penitent behavior in Germany, considered allowing it. Windebank thought it would be a bad idea, as Italy would present too many "inticements to pleasure and wantonness" and ruin the fragile progress Thomas had made.[9] He urged Cecil not to allow it, and if he persisted, to free Windebank from his charge and from the responsibility of trying to oversee Thomas's behavior in the Italian den of sin. At that moment, one of Thomas's young half-brothers died and Windebank renewed his argument that Thomas, the main heir, should not go to Italy, but rather return to England and to his grieving family. Burghley acquiesced, and Thomas's youthful foreign adventures ended.[10]

Thomas Cecil (see Fig. 1.1), one of the main people involved in the later disputes with the Lakes, was not quite the useless and immoral spendthrift his father initially feared him to be. He never rose to the same prominence as his father at Queen Elizabeth's court but made his mark as a soldier and occasional courtier. He also served as an MP in the Commons until his father's death, when he inherited the title Lord Burghley and thenceforth sat in the House of Lords. His most significant Elizabethan appointment was as Lord of

Fig. 1.1 Thomas Cecil, earl of Exeter. Unknown artist. © National Portrait Gallery, London.

the Council of the North from 1599 to 1603. While King James did not renew that appointment after he took the English throne, he recognized the importance of the Cecil family and ensured that Thomas became a member of his Privy Council. He remained a Privy Councilor until his death in 1623, although never holding any additional ministerial posts.[11]

Since Thomas seemed more suited for soldiering, Burghley pinned his political hopes on his younger son Robert, whom he groomed to take his place at Elizabeth's court. Thomas appeared to realize his limitations and his brother's superior bureaucratic and political abilities. He later wrote to Robert that "God hath bestowed rarer gifts of mind upon you than on me. I know you have deserved far greater merit both of his Majesty and your country."[12] Sir Robert Cecil became a Privy Councilor in 1591 and increasingly took over his father's duties of Secretary of State. Queen Elizabeth formally titled him such in 1596. He also became Lord Privy Seal when his father died in 1598. Sir Robert remained Secretary of State when King James succeeded Elizabeth in 1603 and became the most powerful adviser of James's early reign (he died in 1612). Since his elder half-brother Thomas inherited their father's Burghley title, King James rewarded Sir Robert with noble titles of his own. He became Baron Cecil of Essendon in 1603, Viscount Cranbourne in 1604, and then earl of Salisbury in 1605. Also in 1605, James created his elder brother Thomas earl of Exeter. Thus, Sir William Cecil managed to rise to the peerage through his service to Queen Elizabeth, and his two sons completed the process by both becoming earls. Cecil's daughters and granddaughters also married into titled families, firmly establishing the Cecil family at the top of the English elite.[13]

By the time Sir Thomas Cecil became earl of Exeter in 1605, he was already married and had many children of his own. He married Dorothy Neville shortly after returning from his foreign travels and the fecund couple had ten children—four sons and six daughters—who survived to adulthood.[14] His eldest son William took over the title of Lord Burghley when his father became the earl of Exeter. William, the 2nd Lord Burghley, also played a role in the Lake-Cecil feud, although he generally allowed his father to take the lead in the lawsuits that it produced. The early modern practice of recycling the same first names in multiple generations, and the change in titles, can make keeping up with the various persons confusing. To promote clarity, I will refer to Thomas Cecil as "Exeter" from now on, even when referring to a time before he received his title.

Like his father, William Cecil (2nd Lord Burghley, or simply "Burghley" from here on) also traveled abroad in his youth. In the mid-1580s, he spent time in France and Italy. He also caused his father some concern, as he did not always keep him informed of his movements, spent too much money, and went to Italy without his father's or grandfather's express approval. Italy, the center of the Catholic Church, could prove a dangerous place for young Protestant men, especially if they, like Burghley, had powerful relatives. The English feared kidnapping, or worse—conversion to Catholicism. In the end, Burghley's Italian sojourn proceeded without such dangers. He was loth to end his travels and dragged his feet in France when his father called him home.[15]

In 1589, Burghley married Elizabeth Manners, the only surviving child of the recently deceased earl of Rutland. Elizabeth was a ward of the crown and a very tempting heiress. The twenty-three-year-old Burghley snagged the prize: he secretly married Elizabeth, who was fourteen at the time. Elizabeth was legally old enough to marry (the legal age of consent for girls was twelve), but since she was a ward, she should not be married without the consent of the guardian. Burghley appears to have been fined—and perhaps even briefly imprisoned—for the offense, and the mother of the bride had to deal with the legal implications for several years afterwards.[16]

The marriage proved brief. In the year following the wedding, young Elizabeth gave birth to a son, christened William, after his illustrious great-grandfather, the first Lord Burghley.[17] Elizabeth became pregnant again almost immediately but did not survive her second pregnancy. At age sixteen, she died in childbirth and was buried on May 19, 1591.[18] Elizabeth's father had also held the title of Lord Roos. As a woman she could not inherit the earldom of Rutland—it went to a male cousin—but she was able to inherit the title of Baroness Roos (her cousin later disputed it but lost). When Elizabeth herself died, she passed the title Baron Roos to her toddler son, thenceforth known as William Cecil, Lord Roos, one of the main characters in the tale of the Lake-Cecil feud.[19] Throughout this book, I will refer to him as "Roos."

After the death of his mother, Roos's father married Elizabeth Drury. The couple had three daughters, but no sons.[20] As a result, Roos continued in his position as his father's heir. The earl of Exeter had several other sons, but Roos's father was the eldest. Hence, Roos was also the second-generation heir to the titles and vast estates of Exeter. Born to enormous privilege, Roos's family held high expectations for him.

Lord Roos's Travels

After his education in England, Roos was sent abroad to complete his training.[21] As his father and grandfather before him, Roos needed to be properly prepared for a career of service to the king, which hopefully would lead to even greater power, wealth, and status for the family. His powerful great-uncle Sir Robert Cecil, earl of Salisbury, King James's influential secretary and adviser, supported the plan as well and ensured that the Privy Council issued the required travel license.

Roos was fifteen years old when he set off in 1605. Most young lords and gentlemen, like Exeter and Burghley, stayed abroad for two or three years. Roos, however, mostly remained abroad for a full decade.[22] Roos thus spent his most formative years—from age fifteen to age twenty-five—outside of England. As others later observed, Roos became more comfortable and familiar with continental European cultures and customs than with his own home country. These travels and experiences abroad featured prominently in the later feud and fighting between the Lakes and the Cecils, in how Roos himself behaved, and in how others reacted to Roos's actions. His travels and experiences matter to the story.

Roos's traveling tutor was named John Molle. Like so many other tutors of traveling young lords, Molle found it difficult to control his charge. Tutors held a precarious and ambivalent position: they were hired by anxious parents to ensure that the sons were studious and well behaved. Parents wanted the significant financial investment of sending their sons abroad to pay off. At the same time, tutors often came from a lower socio-economic position than their charges, which made it difficult for them to enforce their authority. They admonished but could not always give direct orders. They could make travel arrangements and try to control the purse strings, but young lords could often find others who were willing to lend them money or serve as travel companions. The tutors could—and did—tell the fathers of their sons' misbehavior and hoped that stern words from a parent would lead to reform, but even that was problematic, since it also revealed the tutor's inability to perform the assignment duties.[23]

Roos began his foreign sojourn in France. He studied French, saw the sights, and visited the royal court, where according to observers the French king received him kindly and with much honor.[24] Less than a year into his stay in France and foray into French high society, he fell in love. The sixteen-year-old Roos wrote earnestly to his uncle Salisbury that if the woman in question had not been of such a high status, he "might perhaps have gone about to marry her unadvisedly," to "satisfy" his "own passion." However, considering the high "birth, quality, wealth, and rank" of the lady, Roos "had so much wit as to think she would not be carried with a simple love." He asked Salisbury, whom he considered "one of my nearest and most honored parents," for his approval, and for his assistance in getting King James's permission for the marriage as well. He believed the lady would be very pleased with a match in Salisbury's powerful family, and, since she was also a powerful Protestant noblewoman in a mostly Catholic France, King James would probably find the marriage politically useful. Roos assured Salisbury that he would do nothing without his express approval. Clearly, no such approval was forthcoming, as there was no match. Who was the woman who had captured the teenager's heart? Roos only mentioned that she was the widow of the "late Duke Latremouille." This probably referred to Charlotte-Brabantina of Orange-Nassau, widow of Claude La Trémoille, duke of Thouars. The duchess was ten years older than Roos and had already given birth to four children before her husband died in 1604. There is no evidence to suggest she returned young Roos's ardor, but none to the contrary either.[25] Salisbury, perhaps wise to the experiences of Roos and his half-brother before him, made sure that his own son, Lord Cranbourne, was properly married before he completed most of his educational travel, perhaps to avoid any unwelcome foreign attachments and temptations.[26]

By the fall of 1607, Roos was in Italy, where he stayed almost two years. He spent time in Venice and later also went to Rome. Sir Henry Wotton, English ambassador in Venice, strongly advised him against going to Rome, as he believed it might be dangerous for such a well-connected young English Protestant nobleman to visit the center of Catholicism. Yet, Roos insisted and went against Wotton's objections. This rash action had a heavy cost, but not for Roos himself. Roos's tutor Molle was a staunch Protestant and had published works against Catholicism. The Roman Inquisition promptly arrested and imprisoned Molle as they arrived in the Eternal City. Separating young Protestant travelers from their tutors was also a tested strategy in Rome: removing the influence of the tutor made the young man more vulnerable and exposed, and then priests and other converts could more easily persuade him that Catholicism was the true religion.[27]

Exeter and other members of the Cecil family lobbied for years to get Molle out of his Roman prison, but in vain.[28] After a full thirty years of imprisonment, and continued resistance to any overtures of Catholic conversion, poor Molle died in his Roman prison. Roos, however, left Rome unscathed and continued his sightseeing, enjoying his favored status as Salisbury's nephew. Back in Venice, he was formally presented to the Doge and Senate and allowed to view the "jewels of the Sanctuary and the Hall of Arms."[29] Roos did not appear to express much regret or sympathy for his tutor's plight, even though his insistence on traveling to Rome had put Molle in such a bad spot. At this early stage, he did not know the full long-term consequences of his actions yet.

There is no mention of another tutor being assigned to Roos, so he probably continued his travels in the company of various friends and acquaintances instead. While in Venice, Roos asked for a letter of introduction to the Venetian ambassador in Prague, as he planned to travel first to Bavaria, and then onwards to Prague, but he knew no one in the city and there was no English ambassador there either. The Venetians courteously obliged. After his brief stint in Prague, he returned to northern Italy.[30]

In April 1609, Roos "sailed from Genoa to Marseille and from there he went to Arles and then Avignon, where he celebrated Easter (16 April) with the Jesuits."[31] He traveled for part of the way with Tobie Mathews, an English Catholic in exile. Mathews went back into Italy from Avignon, while Roos continued to Montpellier. In June, he was still in Montpellier, but by early August he had moved northward to Paris. A month later, he left for Lyon.[32] Roos's friendship with the Catholic Mathews and his visit with Jesuits, by the English considered the most insidious and dangerous of Catholics, were early signs of his association with Catholicism that continued throughout his travels, carefully noted by worried family and observers at home.

Late in 1609, Roos left France for Spain. He had heard much about the country and wanted to see it with his own eyes, but he seems to have undertaken the journey without consulting his family.[33] Spain was not a common destination for educational travel in the early 1600s. The active involvement of Spain in trying to return England to Catholicism in the previous decades was no doubt the most important consideration. The fear of being associated with Catholic conversion or some sort of spying or plotting was too great. Sir Francis Cottington, the resident English ambassador in Spain, lamented that except for Lord Roos, he had "never seen one honest [English]man of them that come to see and learn the language as in other parts."[34]

Undaunted, Roos first went to Salamanca, believing it would be a beneficial place to practice his Spanish language skills, since there were no other Englishmen there. In all, he traveled throughout Spain for about eight months, with a brief foray into Portugal.[35] By mid-March, he received word from an angry uncle Salisbury, who argued that Spain was only a place to visit briefly and not a fitting place to tarry too long. Salisbury had heard rumors of Roos's Catholic conversion, but to Roos's relief, did not believe them. The rumors were enough to make Salisbury want Roos out of Spain as soon as possible, however. Roos, who thoroughly enjoyed his stay in Spain, seemed annoyed that his uncle wanted him to cut his stay short and dragged his feet. On May 20, after another angry letter from his uncle, Roos wrote and said he would return to Paris.[36]

A few days later, word reached Madrid that King Henri IV of France had been assassinated on May 14, leaving the situation in France tenuous. Roos wrote again to Salisbury, emphasizing that while he certainly wished to obey his great-uncle, he worried the tumult in France might make it dangerous to travel there for the moment. He intended to go to the Spanish French border, check out the situation, and then decide what to do. By the end of July, he was still in Spain. He tried to appease Salisbury by sending him a long account of his travels in Spain. It was not written in Roos's own hand but was entitled "A discourse of the Er. Roos his travails in Spain," and undersigned W. R. [William, Lord Roos]. Clearly, he wanted to show Salisbury that his journey had been instructive and that he had used his time well by learning not only the language but the culture and geography of Iberia as well.[37] He must have left the country to return to France shortly thereafter. By November, he had arrived back in Paris, planning to spend a few months there. His sojourn in Spain had made him "altogether after the Spanish fashion," according to one observer.[38]

In the spring of 1611, Roos traveled through the Low Countries.[39] Roos claimed that his grandfather the earl of Exeter ordered him to take the trip but did not say why.[40] His behavior on this journey left a deep impression on Thomas Lorkin, tutor to Sir Thomas Puckering. Puckering had been studying in France, where he made Roos's acquaintance.[41] The two decided to tour through the Low Countries together and Lorkin reluctantly agreed. However, the tutor quickly changed his mind about the suitability of Roos as a travel companion for young Puckering. In a candid and lengthy letter to Sir Adam Newton, Puckering's brother-in-law, Lorkin described their journey and his perception of Roos's problematic and disturbing behavior.[42]

The company set out from Paris on March 29. They passed through the towns of Peronne, Cambrai, Valeciennes, and Mons, before arriving at Brussels. In Brussels, they met up with Lord Cranbourne, Salisbury's son and Roos's cousin, on his way back from his own travels in Italy and Germany. So far, so good, Lorkin tells us. The only issue he had during this part of the trip was Roos's "unsavory & obscene discourse, wch my Lord usually fell into, able to corrupt a very chast mynde." Next on their journey was Antwerp. They spent a few days seeing worthy sights, of which Lorkin approved, but the rest of the time in Antwerp was "squandered away in play," overindulgence in food, and sleeping late. They kept bad company: especially troubling was the Catholic priest—who Lorkin had heard had acted as a spy for Spain when in England—and two English captains who were "notorious for their insolent carriage towards his Ma[jesty]."

Back in Brussels, the revelry continued. They did do something edifying by visiting the court of the *Infanta* Isabella Clara Eugenia and Albert, archduke of Austria, Regents of the Spanish Netherlands, three or four times, where they were well received. William Trumbull, the English agent at the archduke's court in Brussels, had been forewarned of Roos's coming. Since Roos was so closely related to Salisbury, Lord Treasurer and the king's most trusted adviser, Trumbull was asked to ensure that the young Lord would receive an honorable reception at the court in Brussels.[43] Lorkin no doubt thought this aspect of his charge traveling with the well-connected Roos was useful. Other than their courtly visit, the young men mostly wasted time by drinking until midnight, sometimes even until two or three a.m., and then not rising until nine or, more commonly, ten in the morning. "This grieved me much," Lorkin observed. Apparently, Roos's old travel companion, the Catholic convert Tobie Matthews, as well as his uncle Sir Thomas Cecil, were also present in Brussels at the same time.[44]

Parental fears of foreign women and foreign religion persisted in English Protestant minds. They viewed the continental Catholicism as potentially dangerous. Roos's father was at one point accused of having converted to Catholicism while abroad, and his grandfather's tutor had worried that his charge spent too much time in the company of Catholic Frenchmen, and not enough in the company of properly Protestant Englishmen while abroad. Likewise, as witnessed in Salisbury's concerned and angry letters to Roos, rumors flew that Roos was getting too chummy with Catholics while in Spain, and that he seemed drawn to characters known to work to convert Protestants. Lorkin worried especially that young Puckering might be seduced by the Roman faith. His worry increased when Roos insisted that they stop at a monastery with English Catholics along the way from Antwerp to Brussels. Disapprovingly, Lorkin observed Roos take leave of the prior of the monastery by bowing almost to the ground and kissing the hem of his garment. Clearly, he thought Roos was showing too much reverence to a Catholic clergyman.

At Brussels, Roos excluded Lorkin from the company's dinners, using the excuse that there was not enough space in his quarters to accommodate them all. While Lorkin did not mind a bit of a break from the boisterous young men, he was concerned about not being able to counter religious discussions for Puckering's protection. Roos invited Catholic priests and others, who Lorkin knew worked hard to convince Puckering to convert. Lorkin warned his charge and told him simply to remain quiet and not respond if the discussion turned to religion, or to try to change the subject. Puckering did not heed his tutor's advice and not being present during these discussions worried Lorkin a great deal. (Lorkin explained to Newton that he knew what they were discussing even though he was not present, because his chamber was next to the one where the party had their dinners. The walls were thin, so he could hear their conversation. He was eavesdropping on the young men.) Lorkin tried to convince Puckering that it was time to leave Roos's company, but "founde as good success here, as I had formerly done in laboring to dissuade from the journey itself," that is, none.

The other big problem with Roos was his love of everything Spanish and his growing disdain for England. Lorkin confided that he "never yet heard any so highly magnify any nation or country, as he doth this [Spain], with the vilifying not only all other stranger countries, but even of his owne." Roos was opposed to the Dutch Protestant rebellion against the Spanish crown and believed all those who supported them to be "no better than damned persons." Roos's embrace of Spain also extended to his own household: he had a Spanish attendant and he insisted that "no drinck [tastes] well but that which he [his Spanish attendant] brings him." Roos later had a most trusted and favored Spanish servant, Diego da Silva, and he is probably the person Lorkin was referring to, even though it is not entirely certain when he entered Roos's service. Da Silva returned to England with Roos and married an Englishwoman named Frances James. He also became an important witness in the Lake-Cecil feud.

After all the dissolute living, Puckering fell ill while at Brussels. The young man did not heed the doctor's orders, and when Lorkin insisted that he refrain from acts that would make him worse, Puckering responded by calling his struggling and wounded tutor a "foole." After Puckering's recovery, Lorkin renewed his request that they return to Paris, especially since the doctors argued that the air in the Low Countries was "aguish" and likely to cause a relapse. Puckering and Roos finally agreed, although their departure was further delayed when "the merchants refused to furnish my Lord [Roos] with any more mony." Roos then went to the English agent Trumbull and asked for a loan so he could travel, to which Trumbull reluctantly acquiesced. Trumbull did not have all the money available himself but managed to convince English merchants in the region to advance the funds, promising that they would receive their money back swiftly.[45] Like so many other of Roos's creditors, Trumbull would come to regret his generosity, but it was difficult to say no to such a well-connected young lord.

Roos intended to head home to England rather than back to Paris, so the company decided to take a coastal route, and then part ways at Calais. At long last, they set off on May 16, passing through Ghent, Bruges, Sluis, Ostend, Nieuwpoort, and Gravelines, before arriving at Calais on May 21. Lorkin also told Newton that this whole journey was evidence of how little sway he had over Puckering at this point, who chafed at the idea of being told what to do as "schoole-boy-like." While he believed that Puckering had great promise, he feared that his willfulness and bad choice of company might lead him astray, unless Newton could convince him to reform his behavior.

As a final salvo to illustrate Roos's depravity and bad behavior, Lorkin also recounted an event that had happened while they were in Sluis. Roos, disagreeing with the Dutch rebellion against the Spanish, wanted to mark his displeasure in the town, the only part of the Dutch Protestant states they had entered on their long journey. Before they arrived, Roos promised some mischief. As they were at the ferryboat which had taken them into town, Roos took out "his privy member [penis] in the presence of divers men & women," and "shewed them openly 5 or 6 times." This genital display was not quite enough for Roos. Once in town, they visited the church, where Roos loudly uttered profanities against the "Hollanders." Lorkin told Newton that he realized this was "not the cleanliest discourse, though [he] had contrived it into as cleanly termes as I can." He told Newton of the incident so that he could "understand him thoroughly" and, he added with a dose of sarcasm and exasperation, see "the good choice Mr. Puck: hath made of his company."

After this trip, Roos returned briefly to England, perhaps because he had run out of money and credit, or because his license to travel was expiring. He remained in England until the following spring. Throughout the summer and fall of 1611, Roos was repeatedly dodging the attempts of Trumbull's London agent to collect the debt he owed. Roos, who had promised to pay Trumbull back promptly upon his return to England, did not complete the payment of the funds until early November, and then only after increasing pressure from Trumbull's agent and friends.[46] In October, Roos wrote Prince Henry a letter from Nonsuch, fishing for an appointment within the prince's recently established household. He was unsuccessful, but not deterred. He may have believed that his friendship with young Puckering would help his cause. Puckering's brother-in-law, Sir Adam Newton, had served as Prince Henry's tutor, and Puckering had participated in the lessons as a companion to the prince. By 1611, Newton had become the crown prince's secretary. As Newton was also the recipient of Lorkin's missive describing Roos's bad behavior, the connection may not have been as beneficial as Roos believed. In January 1612, Roos sent his apologies to the earl of Rutland (a relative on his mother's side) that he had not visited him "when he was in the country."[47]

Roos received a new license to travel for three years on April 24, 1612. After another sojourn in the Low Countries, he planned "to be at the inauguration of the emperor."[48] The Holy Roman Emperor Rudolph II had recently died, and his brother Mathias had been duly voted the next Habsburg emperor to succeed him. Mathias's coronation was to be a stately affair, held in Frankfurt in late June 1612. On this occasion, Roos received his first diplomatic assignment from the English king, probably suggested by Salisbury. King James tasked Roos with presenting the English king's formal and official congratulations to the new emperor. Roos wrote to Secretary Lake on July 3, 1612, and thanked him for the opportunity to serve the king.[49]

While performing his duties abroad, Roos lost his main protector at home. Salisbury died in May, leaving the Cecils without their powerful representative in the Secretary of State position, and court politics shifted toward the numerous Howard clan instead. Roos's grandfather the earl of Exeter now served as the most senior patriarch of the Cecils, as Salisbury's son Lord Cranbourne (now 2nd earl of Salisbury) was still young and inexperienced.[50]

After attending the imperial coronation in Frankfurt, the peripatetic Roos set off again, this time toward Venice, arriving in early August.[51] By November, he had moved on to Florence. He was again looking to show himself useful to Prince Henry. The idea of a marriage between Prince Henry and the Medici duke's sister had been considered at the English court. Roos wrote an account reporting on the situation in the dukedom of Grand Tuscany and sent the account to one of the prince's close officials, Sir David Murray. The accompanying letter also exemplified Roos's abilities to play politics: Murray was no fan of a Catholic bride for Prince Henry and Roos warned him that people at the court in Florence had been told of his dislike. If the match went forward, Murray needed to be on guard against potential Florentine enemies.[52] None of Roos's efforts to ingratiate himself with Prince Henry paid off, however, as the prince had just died. By early December, the news of Henry's death reached Lord Roos in Florence. The avenue toward a court career in the prince's household was now permanently closed.

It is not clear where Roos spent most of 1613. He was in Florence late in the year. By late December, he was back in Venice, one of his favorite places. He found the city's festive and raucous carnival season particularly appealing. On January 3, 1614, Sir Dudley Carleton, English ambassador in Venice, informed John Chamberlain that Roos had "made haste from Florence to be present with us at our Communion on Christmas day," preceding Carnival. Carleton's household was furnished with an English Protestant priest to minister to both the ambassador as well as the many English visitors. Carleton was glad of Roos's participation, as it was evidence that he remained properly Protestant and Anglican. Carleton added that this was not welcome news in Rome, as "they have long had this young lord in their catalogue as one of their converts."[53]

Roos may have stayed in Italy throughout the next year as well, indulging his interest in art and collecting, purchasing both statues and paintings. At some point while in Venice, Roos had his portrait painted by Domenico Tintoretto, which unfortunately does not survive. Other English who stayed in Venice, like the ambassadors Carleton and Wotton, also hired Tintoretto, a popular portraitist.[54] Roos appears to have taken part in a developing culture of early Stuart art connoisseurs and collectors. While in Italy, he befriended Thomas Howard, earl of Arundel, and his wife, the rich heiress Alethea Talbot, both of whom were avid travelers, art patrons, and collectors. They were also Catholics, although Arundel later converted to Anglicanism. A few years later, the king's favorite, the duke of Buckingham, as well as Prince Charles (both as prince and later as king), also developed an interest in art, specifically painting, and used their art patronage and collecting as a way to shape their noble and royal images. Diplomats like Carleton, Wotton, and William Trumbull also understood the importance of art for courtiers and politicians, and often served as go-betweens for English patrons and foreign artists. Roos's interest in art connected to his aspirations to become a culturally sophisticated and politically adept servant to the king.[55] Ultimately, his art collecting, like his nascent political career, did not last.

Roos left his business in England in the hands of his servants, some of whom later rejoined him in Italy. In October 1614, the gentleman servant Giles Dunscombe received a pass "to repaire into Italy to the Lord Ross."[56] Around the same time, Roos's Spanish servant Diego da Silva returned briefly to England, presumably to do some errands for his master. He received a license to travel back to Roos in Italy in late December 1614, and to bring "suche trunckes of apparell and other necessary provisions (not prohibited) as he shall have occasion to carry over for his use."[57] Carleton, then still ambassador in Venice (although he was about to leave), asked Chamberlain if he had any news of "Don Diego." By December 22, Chamberlain reported that Diego had visited the earl of Exeter in England, but that was all he knew.[58]

Roos may have either purposefully or unwittingly caused problems for one of his traveling acquaintances and fellow art enthusiasts, Lord Arundel. On January 5, 1616, Chamberlain reported to Carleton that the king had questioned Arundel regarding his loyalty and religious affiliations while traveling in Italy. A recent Catholic, Arundel had converted to Anglicanism during Christmas 1615. "Yt is whispered abrode that your Don Diego's master gave very malignant intelligence of the Lord of Arundells beeing in Rome and of his entertainment and conversation there," Chamberlain noted. After being "put to his aunswer," Arundel "gave goode satisfaction" and presumably escaped censure at the time.[59]

During the early months of 1615, Roos headed northward. He had an unpleasant experience in northern Italy on his way home. Carleton had given da Silva "an item of some danger" to transport, which had led the Spaniard briefly to part company with Roos, perhaps to protect his master. The precaution proved necessary. In the town of Novara, an officer from Milan backed up by a company of forty soldiers forcefully entered Roos's chamber, looking for the absent da Silva. Considering these circumstances, Roos decided to skip visiting Milan and head straight through Switzerland instead.[60] By February 23, he was in Flushing, but then backtracked and went to Heidelberg in April and May, visiting the court of Frederick of the Palatinate and his English wife, Princess Elizabeth.[61] He was back in England by the summer of 1615, ready to settle down and to get serious about pursuing a political career.

A New Wife for Exeter

While Roos traveled throughout Europe, significant changes occurred in his grandfather's household. In March 1609, Exeter's wife Dorothy, Roos's grandmother, died.[62] Exeter remarried the following year. The earl had plenty of children (four sons and six daughters), so he did not remarry for the lack of heirs. Exeter was also immensely rich, so he certainly did not need to marry for money. He was already sixty-eight years old and his family well established, so he was not marrying to increase his political potential or power. He appears to have chosen his new bride primarily out of personal preference and desires. Thomas Screven informed the earl of Rutland on December 3, 1610, that it "is most sure that the Erle of Exeter is newly maried to the young faire Lady Smythe, the widow of Sir Thomas Smythe, Clark of the Counsell, and sister to the Lord Chandois, as I take it."[63] Exeter's beautiful new wife, the recently widowed Lady Frances Brydges Smith, would play a central role in the future Lake-Cecil feud. She became Roos's step-grandmother and was the main target for the Lakes' accusations of adultery and murder once the feud began to heat up.

Born Frances Brydges in 1580, she was the daughter of William Brydges, Lord Chandos and Mary Hopton. Sometime before 1604, Frances married her first husband, Sir Thomas Smith, the king's Latin Secretary who also became Master of Requests by 1608. The couple had two children, Robert and Margaret. When Robert was born in August of 1605, Salisbury became his godfather, suggesting friendly ties between the Smith and the Cecil families. Margaret was born sometime between 1606 and 1609. In addition to her husband's service at the Jacobean court, Frances also had ties to the court through her brother Grey Brydges, 5th Baron Chandos of Sudeley. Chandos was active in court entertainments in the early Jacobean period.[64]

In 1609, Sir Thomas became ill with a lingering disease. He tried the waters at Newnham, but it did not help. The colder weather of late fall seemed to make his condition worse, and by November, he was bedridden. He died on November 28 and was buried at Fulham on December 7.[65] His grieving wife erected a funeral monument for him in the local church.[66] Smith left his estate at Parsons Green in Fulham to his son Robert, but gave Frances the profits from it during life, as well as made her the sole executrix of his will, signaling a good relationship between the couple.[67] Frances was now a twenty-nine-year-old widow with two young children.

Frances's first husband had been twenty-four years her senior, so she was already used to an older husband when the almost four decades older earl of Exeter came courting. In addition, the exalted title, high political and social position of the Cecils, and Exeter's wealth made an attractive proposal. According to the Lakes, the widowed Frances had other suitors and had even accepted the proposal of Francis Crane, one of her husband's men, before she was aware of Exeter's interest. The Lakes argued that Frances had callously cast her betrothed aside and agreed to pay for his silence in order to pave the way for the much more prestigious marriage to the earl of Exeter. It is not clear if there is any truth in those accusations, as the Lakes made them at a time when they were trying to discredit the then countess of Exeter by painting her as a gold-digger and oath-breaker. Both Frances and Crane later denied having ever been betrothed. In any case, Frances accepted the earl of Exeter's proposal. In December 1610, she became the new countess of Exeter. Eight years later, her step-grandson's wife would accuse her of adultery, incest, and attempted poisoning.

The Lakes

Unlike the Cecils, the Lake family had more recently risen to prominence, and it was largely due to Sir Thomas Lake's own abilities, hard work, and good fortune. Lake's father, Emery Lake, was a customs official of little influence in Southampton. Young Thomas Lake was educated at a local grammar school and became very proficient in Latin. Later, he attended Oxford University. His political career began under the tutelage of Sir Francis Walsingham, Queen Elizabeth's spymaster and Secretary of State (after the 1st Lord Burghley had become Lord Treasurer). Lake was a lowly assistant at first, but then became Walsingham's clerk. His nickname "Swiftsure" described his speedy and accurate work. The first court appointment as Clerk of the Signet came in 1589. When Walsingham died in 1590, Lake searched for new patrons and found them in the Cecil family, specifically in Sir Robert Cecil (later Salisbury).

With the help of the Cecils, Lake was also returned for Parliaments in the early 1590s. He continued to be an MP during the reign of King James.[68]

By the time of James's reign, Lake made further advancements. When Elizabeth died, Lake was among the select group dispatched to Scotland to inform James of the news and his own ascension to the English throne. James favored Lake, knighted him in 1603, and retained him as Clerk of the Signet. In addition, Lake often accompanied the king on his frequent hunting trips. Like many other early Stuart officials and courtiers, Lake took advantage of his position by making money in other ventures. He and his father-in-law profited from buying parsonages from the crown and selling them at a profit. He also managed Queen Anna's impositions on sugar imports to his personal benefit. King James appointed Lake Latin Secretary after the death of Sir Thomas Smith in 1609 (Frances Brydges Smith's first husband).[69]

Lake had some trouble achieving his ultimate goal of succeeding his patron, Sir Robert Cecil, earl of Salisbury, as Secretary of State. He had hoped for it as early as 1605, when a friend wrote to Ralph Winwood that Lake certainly seemed fit for the office, but worried that it might be "too great a step for him," referring to his humble origins.[70] Lake's insufficient foreign language skills and knowledge of foreign politics and culture also hindered his advancement. He was a skilled Latinist but did not speak or write other languages very well, making the king doubt that he could take over the role successfully. When Salisbury died in 1612, Lake was disappointed that King James decided to be his own secretary, although it was the king's favorite, Robert Carr, earl of Somerset, who did most of the actual job. Two years later, King James finally tired of the ad hoc arrangement and decided to appoint a regular secretary. To Lake's chagrin, James chose Sir Ralph Winwood, Lake's main rival at court. Lake did become a Privy Councilor in the same year (1614), which was a step upward. After much machination and continued disappointments, Lake finally attained his long-held dream in January of 1616, when James decided to have two secretaries: Winwood continued in his position, dealing with foreign correspondence, and Lake became junior Secretary of State, allotted the domestic correspondence. While Lake had thus risen to prominence, his brother Arthur Lake made a career for himself in the church. He was a studious man who eventually rose to become bishop of Bath and Wells. The two brothers managed to do very well for themselves.[71]

Sir Thomas Lake married Mary Ryder in 1591, the daughter of Sir William Ryder of London. Lady Mary Lake became one of the main driving figures in the later Lake-Cecil feud. Mary Ryder did not come from the nobility, but her father was a person of note in the city of London. He was a wealthy haberdasher who served in various offices of note: sheriff, alderman, and Lord Mayor of London. Ryder had no sons living, so Mary and her sister Susan (who married Sir Thomas Caesar) were co-heiresses to their father's fortune upon his death in 1609. Over the course of their long marriage, the Lakes had several sons and daughters. The sons included Thomas (b. ca. 1595), Arthur (b. 1598), and Lancelot (b. 1609). The family had at least three daughters: Anne (b. 1599), Elizabeth, and Bridget (b. 1616).[72]

Even before the trouble began between the Lakes and the Cecils in 1617, Mary Lake had acquired a reputation of being a "difficult" woman. Seventeenth-century expectations for ideal female behavior included silence, obedience, meekness, grace, and humility. Women who were too assertive, too loud, or too ambitious were often perceived as problematic. King James was especially troubled by assertive women and heartily disliked the fashion that developed in the 1610s, when some women wore masculine hats, cropped and curled their hair, and wore little rapiers at their waists.[73]

In 1612, Chamberlain remarked that Mary Lake's behavior was the cause of the seemingly stalled career of her husband. Chamberlain called Mary Lake Sir Thomas's "Xantippe," which referred to Socrates's "spirited" wife. By the early modern era, the moniker was a synonym for a dominating shrew. Chamberlain noted that in addition to Lake's suspected Catholicism, it was Lake's wife who "is so well-known and blased, that I thinke she is a principall barre to his preferment." To illustrate his point, he also added "indeed they say she hath plaide her prises of late and beaten her eldest sonne outrageously, who is already contracted to Master Watsons daughter."[74] The son, Thomas, was seventeen at the time, so Chamberlain clearly believed that he should be too old for beatings from a mother, especially since he was betrothed and about to become a married man. (Although he did not actually marry until 1633, when he was a full thirty-eight years old.) In his book about James I and his court, James's contemporary Godfrey Goodman (ca. 1582–1656), bishop of Gloucester, relayed a rumor that Lady Lake beat and "overawed" her husband, but then went on to explain that that rumor was not true. He guessed the rumor had started from assumptions, because Lady Lake was "a woman of great courage" and her husband was a man of "weak, thin body."[75] The rumor may have stemmed from a combination of Chamberlain's report of the alleged beating of the son, coupled with the period after the court cases, when Lady Lake was found guilty of slander and forgery, and Lake was faulted for having gone along with his wife's charges against the countess of Exeter.

Lady Lake certainly appears to have stood up for what she believed was hers. In 1613, she had a dispute with her sister and co-heiress, Lady Caesar, over some of their deceased father's rents and property, which ended up in the Court of Wards. Chamberlain reported to Carleton on January 28, 1613, that Sir Walter Cope "made me a long relation of the great cause now before him twixt the Lady Lakes and her sister the Lady Caesar, wherin he shall have much ado to carrie himself so even between wind and water, that he displease not Sir Thomas or Master Chauncellor [Sir Julius Caesar, Lady Caesar's brother-in-law]."[76] By November of the same year, the dispute appears to have been mediated. The Court of Wards had come to a decision on November 13, and Sir Thomas Lake also found out that Lady Caesar was ready to compromise with her sister, which apparently necessitated destroying their father's will.[77]

All three Lake sons received a good education: they went to university (Oxford and Cambridge) and received legal training at the Inns of Court.[78] The two eldest sons traveled abroad. Both Thomas and Arthur traveled in Germany and the Spanish Netherlands in 1613, and Arthur also went to France from 1615 to 1617.[79] Lake surely wanted to give his sons a better opportunity than he had. Lake probably felt keenly his lack of language skills, save Latin. During the formal reading of the marriage contract between Princess Elizabeth and Frederick, Elector Palatinate in 1612, Lake had been humiliated when he was forced to read French to the whole court. He had "translated the wordes of our communion booke into French so badly, and pronounced them worse, that yt moved an unseasonable laughter as well in the contractors as in the standers by."[80] Unlike his two elder brothers, the youngest Lake son Lancelot does not seem to have gone abroad, perhaps because his family had fallen from favor before he reached the age to do so.

Anne Lake was born in November 1599, the eldest daughter of Sir Thomas and Lady Mary Lake.[81] Anne Lake became one of the countess of Exeter's main accusers during the Lake-Cecil feud. As is the case with many early modern girls who did not receive formal education, we know next to nothing about Anne's childhood and early youth. In addition to a London house in Charing Cross, her father had purchased a property in Little Stanhope called Cannons by 1604, where he built a new brick mansion. Anne may have spent her youth in either of the two houses, or both. When she was a mere five years old, her future husband Lord Roos (then fifteen) left England for his decade abroad. It is fair to conclude that Anne had a much more sheltered upbringing than her husband.

By the mid-1610s, the up-start Lake family and the settled, wealthy, and powerful Cecil family had been linked through ties of courtly service and patronage for several decades. In early 1616, they were joined more directly through the marriage of William Cecil, Lord Roos, to Anne Lake. Disagreements within and about the marriage became the main impetus for the feud between the Lakes and the Cecils. The primary people involved in the disputes included the young Lord and Lady Roos, Sir Thomas and Lady Mary Lake and their son Sir Arthur Lake, and Thomas and Frances Cecil, the earl and countess of Exeter. However, as the feuding developed, heated up, and exploded, further family members, friends, associates, clients, servants, and innocent bystanders would get pulled in by the maelstrom. King, court, council, ambassadors, and agents both in England and abroad would have to contend with the consequences and fallout.

2

Wedded to Trouble

> Upon Monday ye 12th my Lord Roos was married to Mrs Anne Lake, the Secretarys daughter.
>
> Diary of Anne Clifford, February 1616[1]

By the early summer of 1615, Roos's long educational travels were finally coming to an end: in May, he left Germany and headed toward England.[2] In July, he attended the English court and was given the honor of carrying the sword in front of King James, a task reserved for noblemen.[3] Roos's appearance at court signaled his readiness to establish himself at home as a proper Cecil heir: at age twenty-five, he now hoped to follow in the footsteps of his illustrious relatives. By the spring of 1616, he seemed poised for success, receiving his first official royal diplomatic appointment as an extraordinary ambassador to Spain.

Roos also needed a wife. Both his grandfather and his father had married promptly after returning from their foreign travels, and no doubt expected Roos to do the same. The marriage alliance that Roos and his family eventually forged with the new Secretary of State became the link that tied the Lake and Cecil families together. That marriage, which initially seemed so suitable and promising, instead became the foundation and origin of the years-long fierce feud.

The Marriage

Marriage was expected of most, of course, as marriage signaled maturity and entrance into full adulthood. It was especially important for noblemen to continue and pass down noble lineages, titles, and estates. In addition, the notions of masculinity and manhood for nobility included heading a large household. A complete noble household certainly required a wife and children, but it also included servants, staff, tenants, a network of clients, and other reliant men and women. To be a man meant controlling others, especially women, and a nobleman ruled like a king over his extensive household.[4]

Family and Feuding at the Court of James I: The Lake and Cecil Scandals. Johanna Luthman, Oxford University Press.
 DOI: 10.1093/oso/9780192865786.003.0002

It is possible that the earl of Exeter had considered a wife for Roos as early as 1607. He had negotiated with the countess of Cumberland for her young daughter Anne Clifford, a wealthy heiress after the death of her father. Those negotiations came to naught: Anne Clifford married Sir Richard Sackville instead and Roos continued his travels for the better part of eight more years.[5] Briefly interrupting educational travel for a marriage was not unprecedented in Roos's circle. His cousin and namesake William Cecil, Lord Cranborne (eldest son of Robert Cecil, earl of Salisbury), briefly returned home to marry Catherine Howard, daughter of the Earl of Suffolk, in 1608. After the wedding, he departed again, traveling for several more years. Similarly, the young Robert Devereaux, 3rd earl of Essex, married Frances Howard, another of Suffolk's daughters, and then set off for educational travels before returning to his bride. Roos had remained a bachelor while traveling, but in the fall of 1615, he and his family began casting about for an appropriate candidate in earnest.

While Roos was re-adjusting to life in England and searching for a bride, the politics at court began to shift as the sordid details of one of the worst scandals at the court of King James became public. In fall 1615, the news broke that the death of Sir Thomas Overbury in the Tower two years previously had not been due to a disease—but murder. The most scandalous part of the news was that the persons who had orchestrated the murder were none other than Robert Carr, earl of Somerset, and his wife Frances Howard (previously married to the earl of Essex). Somerset had been King James's great favorite since the early 1610s. Upon the death of Roos's great uncle Robert Cecil, earl of Salisbury in 1612, Somerset had taken over not just the king's affections, but also a great deal of political power at court.

Throughout the fall of 1615, the servants and other persons who had carried out the practical business of procuring and administering the poison to Overbury two years prior were tried, convicted, and executed. The trial of the earl and countess of Somerset happened in May 1616. The countess declared herself guilty at trial, but Somerset insisted on his innocence. Nevertheless, both were convicted and condemned to death, but rather quickly pardoned and imprisoned in the Tower for several years instead.

While the fate of the former favorite was fading, Sir Thomas Lake's political star was on the rise. As early as September 1615, rumors of his impending appointment as secretary began to spread.[6] By January 1616, he formally and officially received the long-coveted position along with the royal seal. At the time, King James decided to have two secretaries, so Sir Ralph Winwood, sole secretary since 1614, now continued in the role of secretary of the foreign correspondence, whereas Lake became the secretary for the king's domestic correspondence.

Winwood and Lake were rivals and not particularly fond of each other: Winwood was a staunch Protestant, did not like Lake's Catholic leanings, and had been appointed to be a counterweight to the powers of the Howard family. Winwood had also been preferred to secretary before Lake, even though they had both competed for the same position. Winwood did not want to share his role as secretary and was not pleased when Lake received the honor of having the same "diet" at court as he did. (The courtly "diet," or how much food the king allotted you and your servants while at the royal court, was a sign of rank and royal favor.) Perhaps James thought the two might create a needed balance in court politics and on the privy council. The appointment positioned Lake firmly in the inner circle of royal power. His friends and well-wishers congratulated him on his good fortune, while disappointed rivals had to wait for other opportunities.[7]

By late 1615, the idea of a marriage between Roos and Lake's eldest daughter began to take shape. Anne Lake was fifteen, a full decade younger than Roos. On average, women married in their mid-twenties, and men in their mid- to late twenties in early modern England. Anne was unusually young when compared to the average of the population, but not when compared to women from wealthy families. Young people usually had to work for a time to save money before marriage, to be able to set up independent households (the so-called Northwestern European marriage pattern). The daughters and sons of the wealthy, who did not have the same financial concerns, often married younger, in their mid- to late teens. Roos's own family serves as evidence. Roos's mother had been a mere fourteen years old when she married, fifteen when she gave birth to him, and sixteen when she died in childbirth. Roos's cousin Frances Coke was sixteen when she married in 1617. His grandmother Dorothy Neville was fifteen when she married his grandfather, and his great-aunt Anne Cecil was likewise fifteen when she married Edward de Vere, earl of Oxford. The Lakes would not have been concerned about Anne's young years: her mother Mary Ryder was sixteen when she married her father.[8]

A marriage between Lake's daughter and Exeter's grandson was a good one in theory. Lake was an untitled newcomer in the halls of power and found the match with the Exeter branch of the Cecil family a good alliance with an established, and very rich, noble family. The Cecils had been his political patrons since the 1590s, although those ties had weakened after Salisbury's death in 1612, after which Lake had mostly allied with the Howards at court. The Cecils and Howards were also linked, having created two marriage alliances between their families. Roos's cousin Lord Cranbourne (Salisbury's son) married Catherine Howard, daughter of the Treasurer, Thomas Howard, earl of Suffolk, in 1608, and Roos's half-sister Elizabeth Cecil married Suffolk's son Thomas in 1614.[9] A marriage between Anne Lake and Roos thus strengthened Lake's ties to both the Cecils and the Howards. In addition, the young Roos stood to inherit both an earldom and a fortune upon the deaths of his grandfather and father, which meant Lake's potential grandchildren would become part of the high nobility. Such marriage alliances presented a common path for the newly powerful to weave their way into the titled elite.

The earl of Exeter and Lord Burghley no doubt found the alliance with the daughter of the soon-to-be new Secretary of State a good connection to get Roos established in a future career as a courtier and a politician. Although Exeter was a Privy Councilor, he had never been as active and influential in politics as his half-brother. Since Salisbury's death in 1612, the Cecils had been moved aside by the powerful Howard family, causing the young 2nd earl of Salisbury not to be able to mirror his father's influence. In late 1615, with the uncertainties of the Overbury scandal hanging over the court favorite and his closest associates among the Howards, it was a strategic move for the Cecils to also create a familial connection to the brand-new secretary.

Apart from the considerations about wealth, status, political power, and connections, Roos may have also liked the prospect of hitching his wagon to Lake's family since they shared his affinity for Spain and for Catholicism, even if none of them were openly Catholic at the time. Roos had made no secret of his love for all things Spanish. The Spanish ambassador to England had recognized Lake's potential usefulness as early as 1614, when Lake began receiving an annual pension from the diplomat. That was not an unusual arrangement: Spain paid annual pensions to several other persons at the Jacobean court, such as Suffolk's countess. It did not mean those people always acted in Spain's interest, but the ambassador certainly believed it would help him achieve his goals.[10] When King James began contemplating a Spanish princess as a bride for Prince Charles, Lake certainly was supportive. No sources mention Anne Lake's views, so we cannot know if she shared this affinity for Catholic Spain. In any case, the young and inexperienced Anne's views would probably hardly have mattered to the patriarchs negotiating the match.

By late January 1616, the families had concluded the negotiations. Reports differed slightly, but Anne's dowry amounted to either £5,000 or £6,000, a substantial, but not an astronomical sum.[11] (For comparison, Roos's cousin Frances Coke brought her husband an unusually generous dowry of £15,000 in 1617.) Both the Lakes and the Cecils seemed very pleased with the match and the agreement.[12] Initially, the wedding had been set to take place after Easter, but the groom's father thought it too long a wait: he worried that something might intervene and disrupt the agreement.[13] Since weddings were not supposed to take place during Lent, the ceremony was moved up to the day before Shrove Tuesday. Thus, on that particular Monday in mid-February, Anne Lake and William Cecil became a married couple, thereafter known as Lord and Lady Roos.[14] (I will refer to Anne Lake as Lady Roos throughout the rest of the book.)

Roos had managed to outmaneuver a friend when claiming his bride. Sir Thomas Puckering, his young travel companion with the disapproving tutor, had looked to marry Anne Lake as well. He had begun negotiations before Roos swooped in. Perhaps Anne's other eager suitors made Burghley want to clinch the deal as soon as possible. Roos won the prize, and Adam Newton, Puckering's brother-in-law, believed that "no man was thought to have greater wrong by that marriage" than Puckering.[15] Puckering was disappointed, but found another bride a few months later, also with a £5,000 dowry.[16] A couple of years later, after considering the terrible feud the Roos-Lake marriage engendered, Newton noted that in the end, Puckering should "thank God that you missed of that bargain."[17]

An Unexpected Pregnancy

Sometime before Roos's marriage to Anne Lake, his step-grandmother, the countess of Exeter, fell pregnant. By March, the pregnancy had proceeded to the stage of "quickening," the moment when a woman could feel the fetus move in the womb. For seventeenth-century people, the quickening also generally constituted the moment of ensoulment of the fetus, and the first truly reliable confirmation of a successfully progressing pregnancy. News about her condition began to spread.

On March 17, 1616, Chamberlain wrote to Carleton that the Lady Exeter was "quick with childe" and that this information "runs up and down for great newes."[18] Chamberlain regularly reported pregnancies and births among the great families, but this note was different. It was not an issue of reporting on a potential new heir: Exeter had plenty of adult children from his first marriage, both sons and daughters. At the time of the birth of a daughter in July, the countess was thirty-six and her husband was seventy-four. It was the first reported pregnancy after six years of marriage. Both the countess and the earl had children from previous marriages and so do not seem to have suffered from difficulties conceiving in the past. The extra notation of the pregnancy as newsworthy implies that some were surprised that the countess was pregnant, especially considering the advanced age of her husband. Edward Sherburn was more direct in his letter to Carleton: "The report of my La of Exeter being wth child is certainly true, a blessing beyond expectacion to that good & noble Lady; by so aged a Lord."[19]

Two diarists also noted the birth of the Exeter child that summer. Anne Clifford, who wrote mostly about the private affairs of herself, her family, and friends in her diary, also recorded a few other items that she found newsworthy. Among those was a brief entry for August 1616, which read "about this time, my Lady Exeter was brought to bed of a daughter."[20] The countess was not in Clifford's circle of family and friends, so she clearly thought the birth newsworthy (she later recorded information about the Lake-Cecil feud, greater scandal, and court trials as well). William Camden, who mostly took note of political events and appointments in his diary, specifically wrote under July 1616 that a "little daughter was born to the earl of Exeter, now 72 years old."[21] Camden was two years off since Exeter was actually seventy-four at the time of the birth. Camden found it noteworthy that such an old man would become a father.

While Chamberlain, Clifford, and Camden were only hinting at the—in their eyes—unusual pregnancy, others appear to have been more direct. They believed that the old earl was not the father, but rather that the recently returned Lord Roos was responsible for the countess's condition. Letters in 1616 did not mention this rumor outright, but a later one referred to it once the larger scandal had broken in 1618. At that point, George Gerrard assured Carleton that just like most did not then believe Lady Roos's accusations of adultery and poisoning against the countess of Exeter, the "scandal also that my Ld Rosse should get that childe the Lady of Exeter had last, not beleaved."[22]

At around half an hour past nine in the morning on Saturday, July 13, the countess successfully gave birth to a baby girl.[23] According to the parish register in Wimbledon, the girl was named Georgi-Anna, although her later burial lists her as Sophia Anne. Elizabeth Gresham, the countess of Exeter's gentlewoman servant, called the little girl "the Lady Anne Cecill" in a later document, so her family may have simply called her Anne. Normally, parents requested three godparents, or "gossips" for their newborns: two godfathers and a godmother for boys, and two godmothers and one godfather for girls. Unusually, Georgi-Anna only had one godmother, but an exalted one: Queen Anna agreed to the role. Edward Somerset, the earl of Worcester and King James's Lord Privy Seal, became her godfather. Although the first part of the girl's name may be a bit uncertain, no doubt the second name was in honor of the queen. The baptism, performed by the bishop of London, was held in the afternoon on July 30 at Wimbledon.[24] The countess of Exeter did not attend. Mothers were generally not present at baptisms, as they did not participate in religious ceremonies or social events until they had gone through "churching." The churching usually took place about forty days after the birth. It blessed the new mother after childbirth (or cleansed, in some interpretations, based on Jewish ritual cleansing), marked the end of the secluded lying-in period surrounding the birth, and the new mother re-entered society afterwards. As she was recovering from childbirth, the countess also received the sad news that her sister Eleanor, Lady Turville had died of smallpox.[25]

Was Roos the father of the countess of Exeter's little daughter (see Fig. 2.1)? The short, and admittedly rather unsatisfying, answer: there is no way of knowing. Georgi-Anna was born within the bounds of marriage and English law generally recognized a child as legitimate as long as the mother was married and the husband resided within the country's borders at the time of conception.[26] Georgi-Anna's legitimacy was never legally questioned even in the later slander lawsuits. She also did not live long enough to inherit or marry or get involved in any other legal matters.

Lady Roos and her family later insisted that Roos had a relationship with his step-grandmother, and the countess and her husband insisted that he did not. When the feud heated up between the Lakes, Roos, and Exeters in 1617 and 1618, Lady Roos began to tell a dark tale of adulterous love between her husband and the countess of Exeter. She claimed she had become aware of the illicit relationship during the summer of 1616, the same summer that the countess gave birth to Georgi-Anna. During that first summer as a married woman, Lady Roos resided with the countess of Exeter at Wimbledon, the Exeter estate outside of London. There, Lady Roos claimed, Roos and the countess admitted to having an affair, and the countess especially asked Lady Roos for forgiveness and promised it would not happen again. Moving forward, Lady Roos certainly seemed convinced that the countess continued her "unseemly coveting" of her husband notwithstanding her promise to stop. In hindsight, Lady Roos's tale grew more sinister, and Chapter 6 explores that story further.

The accusations of adultery between the countess of Exeter and Roos included the crime of incest. The countess of Exeter and Roos were not relatives by blood, of course, since the earl's first wife, Dorothy Neville, was Roos's grandmother. It would have been a biological impossibility for Frances Brydges to have been Roos's grandmother anyway, since she was a full

Fig. 2.1 A portrait of a child, said to be Georgianna Cecil. Cornelius Janssens van Ceulen, 1617. The Burghley House Collection. In the top right corner, it says "Aetatis 1 ¼ An. 1617." Georgi-Anna would have been a little over a year old in the fall of 1617.

fourteen years *younger* than her step-son, Roos's father Burghley. (Burghley was born in 1566, and his stepmother in 1580.) However, the definition of incest was more expansive in the seventeenth century, generally also encompassing relations through marriage. Relationships between step-children, step-parents, or in-laws were also considered incestuous.[27]

Even though Lady Roos and the Lakes accused the countess and Roos of having an affair, they never mentioned the paternity of Georgi-Anna specifically. When the earl and countess of Exeter eventually won their slander court case against the Lakes three years later, the general opinion swung in their favor. After their court victory in 1619, many believed the accusations of adultery against the countess were entirely false together with all the other accusations. It was potentially costly to write down clear accusations of misbehavior, as suing for slander and libel had become more common during the early Jacobean period (see Chapters 10 and 11). Letter writers commonly informed the recipients of their missives that information considered especially sensitive would be relayed by "the bearer" of the letter instead. It was safer to write only vague innuendos and save particulars for private conversations largely lost to posterity. For example, Sir John Throckmorton wrote about the Lake-Cecil feud to Carleton in 1618, telling him that his other friends would "undoubtedly give you much better account of this busyness than I can doe, yet if I durst commit it to paper I would." He cautiously added that he "had rather you shoulde heare it from others, then from me."[28]

In 1616, the rumors of the noteworthy pregnancy were vague: it is not clear if they were based on any specific behavior or knowledge, or even where the information originated. Some might have found it easy to think that Roos, a vigorous young man in his mid-twenties, fresh off his educational travels with many adventures to tell, would be more exciting company for the countess than her elderly earl.

Early modern people believed that a marriage with a very large age difference between the spouses was not ideal and might lead the younger spouse to commit adultery. When the Jacobean courtier William Sanderson described the marriage of the earl of Exeter to Frances Brydges Smith, he said Frances was "a youthful" and "vertuous widow," who "became bed-fellow to this aged, gouty, and diseased, but noble earl."[29] An elderly husband might not have the energy or physical capacity to sexually satisfy his more vigorous young wife, leading her to look elsewhere. In addition, such a marriage might not produce children, robbing the young wife of the joys and responsibilities of motherhood.[30] Furthermore, the age difference could make for a less companionable marriage, as the couple might have different interests when in such different life-stages. The elderly husband was likely to suffer poor health, leading the young wife to serve more as a nurse than wife. For all these reasons, a May-December coupling was risky, as the old husband might became that most ridiculed of early modern figures: a man with an unfaithful wife, a horn-wearing cuckold.[31]

Lack of sex, or lack of vigorous sex, could also be considered physically problematic for a woman of childbearing age, potentially causing illnesses.[32] When the countess of Exeter sought medical attention from the royal physician Theodore de Mayerne in 1614 for melancholy, gastric upset, and swelling of the legs, he noted first in his case book that the countess was "young of years" and "married to an older man." He also noted that her menses were "flowing," but in a small amount, and "badly colored." After treating her for several weeks, he believed that most of her problems were due to a misdiagnosis and misguided treatment by other doctors after an earlier malignant fever. The treatment he subscribed aimed to provoke greater menstruation, in order to unblock superfluous melancholy humors from her system. Perhaps the countess's condition had prevented her from conceiving, although there is no note about that. In the end, Mayerne did not think it was lack of sexual activity which caused the countess's conditions, but he certainly found the information about the couple's age disparity important from a medical perspective, since he noted it down in his casebook.[33]

What we can tell with some clarity is that Roos was back in England by the time the countess became pregnant. He was in Spain and in France in 1610, the year that his grandfather married the widowed Frances Smith. He returned to England briefly in 1611 and then set off again for three years in the spring of 1612. No one reported any Exeter pregnancies between 1610 and 1615. Roos returned to England in the early summer of 1615 and the countess became pregnant roughly around October or November of the same year. Chamberlain also reported a second pregnancy in early December 1616. That would have been rather fast after giving birth in July, but not impossible.[34] Either that was a false report, or the pregnancy ended in a miscarriage. No one else mentions a second pregnancy or birth, and considering the stir of the first one, one would expect that a second so soon after the first would not have gone unnoticed. In short, Roos was in England when his step-grandmother became pregnant, but pregnancy certainly requires a bit more than proximity. It is also possible that the simple fact that the countess's surprising pregnancy coincided with her stepson's return caused tongues to wag.

Apart from the rumors and speculations about the countess of Exeter's young daughter, the diarist Anne Clifford also made an evocative note regarding the countess and Lord Roos in early 1617. Clifford was unhappily married to Richard Sackville, earl of Dorset. They quarreled regularly over the issue of her inheritance from her father, how to run the household, and the company Dorset kept. Clifford also disliked that he sometimes restricted her movements and social interactions, in addition to flaunting his mistress. Dorset regularly attended the court and partook in gambling, such as the cockfights so beloved by King James. In a diary entry for April 8, 1617, Clifford noted that while sitting in a chamber with her husband and brother-in-law Sir Edward Sackville, she heard the two men discuss "many businesses." Among them, she "perceived that he [not clear if this refers to Dorset or his brother] was entered into a business between my Lady of Exeter & my Lord Roos of which he will not easily quit himself."[35] Frustratingly, she did not explain this "business" further. Roos had recently come home from a trip to Spain when the Sackville brothers had this conversation. Interestingly, Clifford made this note *before* the major public feud broke out between the Lakes and the Cecils, and before Lady Roos and the Lakes began to accuse the countess of adultery more openly, which suggests that she was not influenced by those later rumors at the time of the diary entry.

The Embassy to Spain

If he heard of the rumors of Roos's possible involvement in the countess of Exeter's pregnancy, the king did not let them deter him from awarding the young man a diplomatic appointment in 1616. The kings of Spain and France had concluded a significant alliance in 1615 via two marriages: the Spanish princess Anna (known as Anne of Austria) married the French King Louis XIII, and Louis's sister Elizabeth married the Spanish *Infante* Philip (later Philip IV). King James thought it wise to note the occasion and send extraordinary ambassadors to both France and Spain officially to offer the English king's congratulations on the marriages. In late April 1616, King James appointed James, Lord Hay to go to France, and Roos to go to the Spanish court. No doubt, Roos's appointment was a result of his new father-in-law's influence as well as Roos's own familiarity with the country.[36] After all, as the Venetian ambassador in England reported, Roos was "by education and habit entirely Spanish."[37]

Roos was excited about the opportunity. It was exactly the sort of job for which his many years of educational travel had prepared him. He wanted to do well, and he wanted to impress. The Venetian ambassador to England remarked that "from a sure source I know that Lord Roos" had "hopes of acquiring great reputation by concluding this business" and that "he is very gratified at receiving this charge, although he cannot hide from himself that it will be entirely at his own expense"[38] Chamberlain likewise told Carleton that this "honour he and his new father in law take so to heart, that they make profession to performe yt very honorablie and to spare no expense."[39]

Roos received his appointment in April but did not actually leave for Spain until early November. By that time, Hay had already made it to France, proffered the English king's congratulations, and returned to England, although his formal report about his embassy had to be put off by a couple of days as he was hit in the eye while playing tennis.[40] Part of Roos's delay may have been James playing politics: he wanted to give preference to the French king and was slower in giving Roos his formal order to leave. In fact, the Spanish had initially been relieved to hear of his plan to send Roos at all, because they had feared "that France would be honoured with such an envoy but not Spain."[41] On July 10, the archbishop of Canterbury told Trumbull that Lord Hay was about to leave, and that Lord Roos would "be sent to Spain" toward "the end of August."[42] By August 28, Roos had gone to court to formally take his leave of King James before setting off for Spain, but still he tarried.[43]

In Spain, preparations were also underway for Roos's arrival. On June 6, 1616, Francis Cottington, the regular English ambassador to Spain, wrote from Madrid: "We are expecting Lord Ros on a special mission to congratulate the King on his children's marriages. I have given official notification of it, and judged by the general satisfaction, he will be well entertained."[44] By September, Cottington reported that the Spanish court had prepared a house for Roos, and that he was sure Roos would "be gratified by the reception here."[45]

And yet, Roos remained in England throughout most of the fall. Others noted the slow progression of Roos's preparations. In May, Sir John Throckmorton reported to William Trumbull that "Lord Haye advanceth his great preparations for his imployment into France, but my Lord Roos dothe goe on *pian piano* [Italian, "slowly"] with his into Spain."[46] The main reason for the delay was the fact that Roos had trouble raising the funds needed. If he wanted to impress, he needed to dress the part, and he needed as large a retinue as possible, also richly outfitted. He needed to travel in style, and stay in appropriately fancy lodgings, and so on. The Exchequer provided some funds toward the project, but it is not quite clear how much.[47] In any case, embassies were chronically underfunded, and ambassadors constantly had to lobby to get their meagre pay. An extraordinary ambassadorial trip was also viewed as an honor and rulers expected that their appointees would spend liberally from their own coffers.

Roos, the rich young heir to even more fortunes, was never any good with money. He had run out of both money and credit during his travels but had probably been rescued by his father and grandfather, or perhaps by his uncle Salisbury. He appeared to be constantly in debt, and he learned to hide it from his family. He borrowed money from Trumbull in 1611 and spent the next few months dodging repayment, so much so that his friend Toby Mathews apologized to Trumbull for having suggested that he lend Roos the money in the first place.[48]

In 1615, before negotiations with the Lakes for a marriage had even begun, Roos had used some of his estates as collateral for loans. When this came to light a year later, it caused endless disagreements between Roos, his in-laws, and his father and grandfather (see Chapters 3 and 5). During the summer of 1616, while trying to raise money for his upcoming embassy, Roos quarreled with Burghley. Carleton, who knew Roos from his travels, noted that the young man did not get along well with his father.[49] Notably, Burghley and Exeter did not contribute any money to pay for Roos's embassy. Roos did raise some money, and angered his new wife and in-laws, by selling or pawning her jewelry, most of which she had in her possession before her marriage.[50]

The main source of the money needed consisted of his father-in-law Lake. Roos and the Lakes later presented vastly different accounts of the financial agreements they struck prior to Roos leaving for Spain. Here, we will look at those different versions; first the events according to Roos, and then the Lake version.[51]

According to Lord Roos, the Lakes showed their true colors early by betraying him. Rather than assist their new son-in-law in his first significant political appointment, as should have been the natural behavior of kin, they used his financial predicament to their own benefit. Although Sir Thomas Lake was Secretary of State, he refused to help Roos raise money unless Roos would make over his estate of Walthamstow to his new wife. Walthamstow was a rich property in Essex, which included two manor houses, substantial acreages of fields, arable land, meadows, woods, and paying tenants.[52] Roos initially hesitated, as he knew it would displease his powerful grandfather and the family patriarch, the earl of Exeter. However, he desperately needed money fast. Hard pressed, Roos finally accepted very disadvantageous terms for a £6,000 loan from Lake, with Walthamstow as collateral. What he did not realize until later was that the Lakes had tricked him into giving up his rights to Walthamstow altogether, rather than having simply—as he thought—mortgaged the estate.

On the other hand, according to the Lakes, they were acting in the best interest of their daughter Anne, Lady Roos. They argued that Sir Thomas had lent Roos £6,000. Roos had used Walthamstow as collateral for the loan and added some of the income from the estate to the annual sum for his wife's maintenance. The agreement stated that if Roos defaulted on the loan, the lands would then go to the future children of the Roos marriage, and if they had no children, to Lady Roos and her heirs. The Lakes argued that they had observed all the legalities in the financial agreement, and they had properly and officially recorded all the deeds and papers. Furthermore, Roos had readily agreed to the deal because he was naturally motivated by a great love for his wife and the hope of future children inheriting and perpetuating his estate and titles.

Even though the full disagreement of the interpretations of the financial arrangements did not surface until the following year, Roos still felt that he had been unduly pressured into borrowing so much money from his in-laws. Increasingly, he became friendlier with Lake's colleague and main rival at court, Secretary Sir Ralph Winwood (see Fig. 2.2). This shift marked quite a turnaround. As late as April 1616, Roos and his stepmother Lady Burghley had said something slanderous about Winwood, but the secretary had magnanimously agreed to forget about it, rather than bring it to the law, once they apologized.[53] By October, as his voyage drew near, Roos had reportedly "grown great with Winwood" and that "some say he [Roos] relies more on him than father-in-law Lake."[54] Carleton thought Roos's increasingly negative feelings toward his father-in-law fit with the young lord's character, but thought it "strange how he could insinuate himself where he loves so little and where he is so well known." The staunch Protestant Winwood, who was no fan of Spain and the idea of a Spanish match, seemed an odd mentor and companion for Roos, who was so fond of Spain and Italy both. "I hope our good friend will be wise and wary enough for being overtaken," Carleton concluded, referring to Winwood.[55]

Signs of Roos's newfound affection toward Winwood continued to emerge. Roos himself later said that Winwood had generously offered to lend him money for the journey, but Roos felt compelled to work it out with his in-laws at the time.[56] Before Roos left for Spain, he sent Winwood a rich present as a token of their newfound friendship, although Chamberlain's reports about the specifics of the present varies. On October 12, he said Roos had sent Winwood plate worth £200 pounds, and on November 14, he said it was a diamond worth £40.[57] Winwood no doubt relished having won the affection of his rival's son-in-law and probably did not mind the presents either.

Indeed, Roos was very generous in the months leading up to his embassy to Spain. Chamberlain commented that he seemed desirous to "buy frends" with lavish gifts, such as those to Winwood. Perhaps Roos was hoping to help his

Fig. 2.2 Sir Ralph Winwood. Michiel van Miereveldt. © National Portrait Gallery, London. Winwood, King James's Secretary of State tasked with the foreign correspondence, was Sir Thomas Lake's colleague and rival. To Lake's chagrin, Winwood befriended Roos.

budding career by cementing strong connections with important people through his gift-giving. During the summer of 1616, Roos made a very grandiose gesture toward Thomas Howard, earl of Arundel. As mentioned, Roos and Arundel knew each other from their travels in Italy and shared an interest in art collection. Now, Roos decided to give Arundel all the antique statues he had acquired during his travels. (Arundel's collections of marbles, and thus also Roos's collection, one presumes, were later donated to the Ashmolean Museum in Oxford, where they are still on view.) Others found Roos's generosity annoying, like Carleton, who had hoped to sell some of his own statues to Arundel. Now, his friend Edward Sherburn noted, Roos had "spoiled" the sale, since Arundel was less likely to pay a high price for Carleton's statues, after receiving all of Roos's for free.[58] Arundel had been favored by the king since his return from Italy and conversion to Protestantism, and he was raised to the position of privy councilor shortly after Roos's generous gift. Right before Roos left for Spain, Chamberlain also noted that Roos "reposeth such confidence in [Arundel] that he hath left in his hands all the entailes of his land and other writings of greatest moment."[59]

By late October, Roos finally set off, leaving London for Portsmouth.[60] Once there, he was initially further delayed by contrary winds, which did not allow his ship to leave port.[61] His retinue included twelve gentlemen, six footmen, eight pages, and twenty "ordinary servants" to attend. Roos spent £50 per person on livery for the footmen, and £80 per person on livery for the pages, as well as an undisclosed sum to outfit the servants. He gave each of the twelve gentlemen £100 "to provide themselves," and he spent over £1,500 on twelve sumptuous outfits for himself.[62] The Venetian ambassador reported that a "single coat is worth 32,000 crowns, owing to a rich embroidery of pearls."[63] Roos also had among his possessions a hatband set with fifteen diamonds and fifteen rubies, a chain of diamonds, and at least seventy-nine gold buttons set with diamonds.[64] Magnificently bejeweled and attired, Lord Roos and his group finally set sail on November 3 aboard one of the king's ships, the Dreadnought.

After the lengthy delays, the sea journey from Portsmouth to Lisbon was swift, as the company were finally lucky with the weather and had winds "as fayre" as "ever blew."[65] They disembarked in Lisbon on November 25. They took some time to see the sights, remaining in Lisbon for several weeks.[66] Chamberlain reported in February that he heard that Roos "visited all the monasteries within Lisbon and without," which was also a pointed suggestion that Roos remained suspiciously interested in Catholic centers of worship.[67] While in Lisbon, Roos was "handsomely entertained" by the viceroy of Portugal (Portugal was ruled by the Spanish king at the time). He had originally planned to be in Toledo by Christmas to meet up with Francis Cottington, the regular English ambassador in Spain, but his slow pace ensured that he spent Christmas at the Portuguese town of Elvas, close to the

Castille border. The Portuguese viceroy generously paid for Roos's expenses as he traveled through Portugal. Roos was also pleased with the great honor he received in Portugal: as he approached each new town, the town magistrates and local cavaliers came out to meet him and bid him welcome. As he crossed the border into Castille, representatives from the Spanish king, as well as local nobles, greeted him outside of the first of the Spanish towns. The king's representatives ensured that Roos had appropriate lodging and everything else he needed while he traveled, but the generosity of the Portuguese viceroy was not repeated: Roos now had to pay for the travel costs for his large retinue himself, "which hath been a huge matter," he admitted.[68]

Roos met up with Cottington in Toledo as planned, albeit delayed. The English retinue then continued toward Madrid, where they arrived in early January. Roos thoroughly enjoyed the pomp of the situation. The count of Salazar, accompanied by other noblemen of note, met Roos at the outskirts of the city and then ceremoniously escorted him to the prepared lodgings in the city in the Spanish king's own coaches. To Roos's great relief, the cost of the richly furnished lodgings in Madrid, as well as other expenses, were paid for by the Spanish king. As a representative of the king of England, the Spanish treated and "entertained [him] royally" while in Madrid.[69]

For the next couple of days, various royal officials and other noteworthy persons visited Roos in his lodging, both to greet him and to prepare him to meet the king. On the day of the first audience, Roos was led through the royal palace until he arrived in the presence chamber where the meeting was to be held. Philip III, dressed in all black, received Roos in a room with rich tapestries on the walls and a bed outfitted with black velvet. As evidenced by Spanish royal portraiture, the Habsburg rulers favored black and an austere, unadorned presentation: the great imperial powers of the Spanish king were believed to be sufficient in and of themselves, without much additional adornment and symbolism.[70] Roos, who had visited courts throughout Europe, was used to more magnificence and felt the king looked like someone in mourning. Philip's queen had died in 1611, and he had not remarried. The black velvet bed was the symbol of a widower, according to Roos.[71]

The first audience was very formal: Roos delivered letters from King James and Queen Anna, and verbal greetings from James, Anna, as well as Prince Charles. The king received all, and courteously asked after the health of each of the English royal family. After this initial exchange, Roos asked for another audience, where he could speak more at length regarding his king's messages. The king readily agreed. Roos then continued to another room in the palace, where he paid his respect to the other members of the royal family. He first met Prince Philip. While the meeting was courteous, Roos noted that the prince took after the curiously stoic style of his father. Both had spoken to him without revealing any expression of emotion in their faces, and they had both stood as still as statues while speaking, leaning on a table. The prince was not dressed quite as somberly as the king, sporting a suit in green topped with a black cloak. While the king had no adornments, the prince wore a sword, an "indifferent good chain," and his velvet cap was decorated with a heron's feather and a hatband of diamonds, which Roos did not deem "very rich." Roos also described his audience with the French princess Elizabeth, married to Prince Philip, but did not note any of her dress or surroundings. Roos did not disclose how he himself was dressed for the audience but considering how much he had spent on his own preparations, perhaps he felt unimpressed by a perceived lack of Spanish royal splendor.[72]

Roos's only orders were to congratulate Philip on the royal marriage alliance with France and to offer to mediate in the ongoing dispute between Spain and the duke of Savoy. The congratulations were soon proffered and received in follow up audiences, but while Roos and Cottington both tried their best, the Spanish king was not particularly receptive to their mediation. At the end of Roos's stay in Madrid, the king of Spain also presented him with a jewel in gold set with diamonds, "in the forme of a greate Roman A" worth an impressive £5,000. Not even that large a prize could make up for what he spent on the journey.[73]

Roos had wanted a weightier task. By the fall of 1616, King James had again begun considering marrying Prince Charles to the younger Spanish princess, Maria Anna. Some observers believed that Roos had been tasked to begin these negotiations secretly while in Spain. Roos certainly hoped that James would allow him to do so. However, James did not intend to leave such an important matter in the hands of an inexperienced diplomat, no matter how used he was to travels and how familiar he was with the Spanish. Instead, he planned to send Sir John Digby, who had previously served as regular ambassador to Spain for the negotiations.[74] In fact, the king even sent a messenger after Roos expressly to forbid him from discussing or even mentioning the idea of a marriage at all.[75]

William Sanderson, a secretary to Lord Roos in the Spanish embassy, later argued that while he was in Madrid, he had received a letter from England that detailed a story of a "deadly feud" having developed between Lady Lake and the countess of Exeter in Lord Roos's absence. Sanderson initially dismissed the reason for the feud at the time ("'tis no matter for what," he said of the cause.) However, he then went on to tell of the "youthful widow" Smith who had married the "aged, gouty, diseased, but noble Earl" and that her "preferment had made her subject to envy and malice." He thus suggested that the feud had something to do with the later open accusations of adultery. In any case, Sanderson showed the letter to Roos, who might then have known about familial disputes brewing at home.[76]

Roos left Madrid in early February. He decided to take the much longer and slower land-route through France on his return voyage. He wanted to extend his journey as much as possible. Perhaps the family news conveyed by Sanderson made him reluctant to return, or perhaps he simply wanted to keep doing what he loved: traveling, especially now when his journey had the added sheen and pomp of an official royal embassy. Cottington remarked that Roos was "travelling so slowly and covering such short distances that he will be a long time on his journey."[77]

Roos and his company reached Paris a month and a half later, around mid-March. Tobie Mathews, one of Roos's previous travel companions, was very keen to learn when Roos was expected in Paris, as he wished to meet with him. Tobie Mathews was a former MP and sometime courtier who had traveled extensively in Catholic Europe during the same time as Roos. They had been travel-companions in Italy and southern France in 1609 and had met intermittently at other times.[78] Mathews had converted to Catholicism in Italy and had been imprisoned in England as a result on his return. After about six months, he was freed and allowed to leave England. Now, he was looking for a way to return to the country of his birth and observers guessed that he was trying to get Roos to intercede with him for the king.[79] Observers were keenly noting Roos's every Catholic connection, suggesting that the suspicions about his religious affinities continued.

Roos hoped for further tasks from the king. He wrote to James and noted that there was no regular English ambassador residing in France at the time. Thus, if the king needed something done, like diplomatic discussions with the king of France, Roos would be more than willing to perform it. He would wait in Paris for the king's further instructions. James immediately dismissed the idea, brusquely told Roos to leave Paris for England at once and cease any "meddling with what did not concern him."[80] Chastened and no doubt disappointed, Roos continued toward home.

By late March, Roos was back in England.[81] James had just begun a long-planned trip to Scotland, so Roos had to travel north all the way to Lincoln to give the king his formal report. In the end, the Spanish venture would not be the start of a shining diplomatic career for the ambitious Roos. The consensus of his abilities and performance was that it was lackluster at best. The Venetian ambassador, who had already noted that Roos was "very lightbrained," reported that James was "highly dissatisfied with the entire embassy of that nobleman."[82] Chamberlain told Carleton that the expensive jewel Roos received from the Spanish king was the only positive outcome of the whole journey.[83] Edward Sherburn also told Carleton that Roos had "succeeded ill in his negociation in Spain," which he found was yet "another argument of his great weakness."[84] Having failed to make a significant professional mark, Roos would find only more troubles in his private life once home.

3
The Riot at Cannons

> There is a warre likewise twixt the Lord Rosse and his mother[in-law] the Lady Lake, insomuch that he made an attempt to steale away his owne wife, but fayling in the successe, your old servant Dupper [Duppa] and three or fowre of his fellows were hurt in the service.
>
> John Chamberlain to Sir Dudley Carleton, June 4, 1617[1]

Although the trip to Spain was professionally a disappointment, Roos had enjoyed the traveling. If nothing else, it had given him a temporary respite from his troubled finances and increasingly strained relationship with his in-laws. The interlude was over once he returned to England. In fact, the simmering tensions between Roos and the Lakes were ready to blow up. At one point, the fighting turned physical, with an all-out brawl between Roos and Lady Roos's brother Arthur Lake and their men. The fight broke out in early May 1617, as Roos was trying to remove his wife from Cannons, the Lakes' estate outside London. The events at Cannons, as well as those in the following months, signaled the escalation of the feud between the Lakes and the Cecils. At the time of the Cannons incident, the fighting primarily occurred between Roos and his in-laws. Roos's father and grandfather, not pleased with his grandson's financial decisions, hesitated to get involved. The countess of Exeter, later the main target of Lady Roos's and the Lakes' most serious accusations, was also not yet involved.

Roos and the Lakes had vastly different explanations for what led up to the fight at Cannons, as well as what exactly happened at the estate that early morning. They related their versions in a court case that was filed the following year, in 1618, as well as in other venues. Although it is difficult to discern objectively exactly what happened, historians such as Natalie Davis and Cynthia Herrup have long since proven that analyzing courtroom accounts is an especially effective method to gain greater insight into early modern society and mentalities.[2] Both Roos and the Lakes interpreted the failures of others mostly in gendered terms, arguing that problematic behavior was the result of failing to live up to the seventeenth-century standards of masculinity and femininity.

Family and Feuding at the Court of James I: The Lake and Cecil Scandals. Johanna Luthman, Oxford University Press.
 DOI: 10.1093/oso/9780192865786.003.0003

The recreated tales of Roos and the Lakes here are based on several sources. The main ones consist of court documents in a suit in the court of Star Chamber, which the earl of Exeter brought on behalf of his then-absent grandson a full year *after* the Cannons episode. When Exeter filed the suit, Roos was no longer in England, having left the previous fall. Exeter sued the Lakes for fraudulently having seized Roos's Walthamstow estate and included the Cannons "riot" as part of those accusations. The surviving documents in this suit include Exeter's original complaint, and the answers of Sir Thomas, Lady Mary, their son Arthur Lake, and two of their servants. The Star Chamber court records do not include interrogatories or witness depositions, which were also part of the usual legal process. The final judgements are also missing, but it is in any case likely this suit was dismissed after the complaints and answers were recorded and that it did not move to the stage of deposing further witnesses (for more on Star Chamber procedure, see Chapter 9).[3]

Exeter, who was not present at Cannons, in turn based his complaint on a now lost document that Roos had written and given to his grandfather shortly after the events. Roos's document detailed his experiences before, during, and after what the young lord termed "the riot" at Cannons. In other words, Exeter's complaint was based on Roos's story, albeit mediated and shaped by Exeter and his lawyers.[4] A year after the Cannons incident, Roos also described portions of his version of the events directly in a long letter to King James.[5]

I have based the Lakes' story on Sir Thomas, Mary and Sir Arthur Lake's answers, as well as the answers of two of their servants, William Sanford and John Falconer, in the Star Chamber suit.[6] Original complaints from two other Star Chamber suits begun by the Lakes and Lady Roos against Roos's and Exeter's employees in November 1617 and February of 1618 also fill out part of their story.[7] Notably, Lady Roos was not named as a defendant in Exeter's lawsuit, and thus she provided no answer. In fact, she never mentioned the Cannons incident in any of her complaints and responses in other suits. Despite being centrally involved in the action, Lady Roos thus remained curiously silent on this episode, although we will certainly hear from her in later disputes.

Lord Roos's Tale: The Injured Husband and the Menacing Mother-in-Law

Once Roos returned from Lincoln, where he had given his official report for his Spanish embassy to King James in March 1617, he went to London. Since his young wife had been living with her parents in his absence, Roos headed to the Lakes' London home at Charing Cross to see her. Everything initially appeared normal: he had no indications that something was amiss. When he went to bed later that night, he naturally thought his wife would join him. The young couple had been apart for months and Roos was "hoping after his longe travel to receive a loving welcome from his newe married wiefe."[8] But the Lakes focused only on their own greed instead of "respectinge the Godly and happie uniting of the hartes and affections of the said Lord Roos and his Lady." Instead of a welcoming wife, Roos was confronted with a menacing mother-in-law. Lady Lake ordered her daughter, "who otherwise seemed then willinge and desirous to accompany her said husband," to stay away from him. Lady Lake entered Roos's bedroom and began speaking to him with "many threatenting and uncivell termes." She told Roos "in violent fashion" that he would never enjoy the company of his wife (that is, have sex with her) unless he signed some papers she held in her hand. The papers essentially ended his rights to the estate of Walthamstow and instead gave them to future children of his marriage, or to his wife, if he died before her.

Roos did not fully understand the meaning of the papers at that moment, but it became apparent to him later that the Lakes were trying to cover up the fact that they had tricked him before his Spanish trip. They had already ensured that Roos had unknowingly given up ownership of Walthamstow when he signed the financial agreements for the £6,000 loan he had received from Lake before going to Spain. Five months after the original agreement, they wanted to pretend that had never happened, and that Roos was only now giving up Walthamstow to Lady Roos.

In addition to keeping his wife from Roos, Lady Lake also threatened to make an already existing rift with his grandfather permanent, ensuring that Exeter would disinherit him entirely. (Exeter's complaint admits that Exeter was displeased with Roos at the time but does not mention the reason for it.) Roos, "verie fearfull of the Continuance of the displeasure" of his grandfather, "much troubled upon such suddaine demeanure and menaces" of Lady Lake, and desirous to have the "society" of his wife, acquiesced and signed the papers.

Even after he signed the papers, Roos did not get to "enjoy the company" of his wife. The Lakes continued to keep Lady Roos from him, arguing that he needed to pay off all loans fully before they would consent to the couple cohabiting again. At the same time, they spread rumors that Roos purposefully avoided and ignored his wife, implying that he was a poor husband rather than a mistreated son-in-law. While away from the Lakes, Roos prepared his own London manor, Charterhouse Yard, to be a proper home for both him and his wife. He informed Lady Roos of his plan and she "promised to come thether & cohabit with him." The Lakes then moved Lady Roos from Charing Cross to Cannons, their estate in Middlesex, some ten miles northwest, in order to keep her even further away from her husband. At that point, Roos received what appeared to be a desperate plea from his wife. In a message, she told her husband that "her mother was a strange woman," and she begged him to please come and fetch her away but take care not to let her mother know about this plan.[9] He readily agreed and set out for Cannons at night in early May.

Roos and his men traveled in two coaches and arrived unannounced at Cannons very early in the morning. Sir Thomas and Mary Lake were not there: Sir Thomas was attending the king in his journey to Scotland that summer and Lady Lake was at their London home. Roos had been to Cannons before and knew his way around. He went into the house and made his way to his wife's room. Lady Roos made herself ready for the journey, after which Roos was "peaceablie leading his said Lady downe from her chamber towards his coach." At that point, Lady Roos's brother Arthur Lake, as well as several of the Lakes' servants, burst forward with swords, daggers, pitchforks, spits, and other weapons at the ready. Unbeknownst to Roos, they had been lying in wait for him, as his treacherous wife and her brother had planned this trap.[10] Arthur drew his sword and held the sharp point perilously close to Roos's chest "vowing to thrust it through him unlesse hee wold there leave his wife behind him." Meanwhile, Lake's servants also attacked Roos's unarmed servants, drawing blood and "greavously" wounding Giles Dunscombe and John Duppa. Arthur Lake and his men "forcibly" wrenched Lady Roos from Roos's grasp and then made Roos leave without her.

Away from Cannons, Roos was stewing over this grave "owtrage and violence." He wished to bring the matter to the law and have the Lakes tried in the court of Star Chamber for causing a riot against him. When Lady Lake got wind of his intentions, she threatened him yet again. She told Roos that he did not stand a chance at bringing them to the law, as her husband's great influence with the king would ensure that no lawyers would even take on his case. Furthermore, at her "commandment," Lake would suborn "false witnesses to procure me speedily to be committed to the Tower" if he proceeded, although Roos admitted that he had "no solide proofe" of this. As his honor "laying thus a bleeding," Roos could not figure out how to respond to these affronts at the time.[11]

The Lakes' Tale: The Protective Parents and the Ne'er-Do-Well Son-in-Law

According to the Lakes, they had acted in the best interest of their daughter.[12] They argued that before Roos's departure to Spain, Sir Thomas had lent him £6,000. Roos had used Walthamstow as collateral for the loan and added some of the income from the estate to the annual sum for the maintenance of his wife. The agreement was that if Roos defaulted on the loan, the lands would then go to the future children of the Roos marriage, and if they had no children, to Lady Roos and her heirs. The Lakes refuted the idea that they had tricked Roos in any way. Instead, they believed Roos had agreed to the deal because he was motivated by love for his wife and the hope of future children to inherit and perpetuate his estate and titles. They argued that they had observed all the legalities in the financial agreement, and they had properly recorded all the deeds and papers. Exeter's charge regarding fraudulent property arrangements lacked any standing, "and therefore the said matter as it is alleadged for want of sufficient certainty is not a Case Criminall or examinable in this hono[ra]ble Court," the court of Star Chamber.

The Lakes found out that their daughter's health and life had been in danger while she had been staying with her husband at the Wimbledon estate of the earl and countess of Exeter during the summer the previous year. Fearing for their daughter's well-being, they had requested for her to stay with her parents while Roos was in Spain, and that the young couple would live in one of the Lakes' houses after his return, until such time that "some greater hope and better proofe from the said Lord Roos should be given for her better usage and securitie." As Sir Thomas Lake would be traveling with the king to Scotland during the spring and summer of 1617, "out of a fatherly care" he wanted to ensure his daughter's safety at the time of his absence. Lord Roos had readily agreed to these living arrangements and had not mentioned any plans for removing his wife from her parents' house. Furthermore, Roos had specifically consented that his wife stay at Cannons, while he mostly remained in the city. He had even traveled to Cannons with her, stayed a couple of days, and then left her there and returned to London. According to Lady Lake, Roos had been with her in the Lake London house in Charing Cross until nine o'clock in the evening the night before the row at Cannons. He had not then mentioned anything to her about going to Cannons just a few hours later. He had said nothing about his plans to move his wife to his house in Charterhouse Yard either. Since none of the Lakes had any knowledge of Roos's plan to remove his wife, they could not possibly have planned any riot.

Neither Lady Lake nor her husband were present at Cannons and did not hear about the fighting until Roos returned to Lady Lake in London later that same day and told her about it himself. Roos recounted to Lady Lake "the passages and proceedings" at Cannons, but that it had only been an "accident" and misunderstanding. The brothers-in-law had cleared it up, breakfasted together with Lady Roos and "druncke healths one to another in a friendly and kinde manner," and then Roos had left. Roos assured Lady Lake that there was "no hurt done or intended" and he loved and respected Arthur. When Lady Lake asked why he had not told her anything about the plan to remove his wife from Canons, he excused himself by saying he had been "sett on and advised soe to doe" by others, which he had never mentioned to her before.[13]

In May of 1617, Arthur Lake had recently returned from his two-year stint of educational travel in France and had only briefly made his brother-in-law Roos's acquaintance before the Cannons incident.[14] He was at Cannons with his sister when Roos arrived. A servant woke Arthur at three o'clock in the morning, informing him of the unexpected arrival of Lord Roos. Surprised, Arthur rose and dressed quickly, in order to greet his brother-in-law. When Arthur asked Roos "why he suddainly surprised them," Roos replied that "his occasion was only to see his wife." Arthur then walked with him to his sister's chamber and left the couple alone. His sister soon came to tell him that her husband intended to take her away "at that unseasonable tyme against her will without the knowledge of her frends." Arthur tried to reason with Roos, reminding him of his former promise to allow his wife to live in her parents' house. When that had no effect, Arthur then asked Roos to wait at least three or four hours, so they could depart at a decent hour. Roos refused any delay. He "tooke his said Lady by force and dragging her upon the ground offred to drawe her to the coach." Arthur, "not being able to brooke to see his sister soe used in her fathers house," turned around left the couple "in that manner."

At that point, Roos called for his men, who came running with swords drawn. In response, Arthur "for his owne securitie in like manner drawe forth his sworde" toward Roos's incoming servants, but he never threatened Roos with it. Instead, Roos's servants assaulted Arthur and wounded him in one arm. The violence ended abruptly, and the brothers-in-law instantly made up and became friendly again. Roos, Lady Roos, and Arthur decided to go back into the house and have breakfast together. During the meal, they each drank to each other's health in a convivial fashion, and Lord and Lady Roos "were then good friends again." After breakfast, Roos took leave of both his wife and her brother. Before the departure, one of Roos's men came up to Arthur and "seemed to be very sorry for that which was done, desiring" Arthur to "excuse him for that he would not have done any thinge but he must obey his Lords commandment." Arthur absolutely denied that he had any prior knowledge of Roos's arrival, or his plans to remove Lady Roos, and he denied that he had told any men at Cannons to lay in wait for Roos. If anyone was guilty of premeditation, it was Roos, who had come there unannounced so early in the morning, in hired hackney coaches instead of his own, which implied that he did not want anyone to recognize him along the way. The fact that his servants were armed also implied that "it should seeme his Lo[rdship] then came thither rather to commit a riot," turning that accusation against Roos instead.

William Sanford and John Falconer, two Lake servants named in the original complaint, also provided answers in the suit. William Sanford, employed as a butler at Cannons, denied having had any part in planning an attack on Roos. He said he had been woken up by another servant between three and four in the morning. The servant told him that Roos had arrived, so Sanford got dressed and began to prepare Roos's breakfast. When breakfast was almost ready, Sanford went into the parlor to start a fire. While Sanford was in the parlor, Lord and Lady Roos came into the room "and there walked a good space togeather." After that, as Sanford returned to the buttery, he saw the couple and Arthur Lake go toward the door, out into the kitchen yard. As Sanford was heading toward the kitchen, he heard Roos, then out in the kitchen yard, "call his servants to unto him." Then he saw some of Roos's men with "drawne swoordes" against Arthur Lake in the yard. He did not know what was going on, and he was not armed himself. When another of Roos's men came from inside the house, also with a drawn sword, heading out into the yard with the others, Sanford stopped him and wrestled with him, but neither man threw punches, and no one was hurt. After this episode, Lord and Lady Roos, Arthur, and Lord Roos's men returned into the house. After a little while, Roos, his wife, and Arthur went into the parlor and had breakfast "in good and friendly sorte, duringe all wch tyme" Sanford could not "perceive any displeasure betweene the sayd Lord Roos or the sayd Lady or in Arthur Lake." After breakfast, Arthur and Lady Roos accompanied Roos out to his coach "and there took their leave in friendly sorte soe farre as this def[endan]t could then perceive."[15]

John Falconer served as a bailiff at Cannons. He had been out early, looking after a hawk that he was training. Sometime between three and four in the morning, he saw two coaches approaching. He did not recognize them. The drivers were poorly dressed and unknown to him, leading him to believe that the coaches were hired. He told the coachmen they must be lost and going the wrong way, as no one at Cannons was expecting visitors at that early hour. Roos then leaned out of the coach and said: "Good Morrow John Falconer." Perceiving who it was, John immediately went to wake up a maid so that she could open the "greate doore" for Lord Roos. After this, John Falconer went about his business, making sure that the coach horses were stabled, watered, and fed properly. He did not see or hear of any commotion in the kitchen yard: he only saw "the Lord Roos the Lady Roos and three of the Lord Roos his servants or attendants going into" the house. He did not witness any "blowes given on any parte neyther did this defendant give or offer any blows or make any assaults against any person or persons then and there present." He knew that Lord and Lady Roos and Arthur Lake had breakfast together in the parlor of Cannons, because he had been required to help serve them while they were at table. He said they "were all very pleasante and merry and did drinke one to another in friendly sort."[16] After they had finished breakfast, John went back to his outside duties, and did not see Roos leave.

The Meanings of the Tales

Given that the tales are so divergent, it is not possible to know exactly what happened at Cannons. There are a few facts that both sides agree on, which can serve to give us the broad outline of the events: Roos had made financial agreements with the Lakes before he left for Spain, which at minimum included him giving up some rights to Walthamstow and other lands. He had not informed his grandfather of these agreements at the time. When Roos returned from Spain, Lady Roos was living with her parents, and Exeter was displeased with his grandson for unknown reasons. Roos was mostly apart from his wife after his return in late March and until the Cannons incident in early May. Some sort of physical fight occurred between Roos and his men on the one side, and Arthur Lake and some Lake servants on the other. Roos then left without his wife.

However, the tales show us how each side in the dispute wanted to explain and defend their behavior and to vilify that of their opponents. Notably, both sides utilized heavily gendered language to present and bolster their cases. Roos primarily presented himself as an aggrieved husband, who's evil and unjust in-laws conspired to keep his wife from him and to defraud him of property. However, in order to explain and defend his own actions, Roos had to admit that his mother-in-law had successfully both threatened and outmaneuvered him and that he depended on the approval of his grandfather. Roos's in-laws used this situation to their advantage. They skillfully painted a picture of their son-in-law as a person who did not fit the seventeenth-century standards of masculinity.

Perceptions of masculinity were based both on performance and physical attributes. A man had to perform certain acts in a certain way for others to consider him masculine: being an ideal man was largely based on what you did, in other words, as well as others' perception of those actions. In the early modern period, an ideal man should be the head and authoritative figure in his own household, be financially responsible, honor his word, use violence only when necessary and with measure, control his emotions, be sexually virile, support his family, and be a good steward of family resources passed down to him.[17] According to the Lakes, Roos had few of these qualities: he did not head his own separate household, he was financially irresponsible, did not keep his word, used violence in an inappropriate manner, and was weak, easily influenced, and intimidated.

Physical strength and sexual virility were also important markers of masculinity. As we have already seen, old men were often ridiculed as less manly because of their weakened bodies and lack of the necessary heat to generate sexual desire and ability to complete intercourse and father children. Similarly, inability to perform sexually and procreate at any age also threatened manhood.[18] Rumors about Roos's impotence circulated at the time of the Cannons incident, further putting his manhood in question.

On the other hand, Roos argued that he was the wronged party, and that the Lakes had in essence prevented him from fully performing his role as a husband by keeping him from his wife. However, when defending himself, he also had to admit actions and behaviors which also put his masculinity in question. In short, Roos found himself in a gendered double bind, where both the accusations against him, as well as his own defenses and explanations, emasculated him in the eyes of observers and thus eroded his support. As Susan Amussen has pointed out, masculinity and manhood were slippery concepts, since "the same actions that disrupted masculinity were also used to control it," and therefore "the same acts and behaviours could be perceived by different observers to both support and undermine patriarchy."[19]

Employing the term "riot" to describe the events at Cannons and accusing Lady Lake of using "threats and menaces" to keep him from his wife and defraud him of his lands was a particular legal strategy that Roos, the earl of Exeter, and their lawyers used, as these terms denoted specific crimes. A riot, when three or more men "does any unlawfull act, as to beat any man," was a felony, punishable by fines, forfeitures of property, and in some cases even with death. Furthermore, a person who had been induced to act against his will through "threats and menaces" could be found not responsible for his actions.[20] By applying the term in the accusations against Lady Lake specifically, Roos's side was trying to negate the property agreements he had signed. Furthermore, Exeter's complaint described the weapons Arthur Lake and the Lake servants used as "invasive," meaning specifically carried to be used in an attack, implying that their violence was planned. Roos himself had not been armed, he said, and only one of his servants even knew that they were going to fetch his wife, implying that there had been no planning for violence on his part. The only violence he committed had been in defense of his own person and of his men.

Roos's primary argument was that he was a wronged husband. As a married man, he should have control over his wife, but his in-laws had, through their threats, trickery, and violence, kept him from his wife. They had subverted the "natural" order of marriage, by intervening between husband and wife. Roos and Exeter were not the only people who thought the situation out of the ordinary. Chamberlain told Carleton that Roos had "made an attempt to steale away his owne wife," suggesting that he found it odd that a husband had to resort to such drastic measures to have access to his own wife.[21] In the Star Chamber complaint, Exeter argued that by keeping Roos from the company of his wife, the Lakes were also denying him the chance of having children and continuing his family line, which should also be his right as a husband.[22] Having children was also a "central component of adult male authority," as Alexandra Shepard has pointed out.[23]

Furthermore, the Lakes had turned Roos's own wife against him, instead of respecting the love that should exist between spouses. Initially, Roos believed that his wife loved him and wanted to live with him, and that it was just her parents', especially her mother's, direct orders that kept her away.[24] The fact that her parents' wishes weighed heavier for his wife than her own husband's wishes certainly weakened the perception of Roos's husbandly authority. Roos later changed his mind about his wife's motivations and believed that rather than being a dutiful daughter, her mother had turned her into a "devilish temptation." Writing to the king about the Cannons incident a year later, Roos related how his wife had written to him with "Crocodille teares" to please come and fetch her, while simultaneously conspiring with her brother to attack him.[25] Roos had acted, as a husband should, trying to protect his wife from evil influences. In the same letter, an entirely disillusioned Roos also described his mother-in-law as both "satanical" and "diabolical," and Lady Roos as a "younger imp of hell," "wicked and abominable," an "impudent whore," and a "shameless brat of hell."[26] He had come peacefully to claim what he thought would be a loving and grateful wife at Cannons, but as he believed after a year's hindsight, she was already beyond redemption at that time. It also meant that Roos had to admit that he had failed as a husband, as he had no real influence over his wife.

Since Lady Roos was such a central figure in the Cannons incident and in the later feud, her silence on the episode is odd. She could have provided vital testimony, but, instead, Exeter's suit only asks for answers from Thomas, Mary, and Arthur Lake, and five Lake servants. Roos may have minimized her role in his first description of the Canons incident to his grandfather. In fact, Exeter's suit, based on Roos's first account written shortly after the event, does not mention Lady Roos's involvement in the plotting to get him to Cannons so that her brother could attack him. Exeter's suit claims that it was Arthur who plotted the riot, but leaves Lady Roos out of it entirely. Instead, it presents Lady Roos as willing to live with her husband but prevented by her parents from doing so. Roos added the tale about Lady Roos sending a message asking him to come and get her in his later letter to the king, sent shortly after Exeter had already filed his suit. By that time, Roos had changed his mind about his wife, considering her just as bad, if not worse, than her parents.

It is certainly possible that Lady Roos was a hapless victim in the fight between her husband and her family in the Cannons incident. In her later tales about her marriage, Lady Roos argued that she had always been a loving, willing, and loyal wife, who had never given her husband any reason to complain about her behavior. In any case, about half a year after the Cannons incident, Lady Roos would be a hapless victim no longer, as she began telling dark tales about her husband and the countess of Exeter.

Since Roos was presenting himself as an aggrieved husband, the Lakes had to try to counter the fact that they *were* in fact controlling Roos's wife in their tales. They did that by emphasizing their roles as concerned parents, looking out for the physical safety and financial well-being of their daughter.[27] Lady Roos was still very young: she had just turned seventeen when Roos left for Spain. According to the Lakes' answers, Lady Roos had shared with her parents some of her fears that the countess of Exeter wished to harm her and that she had not been well after her visit to Exeter's Wimbledon House during the previous summer of 1616. This argument might have been construed after the fact for the benefit of the legal defense. In other court documents, the Lakes contradict themselves about when they learned about the countess's attempted poisoning of their daughter, saying that they did not know about it until the fall of 1617, several months after the Cannons incident.[28] The Lakes also argued that Roos had agreed to his wife's living arrangements and they refuted that Lady Lake had made any threats to keep the couple separated. They had only asked that the two of them remain under the Lakes' roofs. Instead, it was Roos himself who had kept his distance and neglected his wife.[29]

The Lakes believed their concerns about Roos's financial situation were warranted. In fact, these concerns appear to be what made the Lakes so hostile toward Roos when he returned from Spain.[30] In or before March 1617, presumably shortly before Roos's return, a man named Peter Chapman came calling on Sir Thomas Lake with a disturbing story to tell.[31] According to Chapman, the estate of Walthamstow, the very same estate that Roos had used as collateral for the loan from Lake, had promised as part of his wife's jointure at the time of his marriage, and the income from which was supposed to pay for part of his wife's maintenance, was not Roos's estate at all, and had not been since *before* Roos was married. Chapman told Lake that Roos had deeded the estate of Walthamstow to him back in 1615, as payment for loans that Chapman had taken out at Roos's behest. Lake was not happy to hear this piece of news. If true, it meant that Roos had been lying to him and his family from the very beginning, making false promises about Walthamstow as part of the marriage negotiations, not to mention being deceptive about the loan agreement for his Spain money.

When Lake later confronted Roos with Chapman's statement, Roos claimed that Chapman was lying and that he had only given Walthamstow to Chapman as security but had not given up ownership of it. Ironically, it is the same argument he used against the Lakes' claims to the property. The bill of sale Chapman had showed Lake was fraudulent, Roos assured. Lake chose to believe Roos, probably because if Chapman really owned Walthamstow, Lake's machinations to secure it would be all for naught. Half a year later, Chapman claimed that he had been willing to give up Walthamstow to ensure that the rift between Roos and the Lakes could heal. He magnanimously accepted a different estate in its place, although he was not too happy with the replacement, since he judged it was not worth as much.[32] Chapman's tales only strengthened the Lakes' belief that Roos was fiscally irresponsible. The Lakes argued that their actions to secure lands and income for their daughter was justified under the circumstances.

The Lakes also dismissed the idea that Lady Lake successfully threatened Roos as ridiculous. The legal term "threats and menaces" usually referred to a situation where a person's actions could be excused because he feared the loss of life or limb.[33] Here, the Lakes utilized ideas about masculinity to their own advantage. How could Roos, a married adult man, be "threatened and menaced" by a mere woman like Lady Lake? The king had believed Roos mature enough to appoint him to represent him abroad in the Spanish embassy, so there "was not likelihood or probabilitie that he could be drawne and forced by threats and menacies of a Lady," Lady Lake insisted.[34] The Lakes were implying that a woman could not physically threaten a "real man." Thus, if Roos wanted to argue that he was frightened by Lady Lake to the point that he could not be held responsible for his actions, he had to admit to being less than a man.

The Lakes were thus referring to the trope of the man ruled or "overawed" by a woman, which was a stock figure of ridicule in early modern English literature, on the stage, and in real life. The popular shaming rituals of charivaris (sometimes also called skimmingtons or rough music) generally focused on such men. In charivaris, crowds of often young men seized a person deemed "unmanly" and therefore dishonorable, dressed him up as a woman and/or with the horns denoting a cuckold (or sometimes "naked," meaning in just a linen undershirt), put him backwards on a horse or donkey, and paraded him around the village or town while banging on pots and pans to make sure that everyone noticed his disgrace. Local authorities disliked these rituals and tried to prevent them, as they were sometimes violent and deemed disorderly.[35]

The Lakes also insisted that Roos had exaggerated and lied about the level of violence during the Cannons incident. Lady Lake, Arthur Lake, the butler Sanford, and the bailiff John Falconer all insisted that Roos had breakfasted with Lady Roos and Arthur after the melee in the kitchen yard. Roos's account does not mention a meal, only that Arthur made Roos leave without his wife after having threatened to stab him. The fact that the Lakes and their servants emphasize that Roos stayed for breakfast was meant to show that Roos himself did not interpret the actions at Cannons as serious at the time. The idea of the planned riot was ridiculous in the Lakes' view: rioters do not invite their targeted victims to breakfast. According to the Lakes, Roos had made up the charge of a riot afterwards, to cover up for his own bad behavior.

Roos, his grandfather, and their lawyers did have some trouble explaining exactly why Roos found his mother-in-law so terrifying and how she could seemingly manipulate him so easily. When Roos wrote about the incident in the letter to the king a year later, he emphasized what he believed to be the sheer hellish evil of the Lakes, specifically Lady Lake. The explanation that the earl of Exeter and his lawyers found the most palatable was that Roos, as a good grandson should, feared further displeasing the family patriarch, his grandfather. Thus, when Lady Lake threatened to eliminate the chances of a reconciliation with his grandfather (and jeopardized his inheritance), Roos was worried that her "violent information" may be able to do so. Exeter admitted that his grandson was persona non grata with him at his return from Spain, but he never divulged the reasons why.[36] Others suggested it was due to Roos's heavy debts and unwise financial decisions. No source brought up the former rumors that Roos may have impregnated Exeter's wife at this juncture, but it would pop up again later.[37]

However, in trying to help Roos, his grandfather unwittingly also emasculated him, revealing the inherent intergenerational tension in a patriarchal society. Younger men were supposed to defer to the elder family patriarch, but they sometimes chafed at having to wait for their turn at the helm, especially if the elder man was stubbornly long-lived. In Roos's case, he had two generations of men, his father and his grandfather, ahead of him. He did not get along well with his father, according to at least one observer, and his grandfather was displeased with him as well. As a result, Roos was a "patriarch-in-waiting," which meant that many might not view him as a fully adult man.[38]

Since his marriage, Roos and his wife had lived either in his grandfather's or in Lake's houses and households. In England, most new couples waited to marry until they had sufficient resources to set up independent households. This arrangement was one of the reasons why the average age at marriage was relatively high, but also why heading your own household was seen as an important marker of manhood. For the men and women of the elite who married at younger ages, young couples sometimes lived with parents or relatives for a time, but these arrangements could be contentious, as parental authority and spousal authority could be at loggerheads. In the complaint, Exeter and Roos argued that Roos was going to get his wife at Cannons precisely because he had now arranged a separate house for them at Charterhouse Yard. Roos was thus trying to establish his own household, and himself as its ruling patriarch, but he failed: the violence of the Lakes prevented him.

Exeter's complaint also emphasized that the Lakes had forced Roos to agree to the property arrangements while "Lord Roos [was] kept wthowt any Councell of his owne," suggesting that Roos was not capable of understanding the ruse himself. In the document provided to his grandfather, Roos also admitted that he had no copies of any of the agreements. The Lakes certainly pounced on this interpretation and played on the sensitivities of the younger man. In their official answers in the court documents, the Lakes emphasized that Roos was "of full age" and "duly married." Furthermore, he had been trusted as "his [Majesty's] Ambassadour into Spaine upon his [Majesty's] affairs." As a result, it appeared to the Lakes that Roos was "of sufficient wisdom and discretion" to "manage his own affairs."[39] If Roos wanted to be viewed as a man, he should be able to understand property and financial agreements and not need the constant acceptance, guidance, and approval of his elderly grandfather in his every business dealing.

The rumors of Roos's supposed impotence which circulated also negatively affected Roos's honor and manhood. Early modern people generally viewed impotence with derision and shame, as being able to have sex and father children formed important aspects of manhood.[40] Neither side mentioned impotence in their court depositions about the Cannons incident, but contemporary letters reporting the news of the city and court discussed it. According to Sir George Gerrard, who described the fray at Cannons in a letter to Carleton, Roos had agreed to convey some of his lands to Lady Roos, because he wanted his wife and in-laws to conceal the fact that he was impotent. Gerrard believed that Roos's impotence was not permanent, but rather a result of "former deboshments [debauchments]," implying that Roos had contracted a venereal disease.[41] Similarly, Chamberlain, who personally knew some of Roos's servants involved in the Cannons fighting and probably heard about it from them, also reported to Carleton. Chamberlain related:

> his poore Lordship [Roos] is decried out of all crie, and his mother in law hath so baffled him that she hath got him to assure 800li in land a yeare upon her daughter and her heires, for feare she should publish his insufficiencie [impotence] and so come to a nullitie; which now is come to passe that it is as generally spoken of as yf yt were in print.[42]

The rumors Chamberlain reported also added that the Lakes might try to seek an annulment of the marriage. No other evidence points to the Lakes ever seeking an annulment. Lady Roos certainly did not want an annulment: in all her later statements, she was adamant about her love for her husband, desire for reconciliation, and distress at others' attempts at destroying her marriage. The rumors of Roos's supposed impotence, and his being "baffled" (outwitted) by his mother-in-law, certainly led to his further disgrace.

Why did the rumor mill discuss Roos's impotence when the later legal accounts mostly were silent on the matter? Roos was not likely to include it in a report to his grandfather. The embarrassment would have reflected badly on him, especially if he did indeed suffer from a venereal disease and/or impotence. Part of Roos's and Exeter's argument was that the Lakes were illegally keeping a wife from her husband, and thus also preventing him from his conjugal rights and his rights to have children and heirs by her. Impotence would have rendered these legal points moot. If the Lakes were trying to place themselves in the best light possible, it would have behooved them not to mention Roos's potential impotence either. Throughout much of 1617, the Lakes were trying to patch things up with the earl of Exeter and Lord Burghley, blaming problems mostly on Roos's bad advisers, servants, and associates. Much of Roos's expected wealth would come from his father and grandfather, after all. The matrimonial alliance had been intended to tie the two families together: it was not yet time to try to break it.

The rumors of Lady Lake threatening an annulment may have been a result of the ghosts of the Overbury murder scandal from a few years earlier, which had begun with accusations of impotence and an annulment. When the king's favorite Robert Carr, later earl of Somerset, and Frances Howard, countess of Essex fell in love in 1613, they hoped to be able to overcome the fact that she was already married. Divorce was not possible in England at the time, but a marriage could be annulled if it were deemed to have been invalid for reasons such as fraud, pre-contract, consanguinity, and so on.

Frances Howard argued that her marriage to the earl of Essex should be annulled, because the couple had never managed to consummate the union. Non-consummation was not an established reason for an annulment, so the case became contentious and controversial. The ensuing church court proceedings were sensational and scandalous, dealing with the most intimate details of the earl and countess of Essex's failed attempts at intercourse. The earl of Essex had to admit in open court that despite repeated attempts, he had been unable to complete intercourse with his wife. Frances Howard had to undergo a physical exam to establish her virginity. The king argued with the ecclesiastics for the annulment, and when the panel of judges split evenly, he packed the court with more judges in favor of the annulment. After it had been revealed that Howard and Carr, then earl and countess of Somerset, had conspired to murder Overbury, the annulment and remarriage of Frances Howard was often interpreted as the beginning of her moral downfall.[43] It should be noted here that neither Gerrard nor Chamberlain made any overt comparisons between the two cases. If the shadow of Frances Howard's annulment fell over Roos's fight with his in-laws, it was only implied.

Roos's impotence briefly came up again after his death. At that point, the earl and countess of Exeter reiterated that the Lakes, Lady Roos, and Arthur Lake had all affirmed "the L. Roos to be insufficient and to have no knowledge of his wife."[44] However, Lady Lake vehemently denied ever having said anything of the sort. Instead, she argued that it was the countess of Exeter who had started the rumor about Roos being "insufficient in matters of marriage." Lady Lake claimed to have attempted to silence the countess of Exeter's unfounded tales during the summer of 1617, shortly after the Cannons incident. Through an intermediary, she had asked the countess to desist. If she did not, Lady Lake threatened to start telling people that the countess was doing it only to cover up her own crimes, i.e. her adultery with Roos. If Roos was impotent, he could not be the father of the countess's little girl, Georgi-Anna, born the previous year. Lady Lake also claimed that the two women had written several letters to each other about this matter also.[45]

An Uneasy Summer

The fighting at Cannons ensured that the following months were full of tensions. Roos was already in trouble with his father and grandfather when he returned from Spain. When news about the fight at Cannons reached Exeter and Burghley, it made them even more frustrated with him. Roos was trying to get back in their good graces and he needed their support to help him fight against the Lakes. He appears to have had no luck with his father. On May 30, John Holles informed Lake in Scotland:

> let me have word with yow of my Lorde Rose, whose late indiscretion offering to take my Lady his wife from Cannons, your Lady being at London, and without her knowledge, hath raised sum dust in this babbling town, for theruppon sum stir growing.[46]

After Roos had returned to London from Cannons, Holles said he "writ to his father a most submissive, and a penitent letter, for errors past, which he accompanied with a leace, which heretofore unnaturally he had taken over his fathers head." According to Holles, a friend of Roos's father, Lord Burghley would hear nothing of it, insisting that Roos needed to deal with his own problems: "his father returned him the leace, saying he would spare such another, so they would make him an honest man, and refused to meddle with him in any way." Holles, friendly with both Burghley and Lake, wanted to inform Lake of Burghley's decision to let Roos deal with own problems so that "to your mutuall cumforts yow might understand one another." Holles continued: "glad would I be to ciment yow so together."[47] Holles attempts at mediating between Burghley and Lake may have worked temporarily over the summer of 1617, but it did not last.

Roos also tried to placate his grandfather. He produced a written account of what had transpired both before and during the Cannons incident and sent it to his grandfather, thus explaining that all the faults lay with the evil Lakes. This written account, which Exeter used in his later suit against the Lakes, became yet another source of contestation between the two families. The Lakes claimed that Roos had not actually written the account himself, but rather that Peter Chapman, Francis Featherstonehowe, and Henry Russell had concocted it, brought it to Roos, and told him he could put in or take out words as he pleased. Chapman and Featherstonehowe both served the earl of Exeter, and Russell was probably also within the Exeter sphere.[48]

Packed with falsehoods, the account thus created by Chapman and his accomplices suggested that the Lakes had defrauded and forced Roos to give up Walthamstow and that Arthur Lake had orchestrated the attack on Roos at Cannons. According to the Lakes, Chapman also urged Roos that signing and delivering the papers to Exeter was the only path to reconciliation with his father and grandfather. The Lakes argued that Chapman, Featherstonehowe, and Russell were motivated to push this fraud because they wanted to create a rift between Lord and Lady Roos, and between the Lakes and Exeter and Burghley, so that they could get their hands on Walthamstow and other financial rewards for themselves. The Lakes believed the fact that the three men knew so much about the details of the account was especially suspicious and pointed to their complicity in its creation.[49]

In Chapman's telling of how Roos's written account had come to be, Exeter heard about Roos giving Walthamstow to Lady Roos after the row at Cannons, and he did not like it. He dispatched Chapman to inform Roos to write down the account of what had transpired regarding Walthamstow. Exeter also wanted copies of any legal papers or property agreements regarding Walthamstow, so he could discern the truth that way.

Exeter instructed Chapman to make clear to Roos that unless he was entirely truthful in all matters, he "should never enjoye foote of his [grandfather's] lands." When he received the message, Roos told Chapman that he had no copies of any of the legal papers regarding Walthamstow, but that he would write down an account. Exeter demanded a response the very same day. Around eight o'clock that evening, Roos sent for Chapman to Covent Garden in the Strand. Henry Russell happened to be in Covent Garden at the time when Chapman and Roos were there, and Roos called Russell over to join them. Roos pulled out his written account and proceeded to read it aloud. Chapman and Russell both claimed never to have read it themselves, but only knew about the document's contents since Roos had shared it with them on this occasion. Russell specifically remembered how Roos said the Lakes had through threats and menaces and other "indirect meanes" forced him to give up Walthamstow, and how Arthur Lake and his servants had "wronged and abused him" and his servants when he went to get Lady Roos from Cannons.

After acquainting the two men with the contents of the document, Roos asked Chapman to deliver the account to Exeter. Chapman thought it too late in the evening, as the earl had the habit of going to bed early. He counseled Roos to hold on to the papers and to send them to his grandfather in the morning instead. Roos agreed. The following morning, he sent a servant with the papers to Chapman, who in turn delivered the same to Exeter.[50]

Having provided Exeter with his written statement about the riot and the Lakes' underhanded dealings, Roos had to wait to see how his grandfather would proceed. There was not much he could do without further support from his family. By late June, Exeter might have softened a bit toward his grandson. Holles wrote to Lake on June 15: "I am sorrie my Lord of Exeter is runn into these weaknesses, which were neither pleasing to my Lord Burley, nor my Lady Hatton [Elizabeth Cecil, Burghley's sister, Roos's aunt]."[51]

Exeter had not shared Roos's written account with Burghley or Lady Hatton: the document was kept locked up in a box, and only Lake's rival Secretary Winwood and Roos had the keys. Holles explained the disagreements about how to deal with Roos's problems had caused a rift between Burghley and Exeter. Burghley felt he was being kept in the dark and he was not willing to "lean upon this Aegiptian reed with [Exeter], but coveteth to see his way ear he jump into it." Holles told Lake he hoped the old man would soon see reason and "in short time desenganarse [disengage], and fynding his error, will be as forward to your satisfaction."[52] Exeter seemed willing to perhaps give Roos the benefit of the doubt and support him against the Lakes, whereas Burghley declared himself done with rescuing his wayward child. Lake clearly preferred Burghley's approach.

The earl of Exeter and Lord Burghley had other family troubles that occupied them that summer. The marriage of Exeter's daughter Elizabeth, Lady Hatton to Sir Edward Coke had been volatile for some time. By 1617, their fights, mostly over finances, had become a public scandal, requiring the intervention of the Privy Council in late May, just a few weeks after the Cannons incident. Both Burghley and his wife had been present at the Privy Council hearing, in support of his sister Lady Hatton. The Privy Council was able to come up with an agreement that most observers agreed was clearly in Lady Hatton's favor.

The mediation did not last long. Lady Hatton's marriage to Coke deteriorated further during the summer, because they disagreed on a groom for their fifteen-year-old daughter Frances, Roos's cousin. Coke, who had temporarily lost the king's favor for proposing limits on royal power, was trying to get back on top by marrying his daughter to the royal favorite Buckingham's brother, Sir John Villiers. Lady Hatton vehemently opposed the marriage, as did young Frances herself.

In order to avoid the match, Lady Hatton secretly removed her daughter from the couple's London home and hid her in a relative's house in Oatlands, outside of London. When Coke found out about it, he sent out spies to find out where she was and assembled an armed posse to go fetch her. Informed about her husband's actions, Lady Hatton herself set out toward Oatlands to stop him. At Oatlands, Coke broke down the door of the house, searched, and found his daughter hiding in a closet upstairs. He dragged Frances downstairs and out of the house, and then left for London with her.

Lady Hatton assembled a group of armed men herself and went after her husband. Coke had too much of a head start, and Lady Hatton's horses tired. As a result, the armed groups never clashed. After more back and forth, and more intervention from the Privy Council, Frances eventually ended up in her father's hands. The actions of Coke and his wife divided courtiers and commentators. The king, having been informed of the matter, delivered his verdict from Scotland: Coke's paternal right to his daughter was absolute. Lady Hatton did not give up, continuing to fight Coke, but she lost in the end. In late September, Frances married Sir John Villiers in a lavish ceremony at Hampton Court Palace, with the royal family in attendance and the king himself giving her away at the wedding.[53]

During the contentious summer, Roos became involved in the circus about who should get to control his cousin Frances and her marriage. Lord Holles informed Lake that his son-in-law Roos "is in thes things so busie a man, as though this conduced muche to his own occasion." It is not quite clear which, if any, side Roos supported in the matter. Holles surmised that Roos was relaying information, being "likely the hy way, or the ferry boat betwixt Mr Secretary Winwood, and my Lady Cumpton [Buckingham's mother, and mother of the prospective groom]." Perhaps Roos wanted to be useful to the king as well, making sure that his secretary and the royal favorite's mother were well informed. In his rather Byzantine writing style, Holles suggested that Lake would know Roos's intentions in the matter. "I doubt not," Holles concluded, "but you know how to conjure this spirit, and either qualifie, or cast out the divell."[54] Even though it is difficult to determine Roos's role in the matter from Holles's description, Holles did not approve of Roos's actions, and he did not think Lake would think much of them either. If Roos's goal had been to improve his standing with his father and grandfather by somehow assisting in the fights between Coke and his aunt, it did not work.

Even with the distraction of his cousin's troubles, the pressures on Roos did not let up. He was still furious about the insults offered him at Cannons. He believed his in-laws had cheated and tricked him and that they were spreading lies about him. His brother-in-law had attacked him and injured his men. His own wife remained with her parents, out of his reach. Neither party probably knew it at the time, but the Cannons dispute ultimately broke the marriage between Lord and Lady Roos. Roos had not been able to get any assurances of his father and grandfather's full support. His financial situation became even further strained and more embarrassing, and dishonorable rumors about his impotence continued to swirl. Increasingly desperate and desolate, Roos began to plan an escape from his troubles.

4
Leaving England

> Lord Roos, who six months ago was ambassador extraordinary in Spain, has left England secretly, almost with the appearance of flight, taking with him a servant and a Spaniard whom he had in his house.
>
> Giovanni Battista Lionelli, envoy in England to Doge and Senate in Venice, August 25, 1617[1]

Roos simply left. He left his wife, his family, his in-laws, his friends, his debts, his obligations, his king, and his country. He told none of them of his plans and staged quite an elaborate and highly secretive escape. In late July of 1617, a couple of months after the disputed Cannons incident, Roos was going on a trip north to Yorkshire, where he had some property. He may have also intended to visit his grandfather at Burghley House, northwest of Peterborough, along the way. In either case, he never made it there. He set off from London with a retinue of sixteen to twenty men. Once the group arrived at an inn at Stilton, about seven miles south of Peterborough, Roos informed his men that he had received an urgent message, which required him to return to London briefly. He told them to stay and wait for him in Stilton, in order to speed up the process of traveling later. Only Diego da Silva and one other servant accompanied him as he headed back south toward London.[2]

The Flight

Roos never returned to his waiting men at Stilton. Instead, he went somewhere along the southern coast and crossed over the English Channel. With him, he had as much cash as he had been able to raise secretly and in a short amount of time. He had sold furniture from the house at Charterhouse Yard. He sold and pawned plate and jewels as well. An observer estimated that he had managed to come up with £8,000–10,000 in ready money. At Calais, he sent a French foot-post back to England, with orders to deliver a letter and a sealed box directly to Sir Ralph Winwood. The letter was undated and did not reveal a location. Roos hastily excused himself to Winwood, apologizing for

Family and Feuding at the Court of James I: The Lake and Cecil Scandals. Johanna Luthman, Oxford University Press.
 DOI: 10.1093/oso/9780192865786.003.0004

not informing him about his travels beforehand. Roos blamed his abrupt departure on the "diabolicall dealings of the Lady Lake." He assured Winwood that he would hear from him again within twenty-five days and that he would then describe in more detail the reasons for his leaving. In the box, Winwood found "a graunt and conveyance of certain woods," which Roos claimed were worth £8,000. Roos had previously borrowed £4,000 from Winwood and was supposed to have paid it back by the beginning of August. He hoped the grant of these woods would suffice instead.[3] Others reported that Roos "hath passed over his whole estate to Mr Secretry Winwood for the valewable consideration of paying detts," but that appears to have been an exaggeration.[4]

Winwood informed his fellow secretary Lake, still in Scotland with the king, of Roos's departure. Initially, they kept the information close to their vests, as they were not quite sure what to make of it. Roos's actions were not just surprising to his family and friends, but they were also illegal. Any Englishman or -woman needed a royal license to leave the realm. Issuing licenses to travel was part of the routine business of the Privy Council, and the licenses noted the activity the traveler intended: educational travel, business, family visits, health, the king's business, and so forth. Departing without a license could be construed as a rebellion, since it was assumed that the secretive, unlicensed traveler must harbor bad intent. By the early seventeenth century, these suspicions were often connected to Catholicism, such as conversion, study to become a Catholic priest, enter a Catholic monastery or convent, acting as a spy for a foreign Catholic power, and so on.[5]

If the activities of an English traveler abroad were considered problematic, the king could also revoke travel licenses. Sir Robert Dudley discovered as much when he set off from England in 1605. He had a license, but his travel companion did not. Although he was already married with children, Dudley left his family behind and traveled to the continent with his mistress, Elizabeth Southwell, one of Queen Anna's maids of honor. Southwell managed to escape undetected, dressed as a man during their voyage across the English Channel. Once abroad, the couple converted to Catholicism and married. King James and Queen Anna were not pleased at this affront to their authority. Dudley had also committed bigamy, which had recently been made a felony in England. When Dudley refused to come home to face the music, the king revoked his travel license. Dudley and his new wife never returned to England but ended up serving at the court of the Grand Duke of Tuscany.[6]

By mid-August, the fact that Roos had left became public knowledge and a topic of rumors. Commentators initially expressed surprise. Why would such a privileged nobleman, heir to even greater fortunes and titles, just run away?[7]

One suggestion, encouraged by Roos himself, was that he planned to fight a duel with Arthur Lake. Over the course of the summer, he had been talking about challenging Arthur, no doubt perceiving it as a way of restoring his wounded honor and manhood after the disputes with his in-laws and the fight at Cannons. Inherent in the patriarchal masculinity of the early modern period was the need for a man to be able to dominate others. The controlled and rule-bound violence of private combat, or duel, gave an offended man the chance to dominate his opponent. A victory in the duel therefore weakened the status of the loser's claims or actions and strengthened that of the victor. Since Roos's manhood had been called into question before, during, and after the Cannons incident, many of his contemporaries within the socio-economic elite in England would have viewed a duel as a reasonable continuation of the fight between Roos and Arthur Lake.[8]

Duels had become more common in England during the sixteenth and early seventeenth centuries, largely as a result of the popularity of the courtesy manuals written in Italy, the epicenter of the Renaissance. The English soon also began to produce their own. These books primarily spelled out the appropriate behavior for courtiers, but also those who in general wanted to be esteemed as "gentlemen." Dueling was considered an upper-class activity. Protecting one's honor and reputation was paramount. If another man gave serious offense which could not go unanswered, the honorable way to respond was to settle the matter in a private battle at an agreed upon time and place.[9]

Duelers usually fought with swords and/or daggers, and increasingly more commonly with the gentleman's particular weapon: the rapier, the narrow and needle-like blade of which was meant to deliver sharp thrusts. The deep puncture wounds of the rapier were more often deadly than the slicing of the broad-bladed swords. With the emergence of the rapier, a young English gentleman's education also increasingly included fencing lessons. Fencing was not commonly used as a tactic for soldiers on the battlefield but became popular to defend oneself and others. Should it become necessary, fencing skills would also be essential in duels.[10]

Duels were illegal in England. Rulers disliked the duel because combatants took their disputes into their own hands, rather than relying on royal authority and the law. This created a tension between the need to protect and defend the honor of gentlemen and the requirement to subject oneself to the authority of the ruler. Nevertheless, many argued that defending one's honor was more important than obeying the king, and the fact that dueling became more common in the late sixteenth and early seventeenth centuries supports the view. To avoid breaking the law on English soil, affronted persons would occasionally sneak over to France or to the Netherlands to settle matters of honor. Technically, this was still illegal, but presented more of a gray zone and thus appeased some concerned consciences.

To bolster his renewed 1614 proclamation against dueling, King James published an anonymously written treatise to emphasize the point. In 1617, he again reminded his subjects about the illegality of dueling. In February of that year, King James insisted on sitting in the court of Star Chamber when two young men were on trial for having challenged each other to a duel. They were caught and arrested as they were on their way to cross the English Channel, so they never actually fought. This marked the first time the king had ever personally presided in Star Chamber, so he must have felt the case and the issue behind it was especially important. The king found both would-be duelers guilty, fined them £1,000 each, and sent them to the Tower.[11]

Roos had indeed sent a letter to Arthur Lake, challenging him to a duel in Amiens, France. Winwood reported to Lake that a "personage of great quality" told him that Roos had left England specifically with the intention of fighting Arthur. However, after more details emerged about Roos's challenge, most people dismissed it as a smoke screen, a diversionary maneuver. According to John Castle, the challenge was "couched in such poor termes and so childishly" that no one could take it seriously. Again, Roos's maturity and manhood was questioned.[12]

Sir Thomas Lake dismissed the idea of the duel outright: he had heard those rumors but could not "beleave that if he [Roos] intended any such he wold have left so much speech of it behynde him."[13] Apparently, he had been spreading rumors about the challenge for more than a week before he sent it from Calais, dated August 2. Lake also pointed out that Roos had sent the challenge to London, when he knew perfectly well that Arthur Lake was not there at the time. Arthur was traveling toward Scotland to meet his father and the king. Roos had met him along his own interrupted journey north.[14]

Other aspects of the challenge made Lake question it further. Lady Lake had been at Cannons when the letter with the challenge arrived at their Charing Cross house in London, so the Lake's butler was the one to receive it out of the hands of the "base fellow" tasked with delivering it. By emphasizing the low social status of the delivery person, Lake was noting that a proper challenge should be sent in a more honorable manner, delivered by a second or at the very least by a person of gentlemanly standing, as duels were supposed to be undertaken only by those of a "gentleman" status. That Roos had chosen to send it by a common courier, paid for the task, further pointed to the conclusion that the challenge was not made in a serious manner. When

Lady Lake returned to town a few days later, she found Roos's letter and she sent it onwards to her husband.[15] Lake may have shown the letter to a displeased king also, as James commented on the challenge and "meaneth to put him [Roos] in minde of it whensoever he returns."[16] It hardly made the king better disposed toward the absconded nobleman.

Lake instead believed Roos fled England when he found out his grandfather had decided against helping him in his financial straits. According to Lake, Roos had planned to visit his grandfather at Burghley on his journey north. When Exeter found out that Roos was on his way, he ordered his men to refuse Roos and any of his men to even enter the gates of the estate. Roos, losing hope and realizing he could not rely on his grandfather's support, decided to flee the country instead, Lake argued. Roos's uncle Sir John Holcroft, who had traveled north with Roos, told Lake that Roos had informed his company in Stilton that he had received a letter from his wife, and that he had to return briefly to London so that "the matter between them should be put to endes."[17]

Others believed that Roos had fled his mounting debts. Chamberlain told Carleton in October that Roos was "farther indebted that I thought his credit would stretch."[18] Nathaniel Brent also told Carleton that while he could not "perfectly understand" the "storie of my Ld. Roose," he was "certaine he is indebted more than £20,000, hath pawned his goods, mortgaged much land, is run away." In the same letter, Brent compared Roos's situation with Sir Herbert Croft, who, "being deeply indebted by means of his wives excesse hath closely conveyed himself out of the kingdom, shaven his berd," and traveled incognito "under the name of Mr. Nichols." (He didn't succeed in being incognito, it appears.)[19]

Once outside of England, Sir Herbert Croft had "turned popish." Chamberlain judged Croft's Catholic conversion as "no great marvayle, for desperation hath made more monckes than him."[20] Chamberlain was implying that Croft's financial straits left him few options other than to take refuge in a monastery, making his conversion more practical than reflective of deep spiritual conviction. Croft did enter a monastery in Douai, France, but he also appears to have traveled to other places within Catholic Europe. For example, by next spring, Croft was with Roos in Italy.[21]

What about Roos? Was he a closeted Catholic, like Croft, who now would convert, perhaps pushed to it by financial desperation? Many noted that he left with his trusted servant, confidant, and boon companion, the Catholic Spaniard Diego da Silva. "I confesse I never liked Diego," Lake told Buckingham. To Winwood, Lake noted that da Silva, or "Diego his Spaniard," as Lake called him, was "under cullor of religion" a "very lewd fellow." In addition, he had "been told" that da Silva regularly visited the Spanish ambassador's house, implying that he was drawing Roos toward Catholicism and loyalty toward Spain, or that he was a Spanish spy. Lake informed Buckingham that he was about to discover more about da Silva's connections to Gondomar, but he was interrupted in the process when he followed the king to Scotland. By the time he got back, da Silva "was gone, and had carried his master with him." Lake did not trust him and concluded "these revolters are suspicious to me till I see good proof."[22]

The accusation was a little rich coming from Lake, considering he himself drew a pension from the Spanish ambassador. Others, however, did note the close connections Roos appeared to have with the Spanish ambassador. Later that fall, Chamberlain commented that "the speech goes that he [Roos] is at Rome in great privacie with his holiness by the recommendation of this Spanish ambassador, with whom at his departure he left all his rich moveables that he could not make away on the sodain."[23] A disappointed Exeter also complained about the bad influences of the Spanish ambassador. Exeter had been kind to him, entertained him both in Exeter House in London as well as his country estates, hoping that he would help him free Molle, Roos's long-suffering old tutor, from his Roman imprisonment. Instead, the ambassador "seduced" his grandson away from his religion and family and "sent him to Rome with such recommendation as he [Exeter] is in daunger to be utterly deprived of him."[24]

The Chase

Even though he was close to the Spanish ambassador and left England with his favorite Spaniard, Roos did not go to Spain. What followed instead was a kind of cat-and-mouse game throughout Europe. By the time members of Lake's and Winwood's activated European networks reported Roos's movements and actions back to England, the young lord had already moved on. William Trumbull, English agent in Brussels, became one of the main sources for tracking Roos. Trumbull kept up correspondence with people throughout Europe and had built up a web of useful connections, informants, and spies, which he employed for the benefit of King James.[25]

Roos traveled incognito. He also had men travel separately to assist him in raising and moving money, then meeting up with him secretly. For example, it appears that Roos and da Silva parted ways at some point, and that da Silva joined his master at his destination later. Trumbull reported to Winwood that Roos disembarked in Dunkirk and then went to Antwerp. There, he sold two rich cloaks, one of satin and one of velvet. He then bought a simpler outfit with the proceeds, so he could travel without being recognized. He apparently traveled under the name of Thomson, potentially also making a stop in Brussels. He may have initially intended on going to Spain, or he may have planted false information to shake off his possible pursuers. Trumbull noted that an acquaintance of his had met one of Roos's servants on the road from Antwerp to Brussels and the servant said he had orders to meet Roos in Madrid. Trumbull had also heard from others who claimed to have met Roos that he had told them he was headed to France first, and then onwards to Spain.[26]

Next, Roos showed up in St. Denis outside of Paris. Another of Trumbull's acquaintances had spoken to Roos, who then said he planned to live quietly in the Paris region until he could hear from his friends in England. After that, reports placed him further south in Lyons in October.[27] By late October and early November, he was spotted in Avignon and Genoa. He had waited in Genoa for a few days, until more of his money and goods arrived, somehow smuggled out of England. From Genoa, he and the one servant who traveled with him (which was not Diego da Silva at this point) took ship to Rome. Trumbull had managed to get a hold of the original "billet" which proved the trip. Roos arrived in Rome on November 5.[28]

Roos mostly stayed in Rome in the months that followed, with visits further south to Naples as well. While in Rome, he visited several cardinals and hired a "schollar" to "reade the Mathematicks onto him," in an apparent desire to expand his learning. Initially, Trumbull's contact had heard that Roos had brought large sums of money, upwards of £20,000 or £30,000 and scores of jewels, and that he planned to buy a coach and install himself in a palace in the Eternal City. Since those early reports, Trumbull noted that Roos had scrapped that plan, and decided to live more modestly and privately instead. By December, Diego da Silva had joined Roos in Rome, presumably after having traveled separately and made further financial arrangements for his master.[29] In January, Roos wrote from Naples to Sir Francis Cottington, the regular English ambassador in Spain, whom he had met while there on his own embassy a year earlier and during his educational travels. Roos told Cottington that he hoped "His Majesty will give him leave to travel," that is, grant him a belated travel license. Cottington, a better judge of Roos's situation than the young man himself, told Trumbull: "This I doubt very much." He then added "I am truly sorry for him in his present situation."[30]

Meanwhile, King James sent several couriers to find Roos and deliver the king's message that he was to return to England immediately from his unauthorized voyages. In an official letter from the Privy Council to Roos dated August 24, the offending lord was told that the king found "his suddaine and unexpected departure without [the king's] leave or the pryvitie of any of his Councell" a "high Contempt committed by you."[31] None of James's official messengers managed to locate Roos during the fall and winter of 1617/18. In mid-September, John Castle informed Trumbull that the "King's letters to Lord Ros should have reached him in France by now, but many doubt that he will return home, in obedience to His Majesty's commands."[32] Roos managed to evade the king's messenger. King and council dispatched another courier in October and November but were thwarted again. The messenger "is returned and hath not found Roos," Chamberlain informed Carleton.[33] The fact that messengers could not find Roos meant that they were also unable to deliver the king's writ formally, as it had to be delivered in person to be valid. Some commentators noted increased irritation with Roos's stubborn elusiveness. By December, an exasperated George Abbot, archbishop of Canterbury and a member of the king's Privy Council, wrote Roos, chided him and emphasized he should return from his "idle, ridiculous and discontented journey."[34] The Privy Council wrote him yet another official missive on December 4, telling him that the king took his actions in "ill parte."[35]

Lake and Winwood held different views about Roos. For Winwood, Roos had been a useful and well-connected young friend. His ability to irritate his rival Lake by befriending the son-in-law who had such a troubled relationship with his father-in-law constituted an extra bonus. Winwood certainly did what was required of him when it came to locating Roos: as the secretary of the king's foreign correspondence, he had been the recipient of Trumbull's most detailed early reports. However, he also sent subtle warnings to other people who were friends with Roos. For example, Sir Dudley Carleton had become acquainted with Roos when he served as English ambassador in Venice at the same time as Roos's educational travels in Italy. Carleton had found Roos a charming and cosmopolitan young man. He also had kind things to say about Diego da Silva, judging him "a man of good sufficiency, both learned and intelligent and much esteemed for his honesty and fidelity to his master."[36] When Winwood informed Carleton about Roos's disappearance, he only told him the facts, saying that Carleton's "good friend Lord Roos" had secretly left England with da Silva and that he had "left his estate and family, which was great, at six and seven."[37] However, he did not specifically ask Carleton to provide information about the men. Chamberlain, also aware of Carleton's friendship with Roos, counseled Carleton that it was best not to get involved. "Yf he [Roos] chaunce to come by you" at The Hague, Chamberlain noted, "I pray you take no more notice of this then you shall find convenient."[38]

Lake, naturally, had a personal stake in finding his daughter's troublesome husband. Unlike Winwood, he perfunctorily asked Carleton to be on the look-out. "If your Lordship hear any thing of [Roos's] passage, you shall do well to let us know it," the secretary demanded, adding that Lake had orders from the king to find Roos. Carleton could not ignore such orders, but he did not perform his duties with any diligence. At the very end of an otherwise long and detailed dispatch to Lake, Carleton added curtly "I failed not, according to your honour's desires, to lay wait for my Lord Roose in these parts, but I hear he is passed through France towards Lyons."[39] Carleton's information was late, whether on purpose or not is not clear. At that point, other sources had already informed Lake that Roos was in France.

In late October, Winwood fell seriously ill and died, leaving Lake as the sole royal secretary for several months. Winwood had been responsible for most of the king's foreign correspondence, whereas Lake took care of the domestic side. Winwood's death, and the fact that the king delayed the appointment of a new secretary, meant that Lake temporarily took over both duties. This allowed him to have more direct access to the English ambassadors and agents. When Lake informed Trumbull of Winwood's death and the king's order that Trumbull address his letters to Lake from now on, he did not neglect to add "I would be glad to receive from you any information you may have about Lord Ros."[40] Trumbull was clearly more informative and forthcoming than Carleton. He had already supplied Winwood with details about Roos's movements, but it is not clear how much of that Winwood had shared with Lake before his death. In his next letter to Trumbull, Lake thanked him for the information about Roos, which was "the first definitive information that we have received about him." The grateful Lake wanted to find out more, though. "Please find out from the same source whether Lord Ros tooke Rome only as in his passage to some other place or whether he purpose his residence to be at Rome; what is become of Diego his man, and what sommes of money were made unto him at Genoa and from whome heere."[41]

At one point, Lake questioned Trumbull's sources of information, asking the agent if he was sure that Roos was in Rome, as he had heard a different rumor of his whereabouts. Trumbull was clearly offended that Lake did not trust his work. "To doubt of my L. Roos his being at Rome, were a kynde of heresy," Trumbull noted pointedly. "It is in this Towne, Lippis [as] tonsoribus notum [everyone knows it]."[42] He then when on to outline how he knew, giving an interesting insight into Trumbull's network for collecting information:

> I will assure you, it hath bin confirmed to me by severall ways: namely by [letters] written from Sr. Francis Mac Donnell, Hugh Owen, and the Reader of the Engl, seminary there [in Rome]; to some persons with whome they keepe correspondence, in these parts: being of my acquaintance, or familliar wth some of my friends.[43]

Trumbull told Lake he had heard the same rumor about Roos being elsewhere in France but had quickly concluded that it could not be true, since that region currently suffered from a severe outbreak of plague, leading other nobles to flee it altogether. Trumbull seemed irritated that Lake would think he had not heard or considered this same rumor. The experienced agent gave Lake, not as familiar with the foreign correspondence, a lesson in how it worked. Trumbull concluded by telling Lake that he "may be confident that which I can learne any thinge concerning my L. Roose, worthie yor knowledge I will not fayle to enzelle[enseal] it in ltr of these advertisements." Trumbull noted that this defined his job and his responsibility, as his missives to the secretary were "where I must give yo Lo an account of his Maties service."[44] Trumbull's job consisted of informing the king on important matters of state, and he thought Lake seemed a bit too focused on using the king's resources to get information about Roos for private reasons.

Lake did relay the information from Trumbull to the king, via Buckingham. "I thought it my duety," Lake told Buckingham, "to let His Majesty know what is become of him." If Lake had ever thought much about Roos, he clearly had become disillusioned by this point. He also did not mind telling the king that he "feared now the worst" regarding Roos, probably meaning that he had no intention of returning to England and that he would be converting to Catholicism. In other words, Lake did not try to protect his son-in-law from the king's ire at this juncture, but rather was willing to tell the king that Roos was clearly capable of anything. "What further so unsettled and unconstant a brayn as he hath will doe I know not," Lake complained.[45]

Lake further questioned some of Roos's servants in England, trying to gather more information about their absent master and his goods. Lake learned that George Gwilliams might provide him with more answers. Gwilliams was Diego da Silva's servant. Lake heard that Gwilliams had bragged to others that Roos had left him behind in England so that he could arrange for some of the young lord's goods to be sent after him abroad. Gwilliams was also supposed to join Roos in his journey after these tasks were completed. Lake suspected that Gwilliams had more selfish goals, or perhaps that he was motivated to help his master, da Silva, rather than Roos. Lake claimed that Gwilliams was accused of having stolen goods out of Roos's Charterhouse Yard residence, and then bringing those goods to da Silva's house. When da Silva left England, he also left his English wife, who had recently given birth, behind. Lake believed she might be the recipient of some of Roos's goods.[46]

When Gwilliams was charged with these crimes shortly after Roos's departure, he had fled, supposedly to the Low Countries. Trumbull later confirmed to Lake that Gwilliams had traveled via Brussels and then to Paris.[47] After a stint abroad, he returned to London later the same fall, clearly hoping that the danger had passed. At that point, the king's council had officially charged Lake with ascertaining the unlicensed Roos's whereabouts. As a result, it behooved Lake to investigate all possible leads—or at least that is what he told a court half a year later. He had his own reasons for wanting to secure as many of Roos's goods as possible, considering the precarious situation of his now abandoned daughter. When Lake heard that Gwilliams was back in London, he ordered him arrested and brought to him in Whitehall palace.[48]

When questioned, Gwilliams absolutely denied everything and refused to give any information regarding Roos. When Lady Roos learned that her father had Gwilliams in custody, she also wished to speak to him. She was hoping to learn news of her husband. Lake sent Gwilliams to the Lake townhome in Charing Cross. Lady Roos asked her mother to question Gwilliams for her, likely relying on the greater authority of the more mature woman. Gwilliams still refused to talk.

Since neither Lake nor his wife and daughter could get anywhere with him, Lake had Gwilliams committed to the Gatehouse prison, hoping that prison would soften him up and loosen his tongue. However, Gwilliams stubbornly remained quiet, so Lake released him after a few days. He did have a bond placed on Gwilliams, which ordered that if requested, he should appear before the Privy Council within ten days.[49] Like so many other interactions that had something to do with Roos, Lake's questioning of Gwilliams became a contested issue a few months later, when the feud between the Lakes and the Cecils reached its apex. The earl and countess of Exeter would later claim that Lake's arrest of Gwilliams was more sinister in its intent (more on that in Chapter 7).

Roos in Rome

Meanwhile, Roos was hiding in Rome. His flight puzzled many. He had been given so many advantages in life: he was the only son to an eldest son, heir to the great estates and titles of both Burghley and Exeter. He had more international experience than many of his peers, could boast of useful language skills, and had been entrusted with the king's business on his Spanish embassy. He had influential friends and had contracted what—on the surface—looked like an advantageous marriage with a substantial dowry. Yet, the life that Roos and his family had planned for him had not worked out. His ambassadorial trip to Spain had failed to impress the king and had left his already strained finances in ruins. His marriage seemed broken beyond repair. He believed his evil in-laws were treating him badly, defrauding him of his estates, and attacking him. His family appeared to have abandoned him and wanted nothing to do with him. He had angered the king by leaving without a license, and even further by purposefully thwarting the royal messengers. He had to skulk around in Europe and resort to complex and secretive maneuvers to have access to money.

At least he was now in comfortable surroundings, in a place and society that welcomed the young English lord. Roos had spent his formative years outside of England, from his mid-teens to his mid-twenties. It is perhaps not surprising that when the pressure became too great for him to handle at home, he decided to go where he had experienced happier times in younger, more carefree days. Continental Europe was more familiar to him, and, as others had observed, he preferred it to England. Having spent long periods in Italy, he clearly favored the place.

Perhaps he also indulged in further art patronage while in Italy. The Venetian artist, Odoardo Fialetti completed and published a book of prints dedicated to Roos in 1617. According to Chaney and Wilks, Roos had commissioned these prints from Fialetti.[50] The book was called *Scherzi d'Amore* (*Games of Love*) and consisted of a collection of thirteen relatively simple engravings, depicting Venus and Cupid in various situations, such as at play, at rest, embracing and kissing, Venus spanking Cupid, Cupid building a bow while Venus looks on, etc. Ten of the prints are accompanied by short little verses. Some of the prints have erotic overtones, but eroticism does not appear to be the main theme. The prints were completed rather hastily, and made to appear as individual pieces, so perhaps the book was put together quickly for Roos when he showed up in Italy again in late 1617. It could have been the result of an enterprising artist: it seems a bit odd that Roos would have the time and finances to collect art in Venice during his secretive traveling. Roos had collected art while on his earlier travels, certainly, but this journey was of course very different. Now, he was fleeing, with no clear sense of how long he was going to be gone, or what his financial situation looked like. On the other hand, Roos had not made particularly smart decisions with his money before. The theme of the prints, the sports of love, also seem rather tone deaf for a man who just left his wife and family behind.[51]

The fact that Roos ended up in Rome, the center of Catholicism, was not lost on anyone either. The pope had long hoped to be able to count Roos among successful converts as part of an ongoing public relations campaign against Protestantism. Now at last it seemed that the Catholic Church could claim him. Because of the danger of falling into the hands of the pope and the Roman inquisition, not many Englishmen traveled to Rome. In fact, because of incidents like the imprisonment of Roos's unfortunate tutor Molle, English travel licenses for educational travelers specifically forbade them from going to the city, seeking to protect young lords and gentlemen from undue papal influences. As a result, Rome was a relatively safe city for a person who was trying to avoid English agents. Roos was not as likely to run into other Englishmen besides Catholic converts.[52]

Roos's behavior troubled his family greatly and his reputation in England suffered as a result. One of Trumbull's correspondents, after relaying information about Roos's furtive movements, added that it was "to be regretted that he has not used his talents to serve His Majesty and the public in affairs of state."[53] After Roos's flight, it became more difficult for his family to defend him, should they change their minds about doing so. His behavior during the months before, during, and after the Cannons incident, his illegal flight from all his troubles in England, his flight to Catholic Rome, all made it difficult for people to think of him as an injured party. Instead, public opinion increasingly viewed him as a failure as a man. Although no evidence had come to light of any nefarious seditious behavior, Roos's flight at the very least presented an international embarrassment for the king, considering that he had entrusted the young man to represent him at the Spanish court. Clearly, he had misjudged him. "The world wonders," mused one observer, "how ever he could so much deceave the king as to be trusted with the carriadge of so much as the message of Lewys the XIth his barber."[54]

5
Tangled Estates

> For my L. Rosse we can heare no certainty of him. He hath been at Orleans at Lyon at Avignon, but where he is, no man can tell. He passeth privately where he goeth; is accompanied only with Diego, but here he hath left a most confused and torn estate.
>
> Sir Thomas Lake to Sir Dudley Carleton, October 20, 1617[1]

When Roos left England, he also left his wife, in-laws, and family to try to work out the tangled messes of his finances and obligations. Other than trying to take as much money and valuables as possible with him on his journey, Roos had made few provisions for all those left behind. The property disagreements, accusations of bad faith, the fight at Cannons—coupled with the tense relationship between Roos, his father, and grandfather—made for a scenario where nobody was likely to believe and trust the other. The Lakes wished to get the greatest benefits for their daughter and themselves. Exeter and Burghley tried to protect as much of the Cecil property as possible and ensure it did not slip out of their control.

Roos owed money all over the place, but both sides also worried that unscrupulous people would try to profit from the chaotic situation, illegally hold on to Roos's property, inflate their claims, or pretend to be creditors. The continued disagreements about the Walthamstow estate also worsened the bad blood between the Lakes and Cecils. In Roos's stubborn absence, the Lakes and Cecil initially tried to solve the thorny disputes with the help of mediation, and then through the courts. Both attempts failed and the bad feelings festered.

The Lakes' First Court Case: Evil Servants and Bad Advisers

The families first went to Secretary Sir Ralph Winwood and asked him to mediate in the matter. A powerful person at court, he had also been close to Roos, potentially having more insight into his finances. Winwood had been one of the few people who received a letter from Roos shortly after he left.

Family and Feuding at the Court of James I: The Lake and Cecil Scandals. Johanna Luthman, Oxford University Press.
 DOI: 10.1093/oso/9780192865786.003.0005

After that letter, however, Winwood had heard nothing further from the exile, even though he had expected it.[2]

Perhaps Winwood might have miraculously succeeded in the difficult task of mediation, but he did not have the time. In late October, the secretary fell ill. His good friend Chamberlain reported his rapid decline. Persistent fevers and fainting spells made him take to his bed, where he was let blood, "which was very bad and fowle." Since he was such an important person, his sickbed received a constant flow of visits from people of note. Among others, the countess of Exeter came to see him "and takes upon her great skill in phisicke," Chamberlain noted.[3] Whatever the countess may have suggested or administered for treatment did not work. Chamberlain grew concerned about his friend's unusual talkativeness. It was a bad sign of his mind being affected by the illness, he believed, as Winwood was usually the quiet, contemplative sort. Growing ever weaker, Winwood passed away a week later. Doctors performing an autopsy found "his heart withered to almost nothing, his spleen utterly rotten, one of his kidneys clean gon, the other perished, his liver full of blacke spots, his lunges not sound, besides divers other defects." Indeed, it "was a wonder how he held out so long, and looked so well," Chamberlain concluded.[4]

With Winwood gone and the usual jockeying for an empty post busying the court and court observers, the mediation ended. The Lakes and Cecils went to the law to settle their differences. When one of the suits was argued in court, Sir Francis Bacon, Lord High Chancellor (and formerly the Attorney General) sat as one of the judges. He asked why the parties had not dealt with their differences sooner, and Burghley replied that "yt was undertaken by a worthy counsaillor deceased [Winwood] who yf he had lived till this time was in a way to compound yt to the satisfaction of all sides." Bacon, who did not like Winwood, responded that "yf you trusted him you trusted to a rotten reede who would have failed you in the end."[5]

In late November, the Lakes began the process by submitting a suit against some of Exeter's and Roos's servants and companions. According to Chamberlain, they also put in a suit in the Court of Chancery, but no surviving Chancery record exists.[6] Technically, it was Sir Henry Yelverton, the Attorney General, who brought the Star Chamber suit. It was a criminal case, where the defendants were accused of fraud, conspiracy, and slander. While the state prosecuted the case, the Lakes and Lady Roos brought the information in the complaint to Yelverton.[7]

In this first suit, Lady Roos and her family did not focus their ire directly on Roos, Burghley, or even the earl or countess of Exeter. In fact, according to this complaint, Lord and Lady Roos and both of their families were blameless, victims of evil and ambitious servants and advisers. As a first legal attempt at solving the growing disagreements, it was not a bad strategy. Blaming "bad advisers" was a long-established method to fix perceived problems without offending or fighting directly with the principals involved. If Exeter and the Lakes could agree that a few servants had caused the problems between them, they could patch up their differences and move on with their honor intact and faces saved. In addition, if Roos was also largely blameless, his marriage to Lady Roos might be salvaged, if only he could be persuaded to return to England.

The defendants in this first Star Chamber case consisted of Roos's Spanish servant Diego da Silva, Exeter's servant and the recently knighted Sir Peter Chapman, another Exeter servant named Francis Featherstonehaugh, and Henry Russell, whose association with the main characters is not entirely clear, but who was probably in the Exeter/Roos orbit. Da Silva, abroad with Roos, did not provide an answer. The surviving court documents thus consist of the original complaint and the answers of Chapman, Featherstonehaugh, and Russell.[8]

Lady Roos and the Lakes accused Chapman of fraudulently trying to get control of the manor of Walthamstow, and to combine and conspire with the other three men to continue to keep it away from Lady Roos by stirring up discontent between Roos and his wife, between Roos and his father and grandfather, and between the Lakes and the Cecils. As mentioned in Chapter 3, one of the issues was Chapman's claim that Roos had given him Walthamstow to repay loans Chapman had taken to raise money for Roos. The complaint accused Chapman of having tried to defraud Roos out of the estate, as Roos believed he was just giving Chapman temporary control of the deed to Walthamstow as security for the money he owed him. When Chapman understood that Roos had used Walthamstow as part of Lady Roos's jointure (and then later deeded it to her), he began to work to undo and destabilize the Roos marriage to get Walthamstow back. The complaint stated Chapman was aware that Roos had given Walthamstow to his wife, a "ladie and wife of much vertue and pacience," because of "his great love and affection wch deservedlie he had borne unto" her.[9] Destabilizing the marriage and trying to remove that love thus became part of the method to reach the goal of getting Walthamstow, Lady Roos and the Lakes argued.

As a part of this larger scheme, the complaint also accused Chapman and Russell of conspiring to create a false written account of the events before and during the Cannons incident the previous spring. They had persuaded Roos to sign it by arguing that his grandfather and father would disown him if he did not do so. According to Lady Roos and the Lakes, this document was a false account of how Roos accused Lady Lake of fraudulently and with threatening and menacing words and actions to give up all claims to Walthamstow and hand it to Lady Roos instead. This false account, the complaint stated, had caused Exeter to conclude that Lady Lake had "cousened" Roos out of Walthamstow. Calling someone a "cousener," or a swindler, was serious, as it questioned both their honesty and their reputation. In the later trials, Sir John Holcroft (the earl of Exeter's son-in-law) argued that Lady Lake's malice against the earl and countess of Exeter had begun when "the earl called [Lady Lake] a Cozener."[10]

The complaint also argued that the men were trying to de-stabilize the Roos marriage because they believed it would increase their own influence with both Roos, Burghley, and Exeter. Since Roos so loved his lady, the complaint stated, the men found that trying to separate them "was not so easily to be affected." Instead, they strove "with more secrecy and craft to wynde themselves in to favor with all the said greate Lordes." They thus began telling "false tales and reportes" to try to promote a "separation" between Lord and Lady Roos, or "att least to kindle thereby such a fure of dissention betwixt the said honorable personages and their families."[11] If there was discord between the families, Chapman might also benefit by getting his hands on Walthamstow through his fraudulent machinations.

The complaint also alleged that the four men had slanderously stated that Exeter and Burghley were pressuring Roos to "keepe from his said wife and become divorced and separated from her." If he would not, they would not "accompt him as a child" and the earl and Lord Burghley would both disown him completely, ensuring that "noe part" of their estate "should discend or come unto the said Lord Roos." Not only were the tales false—neither Exeter nor Burghley had said anything of the sort, according to the complaint—but they also slandered Lady Roos, since they suggested that she had "for some crime or falt deserved to be separated & divorced from her husband," which was not true.[12] Furthermore, the defendants had egged Roos on and assisted his flight out of England and they continued to work toward keeping Roos away from his wife.

As a result of the defendants' slanders and frauds, discord abounded. The "Earle & the said Lord Burghleigh are in dislike with the said Lord Roos and the said Lord Roos att discord with his said ladie and wife & the said Sr. Thomas Lake and his familie & frendes" and "the said Earle and the said Lord Burleigh & their families and frendes are like to be at great discension &

variances." Causing disagreements between "man and wife, families and families, subjecte and subjectes of this Kingdome" was problematic, especially when the individuals were "honorable Personages greate Officers or Families." Such "discord or slander" were against the king's laws and could create "a great mischief quicklie subjecting and destroying the whole kingdom." Such acts therefore were "worthie of sharpest punishments answearable to the demeritt."[13]

In their separate answers to the complaint, Chapman, Russell, and Featherstonehaugh all denied these charges against them. Featherstonehaugh's outright denials did not contain any further explanations or stories. Russell denied having ever tried to sow any discord between Lord and Lady Roos or having even heard Exeter or Burghley say they would disown Roos unless he lived apart from his wife. He had not said anything slanderous about Lady Roos, or suggested that Roos had cause to separate from her. Russell did admit that he had been present in Covent Garden when Roos first attempted to give his written account of the Lakes trying to get Walthamstow from him through fraudulent means, as well as the Cannons incident. While speaking to Chapman in the garden, Roos had called Russell over and read what was in the account. Russell denied that he or Chapman had anything to do with writing the account. He also denied that he had anything to do with Roos's leaving the country, or that he was pressuring him to stay away.

Chapman also denied all the charges. We have already explored his explanation regarding his interest in Walthamstow. When he then heard that Roos was including Walthamstow in the jointure for his wife, Chapman reminded him of their previous agreements. He also told Lake about it. All parties agreed that Chapman would return the deeds to Walthamstow and that he would receive some other lands in compensation. This is what happened. Chapman denied having had any part in writing Roos's account or forcing him to sign it: he had only told Roos that Exeter expected it, and then delivered it to him. He knew of its contents because Roos had read it aloud to him and Russell while they met in Covent Garden. He had never tried to sow any discord and had never claimed that Exeter and Burghley had said they would disown Roos if he would not separate from his wife. He did admit that when Exeter sent him to tell Roos to provide a written account of what had happened with Walthamstow, Exeter told Chapman to relay to Roos that Exeter expected complete honesty. If Roos "refused to deal playnely with him in that behalf and to sett downe the trueth that hee should never enioye foote of his lands or words to the same or the like effect." This was the only time Chapman had heard Exeter mention disowning Roos, and it had nothing to do with Lady Roos's behavior, or Exeter pushing Roos to separate from his wife.

Chamberlain noted that the case "upon the aunswer of the parties was dismissed the court."[14] Apparently, the court was satisfied with the defendants' answers and did not find the accusations credible enough to continue the suit. Lady Roos and the Lakes resurrected it again a few months later, with some additional charges against Chapman, but for now, Lady Roos and the Lakes had failed in their first attempt at a solution. The fight over Walthamstow continued, as did feelings of distrust and betrayal between the Lakes and Cecils.

Exeter Strikes Back

Exeter and Burghley made their first official move trying to assist their son and grandson in his troubles later in the same month of November. The two filed a suit in the Court of Chancery. Chancery was a royal court of equity, where the royally appointed Chancellor (or his representatives within the Chancery) decided cases based on merit and principles of "conscience," rather than the strictures of the law.[15] Exeter and Burghley wanted the Court of Chancery to give them administration of Roos's goods in his absence, since they were blood relatives and only had his interests at heart. They also requested that the court send subpoenas to a long list of people, to specify what property of Roos's they had in their possession, or what sort of debts of Roos's they held. The complaint accuses the named persons of having tried to profit from Roos's disappearance, and of fraudulently claiming they owned or controlled Roos's lands or goods.[16]

The first names listed in the complaint were Sir Thomas and Mary Lake. If they provided answers in this suit, they do not survive. Clearly, Exeter, who had read and kept Roos's account about how the Lakes had cheated him out of Walthamstow through fraudulent means and attacked him at Cannons, wanted to know more about those events, and challenged the Lakes' claim that Walthamstow now belonged to Lady Roos. Since the surviving court documents do not include any Lake answers, it is hard to tell if they were somehow able to ignore the subpoena of the court, or if they were not required to reply, or if they replied and the documents are lost. In either case, the Exeter court complaint was a clear salvo in the Lakes' direction. Exeter and Burghley were not willing to go along with the Lakes' presentation of the Walthamstow dispute as a result of conspiratorial and ambitious servants, but rather chose to blame the Lakes for tricking and pressuring Roos.

Diego da Silva and his English wife Frances were also required to reply to the complaint, as was Robert James, Frances's father. Da Silva again did not answer, as he was abroad with Roos (another sign of how close he was to Roos). His wife Frances and her father Robert James of Fitzhead, Somerset, did provide a reply. Unfortunately, the document is severely damaged and only partially readable. Frances and Robert James outline certain leases and properties that Roos had given to da Silva long before his departure from England. Da Silva had benefitted greatly from Roos's largesse, and now Exeter and Burghley accused him and his wife of having taken even more of Roos's lands and goods.

Frances da Silva and her father both denied that they had tried to profit further or take control of something that was not theirs in Roos's absence. They also denied that Roos had given them orders for any of his goods, debts, or any other financial business. Furthermore, they provided an inventory list of goods that Roos had given the da Silvas when they married the previous year (in 1616). It included various household textiles (fine sheets, pillowcases, tablecloths, napkins, rugs, and blankets), a bed with curtains, valances, and other accoutrements to dress it in yellow satin and taffeta, accented with purple and silver lace, five paintings, a matching table and four stools with yellow taffeta and silk embroidery and fringe, hangings, and a wooden cabinet.[17]

This was certainly an impressive wedding present and Exeter's complaint tacitly suggested that da Silva had stolen the items from an unsuspecting Roos. In comparison, the bedroom furniture Roos had provided to outfit his wife's chamber in her parents' house before he left for Spain seemed significantly less splendid. According to Lady Lake, it consisted only of "a bedstead with furniture of blew clothe and some olde hangings and fower or five chayres."[18] Mistress da Silva insisted that the furniture and household goods were indeed wedding gifts and thus she hoped "shee may lawfullie keepe" them "seeing the same were given to her."[19]

In addition, Exeter's suit requested answers from Richard Best, Roos's receiver of rents, three London goldsmiths, a London upholsterer, as well as three other gentlemen, at least one of which had been in Roos's service for five years. Out of these, the Chancery document bundle only contains the answers of Best, one of the goldsmiths, and Roos's gentleman servant Giles Dunscombe. These men's answers partly show the state of Roos's finances and behavior before he left. Best outlined how he had received the rents from Roos's estates as usual and provided them to Roos. After Roos's departure, he had paid the rents "according to the appointment and direccion" of Exeter instead, since no orders were coming from Roos. He was not aware of any of the sales of jewels, plate, or lands that Roos had made before his leaving, except for the sale of the manor of Turmanhall in County York. Best was not familiar with all of Roos's debts, but he did know of about £500 of debts and would be willing to provide a list of persons and sums to detail that. Other than the rents, he said he had no other goods or papers of Roos's in his possession since Roos left the country.[20]

Thomas Havers, a London goldsmith, did confirm that he had sold to—and bought from—Roos, at "divers times before the supposed last departure out of this kingdome." Havers had paid Roos for the plate he had bought from him, and Roos had paid him all except four pounds of what he owed him for purchase of plate. He could not remember the pieces he had traded with Roos nor could he remember the exact times when these transactions had taken place. (One might interpret this forgetfulness as convenient, of course, if Havers had done something untoward.) In the case of Roos, he only dealt with plate, he never bought or sold any jewels. Furthermore, he did not have any of Roos's jewels, goods, writings, lands, leases, or any other thing belonging to Roos, in his possession since Roos's departure. He also did not know of anyone else who held goods, except for Roos himself.[21]

Giles Dunscombe, described as a "gentleman" in the court documents, had served Roos since at least 1612 and may have traveled with him during the period from 1612 through 1615. He had been "att great expense in his Lordship's service," according to his reply. Dunscombe was one of the men who had accompanied Roos to Cannons during his unsuccessful attempt to take his wife away earlier that year and was wounded in the melee. He, along with almost all other servants, had been left behind when Roos left England.

Dunscombe told the court that he had already delivered all the "writings and evidences whatsoever" of Roos's to the earl of Exeter, "not havinge kept so much as any noate of them." Furthermore, Roos owed him £20 for one year's wages, as well as £9 and 6 pence "upon accompts and Reckoninge" when he left the country. These sums remained unpaid. Dunscombe said he had some of Roos's household goods "of little or small value" in his possession when Roos left: two ebony bedsteads, two featherbeds and bolsters, three quilts and a bolster, three blankets, six pairs of sheets and some odd ones, one crimson and gilded bedstead, one pair of brass andirons without spindles, three pictures, one ebony table, one great trunk, one old trunk, and two Bibles (one in French and one in English). When Roos left, Dunscombe did not know how he would get paid, so he went to the City of London court at Guildhall (run by the Mayor and Aldermen of London) and sued to attach the goods. After the goods had been properly appraised, Dunscombe eventually won a judgment in that court on November 27, 1617. Dunscombe provided the Court of Chancery with this document, arguing he has nothing else of Roos's.[22]

It is possible that Exeter's lawsuit was dismissed after the defendants had provided the answers. No other records mention a continuation or a solution of the suit. Exeter began yet another lawsuit trying to recover Roos's property in 1621, so he must have considered some of the issues unresolved. At that point, Roos had died abroad, and Exeter and his wife had won a decisive victory, both legally and in the public eye, against the Lakes and Lady Roos. Exeter's 1617 lawsuit primarily alerted his grandson, as well as others, that he was willing to support him and disbelieve what the Lakes told him. Even though Chamberlain reported that Roos "is thought will soon return yf he find that his grandfather and father mean to sticke to him," the young nobleman continued to stay away.[23]

Roos's Abandoned Creditors

Roos's flight left many others besides his family and in-laws in a bind. Not everyone was as lucky as Giles Dunscombe, who could keep some of Roos's possessions in order to get paid. It was not the first time Roos had shown this kind of irresponsible behavior. Roos abandoned unfinished legal business: he was embroiled in a lawsuit with a tenant when he left.[24] When Roos borrowed money, his creditors, who often in turn created financial agreements with others in order to provide Roos with funds, found themselves in a bind when he did not repay on time. While Roos was on his educational travels, he had benefitted from his familial ties. People were willing to lend him money, because they wanted to get on the good side of his uncle Salisbury, the king's most trusted minister.

Some regretted their decision. Sir William Trumbull, the king's English agent in Brussels, learned this lesson the hard way. When Roos was stuck in Brussels without funds to travel back to England in 1611, he had approached Trumbull and asked for his assistance, as the English merchants had initially refused him. Trumbull had been told to ensure that Roos received an honorable reception at the archduke's court because of his connection to Salisbury and therefore probably felt pressured to help him. Roos's friend Tobie Mathews also asked Trumbull to help. Trumbull put up some of his own money, also pressuring reluctant English merchants in the region to come up with the rest, personally guaranteeing prompt repayment. When Roos reached England, he thanked Trumbull and promised that he would repay him with interest by the date they had agreed.[25]

When Trumbull's London agent attempted to collect, Roos disappeared out of town, and his household servants employed all sorts of evasive and stalling tactics for months.[26] Meanwhile, Trumbull was left trying to satisfy the impatient merchants, taking hits to his own credit and reputation. Even Mathews found Roos's delays distasteful. He wrote Trumbull and said he "know not whether I be more sorry or ashamed to consider how much it was my ill fortune to persuade you to engage yourself for Lord Roos."[27] Eventually, Roos repaid the loan a little at a time, but apparently only the principal, and not the agreed upon interest.[28]

Similarly, when Roos had returned out of his Spanish embassy in March of 1617, he had tried to raise money to repay the loan to Lake by selling and pawning some of the jewelry with which he had outfitted himself before the journey. Roos approached Robert Hooke to assist him in the process. Roos delivered a hatband set with fifteen diamonds and fifteen rubies, a chain of diamonds, and "threescore and nineteen buttons of goald set with diamonds." In addition, Roos also delivered the very jewel the king of Spain had presented him, a "Jewell of goald sett wth diamonds in forme of a greate Roman A." Hooke's job was to use the jewels to raise money for Roos, so the young lord would be able to repay his loans.

Roos provided Hooke with deeds for the jewelry, to show prospective money lenders or buyers that he had come by them legitimately. It appears Hooke did not sell the jewelry outright, but rather pawned them. He argued it was the only way he could come up with the money as quickly as Roos required. The agreements Hooke made bound him to pay interest on the money he raised. When Roos left the country later that same year, Hooke had tried to go to Exeter and ask him to redeem the jewels and let him out of the financial bind he was in because of his grandson, but the earl had not been willing to do so. As a result, Hooke was forced to borrow money and pawn his own goods in order to raise the money to pay the interest.[29]

People high and low felt the effect of Roos's flight. One Edward Webster complained that he had not been paid for the housing and caring for Roos's "caroch," or carriage, since the young nobleman left. Roos's steward had made an agreement with Webster, promising to pay twelve pence per week if Webster kept and maintained the carriage. Apparently, the payments had stopped once Roos left England, which led Webster to keep the carriage as collateral for the unpaid fees. He argued that the carriage was not worth much, as it was old and worn and had "nether bed nor seat nor cushions in yt," and that the keeping of it was now "a great burthen and hindrance" for him. Several years later, he declared that anyone willing to pay him the back-fees for the storage could certainly have the carriage.[30] In the end, holding on to Roos's abandoned property was not profitable.

Roos's Abandoned Wife

When Roos fled, he left his wife in a hopeless sort of limbo. She was tied to him by marriage, but she received none of the benefits that a marriage ideally should provide: financial security, greater autonomy and power as a mistress of her own household, the joy and responsibility of children, a loving husband. Instead, she was tied indefinitely to a person who had summarily abandoned her. She was still living at home with her parents, relying on them for her support and subsistence. (It is not clear if Lady Roos received any of the agreed-upon annual spousal maintenance after Roos left.) She could not hope for children with her husband absent. She did not know much about her husband's finances, and every new revelation seemed to make the situation bleaker and bleaker. Hers was not an enviable position. Clearly this is not what she had imagined, or what her parents had in mind, when she married into the wealthy Cecil family.

In the Star Chamber lawsuit against da Silva, Chapman, Featherstonehaugh, and Russell, Lady Roos was presented as an innocent and virtuous wife, most worthy of the love of her husband, but abandoned as a result of the slanders of evildoers. This was undoubtedly part of the legal tactic. However, Lady Roos's emphasis on Roos's love for her, and how others had intervened to remove or steal that love that was rightfully and lawfully hers, is a theme that runs through her answers and complaints in other lawsuits as well.

In the tales Lady Roos later related, she claimed she had hoped her marriage might improve in the late summer of 1617. The crisis of the Cannons incident had certainly caused a huge rift between Roos and the Lakes, but Lady Roos noted signs that the marriage might yet survive. At some point between his return from Spain and his flight from England, Roos gave his wife a fine jewel. It was a cross of diamonds as "recompence of the many other jewells which the sayd Lady had before her marriage" and which Roos had "taken away and converted to his owne use" during his embassy.[31] Most notably, Roos had pretended to reconcile with his wife right before he fled England. When he unexpectedly returned to London from his interrupted northward journey the previous July, Lady Roos insisted that he had come to see her "wth great showe of love and kindness," which promised better days ahead.[32]

However, when the details about her husband's secretive and illegal flight emerged, Lady Roos realized that the hoped for reconciliation was just a ruse, "wch the promise considered cannot but grieve [her]."[33] Her husband had not only tricked her but truly abandoned her. Since he left, he had not written a single letter, or sent her a greeting or token, or acknowledged her in any way. In her answers to the charges in the slander suit of the following year, Lady Roos noted bitterly that she while she received nothing, she heard that Roos sent letters and messages to another woman, the woman who had stolen her husband's love from her: the countess of Exeter.[34]

6
The Tales of the Summer of (Dis)content

> I doe here confesse that I haue done my ladie Rosse a greate deal of wrong first by abusing my self wth her husband and then attempting her life by poyson for feare she wold reveale it.
>
> Frances Cecil, Countess of Exeter, June 15, 1616
> (according to Lady Roos)[1]

As the first Star Chamber and Chancery court cases were developing rather disappointingly for both parties, the accusations of wrongdoing grew more heated. Exeter continued to believe that the Lakes had defrauded Roos of Walthamstow and had thus driven him to leave the country. The Lakes continued to argue that bad actors had put these ideas into the earl's head in order to cover their own greediness. The Lakes also tried to find out more about who knew and assisted Roos in his departure and who had control of Roos's resources. They questioned Roos's servants and associates, sometimes in quite forceful ways, which would become more grist for Exeter's mill in a few months. A thoroughly disillusioned Lady Roos now also began lobbying sensational accusations against Lady Exeter, which gave the feud a whole new dimension, turning the property disputes and the fight at Cannons into the much more sinister realm of adultery, incest, and murderous poisoning.

A few months after Roos left England in 1617, Lady Roos revealed a dark tale that had taken place during the summer of 1616, the very first year of her marriage and before Roos's Spanish embassy. The young, newly married woman said she had been quiet about most of this before, because she had "hope of amendment" from both Roos and the countess of Exeter. As a good and dutiful wife, she had also been silent for "her lord and husbandes sake," concerned about her husband's reputation and honor, as well as his relationship with his grandfather.[2] Since Roos had now turned his back on king, country, wife, and family, she was ready to reveal the full extent of the countess of Exeter's treachery and villainy. This chapter tells the tales of that disputed summer of 1616 from the vastly different perspectives of Lady Roos and her family and servants on the one hand, and the countess of Exeter and her husband and servants on the other. These tales also implicitly reveal

Family and Feuding at the Court of James I: The Lake and Cecil Scandals. Johanna Luthman, Oxford University Press.
 DOI: 10.1093/oso/9780192865786.003.0006

seventeenth-century ideas about bodies, health, and medicine, and the operations of a large noble household.

Wimbledon House

The drama primarily played out at the Cecil estate Wimbledon House (see Fig. 6.1), where Lord and Lady Roos stayed for a few months together with the earl and countess of Exeter. When Exeter was a child, he had sometimes lived at the Rectory in Wimbledon, as his father had been granted the right to occupy the house by Henry VIII. By the 1570s, Exeter (then still plain Sir Thomas Cecil) had acquired the manor of Wimbledon and proceeded to build a great house in the late Tudor style. The building was completed in 1588. The house does not exist anymore, but several descriptions and drawings of it survive. The house was built of red brick, with tall Tudor-style chimneys and numerous large windows. The gables and roof had fanciful and ornate decorations. It had a grand entrance, with double courtyards and

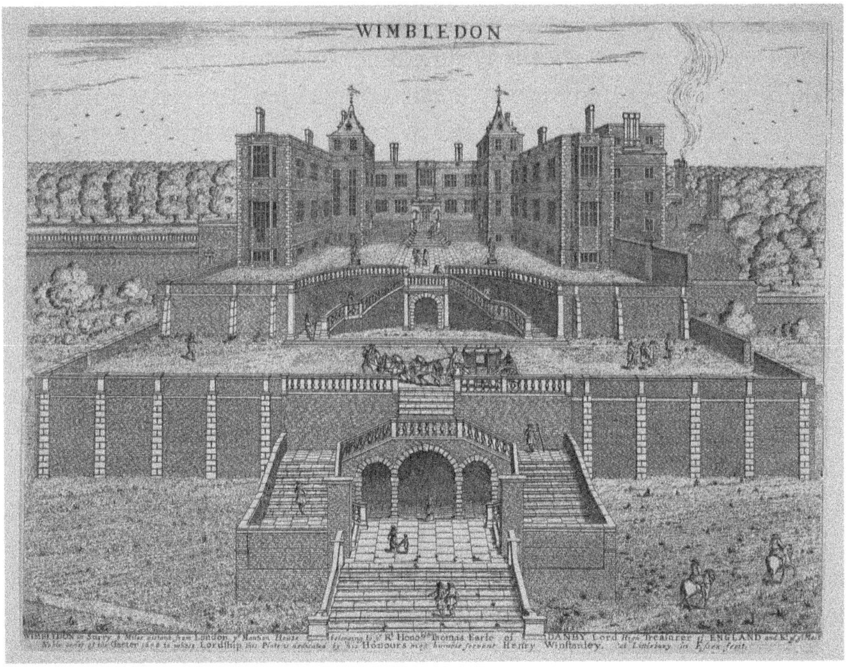

Fig. 6.1 View of Wimbledon House, 1678. Etching by Henry Winstansley. The Trustees of the British Museum. The Tudor period ornate decorations on the roof had been removed by the later 1600s.

stately double stairs leading up both courtyards and to the house. The house was within easy reach of London, yet rural enough to provide a true countryside experience. Exeter hosted both Queen Elizabeth and King James there several times.[3]

Exeter was a keen builder and especially interested in establishing fine gardens for his homes. The gardens at Wimbledon were magnificent. Near one side of the house was a sunken walled garden. Formal gardens, planted in geometric designs, stretched out behind the main house. Among them stood a banqueting house on a raised platform, perfect for entertaining in pleasant weather. Close to the kitchen on the side of one of the wings of the house were the kitchen gardens, producing herbs and vegetables for the table and for medical treatments. Next to the kitchen gardens, a visitor could stroll among the fruit trees of an orchard, interspersed with a variety of roses. Further up on terraces were other fruit trees, including cherries and exotic lemon and lime trees (see Fig. 6.2).[4]

The manor house was luxurious. The central portion of the U-shaped house had a 180-foot-long gallery, with checkered black and white marble floor. The gallery and several other rooms were wainscoted in a green-tinted oak, lavishly decorated with golden stars. In the middle of the long gallery stood a grotto adorned with seashells, with sculptures depicting men, lions, serpents, and other "fantastical" figures. The walls were lined with long benches. The most curious piece of furniture in the room was a 21-foot-long table made from a single piece of wood. A large mirror reflected the splendor of the room, and the ceiling had eight framed pictures.[5]

The summer at Wimbledon in 1616 had been made more exciting by royal visits. The earl of Exeter invited the king to hunt and then dine at Wimbledon. The arrival of the royal party on June 21 must have made for a great flurry of activities in preparation. The king had great success with the deer before the dinner. The new French ambassador was also present, waiting for his first official audience with the king. The countess of Exeter and Lady Roos were seated at the ambassador's table, both given a prominent place. Also in attendance was Lady Hatton, one of Exeter's daughters who sometimes attended Queen Anna's court, and whose husband, Sir Edward Coke, was still the king's Chief Justice of the King's Bench.[6]

The countess was heavily pregnant during the royal visit. She gave birth to her youngest daughter at nine thirty on the morning of Saturday, July 13. On July 30, there was yet another royal visit to Wimbledon when Queen Anna

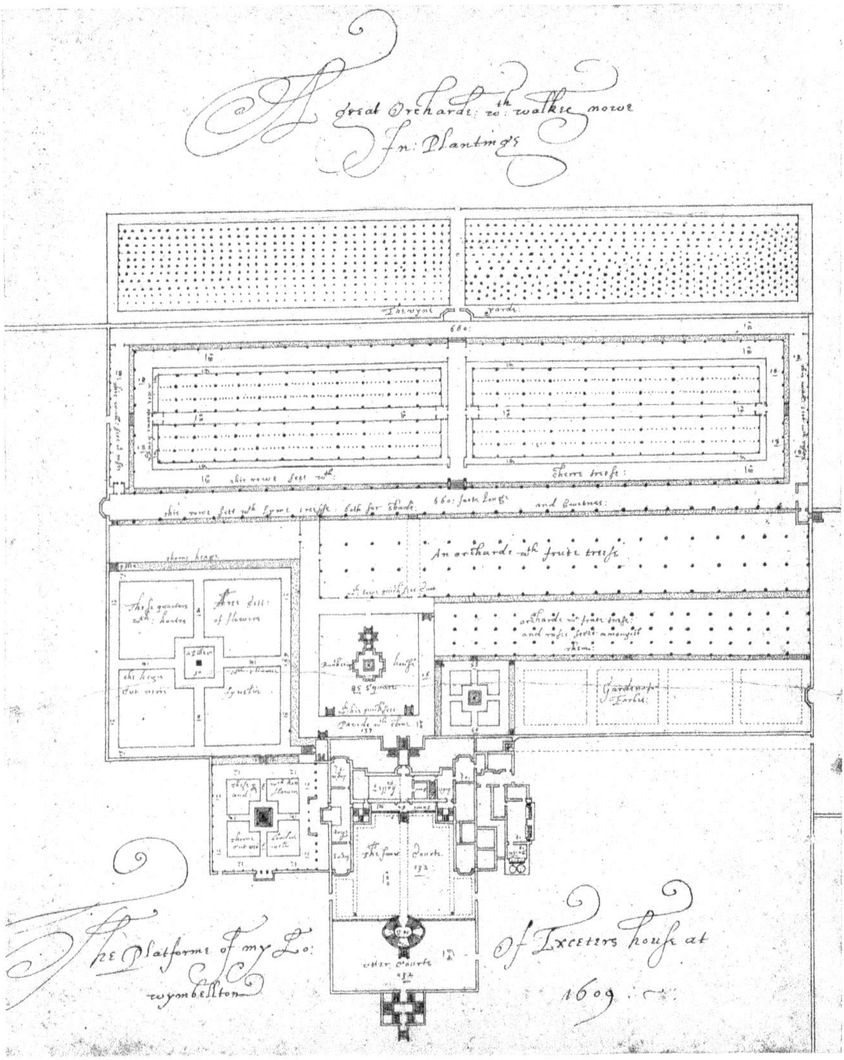

Fig. 6.2 Plan of Wimbledon House and the grounds, Wimbledon. Drawing by Robert Smythson, 1609. RIBA Collections.

attended the baptism and stood as godmother for baby Georgi-Anna.[7] The countess, who was not yet churched, did not attend the baptism. No source mentions if Lady Roos attended, but it seems that it would have been likely, as she was still at Wimbledon at the time.

In this grand, beautiful, and bucolic setting, evil lurked behind the scenes, according to Lady Roos. The sinister actions of the adulterous countess of

Exeter endangered Lady Roos's very life as well as her marriage. For her part, the countess of Exeter insisted that she had been a friendly and cheerful hostess to a grateful Lady Roos, and that she was entirely innocent of any wrongdoing. These divergent accounts warrant a close look.

I have recreated Lady Roos's tale here based on her answers in the Star Chamber slander suit Exeter filed on his wife's behalf in 1618, as well as the countersuit filed by Sir Thomas Lake's son also named Thomas, in the same year. The younger Thomas Lake's complaint, built on the tales of Lady Roos, was even more detailed than Lady Roos's own answers in Exeter's suit. That account must have been based on Lady Roos's telling of events, unless her brother and the Lake lawyers made up further details of their own in the accusations, which is not likely. The latter complaint appears to be designed to tell a more cohesive story and respond to some of the questions raised by the Exeter suit. The answers provided by Lady Roos's servant Sara Swarton in the 1618 Exeter slander suit are also invaluable, as they are the most detailed of any account. I have also included witness depositions from other individuals (mostly servants), which were collected by Lake and his lawyers before the slander suit went to trial in early 1619. The witness depositions survive as abstracts of the summaries presented in the trial, and not in full. (More on the workings of the court of Star Chamber in Chapter 9.)

The countess of Exeter's tale is based on her husband's complaint in the 1618 Star Chamber slander suit against the Lakes and Lady Roos, as well as the answers of the earl, the countess, and the countess's gentlewoman servant Elizabeth Gresham, in Sir Thomas Lake Junior's countersuit in the same year. I have also included witness depositions of other Exeter servants from the later trial.[8]

Lady Roos's Tale

Shortly after the marriage of Lord Roos and Anne Lake in February of 1616, the earl of Exeter invited his grandson and his new bride to come and live with him. The couple first lived at Exeter House in the Strand in London, but the whole household moved to Wimbledon during the summer to enjoy the country air. The servant Sara Swarton accompanied Lady Roos in her new life. Swarton had a long history working for the Lake family, especially looking after the many Lake children. Lady Roos had known her all her life. When she married, Lady Roos asked her mother if Swarton could come join her, and

Lady Lake agreed. It must have been a source of comfort for the mere sixteen-year-old bride to have a familiar and trusted face in her grand new surroundings.

The countess had initially been a gracious hostess, but Lady Roos soon began to observe "many extraordinary signes of too great affection & familiarity" between her husband and his step-grandmother. This grieved her, as she believed she might lose her husband's love and affection. At one point, Lady Roos confronted the countess with her "greate greefe and discontent." Lady Roos believed she had put a stop to the countess's bad behavior by simply confronting her, but that turned out to be a miscalculation. Now that Lady Roos knew, the countess realized that "the same affection and familiaritie" between her and Roos "could not be continued nor eyther of them be free from the publique complaint or accusation thereof by the sayd Lady Roos" unless the countess aimed for the younger woman's "death and destruction."[9]

At one point in early June, Lady Roos decided to take a cooling bath. Bathing was probably not a regular affair for most people. As Susan North has recently demonstrated, that did not mean that early modern people were filthy: in fact, they regularly washed themselves with water, soap, and linen strips as wash cloths, making use of basins of various sizes (smaller ones for the washing of hands and face, larger ones for standing or crouching sponge-baths). They also changed their linen underclothing as often as they could afford it, which might have meant almost daily for the very rich who had enough linens and the servants to wash them. Full body submersion in a tub indoors (as opposed to bathing in rivers, lakes, and ponds outside) also required resources and labor: the expense of a large enough tub, carrying enough water to fill it, potentially heating the water, etc.[10] This, of course, was not a problem for the wealthy.

The purpose of a bath could be medicinal as well as cleansing, adding various decoctions to the bath water to sooth and mend ailing bodies. The purpose of Lady Roos's June bath appears to have been medicinal. According to Sara Swarton, the countess suggested that it would be a good idea for Lady Roos to "open her bodie" further before the bath, by means of an enema. In a slightly different version of events, as told in the account of Sir Thomas Lake, Jr., Lady Roos was not feeling quite well, and the countess suggested that she take an enema.

Enemas were very common medical treatments for all sorts of ailments in the early modern period. The medical treatments of the time were based on the humoral theory, where the body was made up of the four humors: blood, phlegm, black bile, and yellow bile. A healthy body was a body with a harmonious balance between all humors whereas a diseased body had an imbalance of humors. As a result, medical treatments were usually based on the idea of restoring the balance of humors, often through removing excess humors through purges, enemas, bleedings, and so on. Gendered bodies were also believed to have certain characteristics. Male bodies were hotter and drier, and female bodies were cooler and moister. Different organs were often connected with various humors and the hot, dry, moist, cool qualities. The countess's suggestion of an enema in connection to a bath was therefore not unusual. Most people would have been very familiar with this form of treatment.[11]

Having thus declared the need for an enema, the countess told Swarton to go see Elizabeth Gresham, the countess's gentlewoman servant, so that Gresham could give her some "conserve of roses" to put in the enema. The countess said that the conserve of roses would make Lady Roos have "two or three stooles." Swarton did as she was told and gave Gresham an empty "toppe of a Magdala cupp." Gresham went into a closet, and when she came out, she handed Swarton the measure filled with conserve of roses. Gresham told Swarton to add "about the quantity of a Nutt" of the conserve of roses in the mixture to be put into the enema. Swarton did as directed.

When she mixed in the conserve of roses, Swarton noticed that it had a strong smell, and exclaimed "God blesse us yt smelleth like rosacre such as Mrs Anderson would have given her husband," likely referring to a recent case of poisoning. Nevertheless, Swarton did not suspect that the countess had any evil intent at that time and so proceeded. Swarton also enlisted the assistance of Alice Butler, another servant, who prepared the "simples" for the enema. Butler also went to Gresham for a "glister pipe," an instrument necessary for the administration, which she received and gave to Swarton. After mixing up the decoction, Swarton duly administered the enema to Lady Roos. Both Butler and another servant, Robert Marsh, saw the glister pipe and other things in a basin in Lady Roos's room afterwards, which suggested that Lady Roos had indeed been given the enema.[12]

The enema had an extraordinarily strong effect on Lady Roos's body. According to a later report from the trial, Lady Roos claimed the "glister" made her "use 32 tymes in one night," which was certainly more than the "two or three stooles" promised.[13] The night after the administration, she was "grieved and payned all that night," which continued for three or four days afterwards. Lady Roos was so uncomfortable that she could not stay in her bed. Swarton noted that in her desperate state, Lady Roos blamed her servant: she accused Swarton of having mistaken the mixture in the enema. She even beat poor Swarton and said she "was bound to curse" her "whilest she lived for giving it unto her."[14] Lady Roos's brother Thomas argued that it was it was only through "the strength of her youth" that she "escaped the stroake of death intended by the giving of the sayd poyson."[15]

After this experience, Lady Roos began to suspect that it was the countess who was behind her suffering, and that it had been on purpose rather than a mistake. It was not just her husband's love that she was in danger of losing, but perhaps also her life. With "anguish and trouble of mynde," Lady Roos told her husband of the countess's evil actions. Roos was first "loth to apprehend yt" and was trying to convince his wife that the countess had no evil intent. When she refused to give in, and he perceived that she might be desperate enough to tell her family and friends about his incestuous affair with his step-grandmother, he became concerned. He conferred with the countess, and the two figured that the only way to pacify Lady Roos and keep her from telling others about their illicit relationship and dealings would be to offer her a confession and a promise to end the relationship and never hurt her again. They offered this concession only if the younger woman would first be willing to swear an oath not to ever reveal the adultery to anyone. Lady Roos, happy to have a solution, to secure her future safety, and to end the threat to her marriage, agreed.[16]

On June 15, about a week after Lady Roos's painful experience with the enema, Lady Roos called Swarton to her as she was standing in the earl of Exeter's bedchamber next to the parlor. She told Swarton to hide behind some hangings (tapestries) along one wall and listen to what Lady Roos and the countess should say. Lady Roos ordered Swarton to pay close attention and note everything said, but never reveal it to anyone else unless Lady Roos specifically told her to do so. Swarton duly hid. Soon, the countess entered the room with Lord Roos and Diego da Silva. From her hiding place, Swarton heard Lady Roos speak. She accused the countess of having wronged her and of having tried to poison her. The countess answered: "Good Madam, yf you thinke I haue done aniesuch thinge or given you more than was fittinge [in the enema] I pray you forgive mee and I hope god will." Lady Roos replied, "You have often promised not to wronge mee any more but I will not trust you unless you giue itt mee under your hand." The countess answered: "Madam I will soe itt may goe noe further." Lord Roos interjected at this point, telling Lady Roos: "Nan you may thank Diego for this and you maie proue that Diego loueth you," implying that da Silva not only was familiar with the situation but also might have been the one to come up with the compromise. The countess's written confession read:

> I doe here confesse that I have done my ladie Rosse a greate deal of wrong first by abusing my self wth her husband and then attempting her life by poyson for feare she wold reveale it and I do hereby aske gods forgivness and her and have written this to give her satisfaccion and doe thinke this noe other thinge I can doe enough satisfaction for her.
> June XVth
>
> Francis Exeter

After the others left the room, Lady Roos asked Swarton if she had heard what the countess said. She did not ask her to repeat the words, or show her the writing, but instead just told her to keep quiet about it. Swarton did not know that the countess had written anything down: she claimed she did not learn about the written confession until she was being questioned by the Privy Council in the spring of 1618.

Believing that the countess had now reformed her behavior, Lady Roos remained at Wimbledon throughout July and August. In July, Lady Roos felt poorly, like she was coming down with a cold. Stories here conflict: Swarton claimed that the cooling bath was in connection to the first poisoning attempt, but Tomas Lake Junior's account states that the idea for a bath occurred during the second poisoning incident, rather than the first, and that it was the countess who suggested the "cooling bath." In both accounts, the countess also counseled a purge prior to the bath, in the second account specifically to "prepare her body with a purge of Syrrup of Roses taken in whay."

The earl of Exeter had a habit of taking syrup of roses, so this medicine was readily available in the house. At the countess's directions, her maid Gresham provided syrup of roses to Lady Roos's gentlewoman Mary Lake (not a member of Lady Roos's immediate family), who mixed it with the whey a dairy maid had delivered for the purpose, and then gave it to Lady Roos. Again, Lady Roos felt unwell and took to her bed. She became convinced that the countess of Exeter was at it again. For days and weeks afterwards, her head was sore, and she suffered from "cramps and griping" in her stomach, referring to diarrhea.[17]

Sometime after this incident, Lady Roos appears to have traveled with her husband, mother, and sister to Burghley House. Burghley was another one of Exeter's country estates. The description of their interactions on this journey does not provide a date, but it was probably during King James's progress during the summer of 1616, which started on July 19 and ended on August 29.[18] The king went to Burghley on August 3 for three nights.[19] Lord and Lady Roos, who had been living in the same household with the earl and countess of Exeter for several months by this time, would probably also attend at Burghley during the royal visit. Lake often traveled with the king on progress, so it also made sense that his wife would go to Burghley, given Lake's responsibilities to the king and the Lakes' new relation to the Exeters through their daughter's marriage.

Along the way to Burghley, the company stopped overnight at an inn at Ware. The story about what happened at Ware was not included in Lady Roos's, Swarton's, or Lady Lake's specific answers in Exeter's lawsuit, nor in her brother's complaint. Instead, it shows up in the abstracts of witness testimonies from both sides. Just as Roos was ready to take "Coache to goe to Burleigh," he received a letter and became "discontent." Lady Roos "wept" and "became ill" as Roos became discontent. That same night, Elizabeth Lake, Lady Roos's younger sister, claimed to have overheard a conversation through "a Wainscott dore" between Lord and Lady Roos while at Ware. Roos had "confessed unlawfull love and the attempting of the poison, and the recognition [confession] under the Countesses hand." Lady Lake claimed not to have heard about the countess's written confession, but only about the letter, which had caused so much discontent in Roos and sorrow in Lady Roos. Edward Norgate, a Lake servant, deposed that while at Ware, Lady Lake had cried and told him that "the L. Roos would be his Ladyes death at first or last, and complained much of his ill usage of her."[20]

After the visit to Burghley, Lady Roos returned to her parents' house. It is not entirely clear where her husband was at that time, but in any case, he was busy preparing for his upcoming embassy to Spain. As she returned from Burghley, Lady Roos "was sick" and "complained of weaknes." This was now about a month after the latest incident with the syrup of roses. Doctor Henry Atkins, one of the king's physicians, was summoned to care for her, and he gave her some strengthening "cordials," a common treatment for someone suffering from diarrhea.[21] Shortly thereafter, Roos left to go on his ambassadorial trip to Spain.

The Countess of Exeter's Tale

According to the earl and countess of Exeter, they had never invited his grandson and his new wife to live in his household. Instead, they argued that it was the young couple who had "become earnest suytors" to the earl and countess to "permit them to lodge and dyett in their house for a quarter of a yeare (or such a tyme)." Lord and Lady Roos complained that the Lake house, where they had initially stayed after the wedding, was "so straithened in roome, that they disliked much to continue therein." The Rooses promised to pay their way, "to make reasonable satisfaccion, and allowance, for such their entertainment, their estate and company considered." After these pressures and promises, the earl agreed that the Rooses could live with him in the Strand and at Wimbledon for a time.[22]

The outraged countess said she was entirely innocent of any charges of adultery, incest, and poisoning, and claimed the supposed conversation and confession at Wimbledon in June had never happened. She had nothing to confess. She had "neuer demeaned herself otherwise towards the said Lord Rosse, then did well become her in honour, and might worthily become the wife of his grandfather to doe."[23] She argued that Lady Roos was "most friendly and kindly entertayned" during her stay at Wimbledon that summer and that the lady had "made great semblance of a due acknowledgement of a harty, and affectionate report towards" the countess.[24]

In the later trial, witnesses for the countess also argued that Swarton had not even been present at Wimbledon at the time of the supposed confession, so it would have been impossible for her to hide behind the hangings in the earl's room to overhear a conversation that day. Furthermore, they claimed that Lord and Lady Roos had been outside of the Wimbledon estate on that afternoon, and so could not have had a conversation with the countess indoors. Richard Boys and Benedicta Beering deposed that they had both met Lord and Lady Roos on the Wimbledon heath at 4 o'clock that same day, June 15. Boys and Beering were servants of Frances, Lady Tufton, one of the earl of Exeter's daughters. Beering also said she waited on Lady Tufton at Wimbledon for three days around that date in June, and never saw Swarton there. (Lady Tufton was also present during the royal visit to Wimbledon on June 21.)[25] Furthermore, she did not see Swarton in the coach that carried Lord and Lady Roos on the heath that same day. Mary Lake, Lady Roos's gentlewoman, said Lord and Lady Roos left Wimbledon at some point between three and four o'clock that day. She also deposed that Swarton was attending Lady Lake in London in June. Lady Lake was just about to give birth to her youngest child at that point and required extra assistance. John Johnson, whose connection to the principals is uncertain, said that Swarton left Wimbledon at least six weeks before the countess was brought to bed on July 13.[26]

The countess also argued that she had no knowledge of Lady Roos having had an enema while at Wimbledon. The countess had never suggested it, had never ordered one to be prepared for her, and certainly had not ordered anyone to add poison to this non-existent enema. She was not aware of Lady Roos feeling "sicke, or ill at ease" at any time while staying with her, except for having "a Chollicke (wherewith she was usually troubled)" and one occasion when Lady Roos had "distempered herself by goinge abroad in the night tyme in the dew."[27]

On that latter occasion, Lady Roos had felt as if she had a cold, and asked for some syrup of roses to restore her good health. The countess did not know about this episode until after the fact, about two hours after Lady Roos had already taken the medicine.[28] She was confined to her chamber after childbirth still and was sleeping when Lady Roos made her request via a servant. Elizabeth Gresham, the countess of Exeter's gentlewoman servant, did not want to wake up her sleeping mistress, so she went to the cupboard with medicines, took out the syrup of roses, measured five spoonsful, and delivered it to Lady Roos's servant. Gresham did not mix anything else into the syrup, neither whey nor poison. The countess and Gresham both explained that the elderly earl of Exeter regularly took syrup of roses, and Lady Roos received the medicine from the very same "glasse" from which the earl had received doses both before and after, without any ill effects. There could thus not have been any poison in the medicine. When the countess found out that Lady Roos had taken the syrup of roses, she was upset with the servants involved. Lady Roos should not have been given medicine without the "consent and privitie" of the countess, or "without the direction of any physician."[29]

A slew of servants, some of them Lady Roos's, later attested to the fact that Lady Roos did not seem to suffer any bad effects from the syrup of roses. According to Mary Lake, the servant Elizabeth Prince finished what was left after Lady Roos had taken some of the medicine. The syrup worked "as other physic useth to doe," but other than that, Prince was fine. When Lady Lake arrived at Wimbledon that same day for a visit, Lady Roos quickly took to her bed, but not because she was ill. Instead, she did so in order to avoid seeing her mother. After her mother left, Lady Roos got up from bed again, was "pleasant and merry," and then supped with the countess in her chamber, displaying "love and respect" to her hostess. Another servant saw Lady Roos ride in her coach outside the same day, and yet another witnessed her "leape and dance" and that she did not stay in bed the day after. Yet another said another had told her that Lady Roos did "rumpe up and downe immediately after the taking of the Syrrup."[30]

The countess's camp also dismissed the notion that Lady Roos or Lady Lake had heard of anything untoward from Roos while at Ware, during their journey to Burghley for the king's progress visit in early August. John Duppa, Roos's servant, argued that he had not perceived any discontent between his master and Lady Roos, and that there was no way that Elizabeth Lake could have overheard a conversation. The rooms in which they lodged were not next door to each other, as Elizabeth had claimed, because there was a "great chamber" in between them. Another servant argued that Roos had not even lodged in the same chamber as his wife, so Elizabeth could not have overheard a conversation between the couple.[31]

When Lady Roos left Wimbledon and returned to her parents' house, the countess had heard that she mentioned to several persons that she had been "extraordinarily well used by the Countesse." While Lady Roos had complained of weakness and been visited by a doctor, that same doctor later said she had not mentioned anything about any poisons at that time. Dr. Atkins also later deposed that if she had been given the poison roseacre, it would not have been possible to live a full month after. Lady Exeter also argued Lady Roos's head suffered not from the aftereffects of poison, but rather from "lack of combing."[32]

The Meaning of the Tales

Just like the tales of the riot at Cannons, the tales of the summer of 1616 obviously vary widely. The tales only agree on a few basic facts: Lady Roos spent the summer at Wimbledon, as did the countess of Exeter, who gave birth to her youngest daughter there in mid-July. While the countess was in bed recovering from childbirth, Lady Roos felt ill and took some syrup of roses mixed with whey as medical treatment. Syrup of roses was readily available in the Wimbledon household. Lady Roos left the Exeter household after the summer and returned to live with her parents, complained of illness, and received medical care from Dr. Atkins.

Just like the divergent tales of Cannons, these stories have many meanings, both clearly stated and implied, that reveal the early seventeenth-century ideas about health, illness, medical treatments, and poisoning. Most notably, when Lady Roos told the tale of the countess's adultery and murderous intentions, she was using well-known tropes of illicit sex, sin, and poisoning that would have been easily recognizable to her contemporaries. The countess of Exeter countered by arguing that she was a model wife and a hospitable mistress of a wealthy noble household, and that Lady Roos brought her illnesses on herself through her own carelessness.

Lady Roos and the Lakes argued that the countess's behavior at Wimbledon was especially insidious, because she had hidden her poison in medical treatments supposed to restore health, not harm it. She had suggested that Lady Roos take an enema "under a fayned pretense of love" for Lady Roos "and care of her health."[33] Poison was generally viewed as an especially evil type of attack, because it was secretive, hidden, and difficult to defend against. It could be disguised as nurturing food and drink or healing medicines, thus also ensuring that the vile and malicious murderer could appear entirely innocent, caring, and loving. Sir Edward Coke, the great lawyer and the earl of Exeter's son-in-law, thought poisoning the worst kind of murder, "the most horrible and fearfull to the nature of man," because it was the "least preventable by manhood or providence." Another lawyer, Henry Montagu, believed poisoning a "work of darkness"—concealed, sinful, and evil.[34]

Because of its secretive nature, poisoning was also viewed as an unmanly and un-English crime, more suited to women, weak men, and foreigners. Instead of using manly strength, bravery, and a weapon to kill someone, the poisoner needed only secretive and dangerous knowledge, and an opportune moment to trick the victim to take the poison. Women, as mistresses of the kitchen and medicine cabinets, had ample opportunities, the thought went. Sinful women secretly reaching for poison formed a fearsome image in the early modern mind, as "posioning can be said to operate as a means of distilling fears about women into a single felony," as Una McIlvenna has put it. Late Elizabethan and early Jacobean plays and other English literature also often depicted the poisoner as an evil "other," often Catholic, Jewish, Spanish, or Italian.[35]

The most spectacular case of poisoning in Jacobean England was the Overbury case that had just come to light in the fall of 1615 (mentioned in Chapter 2). The earl and countess of Somerset had murdered Overbury in 1613 by ordering their accomplices to procure and administer several poisons while he was imprisoned in the Tower. The poisoning was made even more evil by the apparent care taken in putting poison in the sorts of treats of which Overbury was especially fond, such sweet tarts and jellies, and by adding poisons to supposedly strengthening broth and medical treatments. Under the guise of this thoughtfulness, the Somersets and their accomplices instead killed Overbury. Overbury's death was also especially heinous, slow, and painful, leaving a stinking corpse that was hastily buried for fear of contagion. Two years later, the dark plot was revealed. The sensational trials that followed the discovery of the crimes took place in the fall of 1615 and spring of 1616. The associates who carried out the Somersets' orders were tried, convicted, and promptly executed by hanging.[36]

The much-awaited trials of the earl and countess of Somerset for accessory to murder took place in May 1616, right before Lady Roos spent the summer at Wimbledon. Likely, Lady Roos would have known about the details of the poisoning of Overbury, as the Overbury murder had been the talk of the town for months by the time of the Somerset trials. Overbury had been given different poisons on multiple occasions over a period of several months in 1613. First, he received a deadly poison of "green & yellow color called roseacre" mixed into a broth in May. Secondly, he was given powdered arsenic and told it was medicine. Thirdly, deadly "mercury sollinate [sublimate]" was mixed into tarts which Overbury ate. Lastly, now very ill, Overbury was given an enema mixed with mercury sublimate and more food laced with the same poison. He finally died the next day.[37]

Notably, Lady Roos accused the countess of Exeter of having used roseacre in an enema right after the conclusion of a very famous case of poisoning featuring both the poison roseacre and the method of a poisoned enema. Of course, Lady Roos's story of what happened during the summer of 1616 did not become public until 1618. Lady Roos might have believed that the fact that the countess of Somerset, such a well-known and favored lady at the royal court, had confessed to the shocking poisoning would make it more likely that others would believe that another noblewoman could also commit a similar crime. Alastair Bellany has suggested that Lady Roos's accusations were a copy of the Overbury murder.[38]

However, it must also be noted that Lady Roos never made any overt comparisons to the Overbury case, and neither did the Lakes, or the earl and countess of Exeter. Others who commented on the Roos-Exeter case did not raise the specter of Overbury either, with one exception several months after the conclusion of the trials in 1619. That exception did not directly talk about Lady Roos's supposed poisoning, but possibly referred to the later rumor that the Lakes had Roos poisoned while he was in his exile.[39] Roos's hasty death in 1618, amid the lawsuits between his in-laws and grandparents, was suspected to be poisoning, although there was little actual evidence of it. (See more in Chapter 8.)

It may not have been necessary to state a connection or similarity with the Overbury case, as it was so well known by the time of the revelations of Lady Roos's accusations in early 1618. Most people who kept up with events at court or capital would have heard about it. Interestingly, Sara Swarton referred to an entirely different poisoning case in her answer to Exeter's slander suit beginning in 1618. Swarton related that she had reacted to a "strong smell" in the conserve of roses that the countess had ordered mixed into Lady Roos's enema. Swarton exclaimed: "God blesse us yt smelleth like rosacre suchas Mrs Anderson would haue giuen her husband."[40] However, another of Lady Roos's servants claimed never to have heard Swarton mention anything about an odor of roseacre at the time, so it could have been a construction after the fact, referring to some later case.[41]

Medical treatments that did not go well, or where the patient died, could also give cause for suspicions of poisoning, as could unexpected deaths. In early 1618, the Prince of Orange died after having an enema. His body "is waxen blacke which is a signe there was poyson in it," John Wolley reported to William Trumbull. It is more likely that the prince died because the person who administered the enema made a mistake and caused an internal rupture, but since it was a suspect death, the rumors of poison immediately began to swirl.[42] Similarly, when King James died in 1625, his beloved favorite the duke of Buckingham and Buckingham's mother were rumored to have attempted a treatment without the knowledge and approval of the king's doctors. He had applied a plaster, as well as given the king a syrup or posset or other kind of medical concoction to drink. This stirred Buckingham's enemies, who soon accused him of having poisoned the king.[43]

For Lady Roos's and the countess's contemporaries, the idea that a woman's sexual crimes could lead to attempted murder would have seemed a natural connection and progression. Sexual crimes corrupted a person, especially women: a woman who had committed sexual sins was likely to commit other sins as well. For example, when retelling the tale of the Overbury murder, writers often began the story with Frances Howard's troublesome sexual desires and perceived sexual sin. Frances Howard's desire for an annulment in order to be able to marry her lover was the beginning of her downfall. Since Overbury disliked the relationship and tried to convince Carr to end it, Frances Howard, her virtue already corrupted by illicit sex, slid further into sin by deciding to poison Overbury and get rid of the obstacle. In addition, pamphlets describing stories of female murderers often began with the moment of sin that led to the downfall.[44] If the countess of Exeter had already committed the sins of incest and adultery, many seventeenth-century people would be predisposed to believe that she might also attempt murder.

The main thread in Lady Roos's tale is the story of the countess stealing the love and affection of her husband. In Lady Roos's telling, everything else follows from that adulterous and incestuous desire. Indeed, Lady Roos's testimony across multiple lawsuits continuously circles back to complaints about the countess's "unseemly covetinge and affecting of" Lord Roos, by which she had "taken away and depreved" Lady Roos of "the love and affeccion" of her husband.[45] The countess's sexual sin led her into desperate situations, and she tried to cover them by committing even greater sins, murdering people who knew of her immorality. Interestingly, Lady Roos does not emphasize that the countess's sexual sins with Roos would of course also mean that she is being an unfaithful, adulterous, and bad wife to her husband the earl. Instead, Lady Roos mentions only that the countess has stolen her husband, her husband's love and affection, and thus her rightful place as his wife.

Illicit sex and poison were also often associated with witchcraft in the early modern mind, but this theme was absent in Lady Roos's accusations. The hidden evil of poisoning, and the dark knowledge required to concoct the poisons or their administrations, were easily connected with the workings of the devil or the devil's minions. The period from the late 1500s to the mid-1600s saw the most trials and executions for witchcraft in England. Other Jacobean court women accused of sexual immorality were also connected to witchcraft and dark magic. Frances Howard was accused of having used love-magic to try to render her first husband impotent, and to bind her second husband's love prior to their marriage. Lord Roos's cousin Frances Coke Villiers, viscountess Purbeck, was similarly accused of using the assistance of Dr. Lambe, previously convicted of witchcraft, in order to magically harm her husband as well as her brother-in-law, the duke of Buckingham, in the 1620s.[46] Lady Roos never mentioned witchcraft in connection to the countess of Exeter's alleged poisoning.

Naturally, the countess of Exeter and her supporters presented a very different picture of her. Far from being an adulterous poisoner, she was a model of early modern womanhood. As a wife, mother, and mistress of a large household, she would have been expected to be responsible for looking after the health of her household, as well as be knowledgeable about basic medical treatments. In 1623, Gervase Markham dedicated his book *Country Contentments, or the English Housewife*, to the "the Right Honorouable and most Excellentest of Ladies, Frances, Dowager Countess of Exeter." The book contained recipes and tips for the "inward and outward Vertues which ought to be in a compleate Woman." The good housewife needed to have many skills, such as "in Physicke, Surgerie, Extraction of oyles, Banquetting-stuffe, Ordering of great Feasts, preseurving of all sorts of wines, Conceited secrets, making Cloth, Dying, the knowledge of Dairies, office of malting, Oats, their excellent uses in a Family, Breweing, Baking, and all other things belonging to a household."[47]

The countess also expressed her medical interests and knowledge to others. Godfrey Goodman noted that the countess of Exeter "did much good to all sorts of people by her physic and surgery, and had great skill therein."[48] As noted, when Sir Ralph Winwood lay sick and dying, the countess of Exeter visited his sickbed and suggested treatments. Chamberlain then remarked that the "Lady of Excester was with him" and "takes upon her great skills in phisicke."[49] Chamberlain's note has a hint of disapproval, perhaps suggesting that the countess believed herself more skilled than she was, or more than was considered appropriate for a woman. Markham agreed that women should not pretend to be learned doctors. "Indeed we must confess," Markham wrote, "that the depth and secrets of this most excellent art of phisicke, is far beyond the capacity of the most skillful woman, as lodging onlye in the brest of a larned Professor." Instead, Markham argues that the ideal housewife should be knowledgeable only in "some approved medicines, and old doctrines which have been gathered together, and delivered by common experience, for the curing of those ordinary sicknesses which daily perturbe the health of Men and Women."[50] In Markham's eyes, the countess of Exeter exemplified the proper skills and practice.

The tales do not reveal who made the syrup or conserve of roses that were in the cupboard at Wimbledon. These products could be purchased ready-made at an apothecary shop but were generally simple enough medicines that a skilled housewife could produce them herself.[51] Books like Markham's, as well as other popular herbals, like John Gerard's *The Herball or Generall Historie of Plantes*, W. M.'s *The Queens Closet Opened*, and Nicholas Culpeper's *The English Physitian Enlarged*, contained discussions of the medical uses of various plants and recipes for medicines. Each provided recipes for syrup of roses, conserve of roses, and oil of roses.[52] The herbals argued that wild roses were less efficacious, and therefore told its readers to use cultivated roses instead. The recipes called for quite a large quantity of roses, thus requiring a large rose garden. Only wealthier households could afford to keep such a stock of roses, or purchase the cut flowers, since cultivating the flowers would take away growing space from edible plants. At Wimbledon, a whole section of the garden was specifically dedicated to fruit trees interspersed with rose bushes. If the countess of Exeter, or someone within her household, was making the syrup and conserve of roses, the raw material was available close at hand.

Roses were used for many sorts of ailments, generally believed to have a cooling, strengthening quality. As a result, medicines featuring roses were quite common and many seventeenth-century people would be familiar with them and their functions.[53] Syrup of roses and conserve of roses were sometimes used as a gentle form of purging laxative, believed to be especially suitable for children and the elderly, whose bodies might not be able to handle stronger stuff. Gerard counseled that the "juice, infusion, or decoction of the Roses, are to be reckoned among those medicines which are soft, gentle, loosing, opening and purging gently the belly, which may be taken at all times, and in all places, of every kinde or sex of people, both old and yong, without danger or perill."[54] For example, the elderly earl of Exeter often took syrup of roses, according to his wife and servants, presumably without ill effects. The conserve of roses that Lady Roos and Swarton argued was mixed into the enema would thus have been meant to work as an added, cleansing laxative. Swarton said that the countess had informed her that "there was somewhat in the conserve of roses would make ytt worke and giveteh Lady Roos two or three stooles."[55] The medicines and the treatments that Lady Roos and Swarton mention in their tales were therefore nothing out of the ordinary and followed conventional early modern medical ideas and practices.

In the countess's account, she became upset when she heard that Lady Roos had received syrup of roses without her knowledge, or without the same having been approved of, or ordered, by a doctor. It suggests that she did not think that Lady Roos had the appropriate knowledge to determine whether she should take medicine, but that she believed that she did, or at least that a doctor would. The countess did not say so outright, but implied that she would not have suggested the syrup of roses for Lady Roos. At the very least, as a mistress of Wimbledon, she was responsible for the well-being of its inhabitants, and she should have control over the medicine cabinet. (On the other hand, if the countess *had* indeed poisoned Lady Roos with the earlier enema, or if Lady Roos had accused her of doing such a thing, she might be concerned about Lady Roos taking any further medicines in her house, unsupervised.)

The countess of Exeter implied that young Lady Roos suffered because of her own inexperience and improper behavior. The countess was twice married, had children, and oversaw the extensive household of an important and rich nobleman who served the king. Lady Roos, on the other hand, was just a teenager, newly married, without any experience of bearing or caring for children, or running her own household. The countess argued that Lady Roos's July illness was connected to having walked outside at night and being chilled by the moisture from the dew. This clever comment manages to suggest both that Lady Roos was irresponsible and inexperienced, and that she was gallivanting about outside at unseemly hours.

The countess's servants who said that Lady Roos did "rumpe up and down" after taking the syrup of roses, also used language that suggested childish play, rather than proper womanly behavior. The countess of Exeter's explanation for Lady Roos's sore head likewise served as a double insult. Rather than being caused by poison, Lady Roos's sore head and scabby scalp was caused by "lack of combing," the countess noted. Regular combing of the hair was viewed as essential to cleanliness and health, as it would stimulate the scalp, untangle messy hair, and remove unsightly dirt as well as lice and nits.[56] This comment suggested that Lady Roos neglected basic hygiene practices, either because she was inexperienced and did not know what was required, or because she was a sloppy and slovenly person, or perhaps both. In the countess of Exeter's version, Lady Roos's behavior thus marked her as more of a child than a mature woman.

The Autumn Fallout

After the disappointing and disconcerting summer at Wimbledon, Lady Roos returned to her parents' house again. She lived with them throughout the fall of 1616, while her husband was frantically trying to raise money for his upcoming Spanish embassy. It is not clear where Roos spent his time, whether with his wife at the Lakes in the London house at Charing Cross or at Cannons, or at Exeter House in the Strand. Further changes also occurred within Lady Roos's closest circle: the long-serving and trusty servant Sara Swarton left Lady Roos's employ. Swarton played a major role in the upcoming scandals and slander lawsuits, so the contested tales about her experiences and employments are significant.

Shortly before Roos left for his Spanish embassy in November, Lady Lake fired Sara Swarton, forcing her to leave the service both of Lady Roos and of the Lakes. According to Lady Lake and Swarton, Diego da Silva was the cause of this decision. Da Silva told Lady Lake "secret false practices tales and informacone" about Swarton, managing to turn the mistress against the servant.[57] Neither Lady Lake nor Swarton elaborated on the details of da Silva's information. Lady Lake claimed to have no reason not to trust da Silva at the time and she was unaware of the full extent of the events of the previous summer. As she did not want an immoral person around her daughter or her own family, she promptly fired Swarton.

Swarton happened to meet da Silva not long after she was fired, and he feigned great concern and interest in helping her. He asked if she had been able to find another position, or if she needed anything. He assured her that he would "sell his Cloke before shee should want."[58] She told him she was alright, but in need of employment. Da Silva promised he would speak with the countess of Exeter right away. Swarton waited below while da Silva went into Exeter House. Da Silva soon came back and said the countess "would not entertaine [employ]" Sara "because shee came from the Lady Lake," implying either that it would be bad form to hire a servant whom a relative had fired or that she did not want a former servant of a woman she did not trust or like in her house.[59] However, the countess wished to speak to her. Da Silva escorted Swarton to see the lady. The countess told Swarton she would keep an eye out for an available position and recommend her for a job if she heard of one. Shortly after that, da Silva gave Swarton a piece of gold worth nine shillings six pence.

Swarton soon gained a position as servant to Sir George Wright and his wife, although she did not specifically mention if the countess of Exeter had anything to do with her new job. Lady Wright wanted to know why Lady Roos had let Swarton go, and Swarton told her she did not know, as she was unaware of da Silva's manipulations at the time. Lady Wright promised Swarton that if Ladies Lake or Roos wanted her back in service, she would be willing to let her go back "upon any reasonable warning."[60] Lady Wright would not allow her to break the annual employment contract for anyone else, however.

Swarton worked for Lady Wright for about a year, until "yuletide" 1617. When Swarton heard that one of Lady Roos's maids had married and departed her position around that time, she spoke with Elizabeth Lake, Lady Roos's sister, about returning to work for Lady Roos. The eventful year when Swarton had been gone had certainly changed the Lakes' and Lady Roos's attitudes toward Diego da Silva: the fracas at Cannons and its aftermath, Roos's flight from England together with da Silva, the beginning of the first court cases dealing with Roos's disputed property, and the growing feud between the Lakes and Exeters convinced them that da Silva's information about Swarton had been false. Shortly thereafter, Swarton returned to Lady Roos's service. Swarton argued that she had not been paid or enticed to return to her service, she simply preferred to work there, since she had worked with the Lake family for so long.[61]

Lady Lake later argued that the countess of Exeter, using da Silva as her instrument, had been behind Swarton's firing. The countess was working to discredit and get rid of Swarton since she had been a witness to her June confession of adultery and poisoning during the previous summer. If Swarton was out of Lady Roos's service and orbit, that was one less person with dangerous knowledge to worry about.[62]

According to the countess of Exeter and her camp, Swarton was a woman of "lewed life and behavior," who had been fired for a good reason. They did not elaborate on what, precisely, Swarton was supposed to have done either, but focused instead on painting a picture of a woman of bad character. They did not address the notion that da Silva had been involved in her firing, only stated that Lady Lake had fired Swarton "upon some conceyved displeasure against her." They argued that the Lakes had chosen her as an instrument to present fraudulent witness testimony, precisely because they knew she had a bad character and could therefore be bribed and manipulated into doing and saying whatever they wished her to perform, including making up tales about what happened at Wimbledon.[63]

These competing tales of the events at Wimbledon and London during the summer and fall of 1616 became public early in 1618, and the impetus for yet another titillating and shocking scandal at the court of James I only a few years after the Overbury murder came to light. It would also lead to a deepening of the Lake and Cecil feud, and to one of the most famous, sensational, and documented set of court cases of the Jacobean period.

7
The Scandal Breaks

> Our king and council, at this time, are troubled with no business so much as the foul matter betwixt your good acquaintance, the Countess of Exeter, and the Lady Roos and her mother.
>
> Adam Newton to Sir Thomas Puckering, February 26, 1618[1]

The developing disagreements between the Lakes and Cecils during 1617 had provided interesting fodder for court observers for months. Speculations about the melee at Cannons, the complex property disputes centering on the Walthamstow estate, and Roos's secretive flight from England had all featured prominently in correspondence that described events at court and in the capital. During the winter of 1617/18, when Lady Roos began to speak more openly about her harrowing and humiliating summer at Wimbledon House in 1616, the scandal took on a new, darker dimension.

The dramatic accusations of adultery, incest, and poisoning hurled against the countess of Exeter became the talk of London and beyond. The countess of Exeter quickly responded to the accusations, presenting evidence of her innocence and offering counteraccusations against Lady Roos and the Lakes. The stories that Lady Roos and her parents told again differed greatly from the constructions and explanations of the countess of Exeter and her servant Luke Hatton, who played an instrumental role in the tales. Throughout the early months of 1618, reports about the newest developments exercised many of those who had something to do with the royal court, keeping them guessing on who was lying and who was telling the truth, and what consequences might follow.

The Servant's Tale? Enter Luke Hatton

Why did Lady Roos feel it necessary to reveal the stories of the countess's adultery and attempted poisoning during the winter of 1617/18, when she had been silent about her difficult Wimbledon summer for a year and a half? Lady Roos argued that she felt it necessary to expose the countess of Exeter's

Family and Feuding at the Court of James I: The Lake and Cecil Scandals. Johanna Luthman, Oxford University Press.
 DOI: 10.1093/oso/9780192865786.003.0007

previous misdeeds because she feared she might be the target of the countess's murderous intentions yet again. She claimed that a man named Luke Hatton had come to visit her several times in London during the previous November and December. Hatton had served the earl of Exeter as Groom of the Chamber, but Lady Roos claimed the countess had secretly caused him to be "turned out" of the earl's service. The countess was not aware that Hatton knew about her machinations to have him fired. Every now and then, the countess still called on Hatton to have him perform tasks for her, keeping him in contact with the Exeter household. Lady Roos first hesitated, but as she recognized Hatton from her time living in the Exeter household, she agreed to meet him. She thought he might have information on the whereabouts and actions of her absconded husband. Perhaps people at Exeter House were in communication with Roos?[2]

During one visit, Hatton informed Lady Roos of a disturbing conversation he had with the countess of Exeter. The countess found herself in disfavor with her husband. The earl had learned of a private meeting between Lady Roos and the countess at Durham House, shortly after Roos had fled the country in July of 1617.[3] Now, the earl wished to know what precisely the two women had been talking about at that meeting. According to Hatton, this had made the countess very nervous, since the conversation with Lady Roos apparently had included the countess's adulterous relationship with Roos. She knew if she refused to tell her husband about the conversation, he would "be offended" with her. If she lied to him, Lady Roos might expose her sins to the earl. The earl wanted his wife to swear an oath that she would tell him the truth of what happened. When she refused to swear, the earl angrily called his wife a "strumpet" and would not "let her come to him."[4]

The desperate countess concluded that her only option now was to silence Lady Roos forever. She "resolved to give [Lady Roos] a dramme" of poison. Because the countess was aware how much Lady Roos loved her father and how close they were, she also feared that Lady Roos had already told Lake about the adultery. The countess might have to poison Secretary Lake as well. In her frantic state, she also considered another option to silence and discredit Lake: Roos had told her that he had evidence that Lake had participated in a plot to prevent King James's ascendance to the English throne during the reign of the late Queen Elizabeth. If she revealed that to the king, Lake and his daughter would both be discredited, and no one would believe anything they might have to say about the countess.

Alarmed by Hatton's information, Lady Roos hurried to tell her father about the threats the very same night. Ever cautious, Lake advised his daughter to get Hatton to give the same information in front of credible witnesses, or else to write it down and sign the document. Three days later, Hatton returned to Lady Roos with a written document outlining the same facts:[5]

> upon the 23th of this month my Lady Exeter sent for me and when I came I found her very desperate and she told me she sent for me to to [*sic*] ask my advice for that she never was in so evil case. I asked her what the matter was she told me that she had met my Lady Roos who had enquired of her of a paper that her husband had given his grandfather and divers other things. And that it [the meeting] was come to my Lord of Exeters ears who had enquired of her what end their meeting was. And that she had told him how my Lady Roos had enquired about that paper and divers other things and that now my lord did mean to bring it in question and would have her avow it upon her oath which because she had refused to do he had called her a strumpet and was so much offended with her that he would not let her come to him.
>
> And, saith she, on the other side you know my Lady Roos may undo me wherefore I pray, quoth she, advice me what to do. I answered her that she had carried this business so evil that he knew not what to say to it but he thought it was her wisest course to use all the meanes she could to make her Lord give Mr Secretary Lake satisfaction. She told me there was not thinckinge of that, there was no going about it, and was like a mad woman when I told her so. No, saith she, there was no way for me but to give my Lady Roos a dramme or to catch her in some trick or other. I tould her she had more need to ask God for forgiveness. She asked me if I would make her mad for she had no way else in the world for her. But, quoth she, I hear she love her father wonderfully wherefore I feare she hath told [him] wherefore, quoth she, I have no waye but to make away him.
>
> I told her I would not be her councellor to this wicked business and was going away, but she told me she had thought upon a better way than all this, which was that she remembered a plot that my Lord Roos had upon Mr Secretary Lake, which was certain plot that Mr Secretary Lake had with others against the King in the Queen's time. And, said she, had them in writing and desired me to be a witness to them. I asked whether she had everfound neersuch a villain to do such a thing and told her I would be her faithfull servant in any honest business and so I left her. Luke Hughton[6]

Hatton also shared information about Sir Peter Chapman that Lady Roos relayed to her father. Chapman was the earl of Exeter's man, who claimed that

Roos had given him Walthamstow in exchange for unpaid loans. As outlined in Chapter 5, the Lakes had already accused Chapman of trying to cheat his way to some of Roos's estates and goods, and of trying to sow discord between the families. First, Hatton claimed that Chapman was involved in some dishonest dealings regarding a renewed lawsuit over Walthamstow, having bribed a clerk of the court to get copies of his answers in the previous suit, and coordinated with others to ensure that their responses in the new suit would be consistent. What troubled Lady Roos the most was that Chapman was slandering her. Hatton informed Lady Roos that Chapman was spreading a false rumor that Lady Roos had become pregnant after her husband's flight from England, and since her husband was not only absent but also impotent, it must be another man's child. Chapman had apparently told Lord Burghley and the earl of Exeter this information. Furthermore, Chapman had supposedly been in contact with Lord Roos in his exile, asking Roos to write to establish the treachery of the Lakes, to further "sow discord" between the Lakes and the Exeters.[7]

Lady Roos's account of Hatton's revelations quickly became contested. At this point, Sara Swarton enters the story yet again. As mentioned, Swarton had been fired from Lady Roos's and Lady Lake's service in the fall of 1616, but she had been promised she could soon return to Lady Roos's service around Christmas 1617. On January 7, Lady Lake sent for Swarton, who was still working for Lady Wright at the time. Swarton heeded their call and came to the Lake's house in Charing Cross, presumably, because she knew she would back in their employ soon. Lady Lake asked Swarton to go to Exeter House to tell Hatton that Lady Roos wished to speak with him. Lady Lake explained that none of her current servants were known at Exeter House, so she did not want to send them there. Swarton agreed and promptly went to Exeter House. When she found Hatton, he told her he had been to visit Lady Roos before and had meant to return to see her earlier. He readily followed Swarton back to the Lake abode in Charing Cross.[8]

In her father's presence, Lady Roos asked Hatton to repeat his information about Chapman's shenanigans. At this juncture, Hatton denied ever having said anything about Chapman. To Lady Roos's mounting frustration, he also denied ever having said anything to her about the countess of Exeter trying to poison her or trying to get Lake into trouble. Lake confronted Hatton with the written document he had produced for Lady Roos earlier, but he denied having written it. He also denied having any meetings with Lady Roos. Lady Roos continuously insisted it was all true, and Lake was certainly more inclined to believe his own daughter over someone else's servant. Angered by

Hatton's denials, Lake imprisoned him for several days, hoping he would change his mind and talk again.[9]

At this point, Lake decided to make the countess of Exeter aware of Hatton's actions. He construed it as concern about Hatton potentially spreading libels about his daughter and his employers. Lake could assure his daughter that he believed she was telling the truth about Hatton's revelations to her, while also trying to prevent further rifts with the earl and countess of Exeter.[10] He requested a private meeting with the countess and she agreed to see him the following day. Lake informed the countess of Hatton's accusations and that he "conceived itt to be a wronge to her la[dyshi]p and also to the Ladie Roos his daughter" and that he therefore had detained Hatton. Lake's revelations could also be interpreted as an attempt to show the countess that he had leverage against her, and that she therefore ought to be more helpful in solving their property disputes with the earl. The countess later said that Lake suggested that they have some "pryvate freindes" hear the matter, presumably to mediate between the families.[11] The countess curtly replied that Lake certainly "had reason to comitt [Hatton] and she had reason to cleare herself."[12]

The Countess Tells the King

Realizing "how farre her honor and Creditt and reputacion was touched" and that "no pryvate examinacion thereof could doe her right therein," the countess decided to be proactive.[13] She went to court to speak with the king later the very same day after her meeting with Lake. The accusations against her were serious and she did not intend to let them go unanswered. She needed to defend her honor. Since Lake still had Hatton imprisoned, the countess of Exeter was presently unable to question him herself. She probably wished to take the wind out of Lake's sails. Going to the king right away and informing him of the accusations coming from Lady Roos and the Lake camp meant that they no longer had the threat of public revelation as a bargaining chip against her. Involving the king was a decisive act, from which there could be no return.

Informing the king meant that the stakes were raised, because the accusations would become public. Lady Roos's claims were grave. They put the countess in a very difficult situation, whether she was guilty of any of it or not. If she did not defend herself against them very vigorously, rumors might spread, take hold, and severely harm her reputation and potentially her relationship with her husband and his family. Honor and reputation were fluid, fragile things. They were not simply conferred by birth, station, or title, but also depending on how others perceived a person and their actions.[14] The way to restore honor was to take resolute action against the offender, to be able to convince others that the rumors were not true. Men might risk the king's ire and legal sanctions and defend their honor by dueling the offender, but that avenue was not available for women.

Defending against rumors of dishonorable actions was generally more difficult for women. That was especially the case if the rumors included illicit sexual behavior. Sexual virtue was an important part of female honor, albeit not the only one. Defending one's sexual reputation required a careful balancing-act, as the definition of women's sexual virtue generally meant silence on the matter. A sexually virtuous woman had no need to discuss illicit sex. To talk about illicit sex, even just to defend against rumors or accusations, could taint a women's reputation. In her defense, she had to display potentially dishonorable knowledge and a sexual vocabulary to articulate it. The rumors of illicit sex and the defense against it might cause people to associate the countess with sexual immorality, real or imagined. For the countess of Exeter, taking the matter to the king put her honor in danger, but staying silent on the matter seemed more damaging and dangerous.[15] Because women's sexual virtue was important, questioning a woman's sexual reputation was a common way to inflict damage, even if disputes had non-sexual origins.[16]

In addition to the damage to her public reputation, the countess's marriage could also be in jeopardy. If the earl of Exeter believed Lady Roos's accusations and doubted the virtue of his wife, she might lose her own position within the Exeter household. Divorce was not possible in early Stuart society, but couples might sue in a church court for a legal separation *a mensa et thoro*, or from bed and board. A husband could sue a wife for separation on the grounds of her adultery, although the same was not true for wives, who could only get a separation if their life and limbs were endangered by staying in the conjugal home. For example, in 1605, Lord Robert Rich sued his wife Penelope for a separation from bed and board, on the grounds of her adultery with an unnamed man. Penelope Rich had an adulterous relationship and multiple children with her lover for over a decade, but the lover, Charles Blount, earl of Devonshire, was not named in the suit. After the separation, Lady Rich married Devonshire. The marriage proved brief, as Devonshire died just a few months later. Despite both Devonshire's and Lady Rich's vehement arguments, the marriage was declared invalid, since remarriage after separation was not allowed. Before his death, Devonshire still managed to leave property to Lady Rich and their children by various trusts and other devises in his will.[17]

Unlike Lady Rich, the countess of Exeter could not count on support from an absent Lord Roos if her husband abandoned her. Roos barely managed to support himself with some difficulty in his exile and was certainly not able to care for his step-grandmother and alleged lover. By charging the countess of Exeter with adultery, Lady Roos certainly selected a good weapon for maximal damage.

Women's legal options were more limited as well. Women did avail themselves of the laws against slander and libel, but not all legal courts allowed women to be plaintiffs on their own. The church courts presented an exception, and those courts were cheap enough that women of lower status could use them.[18] The Court of Star Chamber was another option for slander suits, but its high costs meant that mostly only those who were of middling, gentry, and noble status could afford it. *Femme sole*, or legally independent women, could be plaintiffs in Star Chamber or petition the king to prosecute someone. Married women could not bring a suit without their husbands, however, because the legal construct of couverture subsumed the identity of the wife into that of her husband.[19] The countess and her husband eventually did file a suit in the Star Chamber, but not before trying to have the matter settled by the king first.

As expected, people at court heard about the salacious accusations and started to inform others soon after the countess's visit to the king. On January 12, Nathaniel Brent wrote Sir Dudley Carleton that "Lad[y] Ros hathe accused my Ladi of Exeter of some conspiracy to poison" her, but also added that the matter was "soe improbablie founded, as the complainant [Lady Roos] is much privately blamed, & it is sayd willing it should dye out." However, the countess "will not soe let it passe," but wanted "her innocency more planely appear."[20] The king ordered the Privy Council to investigate the matter.

A few days later the countess, her husband, her stepson Lord Burghley, and other members of the Cecil family went to York House to answer questions posed by members of the Privy Council as well as Sir Henry Yelverton, the Attorney General. Brent reported that the countess defended herself against the accusations "very nobly." The Privy Council also questioned Hatton, who continued to deny that he had ever said the countess planned to poison Lady Roos or that he had written an account of it. At the time, the council refused to free Hatton and he remained imprisoned, but now on the orders of the king instead of Lake.[21]

As the countess defended herself, she needed to explain why the Lakes would invent such serious accusations against her. According to the countess, the malice of Lady Lake and Lady Roos against her stemmed from the conflict over Walthamstow. Mother and daughter were especially upset that the countess had refused to mollify the earl of Exeter's anger over the Lakes' attempts to trick and force Roos into giving up Walthamstow for their and Lady Roos's benefit. As a result, their anger and rage turned toward the countess. They began planning their revenge in November, working on producing forgeries and recruiting discontented former servants to create and spread the slander about her.[22]

The countess argued that Lake had started with George Gwilliams, Diego da Silva's servant who had stayed behind in England when Roos left. In November 1617, Lake arrested Gwilliams, using his official powers as royal secretary to do so. Lake claimed to have only questioned Gwilliams about Roos's whereabouts and about his goods, but the countess of Exeter presented another version. Lake, his wife, and his daughter questioned Gwilliams about the countess's supposed adultery and poisonings. When Gwilliams said he knew nothing about it, the Lakes and Lady Roos gently tried to persuade him with "fair words" to repeat what he knew, but as he continued to deny it, the interrogators turned more hostile, threatening to punish him for his silence. Lady Lake waved a paper with writing on it in front of Gwilliams and demanded that he sign it. Since Gwilliams did not know what was written on the document, he refused.[23] In his own answer to Lake's later lawsuit, Gwilliams was much more neutral. He said that neither Lady Roos nor the Lakes had asked him to say anything regarding the countess's supposed adultery and poisoning, and that the countess had not asked him to claim that they had tried to do so either. Instead, he just noted that Lady Lake and Lady Roos were trying to get him to sign a paper, the contents of which he did not know.[24]

Lake then ordered Gwilliams imprisoned in the Gatehouse. No one was to have access to him other than those carrying a token from Lake. During Gwilliams's imprisonment, the Lakes continued to pressure him to tell them what he knew of the countess's crimes, promising both "libertye and great favor" if he would do so. Gwilliams continued to insist that he knew nothing of any crimes. He remained in prison for fourteen days, after which the Lakes gave up and freed him on bond. Gwilliams had to promise to return to prison within a period of ten days if Lake demanded it.[25] Gwilliams may not have been as unknowing about Roos and his master Diego da Silva as he pretended: on January 1, 1618, Trumbull reported that at one point "Diegos man called Gwilliams" had passed through Brussels, on his way to Paris the previous fall.[26]

After failing to turn Gwilliams, the countess of Exeter claimed that the Lakes and Lady Roos then decided that their former servant Sara Swarton, "a woman of lewde life and behavior," would be a "fit instrument" for their plot, and so made her leave her current position before her term of service was out and come back to serve Lady Roos instead.[27] Encouraging a servant to leave before their agreed-upon term expired constituted bad form: employers were not supposed to poach servants from others. Noting that Swarton had left before her contract ended was also meant to display her bad character. She did not honor the agreement, left her employer high and dry, and was thus not trustworthy.[28] After coaxing Swarton back into their employ and control, the Lakes made Swarton promise that she would do and say whatever they told her.

Luke Hatton, the countess claimed, had been "with his friends in the country" for some time during the fall of 1617, and therefore could not have visited Lady Roos. Hatton himself later elaborated on his employment status in a Star Chamber suit against him that Lake initiated.[29] He had requested to be released from the position as the earl's Groom of the Chamber in April of 1617. Part of his duties included carrying the elderly earl around. After Hatton had "gotten a hurte or strayne in his bodye" he was unable to perform heavy labor anymore. After his release, he went to live with his sister and brother-in-law in Wiltshire. In August, he received a letter from young Robert Smith, the countess's son from her first marriage. Robert wrote that his mother wished for Hatton to come and serve him, as he went to school at Eton. Hatton returned to Wimbledon to find out if the job offer was real. He also wished to visit his mother, who had "lived in house" with the earl and countess since their marriage, presumably as a servant. It appears that Hatton and his mother had long ties of service with the countess of Exeter. Hatton's mother had served Frances Brydges through two marriages.[30]

Hatton had stayed at Wimbledon until the beginning of Michaelmas term. At that point, the earl and countess left for London. The day after, Hatton went back to Wiltshire to arrange to have his clothes and other possessions sent to London. He came back to London three or four days before the "feast of St. Andrews," which was celebrated in late November. He had been staying at Exeter House since then, serving young Robert Smith who was still there (Robert Smith does not appear to have gone to Eton that fall, and Hatton does not mention ever going to Eton either.)[31]

According to the Exeters' version of events, the Lakes believed that Hatton's absence from the Exeter household meant that he had been fired from his service "upon offence and displeasure," and was therefore a suitable target for their purposes. A discontented former servant might be a willing plotter to bring down a former employer. The Lakes and Lady Roos put together the writing describing a supposed encounter between Hatton and the countess of Exeter, during which she told Hatton about the desperate state she found herself in, and her renewed and expanded plans of poisoning Lady Roos and her father, as well as discredit Lake with the king. All of it was lies.[32]

On January 7, the Lakes and Lady Roos put the rest of their plan into action. Hatton presented his version of the events that followed. Sara Swarton came to Exeter House, where she delivered a message to Hatton: her mistress, the Lady Roos, wished to speak with him right away. Hatton could not imagine what Lady Roos would have to say to him, since he had not seen her since that summer at Wimbledon in 1616. He said so to his young master Robert Smith. Robert told him to inform his mother about the strange request. Hatton did, and the countess said he "mighte goe to knowe her [Lady Roos's] pleasure." (The countess never mentioned that she knew that Hatton was going to see Lady Roos.)[33]

When Hatton arrived at the Lakes' house, Sir Thomas, Lady Lake, Lady Roos, and Sir Arthur Lake were all there waiting for him. They asked what Hatton he knew about the countess's plan to poison Lady Roos and Lake. When he denied any knowledge, they showed him the document and asked him if he had not delivered the same to Lady Roos before. Hatton denied ever having laid eyes on the document before, having written it, or having delivered it to Lady Roos. He also pointed out that ever since he had learned to write, he had always spelled his last name "Hatton," and not "Houghton," as the document was signed.[34]

The interrogators also asked him about Sir Peter Chapman's questionable actions in the ongoing lawsuit over Walthamstow, but Hatton said he knew nothing about any of that either. The questioning grew increasingly heated, as it became apparent that Hatton was not delivering what they wanted. Lake then again used his powers as royal secretary and had Hatton imprisoned, saying also that he would "bring his ladye meaning the right honourable the Countess of Exeter before the counsayle." During his imprisonment, no one was allowed to speak to Hatton unless Lake gave express permission. Like Gwilliams before him, Hatton endured threats and pressure to do the Lakes' bidding, but he withstood their attempts and refused to lie.[35]

As the countess of Exeter gave testimony in front of the Privy Council and Hatton was questioned, Lake tried to sway the king in his favor via the Marquis of Buckingham. On January 27, Lake sent his son Arthur to inform Buckingham of his daughter's accusations, as well as to deliver a written account by Lady Roos, along with the written account of the countess's murderous intentions that Lady Roos claimed Hatton had given her. Lake asked

Buckingham to show these documents to the king, and then return them to him via Arthur. Lake asked for Buckingham's "favor for even and indifferent proceedings." Since Buckingham's "own nature is just and honorable," he continued, Lake hoped "to me and myne it will be kynde and favorable." Buckingham does not appear to have appeased Lake's worries, as Lake renewed his request for his favor in the matter three days later.[36]

The Privy Council continued to investigate and then provided a report to the king of the two sides' arguments. Exeter was not pleased with the proceedings to date. When the Lord Chancellor asked him to write down his grievances, he refused to do so, perhaps because he was loath to put in writing criticisms of the proceedings ordered by the king. The earl was somewhat mollified when the Chancellor came to see him in person. However, he wanted to deal with the matter more forcefully: he wished to sue the Lakes and Lady Roos for slander in the court of Star Chamber. When King James was informed of Exeter's intentions, he said he should not take it to court, but rather that the king would deal with the matter himself.[37] James clearly hoped to mediate between the two families and put the matter to rest right away rather than allow the feud to fester further through lengthy court procedures.

While the king tried to find a path forward in this messy dispute, more details about the accusations against the countess of Exeter emerged. Lady Roos added a charge that the countess of Exeter was a dishonest oath-breaker and a gold-digger. Before her marriage to Exeter, she had already promised to marry one Francis Crane. Crane had been a servant of her first husband Sir Thomas Smith and was about the same age as the young widow. He had been appointed as Clerk of Parliament in 1606, an office formerly held by Smith.[38] When the elderly earl of Exeter came courting, the widowed Lady Smith realized that she could make a financially and socially much more advantageous marriage. The title of countess of Exeter had a better ring to it than plain Mistress Crane, and the wealth of the Cecil family was undoubtedly tempting. Instead of keeping her solemn promise and upholding her contract to her first suitor, the countess bought herself free with a hefty £4,000 payment to Crane, Lady Roos argued.[39]

Breaking an engagement could be a serious matter and not just a sign of fickleness. A solemn promise of marriage was viewed as a contract, whether it was made orally or in written form. It could also invalidate a future marriage to another partner. Unless made in front of witnesses, or in writing, a promise to marry could be difficult to prove. Nonetheless, betrothed men and women who had been jilted could, and did, sue their former fiancés/fiancées in church courts for breach of contract.[40] The accusation that the widow Smith paid off Crane suggests that the payment was to keep him from insisting that she not break the contract and that he did not challenge the validity of her marriage to the rich and powerful earl or Exeter. That was certainly how John Levington understood it, as he told Carleton "whane me Lord of Exceter was a sutter to her shee gif Sr Frances Crane for the contract back again fowr thowsand pownd."[41] The countess of Exeter denied the charge and claimed there had never been a pre-contract.

In mid-February, King James called for Lady Roos, so he could question her more extensively. At this point, Lady Roos told the king something about Lord Roos in private, something that she presumably felt was too embarrassing to reveal in a more public forum. It appears that she told the king about the adulterous and incestuous behavior of Roos and the countess during the summer of 1616. Realizing that the stakes had grown much higher with the king involved, and that the countess of Exeter was denying everything so far, Lady Roos now produced her trump card. For the first time, she showed the king and council the countess's written confession of adultery and poisoning. This was the document that Lady Roos claimed the countess had written at Wimbledon during the summer of 1616, in the presence of Roos and da Silva, while Lady Roos's servant Sara Swarton stood hidden behind the hangings in the far side of the room.[42]

Frustrated with Lady Roos's continued insistence and escalation, the earl and countess of Exeter, along with the countess's brother Grey Brydges, Lord Chandos, went to the king, kneeled before him, and asked for "justice against the Lady Rosse."[43] The earl clarified that he was not seeking arbitration from the king, but justice. Considering the severity of the accusations against his wife, he could not settle for some negotiated agreement, but needed her to be altogether cleared.[44] Otherwise, the accusations might follow her like a dark shadow and cast aspersion on the earl. People might view him as a pathetic old cuckold, whose aged body could no longer satisfy his beautiful young wife.

Lady Roos was brought in front of the full Privy Council for yet another questioning. The Privy Council specifically scrutinized the countess's 1616 confession, as well as Hatton's written account. They proceeded in a deliberate manner. They collected samples of the countess's handwriting, for comparison against the confession. They interviewed people who regularly corresponded with the countess and asked them to either verify or deny that the countess may have written it.[45]

During these hearings, Lady Roos decided that there were some questions she did not wish to answer. She argued that she had already told the king the answers in a more private setting, and she did not wish to air these sensitive and embarrassing matters again at the council table. As a result of her refusal to answer, the Privy Council decided to place her in custody. Noble persons not yet found guilty of crimes were often held in more comfortable quarters than regular prisons. Lady Roos was sent to be held at the house of John King, bishop of London. Her maid Sara Swarton, who had backed up Lady Roos's stories, was sent to the house of Edward Doubleday, Warden of the Mint, to be kept separate from her mistress. The Privy Council warrants directed both the bishop and Doubleday that the prisoners were not to have access to anyone. A day later, the council relented and sent another warrant to the bishop: Secretary Lake was to have free access to his daughter while she was held at the Lord Bishop's house. A day after, another clarification arrived: the attorney general Yelverton and the Solicitor General Sir Thomas Coventry were also to have access, so they could question the recalcitrant Lady Roos.[46]

Chamberlain reacted to the news of Lady Roos's refusal to talk with disapproval. He had never been fond of the assertive Lady Lake, but now he found the daughter worse. He told Carleton that the gossips and news sources in St. Paul's "described and pointed out" that Lady Roos was "a very pert Lady, and is saide to *matrissare* right, or rather to domineer as much over her mother, as her mother doth over some others."[47]

Lake and his daughter had much to discuss when he went to see her in her confinement. First on Lake's mind was the countess's written confession. He had never seen it and never even knew of its existence before Lady Roos had shown it to the king. Lady Lake was also surprised to learn about it, as her daughter had not mentioned it to her either. The only incriminating piece of writing of which they had been aware was the Hatton document. Now, the countess's confession was part of the growing official documentation of the case and Lake needed to learn more about this explosive piece of evidence. It was a serious matter. The account written by Hatton was second-hand information. Lake had already tried to make Hatton a scapegoat, claiming that his accusations wronged both Lady Roos as well as the countess. Lake even suggested to the countess that they join in a slander and libel suit against Hatton in Star Chamber. The countess had rejected the offer, but Lake proceeded with the case on his own in March.[48] A confession supposedly written by the countess herself really upped the ante: that could not be blamed on any servant with an evil intent. During the discussions with Lake, Lady Roos must have convinced her father that the countess's confession was real. Lake determined that he needed to fully support and protect his daughter against the dangerous countess, the duped earl, and the irresponsible Lord Roos.

While in custody, Lady Roos became ill, possibly due to the stressful situation. The spring of 1618 was unusually cold and wet, so it may have contributed to making health issues worse.[49] Of course, feigning illness was also a way to garner support and compassion, or to avoid having to talk further with interrogating and prying privy councilors. On February 27, the Privy Council issued another warrant to the bishop of London, ordering him to allow a doctor to visit Lady Roos and to give her any necessary medical treatment. They offered Lady Roos a choice of Dr. Atkins or Dr. Winstone. Dr. Atkins was the same doctor who had treated Lady Roos after her long summer at Wimbledon in 1616.[50]

The Public Reacts

At this point, the many conflicting statements and details that were coming out about the case confused many observers, who did not quite know what to make of them. Some of Sir Dudley Carleton's correspondents found the accusations against the countess of Exeter difficult to believe, due to problematic evidence. In addition, Carleton was friends with the countess, and therefore his correspondents may have been more careful about making statements about any potential wrongdoing on her behalf. When informing Carleton of the growing scandal, Nathaniel Brent described the accusations against the countess as "improbable," and added on February 7 that "the best is I thinke none do beleeve" them.[51] George Gerrard told Carleton that while Lady Roos had been committed to the Lord Bishop's house, the countess of Exeter was "scarce questioned" by the lords of the privy council, because "most of them cleare her in theyre harts."[52] Sir John Throckmorton also explained to Carleton that some people "feared to speak out, because Lake is powerful," which implied he believed that most thought Lady Roos and the Lakes were in the wrong.[53]

Some observers did not know what to make of the whole affair, or which side to believe. After Lady Roos's detainment, Chamberlain confessed to Carleton:

> For my part I know not what to conjecture, but yt shold seeme that Sir Thomas Lake and his are falne into a laberinth, whence they know not how to get out, for yt behoves him to make goode proofes of so heinous imputation against a Lady of her sort [the countess], and yt stands her upon likewise to cleere herself from so fowle scandalls of precontracts, adulterie, incest, murther, poison, and such like peccadillos.[54]

Adam Newton told Sir Thomas Puckering, Roos's former travel companion, that there were some foul actors on both sides. "What it will turn to God knows," he stated, "but the indifferent judges do apprehend that, by some subtle and working spirit, there be tricks put upon both parties."[55] John Levington, a Scot who wrote from Whitehall Palace to Carleton, asked him to relay the story of the feud to Levington's mother in the Hague, who he clearly believed would find it interesting. He ended his relation of the accusations by saying "qwhat will be the ende of it god knowis."[56]

Others found the details of the case downright disturbing. Edward Conway called the families' fighting a "strange Riddle," which would have a "shamefull issue" however it turned out.[57] Thomas, Viscount Fenton, called the "besines" between "the Ladye Exeter" and "the Ladye Ross" particularly "evill favored," with Lady Roos accusing the countess of poisoning her "with manye more matters not fit to be talked of." Fenton also thought either Lady Roos or Lady Exeter "must be a strainge creature and not woordye to leive."[58] Fenton thus argued that if Lady Exeter had indeed committed adultery and attempted to poison Lady Roos, she deserved to die. On the other hand, if Lady Roos had such a depraved mind that she was able to imagine and invent those crimes and be evil enough to accuse an innocent person, ruining their honor and potentially have them punished for crimes they did not commit, she likewise did not deserve to live.

Some of the comments were more light-hearted. Scandals were often the source of jokes and sarcastic comments, as it was a way for people to discuss matters that were technically distasteful and sinful. However, joking about matters that could be construed as slanderous was potentially problematic.[59] For example, the Marquis of Hamilton quipped that "the King had need be another Salomon to judge between the harlots." Lady Roos's brother Sir Arthur Lake overheard the marquis, did not appreciate the joke, and promptly declared himself ready to prove with his sword that his sister was no harlot. Lord Hay, also present, vehemently argued that the countess of Exeter certainly was no whore. Hay and Lake would have fought about it, had the marquis not stepped in to reiterate that he had only meant it as a joke and that they should not take it seriously.[60]

While Lady Roos was in custody at the Lord Bishop's house, the council continued to work. They questioned Hatton again. Hatton continually denied having carried any tales of the countess's poisonous intentions to Lady Roos. Instead, he produced witnesses that placed him in the country during the times that Lady Roos claimed he had come to visit him in London. In addition, both the king and the council concluded that the countess's confession did not appear to be written in her hand and must therefore have been counterfeited. Sir Francis Crane, who Lady Roos claimed had been contracted to the countess before her ultimate marriage to Exeter, was interrogated and denied the whole matter as well: there had been no engagement, no breaking of any marriage contracts, no payment. It certainly seemed as if the countess of Exeter was doing well for the time being. For good measure, Gerrard also told Carleton that the "scandal also that my Ld Rosse should get that childe the Lady of Exeter had last, not beleaved."[61] Some now saw the earlier rumors of the potential paternity of little Georgi-Anna in a new light: they, too, must have been made up entirely by the imaginative Lady Roos and her parents.

However, the council was not quite so one-sided. Lake had many friends. On March 7, Nathaniel Brent noted that the fighting between the two families had "made an incomparable faction amongst the Lords, and festereth more every day like an uncurable sore."[62] Lake had been in a good position at the beginning of 1618. The king had mentioned offering him a barony, but when others protested that it would give Lake precedence over all other barons in the country because of his position as Secretary of State, James reconsidered. Sir Thomas Lake was too lowborn for such ranks and James was not willing to upset the social order.

Lake might have argued that James found it unproblematic to make his favorite Buckingham a marquis in January of 1618. Buckingham, a younger son of a minor gentry family, had started his career as plain George Villiers, but ended it as a duke.[63] It was probably wise of Lake not to bring that up if he wished to keep the king's favor. As recompense, the king told Lake that he could still be a baron, but he would have to give up his post as secretary. Lake preferred to remain at his post. His decision is not surprising, considering he had worked so hard to reach it.[64] In hindsight, perhaps it would have been better for Lake to exchange his position for a peerage, but he operated based on what he knew at the time.

Lake also sought the office of Chancellor of the Duchy of Lancaster, which was about to become available, as the prior chancellor lay dying. He asked Buckingham to help him get the appointment. Lake was attracted to the position because it came with "a good howse," which stood "conveniently for his Majesties service." Lake also admitted that the position was especially meaningful to him, because his first patron Sir Frances Walsingham had held it in Queen Elizabeth's time. Lake made the request to Buckingham at the same time as he sent his son Arthur to explain the "case between my La[dy] of Excester and my daughter." Lake was sure that once Buckingham had been "truely informed" he would "rest satisfied" in the matter and they could proceed with business as usual.[65] Lake was wrong. No one was satisfied with the case, and he did not receive the Chancellorship either.

Even though some of Carleton's correspondents found it likely that the earl and countess of Exeter were prevailing against the Lakes with the council, the king finally decided that the matter was too intricate and delicate to solve quickly. The two sides had dug in completely and refused to budge: mediation was not possible. King James had resisted Exeter's insistence on using the courts at first, but he now argued that the matter indeed should be settled in the Court of Star Chamber. As a result, Lady Roos and Sara Swarton were both released from their respective confinements on March 5. Lake, along with numerous supporters, triumphantly brought his daughter home from the bishop of London's house.[66]

Throughout the rest of March and April, both sides began preparing for court. Chamberlain noted that "the wind may be coming about" in the case, because Sir John Epsley, connected to Buckingham, was frequently visiting Lady Roos and the Lakes, giving the appearance that maybe Buckingham—and therefore the king—was favoring Lady Roos and the Lakes over the Exeters.[67] Chamberlain also mentioned that the earl and countess of Exeter, the ones who "began yt so hotly seeme to coole apace, and find themselves in such a brake, as they know not handsomely how to get out."[68] Court cases were often lengthy and costly matters, and the earl was elderly. Chamberlain had already suggested that Exeter had reservations about going to court earlier, because the case "was like to make an end of him sooner than the cause."[69] No matter. To court they went.

8
Interlude
Lord Roos's End

> Ld Rosse, who is the ground of al, troubleth not his head but laugheth at Rome.
>
> Nathaniel Brent to Sir Dudley Carleton, March 7, 1618[1]

Paradoxically, the role of the still-absent Lord Roos in the feud diminished when Lady Roos and the Lakes made their charges against the countess of Exeter public. The further escalation did not make him wish to come home and clear up any potential misinformation either. At some point during the spring, Roos's "kindsman" arrived in Rome and managed to speak to him. After that visit, Roos began to "show himself more openly in the streets," perhaps because he heard the welcome news that his father and grandfather would be on his side.[2] In the end, Roos's renewed hope did not help him in his predicament. By June 1618, he was dead.

The Letter to the King

Chamberlain reported to Carleton at the end of March that the earl of Exeter and the royal favorite Buckingham had both received letters from Roos. Roos asked for assistance to get the king to approve a license for him to remain abroad for three years, so that he could "digest the intolerable wrongs, disgraces and hindrances he hath receved by the diabolical courses of the Lady Lake and her daughter."[3] However, he did not address the accusations against his step-grandmother. At this point, Roos was in the company of Sir Herbert Croft, who had also fled England the year before and promptly converted to Catholicism.[4] Roos's close associations with Catholic converts and exiles did not endear him to the king.

Either Roos was not yet fully informed of all the details of the accusations during the spring of 1618, or he did not take them seriously at first. Chamberlain believed he must not have heard about Lady Roos's insistence

Family and Feuding at the Court of James I: The Lake and Cecil Scandals. Johanna Luthman, Oxford University Press.
 DOI: 10.1093/oso/9780192865786.003.0008

that he and the countess had committed adultery and incest. As a result, Roos focused on the Lakes and their machinations in defrauding him of Walthamstow, as he viewed it. Roos initially appeared to believe that his young wife was not really at fault in the fighting, because she had "been too much misled by them [her parents]."[5] He would soon change his mind about his wife after he learned more. For the time being, though, his wife "hath submitted her self to the K. pleasure for the determination of al matters now in question with great humilitie."[6]

Exeter had hesitated to assist Roos in his earliest disputes with the Lakes, mostly believing that his grandson had caused his own problems. When the Lakes and Lady Roos accused his wife of adultery and attempted murder, Exeter changed his mind and decided to fully support Roos. Perhaps he was thinking that his grandson must be right in demonizing the Lakes, considering his own experience at this point. When Roos eventually understood that he enjoyed his grandfather's full support, he felt more secure.[7] He sent along a power of attorney to his father and grandfather and asked that they sell some lands to pay his debts.[8] Emboldened, he also wrote a letter to King James dated June 1, in which he attempted to explain his own actions, vilify the Lakes, and, by that point, his wife as well. This remarkable letter is worth analyzing at some length here.[9]

When Roos wrote the letter, he had been gone from England for ten months. He had been called home repeatedly by his family and by the king. He opened the letter by blaming Lake for his own long silence and evasion. He emphasized that he had written to the king as early as September of last year, shortly after he left the country, to explain and justify his illegal actions. His grandfather had now informed him that no letter from him had ever arrived for the king. Roos surmised that it must be Lake's doing. In a fit of charity, Roos admitted that he could "not absolutely accuse him [Lake] of that which I cannot prove," but he went on to explain that no one else could have a reason to intercept Roos's letter to the king, given the circumstances. Lake must have "used the power of a secreitarye, to suppresse my first letter to your majestie that he might have time to possess your majesties eares, with such wicked lies, as himself, his wife, and his shameless daughter the bratte of helle could invente." Continuing, Roos argued that Lake was clearly trying to cover his own crimes by concealing the letter, to prevent Roos from telling his side of the story of the "monstrous injuries" the Lakes had inflicted upon him. Roos also worried that Lake was planning to steal even more of his property and insist on a reconciliation with that "impudent whore," Lady Roos.

It is quite the opening salvo. Roos, who earlier believed that his impressionable young wife may have just been misled by her evil parents, now was convinced that his wife was bad and rotten to the core. It seems brazen and rash to call your own wife a "brat of hell" and an "impudent whore" in a letter to the king, considering that other people sued each other for such name-calling sullying their reputations. It also does not give much room for interpretation of Roos's feelings toward Lady Roos at that point.

Roos's insistence that he had written to the king back in September rings hollow. He argued that his earlier letter had expressed the reasons for his leaving, which included how his "land was gotten from me by threats and menaces, in so horrible and shamefull a manner as the like was never donne." However, he also wrote that his "former letter" expressed the "horrible wrongs which are donne to the la[dy] of Exeter." In September 1617, the accusations against the countess of Exeter were not public yet. Lady Roos claimed that the Hatton visits, during which the Exeter servant had told her of the countess' renewed plans to poison her and her father, took place in November, and the public scandal did not break until January, when the countess of Exeter took the matter to the king after her private meeting with Lake.

As a result, there were no open accusations against the countess at the time when Roos claimed to have written to the king. Some witness depositions in the court cases suggest that some of the servants may have been relaying rumors about an affair between Roos and his step-grandmother, but those accounts were all contested by the Exeter side later. Roos insisting that he had already written a letter to the king, and that Lake probably had stopped it, seems to be an attempt to look less irresponsible in the eyes of the king. It is not likely that he ever wrote such a letter.

Roos used flourishing and flattering language to try to placate the king, hoping for the king's mercy and understanding in a situation that had caused his reputation to be shredded. Roos offered to "do your majesties all humble and faithfull servis," perform any command the king would give him, and promised that "I will perform it without putting your majstie to any charge, or expecting any rewarde." If only he could receive the king's mercy and grace, he would "esteeme it as the possessing the greatest treasure in the worlde." While asking the king's pardon for his offense of leaving the kingdom without a license, he immediately followed it by asking the king to give him a license to remain abroad "for some tyme to digeste and right myself of the injuries which have bin donne me." Roos also asked the king to ensure that his grandfather should be allowed to administer his estates in his absence, since it would be a "dishonor both to myself and my whole house that Sir Thomas

Lake should in any sorte meddle with anything that consernes me he being the father of all the devilish plotts and scandalls against me and my familie." With no intentions of coming home and serving as a witness, Roos was happy to leave the work of fighting against the Lakes to his elderly grandfather.[10]

Roos spent most of his long letter vilifying the Lakes and Lady Roos, explaining how they had defrauded him of Walthamstow, and describing the events leading up to, during, and in the aftermath of the Cannons incident of the previous year. Only toward the end of the letter does he address Lady Roos's and the Lakes' charges of adultery and poisoning against the countess of Exeter, now certainly the most pressing issue for his grandfather. After stating that he had already addressed the wrongs against the countess in his previous (supposedly stolen) September letter, Roos offered no detailed defense of the countess or of any of the particulars of the Lakes' and Lady Roos's accusations, other than that the countess's "honor" was "wronged." He only mentioned that after pointing out the "aspersion which is laide upon myself," as well as his "grandfathers honor is troubled." He did not fail to add that his wife was "not worthye to wipe [the countess's] shoes."

The letter ended with a crescendo of fury directed toward Lady Roos. Roos asked the king to ensure that she was prosecuted for her slanders to the greatest extent of the law. He hoped the king would not spare her because of the honor of her title, which derived from him and which she did not deserve. That "younger impe of helle" should be punished as if she were a person of lower rank, "for as her condisions are wicked and abhominable, so her generasion is so base, that my lo[rd] my grandfather might very well in rigour of justice disinheritance me for having brought into his house so base a creature." He continued with a dramatic flair: "I do renounce her before God and man," adding a suggestive notion that he "in time and place will give such reasons, that she ought not to be my wife." He then concluded: "what severitye soever your majestie shall cause to be donne upon her I shall acknowledge myself more obliged unto your majestie for it, then if you gave me a million of goulds."

As a final flourish, Roos noted that Italians would have used a more direct, violent method to achieve justice. If an Italian had his honor traduced in the same manner as Roos and his grandparents, he would not have waited on the law for justice, but rather "would have cutte the adversaries generation in peeces." Other Italians would have approved of such a vendetta and thought the bloody violence "most honorable and noble." Roos implied that the English king's insistence on using the law to solve the dispute between the Lakes and the Exeters appeared toothless and weak in the eyes of those among whom he now chose to live. Roos's admiration of violence as a solution to perceived dishonor was belied by his own actions: he wanted to sue the Lakes for raising a riot against him at Cannons but was discouraged when Lady Lake threatened him. He had also given out that he tried to duel with Sir Arthur Lake a year earlier, but it was clear he never seriously intended to do that. It was easier to imagine a bloody revenge from a safe distance.

As in the dispute about events at Cannons, Roos again found himself in a gendered double-bind. While blaming his troubles on the "demonic" Lady Lake and Lady Roos, he also displayed unmanly attributes in the process. Bested by an evil woman, Roos had chosen to flee rather than to fight. He was unwilling to return, even though doing so could have helped restore both his own and his step-grandmother's reputations. Roos's contemporaries might interpret his emotional outbursts as problematic, as they "identified rigorous self-control as an essential masculine attribute," especially for men of the elite.[11] His imagined violence was also problematic. Targeted violence could in some instances be viewed as a valid response to threatened manhood. For example, the killing of an adulterous wife or her lover could be construed as mitigating circumstances for murder, especially if it was not pre-meditated. Unmeasured violence of the sort Roos proposed (the outright slaughter of Lady Roos and the whole Lake family), was unacceptable, and viewed as unreasonable and unmanly.[12]

No reports exist or survive that can tell us what King James thought about Roos's letter. The king had clearly intended for Roos to come home: he was a major figure in the feud and accusations in the lawsuit, so the king certainly wanted to question him. According to one report, Sir Giles Brydges, one of Exeter's men and probably a relative of the countess, was sent to Rome with official witness interrogatories for Roos in connection with the lawsuits, but it does not appear that he ever reached the young lord.[13] Another report stated that "Lord Roos is sent for home by letters, and an express messenger from his majesty, his grandfather, and father; and the pardon of his contempt [leaving without a license and refusing to return] sent him by the same messenger."[14]

Lord Roos Dies

The king's messengers either did not reach Roos or, if they did make it to Rome, discovered that he was no longer there. English foreign agents had used their networks to ask for further information about Roos. Sir Henry

Wotton, English ambassador in Venice, had no luck finding out more about Roos. He reported on June 1 that "Lord Rosse doth live so close, shifting often his lodgings, as it seemeth that none of my correspondents can particularly say to have seen him of late."[15] The duke of Savoy agreed to have his ambassador in Rome keep an eye on Roos's actions and movements, and the Venetian Doge and Senate did the same. However, Roos somehow got wind of these arrangements and left Rome for Naples before the Savoyard and Venetian ambassadors were able to gather any information.[16]

Shortly thereafter, Roos died. While in Naples, he fell ill, worsened, and died on June 8, 1618.[17] By late July, the news reached Lake and Exeter in England. Exeter had been planning to leave London to spend some time at one of his country estates but remained in the city to learn more about his grandson's fate. In Exeter's household, there was initially some skepticism: was Roos really dead, or was it a ruse? Was he trying to escape yet again?[18] Lake also received reports from Trumbull in Brussels and Wotton in Venice at the same time.[19] Lake and Exeter both sought to find out more. From Venice, Wotton relayed to Lake that Roos had "given what he possessed in those parts to the king of Spain," which Lake believed he had done to protect those goods for Diego da Silva, and to prevent them from being brought to his wife or in-laws. Lake wanted Trumbull to seek out information about the value of some of Roos's "household stuffe and goods" allegedly left in Antwerp.[20] Lake also wished to know if Roos had made any deathbed declarations or confessions. Had he "acknowledged the wrongs he had done his wife," for example? Had he made a will?[21]

Not surprisingly, the death of a well-connected young nobleman embroiled in such a fierce feud, now at a critical juncture, immediately sparked rumors that his death was not natural.[22] Some reported rumors that Lady Roos and the Lakes had ordered Roos's death "by the practice of Irishmenes hand."[23] If Roos returned to England, he might reveal things that could be detrimental to their ongoing court cases. One of Lake's men informed him that he had "heard out of Exeter House" that the earl speculated that Diego da Silva had killed his master for gain, since Roos gave his goods outside England to da Silva.[24]

George Abbot, archbishop of Canterbury, thought that Roos's own "foolishness" led to his death. According to what the archbishop could glean, Roos had become privy to sensitive information about an intelligence scheme of Sir Andrew Wyse, an English Catholic exile who held the position of Grand Prior of England over the illegal order of the Knights Hospitallers. Roos and Wyse were fast friends. Another acquaintance of Roos's in Naples was the Spanish Viceroy, the duke of Ossuna. According to the archbishop's information, Roos had revealed Wyse's secret information to Ossuna, although he did not say whether he thought it was by accident or on purpose. When Wyse found out about Roos's loose lips, he invited the unsuspecting young lord to dinner and put poison in his wine. The archbishop believed this the likeliest course of events, since Roos had fallen ill and died in the prior's house, and because of Ossuna's actions after Roos's death. Ossuna "openly and frequently rayle upon the Grand Prior, saying he was a villaine and an hereticke, and if any man would give him three pence hee would hang a stone about his necke and throw him into the sea."[25] This explanation suggested that Roos had indeed been murdered, but that his death was not connected to the family feud back in England. The archbishop did not say from whom he had received this information. Other than these rumors, we cannot know for sure if Roos was murdered, or if he simply became ill and died young, as so many others did in this period.

What was especially troubling to many in England was the fact that Roos had converted to Catholicism by the time of his death. His actions and travels in his youth had certainly caused rumors of his conversion before. Roos's friendship with the Spanish ambassador to England, his closeness to the Catholic da Silva, his preference of the Catholic southern European countries, his illegal flight and extended stay in Italy, the reports of his audiences with cardinals in Rome, and reports about his associations with English Catholics living in exile in Italy and elsewhere in Europe, had all long pointed in that direction. When the reports of his death arrived in England, they included the details that Roos had regularly kept two Franciscan friars in his household while in Naples, and that he received last rites from a Jesuit. In England, Jesuits were seen as especially problematic Catholics, prone to be disloyal to the crown.[26]

Roos's death also set off a search for, and a fight over, the property he had managed to carry with him, or have sent after him, in his exile. The earl of Exeter claimed that Roos had made a will, and that this will specified that Roos gave his trusty servant Diego da Silva all his goods that were outside of England at the time of his death. It is not clear if the actual document of Roos's will ever surfaced, or if it existed. In any case, Lady Roos and Lake argued that Lady Roos should have the administration of the goods her husband left behind. In the end, Lady Roos managed to secure the king's support to give her such administration, although that was later overturned by a court in 1621 in favor of Exeter.

Notwithstanding the legal wrangling in England, it proved practically impossible to get the goods that were abroad. Lake received reports that some of it was stored in Antwerp, but his men who were sent to retrieve the trunks were unable to do so. Gondomar, to whom Roos had supposedly entrusted goods that he was unable to carry with him during his flight, had brought much of it with him when he left England in July of 1618. "Those of the house of Exeter do not sticke to say that the Embassador had secretly committed to him goods to the valew of 6,000 li being carried away in 19 carts, besides 200 li in ready gold and jewels to a great valew." If Roos left his goods to Diego da Silva, the Spaniard would have quite the inheritance, provided that he could retrieve it from Naples, Rome, Antwerp, Brussels, and Spain.[27]

Roos had not played a direct role in the legal cases which progressed in the Court of Star Chamber during the late spring and summer of 1618. His blistering June letter to King James became his last word about his relationship with the Lakes and Lady Roos, and his death removed him completely from the family feud. The real battle between his wife and in-laws and his grandfather and step-grandmother had only begun.

9
To the Court of Star Chamber

> If all the examinations that belong to it should be read, I thincke all the Starchamber dayes of the Terme would be to fewe. The books on both sides contayne 19,000 sheets. A pretie buisines!
>
> Thomas Locke to William Trumbull, December 1, 1618[1]

As the king and council proved unable to end the dispute between Lady Roos, the Lakes and the earl and countess of Exeter, the case stood to be fought out in the legal court of Star Chamber. The feuding parties had already availed themselves of the courts of Star Chamber and Chancery for their property disputes begun in the fall of 1617. The accusations of incestuous adultery and poisoning changed the tenure of the feud, including legal strategies. The new suits begun in the spring and summer of 1618 focused primarily on slander and fraud, with the property disputes looming in the background.

Commentators in 1618 and 1619 often spoke about the "Starchamber matter" between the Lakes, Lady Roos, and the earl and countess of Exeter as one entity.[2] However, the legal battles included multiple suits. Sir Thomas Lake had filed the first as early as March, in which he accused Luke Hatton of wronging the countess of Exeter by bringing damaging tales to Lady Roos, and of slandering Lady Roos and Lady Lake when he denied those tales. The main case consisted of the earl and countess of Exeter's slander suit against Lake and his wife, Lady Roos, Sara Swarton, and Sir Arthur Lake, which they filed in April. The Exeters accused the defendants of slanderously fabricating tales of adultery and poisoning and of having forged the countess's confession and Hatton's statement. The Lakes countersued, opening a new case in June of the same year. Sir Thomas Lake the younger, Lady Roos's eldest brother and Clerk of the Privy Council, served as plaintiff, suing the earl and countess of Exeter of slander, the countess's gentlewoman Elizabeth Gresham of complicity in slander and poisoning, and George Gwilliams of assisting Lord Roos's 1617 escape and of slandering Lady Roos. A fourth case brought by the earl of Exeter also in June accused the Lakes of defrauding Roos of Walthamstow and of planning the attack on him at Cannons the previous year. The Cannons case appears to have been dismissed after the defendants provided their

Family and Feuding at the Court of James I: The Lake and Cecil Scandals. Johanna Luthman, Oxford University Press.
 DOI: 10.1093/oso/9780192865786.003.0009

answers. Three slander cases—Lake v. Hatton, the earl and countess of Exeter v. the Lakes and Lady Roos, and Sir Thomas Lake, Jr. v. the Exeters, Gwilliams, and Gresham—moved forward.

The legal strategies employed by both sides ensured that the suits focused on slander and libel specifically and that they would fight their battles in the Court of Star Chamber rather than in another court of law. Over the course of the summer, fall, and winter of 1618, both sides collected an enormous amount of witness depositions and other evidence. They parried, sparred, and looked for winning strategies during the drawn-out legal process.

The Court of Star Chamber

The Court of Star Chamber was a conciliar high court designated to hearing both civil and criminal offenses, although criminal cases dominated by the early 1600s. Its name derived from the location where it usually met: a chamber in Westminster Palace with a ceiling adorned with golden stars. The court, its roots in the medieval period, had developed out of the royal Privy Council: initially, the court occurred when members of the Privy Council sat as judges over legal matters, representing the king's justice. Over the course of the 1500s, the court had become more formalized with a legally trained administrative staff. Most judges were still members of the Privy Council, but it also included common law judges. Instead of juries, the judges voted to determine the cases before them. Most cases involved members of the elite as it was expensive to bring matters to Star Chamber.[3] Since most of the judges were members of the royal Privy Council, the people who ended up hearing the Lake-Cecil case in Star Chamber were the very same people who had already investigated it at the king's request.

Star Chamber, like most stationary courts, met for four traditional terms throughout the year. Hilary term started on January 23 and lasted for three weeks. Easter term lasted from Easter to Ascension Day, a little over three weeks. Trinity term was held in June or July, depending on when Easter fell that year. Michaelmas term was the longest session, lasting for seven weeks from October to November, following Michaelmas (October 9). Generally, the court sat only two days a week, Mondays and Wednesdays, as the Privy Councilors also had to attend to the regular business of state while the legal sessions were ongoing. The restricted number of court days also limited the number of cases the court could hear each term. Complex cases sometimes stretched across multiple sessions.

A Star Chamber court case began with the filing of a complaint. If the court deemed the complaint believable, it required that the defendants named in the complaint provide detailed answers by responding to the specific accusations. Next, the plaintiff responded to the details in the defendants' answers (replication). Sometimes, the defendants provided an additional answer to the plaintiff's response (rejoinder). These documents constituted the pleading of a case. At this stage, the court evaluated the merits of the pleading and decided to dismiss or continue. If the case continued, both sides collected proofs. That usually entailed creating interrogatories, or court-approved questions to be put to witnesses. Both sides called sworn witnesses, and their answers to the interrogatories were recorded in court depositions. These written depositions were later presented at trial, and in some lengthy cases, as in the Lake-Exeter affair, condensed and summarized instead of read in full.[4] The Lakes and the Exeters provided answers to the suits throughout the summer and then began the process of collecting witness depositions in the early fall of 1618. The court planned to have the cases go to trial toward the end of the longer Michaelmas term.

The Legal Strategies

Sources about the cases do not specifically mention why the litigants chose the Court of Star Chamber, so we are left to draw conclusions about their strategies from the circumstances of the cases and the legal developments in Jacobean England. The law did not yet distinguish between slander (spoken defamation) and libel (written defamation), so the terms of slander, libel, and defamation were used interchangeably. Commoners more often used the long-established church courts for defamation suits, as those were more accessible and cheaper for the plaintiffs. However, while the church courts' proceedings might assist in restoring a damaged reputation, they did not have the right to impose damages or imprison the offender, only to impose penance and other spiritual punishments.

During the 1500s, the legal actions for defamation of private persons expanded to provide further remedies. If the plaintiff could prove that the defamation had hindered his ability to do business or perform his profession or had endangered him because of a false accusation of a serious crime, he could receive damages in addition to a restored reputation.[5] By the late Elizabethan period, actionable examples of defamation had expanded further, as this definition by Star Chamber lawyer William Hudson illustrates:

> Libels are of several kinds; either by scoffing at the person or another in rhyme or prose, or by the personating him, thereby to make him ridiculous; or by setting up horns at his gate, or picturing him or describing him; or by writing some base or defamatory letter, and publishing the same to others, or some scurvy love-letter to himself, whereby it is not likely but he should be provoked to break the peace; or to publish disgraceful or false speeches against any eminent man or public officer.[6]

By the early Jacobean period, defamation cases became more numerous, especially in Star Chamber. This court, with its prominent judges and proximity to the king, presented an especially good option for the elite to ensure maximum publicity of their hoped-for restitution in cases of slander, as court observers and other interested people often attended the public court proceedings.[7] Lake and Exeter cases certainly received close scrutiny.

These cases fit into the category of "disgraceful or false speeches against an eminent man or public officer," as both Lake and Exeter were members of the Privy Council, and Exeter a nobleman and Lake a Secretary of State. Even before the expansion of actionable defamation, slandering a peer had been illegal in England since the Middle Ages. The offense, *scandalum magnatum*, was serious. Exeter's complaint was especially keen on pointing out the noble status of the earl and countess of Exeter and Lord Roos, as well as Exeter's position as a Privy Councilor and knight of the Garter. The king's "gracious and princely care" to "protect the fames and honor of yo:r highness nobilitie and to redeem them by yo:r royal justice from all scandall" and "dishonours" with which they were "unjustly" charged.[8] Lake suits also emphasize Lady Roos's noble status and Lake's prominent position in the royal administration. Nevertheless, Exeter's suit did not specifically allege *scandalum magnatum*, although Exeter may have considered following up with such a suit later.[9] Considering the leading role of the women in the cases, claiming *scandalum magnatum* might have made the case more difficult, since they were not officers of state.

Why were all three cases slander cases, specifically? Lady Roos accused the countess of Exeter of adultery and attempted murder, but neither she nor her family ever strove to have the countess tried for those specific crimes. Lady Roos and Lake could have filed a complaint regarding the attempted murder to the court directly, via the attorney general. The attorney general could then have opened a criminal suit on behalf of the king against the countess of Exeter. Likewise, an ecclesiastical court could bring an adultery suit against the countess, as the church had the primary jurisdiction over cases of illicit sex and marriage matters.[10]

Lake must have known that it would have been exceedingly difficult, if not impossible, to move forward with an attempted murder or adultery suit. No physical evidence of the attempted poisoning existed. The poisoning had allegedly occurred more than a year and a half previously, and the victim was still alive and well. Likewise, there was no tangible evidence of adultery: the supposed adulterous lover was abroad and incommunicado when the last suits were filed, and precedent did not work in Lake's or Lady Roos's favor. Commoners were predominantly tried for adultery in the church courts, but it was very unusual for noblewomen to be tried in court for adultery during the reign of King James. Generally, the sexual indiscretions of noblewomen and gentry were dealt with more directly by the sovereigns. It was largely considered inappropriate for the ruling classes to be humiliated and chastised for sexual sins in public. Unlike Queen Elizabeth, King James rarely punished the sexual crimes of his nobility and gentry, unless they were also associated with other (in the king's view) more disturbing and serious crimes.[11]

Another of Exeter's grandchildren, Frances Coke Villiers, viscountess Purbeck, became a notable exception when she was tried and convicted for adultery in the ecclesiastical Court of High Commission in 1625–27. The circumstances in the case were unusual. Buckingham, Lady Purbeck's brother-in-law, specifically pushed the case forward with an eye to dissolving his mentally ill brother's marriage and ensuring that Lady Purbeck's illegitimate son would not be his heir. A sick king James had only reluctantly allowed Buckingham to pursue the case, and the king died shortly after the beginning of the proceedings. The evidence was also rather damning, including a hidden pregnancy and a child born under highly suspicious circumstances, while the viscount and viscountess Purbeck lived apart.[12]

By contrast, the countess of Exeter had powerful friends and a husband who stood firmly on her side, willing to use substantial resources to defend her against Lady Roos's accusations. Vague rumors swirled around the birth of the countess's youngest daughter, because of the advanced age of her husband, but no specific evidence of illicit activities appeared. The earl of Exeter never questioned the paternity of the child, at least not openly. Lady Purbeck's husband suffered from mental illness, so Buckingham had taken charge of the prosecution of his sister-in-law. Exeter was in full control of his faculties and would not brook Lady Roos and the Lakes to speak ill of his wife and make him a cuckold.

Lake had proceeded cautiously when his daughter first told him about Hatton's visits and the countess's renewed poisonous plans. Instead of immediately charging the countess with poisoning and adultery, Lake's first response was to meet with the countess privately. The countess quickly forestalled any other legal options for Lake by going directly to the king with her grievances. Once James and the council began to investigate, Lake and his daughter were forced to accept that the king would direct the matter from then on. Naturally, had the king found convincing evidence of attempted or planned murder in his early investigations, he could have ordered the countess charged with the crime directly, but this was not the case.

When the royally ordered Privy Council investigation stalled and sputtered, Lake first attempted to deal with the dispute by suing Hatton for slander. This represented a repeat of Lake's strategies in the property cases begun the previous fall, when he and Lady Roos first blamed the rift between the families on evil and greedy servants. By suing Hatton for slander, Lake could both protect himself and his daughter and lay the blame on Hatton. It was Hatton who was at fault for telling Lady Roos stories about the countess's intentions to poison both him and his daughter. If Lake and the countess could come to an agreement that Hatton was the problem, then Hatton could be punished and their differences about the scandal put to rest. To this end, but in vain, Lake initially tried to get the countess to join him in the suit against Hatton.[13]

Notably, Lake's suit against Hatton only outlined Hatton's tale of the countess's intent to poison Lady Roos and Lake in November 1617. It does not mention Lady Roos's tales of the adultery and poisoning of the summer of 1616. The complaint only refers to Hatton relaying that the countess told Hatton that he knew that Lady Roos "may undoe me," but he did not specify why.[14] Lake's first slander suit tried to mitigate the rapidly deteriorating situation, not to escalate it. He could sue Hatton for slander and protect his daughter's reputation, without getting into a direct conflict with the earl and countess of Exeter. Lake may have found his daughter's tales about the summer of 1616 difficult to believe, or at least not something he and his lawyers were willing to detail in legal documents.

Lake's strategy to blame evil servants had not worked in the fall of 1617, and it did not work in the spring of 1618 either. Moreover, his daughter's actions rapidly escalated the situation into a direct conflict with the Exeters. When Lady Roos pulled out the countess's supposed written confession as proof and showed it to the king, it left much less wiggle-room for her father. Producing and sharing a slanderous writing with others, in this case the king,

Privy Councilors, and others within the English elite, qualified as defamation without question. It also hardened the countess's resolve to fight the accusations. It made any mediation impossible and gave the earl and countess of Exeter more substantial fodder to file their own defamation suit.

The countess of Exeter was technically not able to file the complaint for the slander suit herself, as married women were not supposed to serve as sole plaintiffs in Star Chamber. The rules of couverture meant that married women were "covered" and subsumed by their husband's legal persona, so husbands had to join a suit with them in most courts, except in church courts and in some courts of equity, like the Court of Requests. In the past, the rule of coverture had been more flexible, with some married women suing on their own in Star Chamber, although it remained uncommon.[15] Nevertheless, early modern people knew that the legal requirements did not always reflect practical realities. Many understood the Exeter slander suit specifically as "the countess of Exeter's cause." For example, when the Star Chamber lawyer Hudson mentioned the case in his 1621 treatise on the court, he called it "Thomas Lake v. Lady Exeter."[16] It gives the impression that some commentators believed that countess of Exeter was the main aggrieved party and that her husband was playing a supportive role. The earl was of course also affected by the accusations of adultery of his wife, as it harmed his own honor and reputation.

The earl and countess of Exeter's slander suit was meant to clear the countess's reputation completely and to show that all the accusations against her were false. Begun in April, the complaint detailed the Lakes' and Lady Roos's actions to invent accusations of adultery, incest, and poisoning against the countess of Exeter, and then fraudulently conspired to produce false written evidence for the same. In addition, the complaint accused the Lakes and Lady Roos of suborning witnesses, homing in specifically on Hatton and Swarton, after attempting, but failing, to subvert Diego da Silva's servant George Gwilliams. The Lakes and Lady Roos were guilty of defamation in both speech and writing. They had fraudulently produced and then shown the countess's false confession and Hatton's fake statement to the king and others. The Lakes and Lady Roos had spread these same falsehoods by telling others about it, thus passing along slanderous words. Fortunately for historians working in the court's archives, defamation suits required that a copy of the text of the defamatory writing was included in the complaint.[17]

Once the Exeters had filed their slander suit, the Lakes needed to respond more forcefully. They did so with their countersuit against the earl, countess, Gwilliams, and Gresham. The countersuit was brought by the younger Sir

Thomas Lake rather than his father. By the time of filing of the suit, news about Roos's death had not yet reached England. In the eyes of the law (and to everyone's knowledge), Lady Roos was still a married women and therefore could not file a suit of her own in Star Chamber. Another male relative had to file the suit on her behalf.

Sources do not mention why the Lakes and their legal team chose the younger Lake to be the complainant, so we can only speculate about the decision. Unlike his brother Arthur who had been present at the fighting at Cannons, Sir Thomas Lake the younger was not personally involved in the disputes, and not named or mentioned in any of the complaints or answers. It could be an attempt to present a united front among the Lakes, ensuring that both adult brothers were on board. In addition, it may have been an attempt to insulate the elder Lake to the extent possible. The secretary himself did not have to sue a fellow privy councilor directly. Instead, a concerned brother protected the reputation of his sister, ensuring that Lake could distance himself from the descriptions of the Wimbledon summer events. In fact, while Exeter sued and named Lake directly in the main slander case as well as in other property cases in Star Chamber and Chancery, Lake the elder was not ever a complainant in any court case against either the earl or countess of Exeter.

The Lake, Jr., countersuit was rather convoluted. In his complaint, Lake the younger argued that because the stories about the countess's incestuous adultery and poisonings were true, the Exeters and their accomplices were slandering Lady Roos and the Lakes when they told the king and others that they were lying and had forged Hatton's document and the countess's confession. Since this case was filed after the main Exeter slander case, it gave the Lakes and Lady Roos an opportunity to present a clearer narrative and more details about the events of the summer of 1616 specifically, but also the fall of 1617 and Hatton's revelations to Lady Roos. Previously, they had provided this information in a more piecemeal fashion in answers to the Exeter suit. Now they could smooth out some of the inconsistencies and tell the whole tale from beginning to end. The Lake, Jr., suit provided more detail about the alleged 1616 poisonings and elaborated on how the countess's sexual sins of adultery and incest were at the root of all her evils and further misdeeds.

Exeter's additional 1618 suit about the Cannons incident and all the earlier turns around the Walthamstow property was clearly meant to provide more detailed information about the longer-term reasons behind the Lakes' and Lady Roos's malice against the countess of Exeter. From Exeter's perspective, it would bolster the claim they had made in the slander suit regarding the motivations of their opponents, and further vilify the Lakes as greedy, grasping, deceitful, and unscrupulous. (Lady Roos was not named in this suit.) Some found it difficult to believe that Lady Roos and the Lakes would completely make up such incredibly detailed accusations and perhaps venture to guess that there might be some fire behind the smoke.

The Cannons suit was a clear signal to Roos that his grandfather was now fully in his corner in the fight against the Lakes. Exeter filed it while Roos was still alive, or at least before he or anyone else in England knew he was dead. The suit did not continue: no sources mention the Cannons suit after the summer of 1618. It was not part of the three Lake-Cecil suits that went to trial at the same time in January of 1619. It is possible that it was dismissed as a result of Roos's death. It might have been necessary to have him as a witness, since Exeter claimed the Lakes had defrauded Roos of his property. However, it seems more likely that it was dismissed because it was found to have no merit. Walthamstow remained in the hands of Lady Roos, first in a trust, but then controlled by her directly (see Chapter 14). Ultimately, Exeter could not change Roos's mishandling of his finances and property.

The Witness Depositions

The court cases moved forward with answers, replications, and rejoinders during the summer. By early fall, both sides began collecting witness depositions. When Trumbull's agent John Wolley went to see Lake on business in early October, he found the Secretary "busy with lawyers and the Exsaminer of the Chansery who was sent to take their oaths about the Lady Rooses business."[18] The size of the cases grew unwieldy. By December, Thomas Locke estimated that the "books of both sides contayne 19,000 sheets" and Sir William Smith reported 17,000 sheets.[19] Chamberlain believed it amounted to a more conservative 9,000 sheets but added that Exeter had paid £500 just for the writing and copying of the documents, not even counting the pay to the lawyers. The "other side cannot passe with lesse," Chamberlain surmised.[20] These legal challenges were not cheap.

Unfortunately, the interrogatories and depositions do not survive in the Jacobean Star Chamber records, so historians cannot directly access the thousands of pages of witness depositions. However, because these cases became so famous, other sources can tell us about parts of the process. Observers and people directly involved commented on witnesses and witness depositions in letters. Disputes about some witnesses also generated further actions on both sides. The State Papers contain abstracts and summaries of witness testimonies that were condensed and presented at the trials, giving an overview of the depositions as well as the people called to testify. Chapter 11 discusses the witnesses and their testimonies in more detail: here, we focus on the process of collecting testimony.

The deposition process and the witnesses themselves were sometimes contested. Both sides jockeyed for advantages and accused the other side of tampering with witnesses, or of bringing forth unreliable ones. Abraham Williams relayed a rumor to Trumbull on October 9 that "false witnesses were suborned in this matter involving Excеter, which has reached the King's ears, and that they have taken both great Oaths and great sums of money."[21] On October 10, Buckingham wrote on behalf of the king to Lake's new colleague, Secretary Sir Robert Naunton. Both Buckingham and the king had received letters from the countess of Exeter regarding problematic witnesses. The king wished to assist the countess in her request to investigate, but also wanted to make sure he did not overstep. As a result, he asked the Attorney and Solicitor Generals to look at it and do whatever was "fitt and convenient in lawe to be donne in this case, either for any warrant from his Majestie or deliverie of any writinges or other thinges appertayninge to this proces now in hand."[22]

According to a later letter from Lake to Buckingham, the issue the countess brought to the king concerned a witness named Katherine Maynard. The case of Katherine Maynard illustrates the complexities of the witness deposition process and explains why the cases grew so bloated. Both sides deposed Maynard as a witness and her contested testimony in turn generated a slew of additional witness depositions and discussions.

Maynard had previously worked as Lady Roos's maid. Her employment probably ended when she married John Maynard, also deposed as a witness. (One of Lady Roos's maids had married and left her employ around Christmas 1617: this may have been Maynard.) Maynard had initially provided testimony on behalf of the Lakes in September. Now the countess of Exeter accused Lake of having paid Maynard in order get some compromising letters back from her, as well as to swear her to secrecy regarding certain matters.

The countess of Exeter believed that Maynard had incriminating information about Lady Roos that she might use. According to a witness deposition by Lady Anna Bamfield, Katherine Maynard had told her in conversation in August that "the Countesse had great wronge," but that Maynard was "tied by oath to secrecy" and therefore could not divulge more. She also told Lady Bamfield that while many had been examined about the case, they did not really know anything. Maynard, however, "knew all," and implied that the countess's written confession was forged. She also added that she knew of two people in Secretary Lake's household who "could counterfeit any hande upon view." Lady Roos, she said, "was no more poisoned than she."[23]

Maynard had apparently told other people about her knowledge of the case. She told Alice Eavon that Lady Roos had promised to give Katherine's husband John a lease of land worth £100 or £200 per annum and secure him a position that had an annual salary of 100 crowns. All the couple had to do was to take an oath of secrecy, and another "for performance of promise." Maynard also told Eavon that Sir Thomas Lake had come to her house and carried away some letters, while assuring her of earlier promises of payments. Maynard had confided that "she knewe enough to dashe and ruyne Sr. Tho: Lake and to cleare the Countesse." Maynard had also told the same to Jane Miller, adding that she had promised Sir Thomas Lake that she would not say anything about what she knew before Michaelmas, because Lake had said that "all then would be well." Miller had also heard Maynard say that Lady Roos had given her plenty of money and "used her well."[24]

In a second deposition, Maynard admitted that she had been angry with Lady Roos, because her former employer had promised to stand as godmother to her newborn, but then reneged. Maynard said that she had written a letter or two to Lady Roos, in which she had implied that she would "dishonor her" as a form of revenge. Lady Roos had then promised her £200 "and other rewards" in order to mollify and quiet her. Sir Thomas Lake had indeed come to her in April to take the copies of her letters to Lady Roos, and he had also assured her that she should have what Lady Roos had promised. About five or six weeks later, Sir Thomas Lake the younger had brought her £100, telling her not to let the elder Sir Thomas know about it. This would have been around the time that Thomas, Jr., filed his countersuit in June. Five or six days before Maynard's examination, Lady Roos had promised to pay her the other £100 and procure the office for her husband. John Maynard also gave testimony. He said they had received £100 and that about a month before he gave his testimony Lady Roos had sent another £11.[25]

When further questioned by Lake's lawyers, Maynard promptly denied what Lady Bamfield had said and instead accused the countess of Exeter of trying to bribe her for her testimony. Maynard deposed that she had been told that "the Countesse would be bountifull to her if she would discover any thinge in her behalf." Maynard believed that Lady Bamfield was working on behalf of the countess. She had been "drawne" to Lady Bamfield for the lady to see if she could get anything out of Maynard that would be useful for the countess's cause. Lady Bamfield had asked Maynard to visit her several times, but Maynard had not gone. She denied that she had said anything about Hatton's document being forged. The Lakes deposed three further witnesses who discredited Jane Miller's testimony regarding Maynard's earlier statements. They argued that Miller was a former servant who had left the Lakes on bad terms, therefore had malice against her former employer and could not be believed.[26]

When Lake found out that the countess of Exeter was pursuing Katherine Maynard as a witness for her side and had brought the issue to the attention of the king, he rushed to counter. In a letter to Buckingham, Lake argued that the letters Maynard mentioned had nothing to do with the case of Lady Exeter. He asked that the king read the enclosed copies of the letters for himself in order to see that they were not nefarious in the way that the countess suggested. Lake also sent along a copy of Lady Bamfield's deposition, as well as copies of Katherine Maynard's two depositions. (Unfortunately, none of the enclosed copies survive.) He was presumably trying to show that Maynard was an unreliable witness, as her testimonies were contradictory. Lake also told Buckingham to ask "the bearer" of the letter about the money paid to Maynard around Midsummer. Lake himself had only learned of the payments recently. The bearer of the letter must have been the junior Thomas Lake. It also means that Lady Roos and her brother had acted without Lake's knowledge, or that Lake pretended that they had acted without his knowledge. Either way, it implies that Lake may not always have had full control over the legal strategies, just like when his daughter presented the countess's supposed confession to the king before Lake even knew it existed. In his letter to Buckingham, Lake added wryly that if the payment had been a bribe to stay quiet, "it wrought little effect," since Maynard had received the money around Midsummer and yet she supposedly had talked to Lady Bamfield in August.[27]

Katherine Maynard was clearly a problematic witness, potentially looking to benefit from her intimate knowledge of her former mistress and the Lakes. As discussed further in Chapter 11, servants might find themselves in a difficult spot when asked to testify, as members of the socioeconomic elite could apply much pressure on poorer people. The Exeter side certainly made much of the fact that Maynard received money and other benefits. Lake did not fully explain why she and her husband received so much money. On the other hand, Maynard also suggests that the countess was willing to make good things happen if she would provide useful information. Of course, it is possible that Maynard was playing both sides, seeing who might provide the greatest benefit. If so, she was potentially playing a dangerous game. Giving a false deposition could have serious consequences. The punishment for perjury could include hefty fines, imprisonment, and corporal punishments: time in the pillory, and loss of ears, nose, or branding in the face.[28]

Some people were loath to get involved in the whole affair, but also found it difficult to say no to Secretary Lake, or to the rich and mighty earl of Exeter. For example, when Lake requested that Lady Constance Lucy give a deposition, she was clearly reluctant to do so. In a letter to Lake on October 10, 1618, she said she had very little to add to the matter and that she "could have been content, not to have been questioned in matters I understand noe more of." Furthermore, she said that Lady Lake "truly heard as much as ever I heard," suggesting that it was unnecessary for her to give a statement since she could not bring any new information. Pressing matters at her estates, as well as her poor health, made it difficult for her to come to London, she claimed. Lake understood that it was important to have someone other than his wife, a defendant in the case, provide the information. Notwithstanding Lady Lucy's reluctance, she promised she would "attend your Honor since it pleaseth you to have it so."[29]

As the numbers of witnesses increased and case files grew larger and larger, King James decided that he was going to sit as a judge in Star Chamber personally. This was an unusual move, as the king had previously appeared in Star Chamber only twice, and only once as a judge. The king's direct involvement raised the stakes for both plaintiffs, defendants, and witnesses, delayed the trial further, and left more room for observers to speculate about the outcome.

10
The Political Seesaw

> But it is the impending case between Sir Thomas Lake and the Countess of [Exeter] that is the principal subject of interest, and it is expected to begin very soon.
>
> John Castle to William Trumbull, October 15, 1618[1]

1618 proved a turbulent year at the Jacobean court. In addition to the Lake-Cecil feud involving a secretary and a Privy Councilor, Thomas Howard, earl of Suffolk, Privy Councilor and Lord Treasurer, found himself in disfavor and accused of corruption and graft. The suspicions against Suffolk also made life more difficult for Lake, who had remained close to the Howards even after the downfall of Somerset and his wife Frances Howard, Suffolk's daughter, on the heels of the revelations of the Overbury murder in 1615–16. With Suffolk in disfavor, Lake attempted to cultivate the patronage of the increasingly dominating Buckingham, but without lasting success.

The diplomatic relationship with Spain also grew volatile. King James continued to consider a Spanish match for Prince Charles, but the actions of Sir Walter Raleigh created a political hot potato in the summer and fall of 1618. Raleigh had returned from a troubled journey to Guiana, during which one of his men had led an attack against a Spanish fort in violation of a prior agreement. On orders from the Spanish king, the Spanish ambassador Gondomar called for swift punishment of Raleigh. At the same time, one of Gondomar's men accidently (one presumes) rode down a boy in London and injured him, leading to protests and riots outside the ambassador's house. All these threads were interwoven in various ways with the Lake and Exeter lawsuits.

Lake tried to navigate the political turbulence, while at the same time focusing on the Star Chamber suits. He managed to stay afloat but was left in a state of uncertainty. As the matter dragged on, commentators were following the developments closely, trying to interpret the myriad of signs suggesting which side might be closer to winning. During the summer, some believed that Lake might prevail after all. After more details about the witness depositions came out in the fall, more leaned toward the Exeters. Many speculated that King James favored that side. No one could quite count the Lakes and

Family and Feuding at the Court of James I: The Lake and Cecil Scandals. Johanna Luthman, Oxford University Press.
 DOI: 10.1093/oso/9780192865786.003.0010

Lady Roos out, however, as evidence of possible royal favor kept cropping up too, and surprise witnesses might materialize. Jacobean court politics were complex indeed.

The Suffolk Entanglement

Thomas Howard, earl of Suffolk, came from a noble family of long standing and influence in England. He tied himself even closer to royal power when he supported the annulment of his daughter Frances's first marriage to Robert Deveraux, third earl of Essex. Freed from her first husband, Frances married Robert Carr, earl of Somerset, and the undisputed favorite of James from 1607 to 1615. The king appointed him Lord Treasurer in 1614. Suffolk managed to survive the spectacular fall of his daughter and her husband in 1615 and 1616, when they were found guilty of orchestrating the poisoning of Somerset's former friend and close associate Sir Thomas Overbury.

The comet-like rise of Buckingham as the new royal favorite ensured that Suffolk—and others—was increasingly less influential at court. Buckingham rapidly became a major patron, building a network of kin and supporters at the royal court. Suffolk and his wife and other members of the diminished Howard circle tried to unseat or at least challenge Buckingham by introducing another enticingly beautiful young man, William Monson, to James's court in early 1618. They "took great pains in tricking and prancking him up, besides washing his face every day with posset-curd," and the young man took every opportunity to appear before the king.[2] King James saw through their overt attempt at manipulating his affections, and brusquely told the young man to absent himself from court. Chamberlain judged the scheme too forward, as the Howard faction had not bothered to try to secure Monson an office at court first, which would give him a solid reason to be in the king's presence. Buckingham, realizing the danger, reacted to the challenge by informing the king about the Suffolks' shady financial practices, triggering an investigation.[3]

Jacobean court offices were desirable not only because of the political power and social prestige they conferred but also because they were lucrative. The salaries were modest, but other perks and the power that came with the offices could translate to substantial riches. As a result, ambitious men were sometimes willing to pay large sums for appointments. For example, Lake had offered to pay in order to become secretary after the death of Salisbury in 1612. His offer was rejected, and he had to wait a few more years for his appointment.[4]

The earl and countess of Suffolk had a large family and many expenses: their many sons and daughters needed to be settled in positions and marriages. They were avid builders, buying and enlarging houses and estates in both town and country, specifically the magnificently opulent estate Audley End in Saffron Walden. To increase their income, Suffolk and his wife appear to have required an outsized number of bribes and gifts from people who wished to influence or do business with the treasurer. It was not uncommon to pay for influence at the Jacobean court, but the Suffolks made it much more expensive. Suffolk began to require payments not just in exceptional or occasional cases, but even for the performance of the regular and mundane work of the treasurer, such as getting payments that already had been approved by the king and council.

The countess of Suffolk's involvement became another distinguishing feature: she required gifts and payments to provide access or influence her husband's decisions. A woman's involvement in such matters was seen as especially problematic and immoral. Female greed was more troubling than the male variety, which could more easily be written off as masculine ambition. The countess was also not appointed to the position, so the fact that she was profiting from, and involving herself so directly in official business of state, became problematic. When Buckingham informed James of the situation, the king ordered an investigation in the spring of 1618. James also ordered the countess of Suffolk to stay away from the capital altogether until further notice.

By May, Lady Suffolk tired of the country and came to London, despite the king's explicit orders to the contrary. The king, annoyed with her blatant disregard of his wishes, complained about the willful countess in a private conversation with Lake. Lake turned around and warned Suffolk that it would be best for his wife to leave the capital in order not to test the king's patience further. King James learned of the warning and became upset that Lake had revealed the contents of the king's private conversation. James felt that Lake had betrayed his trust and promptly told him not to come to court either. The king also gave permission for Sir Dudley Carleton to return to England from The Hague, an ominous sign, given that Carleton had openly been fishing for the post as Secretary of State for some time.[5]

At this point, the incident with the countess of Suffolk seemed an even more dangerous development than his daughter's scandal, the Privy Council's investigation, and the initiation of the court cases. Chamberlain informed Carleton that "Secretarie Lake hath of late had so many feathers puld from him, that he fears to be left bare, and therefore no doubt doth *omnem movere lapidem* [leave no stone unturned] to kepe of competitors." Lake had to give up the Latin Secretary position, which he had held for years, to the Scottish Thomas Read, although he retained the post of Secretary of State for the time being.[6]

Lake tried desperately to restore the king's faith in him. He offered to pay Buckingham a hefty £15,000 to assist him in convincing the king that he was still a loyal servant. Lorkin informed his former student Puckering on June 16 that Thomas Lake "continues in the same terms of disfavor and disgrace as before." Lake was told to "retire himself into the country, if he please," but given "permission" to "follow his suits in law—that between Lord Burleigh and him chiefly." Although he "makes large offers, yet is his blow supposed to be irrecoverble," Lorkin surmised.[7] When Buckingham did not seem amenable to his offer, Lake turned to Buckingham's mother instead, hoping that her intervention might change Buckingham's—and then also the king's—mind.[8]

Suffolk's position at court continued to hang in the balance. After the royally appointed commission's further investigation of the situation in the Exchequer, enough troubling information emerged to make the king act. By mid-July, the king determined that he could no longer keep Suffolk as his treasurer. He formally removed him from office, requiring him to return his white staff, the symbol of the treasurer. Both Suffolk and his wife became *personas non grata* at court. The following year, the earl and countess of Suffolk were brought to the Court of Star Chamber to answer for their financial misdoings.[9]

While reporting on Suffolk's removal, some court observers expected that the king's ire about what he viewed as Lake's betrayal of trust would cool. Lake surely would soon be allowed back to court and restored to his place. The signs were encouraging, and it seems that Lake's investment paid to Buckingham's mother might have been useful after all. On July 1, Lord Fenton wrote that Lake's situation looked better by the day, so that he thought it would not be long before he "awaite on his Majestie againe," since he "still excersiss his place."[10] On July 19, Abraham Williams reported to Trumbull, who had returned to Brussels, that "Mr. Secretary Lake hath fayre promises to be restored tomorrow morning, and doth intend to go the Progresse, whereas Mr Secretary Naunton doth intend as yet to stay behind." Furthermore, the ever-hopeful Carleton was sent back to his ambassadorial post in The Hague.[11] An immediate rival for Lake's post was removed for the moment, at least. William Jones, who worked for Lake, told Trumbull that while Suffolk had lost his staff, "My Secretary Lake his criticall day is past." Jones's evaluation came after Lake had received a visit from the royal favorite Buckingham and told that he was "to come to the Kinge at a day assigned." Additionally, Jones declared, Lake now seemed to be employed in his regular business as secretary again, as "Carleton hath bene with him for his dispatch by the Kinges direction." Pleased with the direction of events, Jones concluded: "I make noe doubt but that he shall come to the same place, and it may be with some addition of honor."[12]

Indeed, Lake was so sure that he would soon be back attending on the king in his summer progress that he sent his "stuffe and diette along" in advance, so it would be available for him once he joined the king.[13] At this juncture, the troublesome witness Katherine Maynard claimed that Lake had told her that she just needed to stay quiet until Michaelmas, since "all would then be well." Lake must have hoped that the fire sparked by his unwise warning to Suffolk regarding his wife had been put out.

Yet the king delayed. James was waiting to hear more from Roos regarding Lady Roos's accusations before he decided to invite Lake back to court. Sir Giles Brydges had been sent to Roos in Italy with formal Star Chamber interrogatories, so that Roos's answers could be used as crucial witness testimony in the court cases.[14] Attempts to reach Roos failed, as Roos had already died by the time Brydges arrived in Italy. Both Lake and Exeter found out about Roos's death late at night on July 26, and so did the king, presumably. The hope that Roos would ever provide any further information in the cases was gone, and the king had to make decisions about Lake's reinstatement without it. Despite the delays, Lake's men initially continued hopeful. On July 28, Edward Norgate told Trumbull: "Wee are not yet at Court, but our hopes and likelihoods grow every day greater." He was concerned that Roos's death might work in the Exeter's favor, adding "I suppose this accident will not a little adde to theire growth."[15]

Abraham Williams found the delay in Lake's rumored restoration more troubling, understanding that "these lingering diseases are daungerous."[16] A rumor of restoration that did not materialize could cause more harm than good, as people might interpret it as a sign that the persons relaying the information were misinformed and thus not within the circle of power. As David Coast has pointed out, rumors of potential removals and appointments mattered a great deal, as they could affect court realities when people adjusted to, and acted based on, information they believed might be true.[17]

Lake remained suspended in a state of limbo and James kept everyone guessing. It is "onley in his Majesties owin breist, I think he impairts to noe bodye but to Marquiss of Bukkinghame," Lord Fenton wrote to the earl of

Mar on August 22.[18] In late August, Trumbull tried to cover all bases and sent copies of his official dispatches from Brussels to both Lake and Naunton, since he had not yet heard anything official from the Privy Council about switching the addressee.[19] By early September, Lake noted a troubling development. Ambassador Carleton was now told to send his dispatches to Naunton, per the king's specific instruction. In fact, Naunton was taking care of all the official correspondence. This indicated that the king had no intentions of restoring Lake within the near future, and worse, that he was having others perform his official duties.[20] The king was still on progress and Lake was still not allowed to join, despite his earlier optimistic preparations.[21] Lord Fenton noted that after the dismissal of Suffolk, with Lake still in disfavor and Secretary Naunton inexperienced, the king was "mutche trubled with besines." Fenton thought that if the king would just "recall" the competent and swift "Secreterrye Laike," it would give the king "great ease."[22] Despite the press of work, King James did not do so.

Later in September, observers noted that Lake could probably not hope for a restoration before the Star Chamber cases had concluded. John Castle informed Trumbull in mid-September that the countess of Exeter "has received a message from the King that he will attend the hearing." More enigmatically, the king also told the countess that once in Star Chamber, he would "disclose certain things which neither she nor her adversaries have dreamed of."[23] The king believed he held some secret information that was crucial to the case, and this was part of the reason why he wanted to sit as a judge in court.

The king's decision to appear in court and to wait until after the trial before he determined Lake's fate, gave the trials much added weight and importance. Lake had hoped that the king's ire over his warning to the countess of Suffolk would fade, and that he would be allowed to return to court and to his official duties after an appropriately penitent period out in the cold. If Lake were allowed back at court, the trials might be viewed as slightly less important, a scandalous side-show involving the female members of his family, but perhaps not as a fatal threat to his own position. The fall of Suffolk did not bode well. In the eyes of some observers, Suffolk suffered mostly because of the grasping actions of his wife, although he himself was of an "amiable disposition." As her husband, Suffolk had failed to control his wife's sins and crimes. "Like Adam," Philip Burlamacchi mused, Suffolk "can say 'la femme que mas donnée ma ruiné'," but he had to suffer the consequences nonetheless.[24] Lake was now facing a similar situation.

Raleigh's Return and Spanish Diplomacy

As the Star Chamber court cases began to wind their way during the summer of 1618, Sir Walter Raleigh's return and arrest became a major topic of conversation. Raleigh had come to prominence as one of the "Sea Dogges" during the reign of Queen Elizabeth, mainly as a voyager and as a soldier. He was once one of Elizabeth's favorites but lost that status after secretly and without permission impregnating and marrying one of the queen's maids of honor in the early 1590s. Even though the personal bond was broken after that, Elizabeth still relied on his skills as a soldier and commander, specifically in the war against Spain. In 1603, Raleigh was found guilty of participating in the Main Plot, which strove to replace King James with his cousin Arabella Stuart, and was supposedly backed by the Spanish, eager to return England to the Catholic fold. The evidence against Raleigh was rather flimsy, but he was nevertheless convicted. King James stayed his execution and he was imprisoned in the Tower instead for almost a decade and a half.

In 1617, the king freed him from the Tower and gave him permission to lead an expedition to South America, provided he did not attempt any violence against Spanish interests. A portion of Raleigh's men, including his son, attacked a Spanish settlement in Guiana in violation of these specific orders. Raleigh's son died in the fighting. The Spanish were outraged by the attack and demanded that Raleigh be punished as the leader of the expedition. Upon his return to England in July 1618, he was arrested and imprisoned again. The Spanish were further outraged after it was discovered that a person from the French ambassador's household had tried to assist Raleigh's flight out of England. After lengthy examinations and further consideration, Raleigh was executed on October 29, 1618.[25]

Anti-Spanish sentiments ran rather high in 1618. Raleigh's execution was the result of a reinstatement of his previous death sentence from the Main Plot trial, rather than a new trial. Some thought this a rather harsh way to deal with the issue, and of questionable legality and justice. Raleigh was generally very popular with the anti-Spanish and anti-Catholic crowd, and they tended to view his execution as the result of undue Spanish pressure, as James pandering to Spain because of the planned marriage between Prince Charles and the Spanish *Infanta*. King James had promised Gondomar and his master that Raleigh would be punished.

In addition, in mid-July, a member of the Spanish ambassador's household accidentally rode down a young child in Chancery Lane, "and left it in great danger of death." The neighborhood reacted by rioting outside the ambassador's residence, throwing rocks and breaking windows. The riot did not end until the Lord Chief Justice Sir Thomas Coventry arrived and arrested the rider, essentially taking him into protective custody. The king then accused the Lord Mayor of London of not punishing the rioters sufficiently, and appointed a special commission led by Sir Edward Coke for the purpose. Ultimately, only seven people were found guilty, imprisoned for six months, and fined £500 apiece.[26]

As mentioned, Lake, as well as the Suffolks, had developed friendly relations with the Spanish ambassador Gondomar since his arrival in England in 1613. Indeed, the Suffolks and Lake were part of the group of courtiers who received an annuity from the Spanish crown, paid with the expectation that they would be friendly to Spanish goals and policies in England. One might imagine that Lake would hope to benefit from these ties in his time of troubles.[27]

However, Lake's connections with Gondomar were not always straight forward. For example, when beneficial, Lake and his wife did not hesitate to use anti-Spanish sentiment to their advantage. In letters and in court documents, they accused Gondomar of having assisted Roos in his flight from England, kept Roos's goods away from his wife, and problematized Roos's love of all things Spanish. They argued that Roos's trust in the Spaniard Diego da Silva was misplaced: an Englishman should not rely so much on a foreigner, they implied, which also included the Spanish ambassador, an agent of a foreign and Catholic power. In addition, Lake had previously told Buckingham (and thus the king) that he suspected da Silva was a Spanish spy (see Chapter 4).

Gondomar did try to assist Lake in his troubles later in 1620, but he was not particularly helpful at the time of the scandals and opening of the Star Chamber cases. Partly, it was because he was simply no longer present. After five years in England, the Spanish king gave Gondomar permission to return to Spain in the summer of 1618. As a gesture of goodwill, King James also granted him the right to bring with him several imprisoned English Catholics, who were released from imprisonment on the condition that they left the country with Gondomar. When Gondomar lingered longer than deemed necessary, the king grew irritated, especially as many of the Catholics who were supposed to travel with him had already been released. By mid-July, Gondomar finally left.[28] He apparently also took with him the property that the now-dead Lord Roos had left with him before fleeing, benefiting from the fact that ambassadors' trunks and property were exempt from searches by customs officials.[29]

The Course of the Cases: The Fall Wagers

On October 15, John Castle updated Trumbull on the current news from London. He discussed the worsening outlook for Raleigh (not yet executed at that time), and that the Suffolks' financial misdeeds were being further investigated, with the current focus on the countess of Suffolk's potential misuse of the king's jewels. These weighty and scandalous matters notwithstanding, Castle explained that it was "the impending case between Sir Thomas Lake and the Countess of Essex [sic] that is the principal subject of interest, and it is expected to begin very soon."[30]

Initially, the trials were scheduled toward the end of the Michaelmas term in November.[31] There was a "summary hearing" of the case in Star Chamber, but only to "prepare it readie" for the trials.[32] The sheer size of the cases meant that trials would take several days, and the already packed court calendar could not accommodate it. Normally, the court would hear about four to five cases per day, so these trials promised to be unusual on several accounts.[33] The king's pronouncement that he would sit in the trials also necessitated a postponement. The materials had to be compressed and summarized in order to make it possible for the king to attend the lengthy proceedings. Consequently, the trials were scheduled for Hilary term in late January.[34]

The delay of the case meant more time for observers to guess which way the cases might go, and which side was favored. Crucially, were Lake to fall, the position of Secretary of State would open for another ambitious politician. The jockeying for court positions was especially notable in the many letters addressed to Carleton in his embassy at The Hague. Carleton's correspondents were looking to keep him abreast of news from the court, as he was actively seeking to leave his post and get an appointment at the English court instead. When it became apparent that Lake was potentially in trouble, they were looking to advance Carleton to the position of secretary in his place. They had already attempted to do so at the death of Chamberlain's good friend Secretary Ralph Winwood in October of 1617 but failed.[35] On October 18, the Countess of Bedford informed Carleton that though "Lady Exeter's business is coming to a sentence, it is quite uncertain who will be Secretary in place of Lake." She assured him that both she and Carleton's other friends "that have better meanes to be of use" would do their best for him.[36] More decisively, Sir Benjamin Rudyard concluded that "Sec. Lake's business is to come on next term, and then will be Carleton's time," and Sir Arthur Tyringham thought Carleton's "promotion cannot be delayed longer than the ending of Lake's business, as he has powerful friends."[37] All three clearly believed that Lake would lose his post.

Not surprisingly, Carleton's friends tended to interpret the case in favor of the Exeters. In addition to Carleton's political ambitions, his correspondents undoubtedly knew of his friendship with the countess of Exeter, as well as his fondness for the now dead Roos. Sir Edward Harwood had told Carleton as early as September 23 that "Mr Secretarye Lake his case is desperate," and that the case looks "every day appeare worse & worse for my Lad. Rosse" and "his majestie understand it soe."[38] After the preparatory publication of the case in November, which included some additional news about the various proofs and witness testimonies, Harwood judged that there was "noe question made of the going out of Secretary Lake," especially since he had heard that Lake had offered money to some of his witnesses (this probably referred to the dispute about Katherine Maynard's testimony).[39] Sir William Smith said that those who had read through all the thousands of pages of depositions and proofs assured him that "ther is nothing proved against my La of Exeter eyther for ye supposed poisoning, or incest."[40] In late December, Harwood reported that "My Lad. Exeter hathe reasonable access" to the king, which made him "think he is well perswaded of hir cause."[41]

Some who were not Carleton's correspondents also judged that the case seemed to move in the Exeters' favor during the fall. Castle told Trumbull that he was "inclined to believe that the whole business has been contrived by mother and daughter out of sheer malice." He felt sorry for Lake and wished he could be spared the consequences of the deeds of his wife and daughter. But, judged Castle, Lake "never knew the bottome of their doeings, but from abuse out of over much uxoriousnes to his wife, and shipped himself improvidently without biscuit."[42] In October, Thomas Lorkin informed Sir Thomas Puckering that "the common voice has already given a heavy sentence against" Lake.[43] The archbishop of Canterbury told Trumbull on October 27 that Lake "still maintains his position, but the general opinion here is that his power is declining and that he may fall before the end of the term."[44]

Others were not sure what to make of the case and were reluctant to speculate. John Wolley warned Trumbull not to get involved and take sides, because he believed the "busines betweene the Earle of Exeter and Sir Thomas Lake is likely to prove naught, and as I take it this bearer [the Earl of Exeter's man] is come about it to your worship. I pray God yow may be well ride of it, for I can not see how your worship can carry an equall hand in that troublesome cause."[45] In late December, John More was still speculating about the case:

> The present Star Chamber case is a perplexing one. When wee see Luke Hattons cause set down first to be opened, wee say the Lady Lak will gain her proces. But when we heare Sir Benjamin Ruddiar nominated to be

> secretary, wee say the ladies husband must go down. And so is hee generally cryed down in Court where the opinion is hee will never ryse although hee should escape the censor of the starre chamber.[46]

Even though he reported rumors regarding the case, the archbishop of Canterbury thought it no point speculating until it had been fully heard in Star Chamber, and one could judge it on the merits of the evidence presented by the two sides.[47]

But far from everyone counted Lake out during the fall of 1618. Signs that the secretary might just pull through the crisis and keep his position kept cropping up. His occasional meetings with the royal favorite Buckingham constituted one such sign. Abraham Williams suggested to William Trumbull on September 25 that since "My lord of Buckingham was with Mr Secretary Lake some fower dayes since," there was "yet good hopes of a restoring."[48] Thomas Locke informed Carleton on November 14 that "Sir Thomas and Lady Lake and Lady Roos had a conference with Buckingham," which made him worry somewhat about Carleton's chances at advancement.[49] There could, of course, be other reasons for Lake's meetings with Buckingham, as Wolley pointed out on October 2. Some thought the meeting was about the continued investigation of the earl and countess of Suffolk, and that the king thought Lake had more information about that, given his connection to them. Others believed it might have to do with a rumored marriage between Buckingham's brother and Lady Roos. Whatever the reason, "none doth hold it to be about the restorement of his office of the which I see as yet no appearnance," Wolley concluded.[50]

The rumors about a marriage between Buckingham's brother, Sir Christopher Villiers, and Lady Roos persisted into the fall as well, yet another sign of Lake's potential resurrection. Surely, people reasoned, the ambitious Buckingham would not wish to marry his brother to the daughter of a disgraced secretary. That would help neither his brother's career nor his own. Therefore, if Buckingham was contemplating such a marriage, the favorite must have inside information from the king that Lake might be restored after all. At the end of September, "Wagers are offred to be layd that Mr. Christopher Villiers shall mary the Lady Roos," Abraham Williams wrote Trumbull.[51] Likewise, Captain Thomas Brett reported that "The Lady Ross with a great addition of portion is spoken of for a brother" of Buckingham.[52] Wolley believed that the primary attraction was the large dowry Lake was willing to offer: "The other day the Marquis spent an hour with Sir Thomas Lake, and it is conjectured that their confabulation had to do with a possible match between Mr. Christopher Villiers and the Lady Ros, who is very rich and can expect a further substantial dowry from her father."[53] The courtier Sir Henry Mildmay was another possible candidate for Lady Roos, "but it is sayde he refused it."[54] In the end, there was no match between the favorite's brother and Lady Roos, likely because the king did not support it. (The king had supported the contested marriage between Sir John Villiers, Buckingham's elder brother, and Roos's cousin Frances Coke, and as a result, that marriage went ahead in 1617.)

The fact that the king decided to grant legal administration of Roos's goods to Lady Roos in late September also constituted a positive sign for the beleaguered Lake family. Since Roos's death, Lady Roos, the Lakes and the earl of Exeter had fought over who should have the legal right of administration. A judge had already granted letters of administration to the earl of Exeter, but the king overruled that decision, and gave it to Lady Roos instead.[55] If the young woman was guilty of fraud and slander, would the king favor her in such a way?

The Twist: The Return of Diego da Silva?

Roos had died before Sir Giles Brydges had time to get his answers to the official interrogatories. However, his servant and companion Diego da Silva still lived. The king was especially keen on getting more information from the Spaniard, whom Lady Roos insisted had been in the room when the countess of Exeter wrote her confession. Indeed, according to the complaint in Sir Thomas Lake the younger's suit against the earl and countess of Exeter, it was Diego da Silva who had come up with the very idea that the countess should offer a written confession to placate Lady Roos, give her security, and to keep her from revealing their sins to her family and others. Lake certainly wished to keep a close eye on da Silva's movements, but it is not clear if he worked toward getting him back to England or if he wanted to keep him away, thinking he would only testify in the countess's favor. The earl and especially the countess of Exeter appear to have been most active in establishing contact with da Silva directly.

The earl of Exeter sent a man named Dendy to Naples to persuade Diego de Silva to return to England and provide testimony in the Star Chamber case. Dendy had orders to assure da Silva that he would not be detained but would be able to "come and go at his pleasure." Da Silva initially travelled back with Dendy as far as Lyons. While there, da Silva received a letter from Gondomar in Spain, which told him not to go to England until he had spoken to the ambassador in Madrid. Da Silva changed his travel plans and went to Spain. He argued that he had to do as Gondomar asked, considering that "his whole state in a manner lay in the ambassadors hands, beeing conveyed by him to Antwerp after the Lord Rosses departure."[56] Da Silva had inherited Roos's property outside of England, and, allegedly, Gondomar had brought much of the property that Roos had left in his safekeeping with him when he left England.

If Lady Roos had made up her accusations against the countess and the written confession, da Silva certainly might have revealed her fraud, were he to return. On November 18, Harwood reported to Carleton that da Silva was supposed to come to England to "prove himselfe an honest man, wch the Lad. (I meane my Lad. Rosse, [sic] had I thinke rather he had stayed where he is)."[57] The generally more skeptical Abbott, archbishop of Canterbury, mused that given how close da Silva had been to Roos, he would be a person who would know "as much touching those thinges that are questioned about the Lord Roos as any man in the worlde, but with what fidelity he will report them I cannot tell." The archbishop surmised that Gondomar intended to question da Silva in Madrid, and if his information made things look bad for Lake and Lady Roos, he would keep da Silva from going to England before the case was concluded. On the other hand, if it would make the Exeters look bad, he would speed him along.[58] Harwood suggested to Carleton that it would have been better if da Silva had come to England but thought his staying away would "not hurte my Lad. Ex cause."[59]

The countess of Exeter was especially keen on reaching da Silva. At first, she gave money to Frances da Silva to travel to meet her husband in Brussels, as he had begun his journey from Naples with Dendy. Frances da Silva was the English wife whom Diego da Silva had left behind when he absconded with Roos the previous year. Frances da Silva also traveled with her young child and servants. The countess of Exeter arranged further moneys for Mistress da Silva in Brussels, asking Trumbull to advance her money until she could arrange for a repayment of that advance from the English merchant Philip Burlamachi.[60]

At the same time, Lake also asked the beleaguered Trumbull to inform him of any developments. "If you hear anything of the course that Diego's wife has taken since her arrival there or of his coming, let me know," he wrote.[61] Sir Thomas Leeds, who worked for Lake, also requested updates from Trumbull on Frances da Silva's movements and activities, and whether da Silva appeared in town.[62]

By December 9, Dendy had arrived back in England empty-handed, and Lake again asked for further information from Trumbull:

> There has arrived here a certain Dendy one of Lord Exeter's men who went with Sir Giles Borges [Brydges] to bring Diego back. But I have not heard that Diego has come. There are conflicting reports that he is with you there, that he has gone to Spain, that he will arrive shortly and that he will not come at all. Let me know if he is in your part of the world and what his intentions may be. If he is in Brussels, you will discover them without much difficulty.[63]

As an aside, Lake mentioned that Sir Giles was a suspicious character, who could not be trusted. He is "said to be either dead or to have renounced his religion and become an exile, at least for the present," Lake insisted. "It would be advisable for you to enquire into the whereabouts of Sir Giles," as Lake believed this Exeter connection was now discredited.[64]

The countess of Exeter tried again, this time sending John Duppa, Roos's former servant and "bedfellow," presumably someone who knew da Silva well.[65] Again, the countess relied on Trumbull to assist her. On December 12, she asked him to "Please lend Duppae £20 if the bill of exchange from Burlamacchi does not reach you before this." She was asking for this favor because Duppa "hathe haste of what I implie [employ] him in."[66] While the countess never spelled out specifically what she had asked Duppa to do, it is a fair assumption that she was trying to reach da Silva again. For emphasis, the earl of Exeter wrote a separate note to Trumbull on the same date and thanked him for his assistance, which he promised to "requite."[67]

It seems Duppa was not as reliable as the countess had hoped. On December 18, she wrote Trumbull again, telling him she had "sent a bill of exchange from Mr Burlamacchi for the money which you advanced" to Duppa, thus repaying Trumbull's temporary loan. "I would have sent another," she continued, "but that I harde some thingse sence I rit my last letors that makes me doute whether Duppae will take that corse I desired he sholde, but I hope he will." Since Duppa was not doing whatever it was the countess asked him to do, she was not willing to supply him with more funds. (Duppa may have decided to stay in Brussels. He tried to get a job in his old employer Carleton's household in The Hague the following year, but Carleton had no position available. Carleton asked Trumbull to let Duppa know this, which probably meant Duppa was in Brussels at that time.)[68] All in all, the earl and countess of Exeter paid for the journey of three parties to try to contact Diego da Silva, to no avail.[69] Da Silva was nowhere near Brussels at that time, but rather in Spain.

Da Silva remained tantalizingly out of reach for both the countess of Exeter as well as Lake and Lady Roos. By January 11, Lake received news from Cottington, English ambassador in Spain. Cottington said he had heard of da Silva's arrival in Madrid, but he had not seen him yet himself.[70] Cottington must have met da Silva very shortly thereafter, as he wrote him a letter asking for Trumbull's favor toward the Spaniard.[71] Da Silva did eventually turn up in Brussels, but not until late January, when the trials had already begun in England. On January 31, Trumbull told Lake that "yesterday Diego da Silva arrived here from Spain," reuniting with his wife and child still waiting for him in Brussels. He could not tell Lake anything about da Silva's plans or intentions, but he promised to let him know if he learned anything else that would be useful.[72] A few days later, Trumbull told Carleton in The Hague the same news:

> I will not forgett to let yo L. knowe, that Diego de Silva, the deceased L. Rooses privado, is newly come hether from Madrid. Whether there will be any use made of his testimony or not, I cannot tell. But I have given notice of his arryvall to my frends in England. If his discourse be answerable to his knowledge and conscience, undoubtedly one of the partyes hath donne irreparable wronge to the honor of the other. Yo Lp will [?] with ease, whome I meane and whose side he can saye most in this business.[73]

Trumbull clearly did not feel comfortable writing openly what he thought about the case, instead preferring innuendo, like so many others.

What can we draw from da Silva's elusiveness and actions? Some clearly thought his testimony would help the countess of Exeter's cause, hence the countess's multiple attempts to reach him. Trumbull was more cautious in his evaluation. He knew that Carleton was friends with the countess of Exeter, and that he was looking for an opportunity at the court, which would open if Lake fell. He was suggesting that as far as what he had heard from da Silva, the countess is innocent and has been wronged. However, he prefaced that by adding "If his [da Silva's] discourse be answerable to his knowledge and conscience," meaning that he did not know if da Silva was speaking the truth.

On the other hand, if da Silva had knowledge of an adulterous or improper relationship between Roos and the countess, the earl and countess of Exeter may have had different purposes in contacting him. If Exeter believed that da Silva would clear his wife, it would make sense for him to pay for Brydges and

Dendy to go to Italy and bring him back to England. If the countess feared that da Silva might reveal her adultery to her husband and to the king, she might want to contact da Silva before he made it to England to ensure that he did not say anything detrimental. Admittedly, this scenario is mere speculation and conjecture, as no tangible evidence exists to support it. It does seem odd that the countess was willing to pay for da Silva's wife, child, and servants to go to Brussels to meet him first, before she sent Duppa. If she really intended to get da Silva to England, he would have reunited with his wife and child once he arrived anyway.

Returning to England was not in da Silva's interest. The English master he had served was now dead. He had aided Roos in his illegal flight. If Lake were to prevail, da Silva might find himself in serious legal trouble in England. In addition, with Gondomar back in Spain, no Spanish ambassador resided in England at the time, which meant less protection available. Da Silva held English lands and leases, which Roos had given him previously. As a Catholic foreigner, and with his protector dead, it might have been difficult to lay claim to them again. In fact, he sold the lease of the manor of Morton Grange in York, which Roos had given him, to Trumbull, presumably while he was in Brussels. King Charles later argued this purchase was invalid, since da Silva was "liable to forfeiture of his estate, being a fugitive."[74] Instead, the lease went to the crown.

According to Cottington, who called da Silva "his ancient frend" and "one whom I love," da Silva went to Brussels to collect Roos's goods that his master had left him in his will. Cottington surmised that the goods were in the hands of "a sonne of ye Conde Gondomar," and he asked Trumbull to assist da Silva in his pursuit of Roos's goods, "or what else he shall have occasion, and I wyll esteeme it as a greate obligacon."[75] If da Silva was able to take possession of the remains of Roos's goods, he would probably do better not to risk those gains for an uncertain stint in England that could only serve others. His wife, child, and servants were now also in Brussels, courtesy of the countess of Exeter, severing his familial ties in England. At this point, Diego da Silva simply disappears from the historical record. Lady Roos and the countess of Exeter had to continue to fight without his testimony.

By the end of the year, some observers felt the feud, scandal, and court cases were disruptive and distracting, and wanted them over and gone. The business had been occupying the public for a full year. Sir Thomas Leeds told Trumbull he wished "there were a good end between thes two noble personages, for thes unsavrie sutes do but fill the lawiers purses with money and themselves with gale [gall]."[76] Perhaps Leeds had also heard the same rumor that John More had been privately told toward the end of December. More relayed that "the parties litigant in the star chamber are upon termes of agreement between them selves." Perhaps the trials could be avoided, he surmised, if it were not for the stubbornness of the earl of Exeter. The "old Conte is no thing tractable," More added.[77] The trials would move forward.

11
Trials and Verdicts

> Never was any accused person more clearly acquitted to the great satisfaction of all the worlde.
>
> Sir John Harwood to Sir Dudley Carleton, February 16, 1619[1]

As Hilary term approached in January of 1619, some observers saw signs that Lake might yet prevail. Rev. Lorkin told Sir Thomas Puckering that the "Lakes' business, it is thought, will receive a more favourable issue than was imagined." Again, it was a meeting with Buckingham who had prompted those guesses. Puckering noted that the "marquis [of Buckingham] was within these few days, at his [Lake's] house, to visit him; whereupon men frame and build conjectures."[2] In his next letter on January 19, Lorkin's guess had already changed somewhat: "In point of honour, it is thought the case will incline favourably on my Lady Exeter's side. The issue of other differences will sort suitable to the proofs."[3]

The anticipation of the trial was high. In addition to its political implications, the case had also achieved a celebrity status, with its salacious and sensational details, and the honor and reputation of elite women and men at stake. No matter the outcome, it was sure to cause further political fallout, scandal, and comments. After all, the losing side would be revealed to be remarkably sinful and scheming. Added to that heady brew was the king's own investment in the case and his unusual decision that he would sit in Star Chamber in person.

The Wise and Just King Solomon

In other notable Jacobean court scandals that led to court cases in King's Bench and Star Chamber, such as the Overbury murder and the Suffolk financial corruption, the king specifically did *not* get directly involved in the legal process. He preferred to distance himself, to maintain an appearance of impartiality and allow justice and law to run its course without direct royal interference. Why, then, did he choose to sit in the scandalous Lake-Exeter

Family and Feuding at the Court of James I: The Lake and Cecil Scandals. Johanna Luthman, Oxford University Press.
 DOI: 10.1093/oso/9780192865786.003.0011

case? Over the course of his reign, King James liked to compare himself to the wise and just biblical King Solomon. Others were aware of James's love for Solomon analogies. For example, Bacon compared King James to Solomon in a speech in the Somerset trials for the Overbury murder. In 1616, Richard Montague wrote in his foreword to a new collection of James's tracts that "God hath given us a Solomon."[4] James would have approved of the funeral oration of the bishop of Lincoln, John Williams in 1625, which compared the dead James to the biblical king.[5] It was this desire to display "Solomon-like" qualities which ensured that King James decided to preside over the Lake-Cecil cases in person. (See Fig. 11.1.)

Before 1619, King James had only appeared twice in person in the Court of Star Chamber. The first time was in 1616, when he had already been king of England for thirteen years. At that point, he appeared in the court to give a speech, but he did not sit as a judge. In his speech, he explained that he had not come to any Star Chamber proceedings before this time, because he wanted to learn the process fully first. He also argued that he needed to wait for an appropriate case before he determined to sit in judgment. To make his first appearance "in a small cause had been disgraceable," the king argued, and to "come in a great cause if it had concerned his mony sone or any Great Man in Court it might have been thought he had come to advance his own ends or private comoditie of for particular favour wch he did ever abhorre."[6]

The case between the Lakes and the Exeters fit James's requirements. It was not a small cause, as it involved powerful families and the king's Privy Councilors and a Secretary of State. However, neither of the men were close royal favorites the way Somerset had been, so James could avoid the appearance of favoritism. The Suffolk corruption case clearly concerned the king's money and interest, making him stay away from that when it was tried in Star Chamber later in 1619. The financial aspects of the Lake-Exeter dispute did not involve the king's business or money. Furthermore, the sensational Lake-Exeter feud had drawn much attention and anticipation. It was a question of honor and separating truth from lies, which enabled the king to show off his Solomon-like abilities.

The first time James sat as a judge in Star Chamber was in early 1617, in a case involving two men on trial for intending to sneak over to France to duel illegally. At the time, James was trying to put an end to the extralegal practice of dueling and believed that a personal appearance in the Star Chamber court would demonstrate his serious intent. Both would-be duelers had already confessed, so the trial was speedy and uncontested. James gave a short speech

Fig. 11.1 King James VI of Scotland and I of England. Daniel Mytens, 1621. © National Portrait Gallery, London.

in court, explaining that "he had chosen a cause that concerned the peace of the kingdome," because that was "the chief office of a king."[7]

The second and last recorded time James sat in Star Chamber, was when he heard the Lake-Exeter case in January and February 1619. When James appeared on the first day, he opened the proceedings with a short speech.

He explicitly compared himself to Solomon, and the dispute between Ladies Lake and Roos and the countess of Exeter to the story of the two women who both claimed a baby as their own.[8] Chamberlain reported the speech to Carleton:

> Among other thinges he compared himself to Salomon that was to judge between two women, (for so he saide he would parallel them as women) and to find out the true mother of the childe, (that is veritie) for which purpose he came furnished with all fit instructions wherby he might inform himself, but specially with equitie and unpartiall affection.[9]

James's careful explanation that he "parallel" the feuding women "as women," was necessitated by the fact that most early modern readers of the Bible understood the two women in the Solomon story to be prostitutes. (The previous year, the marquis of Hamilton had used the same analogy without any clarification, and hearing it Sir Arthur Lake and Lord Hay almost came to blows, incensed about the ladies being called "harlots.")[10] Given the accusations of adultery and incest against the countess of Exeter, James certainly did not want to add fuel to the fire and cast dispersions on the women's honor through his analogy. Nonetheless, the Solomon tale was too enticing: he would rather use it with a bit of explanation than not refer to it at all.

In his 1621 treaty on the history, jurisdiction, and operation of the Court of Star Chamber, the barrister William Hudson also noted James's sitting in the Lake-Exeter case as extraordinary, and that the king had acted in the case "with more than Solomon's wisdom."[11] Moreover, Hudson believed the king "pronounced a sentence more accurately eloquent, judiciously grave, and honourably just, to the satisfaction of all hearers, and of all the lovers of justice, than all the records extant in this kingdom can declare to have been, at any former time, done by any of his royal progenitors."[12] Hudson worked exclusively in the Court of Star Chamber throughout his career, and his name appears on some of the legal documents in the Lake-Exeter cases. Specifically, he assisted in the preparation of the answers of the earl and countess, George Gwilliams, and Elizabeth Gresham in Sir Thomas Lake, Jr.'s suit, and the earl of Exeter's complaint against the Lakes and their servants in the Cannons riot suit.[13]

Having Solomon sit in judgment over the fighting courtiers also gave the king a chance to repair the royal court's damaged reputation after the debacle of both the Overbury murder and the scandals engendered by the Lake and Cecil feud. As Alastair Bellany has aptly pointed out, the Overbury affair connected the court with insidious poisoning, harmful magic, illicit sex, and potential popish plots, and these connotations negatively affected the reputation of the early Stuart court for decades and beyond. Lady Roos's accusations against the countess of Exeter again provided evidence to the observing public that additional members of the courtly circle seemed rotten to the core. Bellany also argues that the king and his defenders attempted to counter the criticism appearing in libelous texts and songs after the Overbury scandal by instead emphasizing the king's role as a bringer of justice, a ruler who righteously punished misdeeds and forced sinners to repent and confess, thus enabling their potential salvation.[14] James could not change the fact that the Lakes and the Cecils had brought scandal to his court yet again, but he could attempt to counter its negative effects by re-emphasizing his role as a just lawgiver, this time by serving as a judge himself. The direct royal involvement in the trial certainly ensured that people would be paying close attention.

The Trial Day by Day

Normally, the court of Star Chamber sat only on Wednesdays and Fridays during terms. If there was pressing business, they sometimes met additional days, especially if the end of term was nearing. Early modern trials were notoriously short: Star Chamber usually heard several cases per day. By contrast, the three Lake-Exeter cases took up almost the entire three-week long Hilary term. The Lake-Exeter cases also required other scheduling adjustments. Normally, the morning session lasted for two hours, from nine to eleven, followed by a break for a lavish and elaborate midday meal. After this hefty dinner, the afternoon session commenced, presumably with a few sleepy participants.[15] During the Lake-Exeter trial days, the court began its sessions earlier in the morning and continued later. It does not appear to have met at all in the afternoons, no doubt to accommodate the king and not overtax him.

Since most of the Star Chamber judges were members of the Privy Council, many of the very same men who had investigated the accusations in the spring of 1618 now sat in the trial. In addition to the king, we know that Lake's colleague Secretary Naunton was also on the bench, joined by Sir Edward Coke (eminent lawyer and Exeter's son-in-law), Sir Fulke Greville (Commissioner of the Treasury), the Lord Chief Justice of the King's Bench Sir Henry Montagu,[16] John King Bishop of London, John Lord Digby (who served the king in negotiations for the Spanish match), Lord Chancellor Sir Frances Bacon (Lord Verulam), the Chief Justice of the Common Pleas

Sir Henry Hobart, Thomas Erskine Lord Fenton (Groom of the Stool to James, member of Privy Council, and a witness in the case.) Fenton was not present at the sentencing/censure, but he was there all the other days, according to Chamberlain.[17] Since this was an important case, other members of the Privy Council may also have been included among the panel of judges, but they are not specifically named in the sources describing the trial.[18] The lords sat at a table during the trial, whereas the king sat in a chair of state, elevated above the rest.[19]

In his treaty on the Star Chamber court, Hudson stated that the king was the sole judge when he sat in Star Chamber, and the other judges were mere advisers. He argued that Star Chamber provided the king's judgment, and normally, the judges were serving as the king's representatives. The judges were in effect reflecting the justice emanating from the king. When the king himself was present, the other judges did not have "any power to pronounce any sentence in this court, for the judgment is the king's only." Hudson specifically used the Lake-Exeter case as his example of this principle. As the sole judge, King James then had the power to decide this matter on his own, like Solomon, according to Hudson.[20] James expressed a similar view in the previous 1617 dueling case: he had come to Star Chamber specifically to "give judgment" and "sentence" against the duelers. Sir Edward Coke, who often clashed with the king on the issue of the royal prerogative, would not have agreed that James had such power in the court.[21] While James did pronounce the later sentence, the other judges still debated and voted on the verdict.

Since neither the lengthy witness interrogatories and depositions nor the decisions of the court of Star Chamber for this period survive, historians must use other sources to figure out what happened in court, including the final judgments. The main sources I am using to recreate the trials consist of abstracts of the evidence, arguments, witness testimonies, and the verdict that survive as copies in the State Papers.[22] In addition, several letter writers also described portions of the trial in various detail, the lengthiest one being a letter from John Harwood to Carleton on February 6, in which he described the first two days of the proceedings. Harwood, who attended the trial, also wrote a letter on February 16, summarizing the outcome and sentence. In addition, Carleton received letters about the trial from Secretary Naunton (February 4), Sir William Smith (February 13), Sir Thomas Wynne (February 14), Alexander Williams (February 15), and four from John Chamberlain (January 23 and 30, and February 6 and 13). Naunton was present at the trial, as he served as one of the judges. Chamberlain may have been present one or two of the court days, but otherwise he relied on reports of those who attended.

Thomas Lorkin also wrote to Sir Thomas Puckering about the course of the court cases on February 2, 9, and 16. As a result of this great interest, it is possible to follow the action day by day, almost like in a modern celebrity trial.[23]

The term officially opened on Saturday, January 23. On Wednesday, January 27, the court met to debate a contested issue regarding the first case to be heard: Lake v. Hatton. The king was not present on this day, but the countess of Exeter and Lady Roos attended. Chamberlain reported that Lady Exeter came accompanied by the countesses of Arundel and Bedford, and "a comitiva of I know not how many Ladies more to the number of almost thirty coaches." (The earl and countess of Arundel had been friends with Roos, meeting often in Italy during his travels. The earl of Arundel had also been the recipient of Roos's largess, having received Roos's collection of sculptures before he left for his embassy to Spain in 1616. Lady Bedford had been a favored and influential lady at court since the beginning of the Stuart reign, so to have her support was significant.) Lady Roos had a more modest show of support, but Chamberlain had heard that nonetheless "Secretarie Lake and his followers continue still confident." As evidence of this confidence, Chamberlain relayed yet another rumor of a remarriage for Lady Roos: she was going to marry John, Lord Paulet, heir to the marquis of Winchester and another of Exeter's grandchildren.[24] The rumor proved false.

The dispute about the Hatton case kept the court busy that day. The earl and countess of Exeter strove to get the Lake v. Hatton case thrown out altogether, before the trials formally began. They had tried this strategy as early as November the previous year, when Exeter's son, Sir Edward Cecil, went to Buckingham and requested that the Hatton case be cut "quite away from the rest of the business."[25] At that time, the king referred the matter to legal experts, who determined that the case should proceed.

In January, the Exeters approached the king and tried again to have the case removed from the rest or dismissed altogether. The king contacted the Star Chamber judges and authorized them to decide the fate of the Hatton case. The countess of Exeter argued that Lake should not be allowed to bring this suit, since he was not the injured party of Hatton's alleged actions. Furthermore, she insisted that Hatton had not in fact written any account of their non-existent conversation, so she believed the hearing of Lake's case against Hatton in open court would only serve to further damage her reputation with its outrageous and false tales.[26] Lake implored Buckingham to influence the king in the opposite direction. The Hatton case was crucial for Lake's strategy. He argued that Hatton informing his daughter about the countess's renewed plans of poisoning constituted the beginning of the whole process as far as he was concerned. The Exeter slander case against him could not truly be understood unless the Hatton case was first fully heard in court.[27]

The judges debated. Sir Edward Coke and Sir Fulke Greville argued that they dismiss the Hatton case, since the injured party (the countess of Exeter) was not the one who brought the suit of libel, and that Lake, as a third party, could thus not sue. Coke referred to a previous libel case, which had been thrown out and deemed "frivolous" because it was brought by a third party, who was not deemed immediately affected by the defamation. Sir Henry Montagu, Lord Chief Justice of the King's Bench, as well as Sir Henry Hobart, Lord Chief Justice of the Common Pleas, argued for hearing the Hatton case. They believed that even though Lake was not directly slandered in Hatton's alleged document, it did indeed concern him. If Hatton's document was deemed false, Lake would be considered the creator and spreader of a fraudulent, libelous document, as he was indeed accused of having done in the main slander case. When the judges voted on the matter, the Chief Justices' argument won, and the court ordered the Hatton case to proceed. In a nod to the countess of Exeter, the judges added that "nothing produced in court but what directly made for the proof of the thing in question, providing thereby that the honour of the lady might be salved."[28]

The king arrived for the opening of the formal hearing of the Lake-Hatton case on the following Wednesday, February 3. The king was present from nine am until past noon. After the king's short opening speech, the Lake v. Hatton case commenced and Lake's lawyers began presenting their case. In his letter to Carleton, Harwood judged that Lake's insistence that Hatton had indeed produced a written account of how the countess of Exeter had told him her desperate plans to poison Lady Roos and her father came across as "weakly proued," and the "circumstances soe unlikely as there was noe bodye beleaved any part of it."[29]

Furthermore, Harwood did not find that Lake's side had produced a reasonable explanation or motive for why Hatton would come up with this detailed and serious accusation against his own employer. The Lakes claimed that Hatton was "discontented" with the earl and countess but did not explain why. The Exeter lawyers deferred their answers to the Hatton suit until the next court day, when the main slander case would be presented, so as not to tax the hearers with unnecessary repetitions. No doubt, it also served as a protest against the case having been heard in the first place. At this time, the lawyers only reminded the king, judges, and the audience, that "there was an improbable tale toulde," and that it was "unsufficiently proved."[30]

On Friday, February 5, the second day of the case opened. On this day, the king and judges heard the main case: the earl and countess of Exeter's slander suit against the Lakes, Lady Roos, and Sara Swarton. The king attended from before eight am to one or two o'clock.[31] This case took two full days to hear: the Exeters presented their case and witness testimony on day one, and the Lakes and Lady Roos gave their counter argument on the second day. Clearly, the people attending court understood that this was the main case, as they took more detailed notes.

As the Exeter lawyers presented their arguments, they first needed to explain why Lady Roos and the Lakes would come up with such specific and serious accusations in the first place. Without a clear motive for the invention, people might be more likely to believe that there was some truth behind Lady Roos's dark stories. The lawyers thus told a tale of feminine fury and revenge. Their story began with the dispute over Walthamstow. The earl of Exeter did not agree to give Walthamstow to Lady Roos, was angry with his grandson for seemingly being tricked by the Lakes, and contemplated disinheriting him altogether. At this news, Lady Roos and/or Lady Lake tried to persuade the countess of Exeter to intervene with the earl to get him to accept the Walthamstow deals, which she refused to do. Lady Roos and/or Lady Lake became incensed and "thratyened to cast suche shame on her, as shee would repente she had not."[32] The scene was set for Lady Roos and the Lakes to invent their accusations. Thus began the relentless campaign to produce false witnesses and manufactured evidence to smear the countess.

Court observers sometimes melded the actions of Lady Lake and Lady Roos, as if it did not really matter which one of them did what. This behavior was especially notable in the discussions about the origin of the malice toward the countess of Exeter. In Harwood's February 6 account, Lady Lake was the one angered by the countess of Exeter's denial of assistance. Harwood recounted that the reason for Lady Lake's ire was that the countess would not persuade Lord Roos to retract the written account of his version of events at Cannons, and the larger story about Walthamstow. The witness Sir Thomas Holcroft (Roos's great uncle) elaborated further that Lady Lake was angry because the earl had called her a "Cozener."[33]

The State Papers trial abstract claims it was Lady Roos who first developed malice against the countess, based on the testimony of Lord Wentworth. In her answer to the Exeter complaint, Lady Roos described a meeting between herself and the countess of Exeter at Durham House after Roos had left England.[34] The Exeters' original complaint does not describe or deny any such meeting, or a particular date for the origin of the malice, only that the

Lakes and Lady Roos had become angry at the countess when she refused to pacify the earl regarding Walthamstow. The different accounts have the malice begin at various times. If it was Roos's writing about the Cannons incident that inspired Lady Lake's ire against the countess, it would date it to May 1617, before Roos left England. If the unsatisfactory meeting at Durham House caused Lady Roos's ill feelings toward the countess, it would be dated to August 1617, *after* Roos's flight.

Although the description of the origin of the malice is covered in some confusion, it does not seem to matter much to the observers of the trial. One of the women, or both, had developed the malice, and once present it festered and spread. Lady Lake's and Lady Roos's feminine fury burned as one destructive fire, their mother-daughter ties also making it unnecessary to be very specific. The idea of feminine evil running in the family, and especially in connections between mothers and daughters, was a familiar theme in early modern witchcraft accusations and trials, an easily recognizable pattern for those witnessing and describing the Lake-Exeter trials.[35]

After having established motive, the Exeter lawyers' focus remained on the defendants' alleged forgery of the two crucial documents: Hatton's written account of the countess's murderous intent and the countess's written confession. The Lakes and Lady Roos had shown these documents to both the king and others, and thus publicly libeled the countess. Since the Exeter side had deferred their answer in the case against Hatton the previous day, they began by arguing that Hatton's written account was forged. They pointed to physical evidence: the handwriting in the document did not match Hatton's, and the last name was spelled Houghton, whereas Hatton insisted he had never used that spelling. Furthermore, Hatton had consistently denied that he had ever said or written anything detrimental about the countess at various instances, including in front of the king with Lady Roos present, as well as during a full thirty-eight interrogations in Star Chamber over the course of the preparations for the case. The lawyers also brought up the fact that many reliable witnesses put Hatton in the countryside rather than in London during the period when Lady Roos claimed he had visited her at Charing Cross and provided her with the writing. In addition, the lawyers added that Hatton's social status made it unlikely that the countess had spoken to him about such private and delicate matters. Hatton, a mere servant to the Exeters, "was no fit man to advice a Countesse."[36]

The Exeter lawyers next moved on to disprove the countess's alleged written confession of adultery and attempted poisoning. First, they outlined witness testimonies, which denied that there had been an incestuous relationship between Lord Roos and the countess. They also denied that there had been any poison in the enema or syrup of roses Lady Roos took during the fateful summer at Wimbledon in 1616. Since none of that had happened, the countess would obviously not write a confession. The lawyers also asked the court and audience why, even if she were guilty, the countess would have ever written such a confession, as she would have placed herself at the mercy of Lady Roos? And why would Lord Roos have been present and agreed to the writing, which would "perpetually subjecte him to his wife," and have "utterly ruined his fortunes with his grandfather"? It made no logical sense, the lawyers contended. Furthermore, the date of the letter itself, June 15, made it impossible, since witnesses had placed Lord and Lady Roos outside of the house that afternoon when the meeting and the writing of the confession supposedly took place inside Wimbledon House. Furthermore, Sara Swarton was in London at that time, attending to Lady Lake who was in childbed, rather than hiding behind any hangings and overhearing confessions inside at Wimbledon.[37]

Physical evidence also proved that the confession was a forgery, the lawyers argued. Lady Roos claimed that the countess had written her confession on a piece of paper that Diego da Silva carried in his pocket, which meant that it would have been folded up. However, the document Lady Roos had presented to the king and Privy Council the previous year was written on a whole, unfolded piece of paper. Furthermore, as witnesses had declared, the handwriting did not match the countess's in other texts. The layout of the chamber at Wimbledon also proved that Sara Swarton could not have overheard the conversation between Lord and Lady Roos, Diego da Silva, and the countess while hiding behind some hangings. The king and some members of the council had even visited the room at Wimbledon and discovered that it was not possible to overhear at one end of the room what was said at the far end. Furthermore, the hangings, which had been in place for thirty years in that chamber, did not reach all the way to the floor. As a result, when a person stood behind the hangings, their feet and lower legs would have been visible to others in the room.[38]

The lawyers also presented witness testimony that Lord Roos had denied any adulterous relationship with the countess, and both Roos and da Silva denied that the countess had written a confession. For emphasis, Roos had made his denials "with many deep oaths" while in Rome and had professed his and the countess's innocence in front of an altar while in Naples, and again as he lay sick before his death.[39] Neither Roos nor da Silva ever answered formal court interrogatories or provided testimony under oath: Roos had died before the messenger with interrogatories reached him. Therefore, it is not entirely clear how Exeter's lawyers affirmed their statements regarding oaths in court.

As an added piece of evidence, the Exeter side also argued that Ladies Roos and Lake, and Sir Arthur Lake, had all "affirmed" that Roos was "insufficient" and had "no knowledge of his wife."[40] Consequently, it was physically impossible for Roos to have committed adultery with the countess. This last argument would probably not have suited Roos very much had he still been alive. However, since he was dead, the earl did not need to worry as much about Roos's sexual reputation being tarnished. (Unlike the earl of Essex, a dead Roos would not be able to remarry. In the annulment proceedings in 1613, Essex had to go to extraordinary lengths to prove that he was not impotent in general, but only unable to consummate his marriage with Frances Howard, as he wished to be able to marry again.) The Exeters were primarily concerned about clearing the countess's reputation. Roos's sexual reputation was collateral damage.

The next court day fell on Monday, February 8, when the Lakes and Lady Roos presented their counterarguments. The king, eager to hear the entire case, made sure to get the court started even earlier. He arrived at seven in the morning and stayed until noon.[41]

In response to the Exeter arguments, Lake's lawyers recounted witness testimonies, which did indeed place Hatton in London several times during the fall of 1617, as well as in Lake's London house in Charing Cross. Two persons of note deposed that Secretary Lake had told them about Hatton's written account in late November of 1617. The first of those was Thomas Erskine, viscount Fenton, the King's Groom of the Stool, Privy Councilor, and a judge in the case. The identity of the second witness, Michael Fortescue, is uncertain.

The lawyers also reiterated that witnesses had deposed that they had heard about the adultery of Lord Roos and the countess. Witnesses also stated that Lady Roos had received both an enema and syrup of roses while at Wimbledon and that she had become ill as a result. The lawyers bolstered the truth of the countess's confession by arguing that Lady Lake and her daughter Elizabeth Lake had overheard Lord and Lady Roos arguing about the affair, poisoning, as well as the countess's confession while they were at an inn in Ware, on their way to visit Burghley House in the late summer of 1616.[42] As to the challenges to the two documents, the lawyers dismissed the differences in the handwriting. Both Hatton and the countess had purposefully changed their handwriting, they claimed, precisely in order to be able to maintain plausible deniability.[43]

The Lakes and Lady Roos further argued that Roos's flight from England was a result of his fear that his grandfather would discover the affair. The lawyers presented as evidence witness depositions regarding what they considered a revealing letter from the countess to Lord Roos. In this letter, the countess expressed hopes of meeting Lord Roos at Spa. She also wrote that her "children's porcions were in his handes," suggesting that she had lent him money and thus aided his illegal flight out of England. The letter was intimately undersigned "your frend forever or everlasting frend Francis Exeter."[44]

A witness had seen this letter in Giles Dunscombe's trunk. Dunscombe, one of Roos's former servants, had originally been left behind when Roos left England. Roos had left without paying him his wages and other debts, so Dunscombe laid claim to some of Roos's property as compensation. According to his brother-in-law, he traveled to Italy in 1618 and remained there with Roos until his death, when he returned to England. Presumably, the letter had come into his possession while he was with Roos in Italy. Unfortunately, the letter no longer existed and could not be presented in court as evidence. Dunscombe admitted having had the letter but denied that the countess said anything about meeting Roos after her husband's death. He also claimed that the countess had made a copy of the letter, but seeing "how slightly she accounted of it, he was the less careful to keepe it" himself. Dunscombe had "carried it longe in his pocket, and in the end, he thinketh, lighted Tobacco with it."[45] The potential piece of evidence literally went up in smoke.

After three days of hearing, especially after the hearing of the main case, observers opined that it was going badly for Lake. Lorkin wrote Puckering on February 9: "Hitherto, matters have fallen very foul on Sir Thomas Lakes side, and the world prognosticates a very heavy censure."[46] Harwood believed that Lady Exeter had "the advantage of the cause" and Chamberlain judged that for "ought can be discerned yet the case is like to go hard on Sir Thomas Lakes side, and the proofs and allegations so weake that they fall of themselves to the ground. Hitherto they cast much fowle water one upon the other, but yt is thought the great Lady will easily wipe of the worst and go the cleerer away."[47]

On the fourth day, the court heard Sir Thomas Lake the younger's countersuit against the countess of Exeter. Again, the king showed up at seven am and remained until noon. The court observers did not mention this case much and the court abstracts do not distinguish it from the main case. Lake the younger's suit specifically accused George Gwilliams (Diego da Silva's servant) and Elizabeth Gresham (the countess of Exeter's gentlewoman) of having assisted in Roos's flight and in the countess's poisoning of Lady Roos, and the summaries of Gwilliams and Gresham's answers were included in the abstracts. This lack of interest, and combination of the cases, was likely because many of the details in this case were a rehash of the main case, only with the plaintiffs and defendants flipped.

Chamberlain found a comment by the king at the opening of the fourth day the most notable. King James "made a kind of apologie for himself as yf he had seemed partiall, protesting among things that in this cause he wold neither aske God not man forgiveness, for any partiall inclination on either side: there was straunge stuffe they say delivered, and indeed such as was not to be heard in such a presence insinuated in such a manner as was generally understood."[48] At the sentencing, this cryptic statement became clearer to those assembled.

The Witnesses

Observers found the Lakes' and Lady Roos's proofs and allegations weak because the only tangible physical evidence consisted of the alleged confession by the countess and Hatton's written account. The Exeter lawyers had picked those apart rather skillfully. The rest of the case was based on hearsay, rumor, and witnesses whose accounts were questioned for a variety of reasons. Since much of the case rested on the words of witnesses, it is crucial to take a closer look at who made up the witnesses, and how their testimonies were perceived and challenged.

The abstracts and notes of the main court case name eighty-eight witnesses, in addition to the named plaintiffs and defendants. Considering the vastness of the compendiums of records, there were probably many more witness testimonies that did not make it into the court-observers' notes. It is possible either to identify or to surmise the role of fifty-four of the witnesses, but it is not clear how the other thirty-four are connected to the case. The witnesses present a cross-section of early Stuart society, as well as the hierarchies that ensured that the words of some weighed heavier than others.

Given the intimate nature of the alleged crimes, it is not surprising that many of the witnesses were servants. Servants had information about the details of their masters' and mistresses' actions and behaviors in a way that was not possible for people outside the expansive households. Of the identified witnesses, a full thirty were servants either to the Lakes, Lord or Lady Roos, the earl and countess of Exeter, or Diego de Silva. Two were spouses of servants, and three relatives of servants. The witnesses represented the whole hierarchy of servants. The countess of Exeter and Lady Roos's gentlewomen,

women of gentry status who served mostly as companions and assistants doing lighter tasks, gave witness depositions, as did their chamber maids, and Ellen Picket, the nurse who attended Lady Lake's children. Servants on the lower end of the hierarchy also testified. For example, Elizabeth Prince, Lady Roos's laundress, Anne Pool, dairy maid at Wimbledon, and Daniel, a stable groom who worked for the Lakes, all testified. The female servants who attended to the physical needs of their employers mostly gave testimony about the alleged poisoning. The men's servants testified as well. Hatton and Gwilliams were the most important of the group. William Jones worked for Sir Thomas Lake, and often traveled to continental Europe on behalf of Lake's business. Giles Dunscombe and John Duppa were Roos's servants. The countess of Exeter had also employed Duppa at least temporarily, sending him to Brussels to contact Diego da Silva. Other male servants of both the Lakes and the Exeters are mentioned, but the documents do not specify their roles or duties.

Servants must have felt great pressure from their employers. A good servant performed the tasks their employers gave them to the best of their ability. A witness who was under oath was supposed to tell the truth. A servant might therefore find him or herself in a position when telling the truth and obeying their employer came into conflict. People at the time certainly believed that a servant who was loyal to his or her employer, or who had few means to support themselves outside of their service, was more likely to depose in favor of their employer.[49] A servant who did not was noteworthy: Exeter's lawyers pointed out when Lady Roos's own servants appeared to contradict their mistress's story. Mary Lake, Lady Roos's gentlewoman, had deposed that she never knew that Lady Roos had "taken a glister" or that she was sick while at Wimbledon, or that she had heard Sara Swarton remark that the syrup of roses smelled like roseacre, as the maid had said in her witness testimony (another servant, Alice Butler, contradicted Mary Lake's account). Likewise, Jane Ballard, a maid who slept in the same bed as Lady Roos while she was at Wimbledon, also claimed that she knew nothing of Lady Roos taking an enema, or that the enema had made her have bowel movements multiple times during the night afterwards. Elizabeth Prince, Lady Roos's laundress, also deposed that she had not noticed that Lady Roos was ill, and that she drank the remainder of the syrup of roses, left behind after Lady Roos had first drunk from the same glass.

Servant witnesses could also be manipulated by their employers. The Exeters argued that Sara Swarton was the most significant example. Having once been fired from Lady Roos's service for bad behavior, she was brought back for the specific purpose to be "a fit instrument for [the Lakes and Lady Roos] to worke upon and to imploy to the purpose" of providing false and fraudulent witness testimony.[50] The Exeter lawyers also objected to the testimony of the servant Lettice Williams, arguing that she was only sixteen years old, entirely dependent on the Lakes, and thus even more easily persuaded and influenced.[51]

Discontented and former servants were considered troublesome and unreliable witnesses. If they had developed ill will against their employers or former employers, they might make up stories with the intent to harm.[52] Servants had intimate information about their employers. The Exeters argued that Lakes and Lady Roos had homed in on both Gwilliams and Hatton as persons who could be of use in their plot against the countess, because they thought they were "discontented" with their employers, Diego da Silva and the earl of Exeter, respectively. In a similar fashion, the Lakes and Lady Roos argued that the testimony of Jane Miller, Lady Lake's former servant, could not be trusted, because she had parted on bad terms and had developed a "malice" against the Lakes. Another witness further testified that Jane Miller was a "slanderous woman, and a pilferer, and of suspicious behavior," implying that anything she said should be discounted.[53]

It was not uncommon for plaintiffs and defendants to pay the costs of witnesses who they asked to take time off, and/or travel, in order to attend court or to give testimony. The merchant Philip Watson from Rochdale went even further. He wrote to Lake in February 1619, requesting that he pay his travel costs to London, as well as for costs accrued for the writing of documents, his lost business during his time away from home, and damage to his credit and reputation, all as a result of his "attending the cause of Lady Lake and his daughter."[54] It is not clear what information Watson provided.

Paying the cost associated with testifying was acceptable. Paying people to give specific testimonies was obviously problematic. The Exeters argued that several of Lakes and Lady Roos's witnesses had been paid to give specific testimony. As mentioned in Chapter 9, Katherine Maynard, Lady Roos's former maid who was discontented because Lady Roos had not stood godmother to her child as she had promised, had received payment from the Lakes. The Exeters argued that the payment was in order to ensure that she testified in their favor. They also claimed the Lakes had paid witnesses to testify that Hatton had been in London in November, when he supposedly visited Lady Roos and told her about the countess's renewed poisonous plans.

The Exeters also accused the Lakes of using proxies to influence witnesses: Howard Strachie, an associate of Lake, had ensured a service position for a

Johan [Joan?] Davies, and then pressured her to provide information beneficial to the Lakes in return. It is not clear if Strachie was a servant, or client, but he was working on Lake's behalf. Similarly, the Lakes and Lady Roos claimed that Gwilliams had received £40 from the earl of Exeter after Roos had left. Furthermore, the earl "allowed him his diet in Exeter House," making Gwilliams now a dependent on Exeter and his testimony in his and the countess's favor questionable. Similarly, Frances da Silva had been given free lodging at Wimbledon for a month.[55] The countess of Exeter had also paid Mistress da Silva to travel to Brussels to meet her husband, so she certainly appears to have benefited from the Exeters' largesse.

A few tradesmen were also included, primarily to testify that they had seen Hatton in London during November and early December 1617, the period when Lady Roos claimed he had visited her and told her about the countess's renewed plan to poison her and her father. Hatton claimed he had been in Wiltshire to fetch his goods and take care of personal business before he commenced his service to Robert Smith. He said he had arrived in London three or four days before St. Andrew's Day (November 30), and that he had remained in Exeter House on the Strand after that.

A young barber claimed to have seen Hatton in London during the fall. He said Hatton had been his customer twice, first around All Saint's Day, and secondly toward the end of Michaelmas term. The Exeters objected to his testimony, because he was only seventeen, and therefore too impressionable, that he had been examined without oath, and that it was "not likely he should remember 10 months after the precise time when he trimmed a man he knew not." Edward Masters, a crossbow-maker, also claimed to have seen Luke Hatton in London, but only after having discussed the matter "with his wifes taylor." The tailor had in turn heard it from Lord Lisle, but then confessed that he did not really know anything about it at all.[56]

As in the case with Edward Masters, much of the evidence was based on hearsay, rumors, and secondhand information. Relatives and spouses of servants, as well as several of the unidentified witnesses, reported what they had heard said, rather than what they knew themselves, in their testimonies. Elizabeth Strachie can serve as an extreme example. She was probably the wife of Howard Strachie, who had solicited witnesses for Lake. Elizabeth Strachie testified that she "had heard Susan Dodson say she heard a report that the Lo: Roos said to his Lady Alas poor Nanne, thou have beene poisoned, I love thee too well to have thee poisoned." Robert James, father of Frances de Silva, Diego de Silva's wife, was a source of information as well. Others testified that they had heard James talk about his daughter's belief that

Lady Roos "was much wronged." Strachie also claimed to have heard Frances de Silva say that "there was unlawfull love between the Countess and L. Roos." The Exeter side objected to the testimony of hearsay, especially when witnesses later denied having said what others claimed they had told them.[57]

The Exeter side also depended on hearsay to some extent, as in when they were arguing that the countess had nothing to do with Roos leaving England: their witnesses, servants of Lord Roos, recounted what they remembered Roos telling them. However, the Exeter side did not resort to hearsay testimony nearly as much as the Lakes and Lady Roos.

In one case, the Exeters tried to discredit a witness because they insinuated that he was Catholic, and, it was implied, therefore not trustworthy. William Jones, Secretary Lake's servant had traveled abroad on his master's business. Jones testified that when he met Gwilliams in Brussels in the fall of 1617, Gwilliams had told him that Lord Roos and the countess had had an affair. Gwilliams later denied it. Joseph Boyle, who had also been in Brussels, observed that Jones and Gwilliams had met only briefly, and added that Jones had persuaded Gwilliams to go to Catholic confession, and that he had seen Jones "upon his knees before a crucifix." Furthermore, Jones had expressed a desire for "toleracion of religion" in England, allowing Catholics to worship freely. The treatment of Catholics in England was a very sensitive topic, generally not popular.[58]

Few of the witnesses came from the same social class as the earl and countess, or the Lakes and their daughter. Generally, witnesses of higher socioeconomic status did not testify to the main accusations, but rather more tangential matters. Thomas, Lord Wentworth (later earl of Strafford) deposed on behalf of the countess of Exeter, gave testimony about the malice Lady Lake bore to the countess as a result of the fight over Walthamstow, and because the earl had called her a "couzener," or a cheat and a fraudster. He also argued that the alleged confession was not written in Lady Exeter's handwriting, as did Sir Nicholas Tufton, Exeter's son-in-law.[59] Sir Thomas Holcroft testified that Lady Lake's malice began when Exeter called her a "cozener," since she had not ever mentioned the supposed adultery and poisoning before the fighting over Walthamstow began. Lady Anna Bamfield, whose connection to either party is not clear, deposed about what Katherine Maynard, former servant to Lady Roos, had told her about the innocence of the countess, and a reluctant Dame Constance Lucy deposed that she had overheard Judith Browne discuss having seen the letter from the countess to the Lord Roos that mentioned her meeting him at Spa.

Five medical doctors also appeared in court to provide testimony. Some had personal connections with those involved, and others provided expert testimony regarding the working of poisons. Dr. Winston had attended an ill Lady Lake in November 1617. He said he had seen someone in the Lakes' house that he later came to understand was Luke Hatton, although he did not know him at the time. Dr. Winston also said that "he found the Lady Rosse sicke about Michaelmas at London who complayned that she tooke her sicknes at Wimbleton." Dr. Atkins had attended Lady Roos as she had complained of feeling unwell when she returned from her summer at Wimbledon in 1616 but deposed that she had not mentioned anything about any poison at that time. He had administered cordials to her but had not given her any antidote for poison. Furthermore, he clarified that it was not possible to survive for a whole month if you had been poisoned with roseacre, unless you had been given an antidote sooner. Dr. Atkins, along with Dr. Mumford, Dr. Gwinne, and Sir William Paddy,[60] King James's personal physician, also all served as expert witnesses on poisons. They verified that the poison roseacre worked inwardly in the body, and could not produce a sore and scabby head, which had been one of Lady Roos's complaints.[61]

During the last week of the trial, Lake and Lady Roos went to visit the king "twice or thrice," in addition to writing him several letters. They may have tried to get an idea of which way the king was leaning, or ask about legal issues, or otherwise attempt to get an upper hand in the proceedings. Chamberlain, who reported this rumor, also added "yet if all I heard be true, within these few dayes the King said he was not for his service, that wold presume at this time in this cause to write him lies."[62] The king, it appears, had already made up his mind, and was not susceptible to being further influenced.

The Verdict

> But firste he [King James] stepps to act a monaches parte
> and to the Comforte of each English harte
> in the Starrchamber sitts in supeame sight
> and like a sun, dispelling vapours quite
> prevents the babblinge lawier, where he stands
> keepeinge the Judge from fowlinge of his hands.
> he still preserves the weaker from the greatter frowne:
> yea, to the Contrys honor, and faire joy,
> doth punish all who durst her peace annoy.
>
> From "Fortune's Wheel," an anonymous verse from 1623, commenting on the Lake-Cecil feud and trials[63]

The fifth day of the trial was set for pronouncing the verdict and sentencing. This also coincided with the very last day of the term. On Saturday, February 13, the judges voted and gave their opinion, and the king pronounced his—and therefore the court's—decision and punishments. It was a complete triumph for the countess of Exeter. The Lakes and Lady Roos lost in all three cases. The king explained his conclusions and assignation of guilt and blame as follows:

1. I find the Lady Lake to be the author of this fowl practice, in respect of the business of Walthamstow, then w.of there hath appeared no other grownd of malice in this whole trial and that was hers: and 2ly her speeches to Norgate at Ware and the [?] at Cannons, w.of were long before this suite commenced, doe declare that she was then hatching the accusations w.of afterward were published.
2. I finde the Lady Roos to be the Actor.
3. Sr. Tho: Lake the surety to Gwilliams and Katherine Maynard, and (w.of I am sorry for) to have abused the authority of his place in committing Gwilliams and Luke Hatton to prison in his own cause. It is to be presumed that he was seduced by his Eve but as it saved not Adams turne to say that the woman though gavest me but he was made to sweat for it so I thinke it just that Sr. Tho: should smarte for it.
4. Sr. Tho: Lake the younger [in his case against the countess of Exeter] the Accuser.
5. Sr. Arthur Lake a chief Abettor and accessory.
6. Sara Swarton an impudent and shameless instrument, who sweares what they say: and is convicted of perjury by demonstration.[64]

The king extended the biblical Adam and Eve analogy further. In James's analogy, Lady Lake was the serpent, the origin of evil who convinced Eve, or Lady Roos, to sin. In turn, Eve corrupted Adam, or Sir Thomas Lake, and made him do bad deeds as well.[65] Chamberlain, who was not present at the sentencing, switched the roles slightly, naming Lady Roos as the serpent, and Lady Lake as Eve instead, again demonstrating the merging of the roles of the two women in the minds of contemporaries.[66]

James had been wholly convinced of the Exeter argument that Lady Lake's malice against the countess stemmed from the disputes over Walthamstow, presumably because the countess had refused to influence the earl to accept the agreements Roos had made (under threats, as Roos claimed). In his judgment, James pointed out that "there hath appeared no other ground of malice in this whole trial." The king also ascribed most of the blame on Lady Lake, believing her to be the person who had made up the accusations against the countess, and then making her young daughter go along with the scheme. In other words, according to the king, Lady Roos had no other reason for malice, since the countess had never committed adultery with Roos, nor poisoned her. Somewhat confusingly, the king also argued that Lady Lake's tearful complaint to Edward Norgate in the late summer of 1616—that Roos would be the end of her daughter—provided evidence that Lady Lake had hatched the plans for the accusations against the countess of Exeter very early on. That supposedly happened well before the fights about Walthamstow commenced, so it seems contradictory for the king to point to it as evidence of plans of accusations, when he also claimed it was the later Walthamstow disputes that formed the basis of Lady Lake's malice.

King James clearly put the lion's share of the blame for the idea of the accusations against the countess of Exeter on Lady Lake and the carrying out of them on Lady Roos. Lake's crimes against the countess were of a different nature and seemed less severe to some of the judges. They debated whether Lake should have a lighter sentence. Lord Digby especially believed Lake's offenses milder, as did Sir Francis Bacon, the Lord Chancellor. True, Lake had abused his office by imprisoning Gwilliams and Hatton for his own purposes. However, he seemed innocent of the invention of the accusations of incest, adultery, and poisoning, as well as the creation of fraudulent documents. While the king certainly believed that Lake had been drawn into the whole feud as a result of the machinations of his wife and daughter, he did not think that he should be spared from punishment. Just as Adam had to carry the punishment for allowing Eve to persuade him to eat the forbidden fruit, Lake also should not escape punishment, but "smarte for it." The king told Lord Digby that he had to either vote to "cleere him yf he could or condemne him with the rest."[67]

In order to further explain his reasoning for the sentence, James told the court and audience that he had suspicions about Lady Roos's tales from the beginning. When he examined Lady Roos the previous spring, he had asked her if she would state her accusations against the countess of Exeter under oath. She initially agreed. The king ordered a Bible brought forth. However, Lady Roos "started back" from the holy book and refused to take the oath. The king dismissed her and called for Sir Thomas Lake to come and see him. James told Lake that Lady Roos had refused to take the oath and that Lake should "be advised what he did, and how far he listened to his daughter's speeches." Lake went home and "dealt with his daughter in private." Lake wrote a letter to the king in which he stated that his daughter was now ready to take the oath. He sent Lady Roos herself to deliver the letter. When the king again proffered Lady Roos the Bible for her to take the oath, she "started back as before, and refused [the oath] a second time." King James concluded that it was "an evident argument for a guilty conscience," and that although Lake had ample warning, he insisted that as a father and a husband, he needed to assist his wife and daughter in their troubles.[68] It was probably this knowledge that had led to the king's decision to preside over the trial in person the previous September and to send the cryptic message to the countess of Exeter that he would "disclose certain things which neither she nor her adversaries have dreamed of."[69]

The feud would now prove very costly for the Lakes and their daughter, as they had to pay both fines to the king as well as damages to the countess of Exeter and other persons deemed harmed by their libels. Seven letters and abstracts list the decision. The numbers for the fines and damages sometimes differ slightly (two letter writers, Harwood and Chamberlain, corrected their original reports in a later letter), but they mostly concur. All reports agree that Sir Thomas Lake and his wife were to pay a £5,000 fine each to the king, and that Lady Roos was fined at 10,000 marks.[70] The reported fine for Sir Thomas Lake the younger varies, however: perhaps a sign that observers did not consider this case as significant as the main one. Most reported a fine of 500 marks. Sara Swarton's fine is more difficult to ascertain. It is variously listed as £500, £100, or 500 marks. Any of these sums would have been enormous for a servant. In addition to fines to the king, the Lakes also had to pay damages to the injured parties. The countess of Exeter was to receive a combined £4,000 (£3,000 from Sir Thomas Lake, Mary Lake, and Lady Roos, and an additional £1,000 from Sir Thomas Lake the younger). Luke Hatton was awarded £500, George Gwilliams £200, and Elizabeth Gresham £100. Lorkin totaled the cost to the Lakes at £22,331 6s 8d. The court also decided that Lake should pay the countess of Exeter's court costs, which added £3,400 more.[71] Sanderson claimed that Lake had told him the cases cost him a total of £30,000.[72] In 2022 value, it would have been more than six million pounds.[73]

Sir Arthur Lake, Lady Roos's brother, had also been named in the slander suit, but although James believed he was an "abettor" and an "accessory" to the crimes, the judges felt that there was not enough evidence of his guilt. As a result, he did not have to pay any fines, damages, or suffer other punishments.[74]

The punishments were not just financial. Sir Thomas Lake, Mary Lake, and Lady Roos were also to be imprisoned in the Tower at their own charge. Some reported that the imprisonment was supposed to be "for life" or "perpetual," whereas others said it was to be "during the king's pleasure." The three were also to make a public submission and recognition of their faults and crimes in the Star Chamber and, more significantly, in the presence of the countess of Exeter. This was a shaming mechanism, meant to humble and humiliate the sinners, and to restore the damaged reputation of the countess.

Sara Swarton's additional punishments were very heavy. Swarton, of a lower social class than her employers, would also be subjected to physical punishment. She was to be imprisoned in the Fleet. On two separate days, she was to be whipped through the streets. The sentence specified that this would happen on market days, which would be busy, crowded days and therefore inflict maximum shame and humiliation. One day she was to be whipped from the Fleet westward, toward Westminster, and the other day from the Fleet eastward, toward Cheapside, maximizing her exposure. She would be branded with the letters FA on each cheek, signifying to all who ever met her that she was a False Accuser. After this, she was to be sent to Bridewell prison for life. Swarton's severe punishments certainly show the stark inequities between socio-economic classes. Her sentence was not unique, but rather common for convicted perjurers of her social standing.[75]

The sentence was also an incentive for Swarton to turn on her employers: she was told in court that none of these horrifying punishments had to happen at all if only she revealed all that the Lakes and Lady Roos told her to say and do.[76] In the courtroom, Lady Lake told Swarton to "redeem herself [...] upon any condition, without regarding them at all," which Chamberlain found both "craftie and malicious counsaile," suggesting that Lady Lake was trying to guilt Swarton into silence. Sir Thomas Lake also told Swarton that he "wisht her to be constant in the truth, but whether she did or no, she shold not want while he lived." In other words, the Lakes were trying to bolster Swarton, ensuring that she would stick to the tales she had told to the court all along.[77] The pressure campaign against Swarton continued in the weeks after the trials concluded.

The King's Big Secret

King James was keen on being viewed as a wise Solomon, and he was also fond of exposing frauds and falsities.[78] King James had explained in court that he had suspected that Lady Roos was lying since she had refused to take an oath the year before. However, the king did *not* share the fact that Lady Roos *had already confessed* privately to him that the countess's confession, as well as Hatton's document, were both forgeries! She had done so at some point over the Christmas holidays, which meant that James knew about the forgeries before the trial of the cases formally began, although not before he had decided to sit in Star Chamber. This situation is quite remarkable: *King James went into the trials already knowing that Lady Roos had confessed to forgeries.* When Lady Roos made this confession, Prince Charles, Buckingham, and Secretary Naunton were also present at the time. Naunton sat as a judge in the trials, but never mentioned it.

The king did not even reveal this confession during the verdict and sentencing. In fact, he did not reveal it at all until almost half a year later, in June 1619. The king then explained that he had kept Lady Roos's confession to himself, since it had been "extraiudiciall [extrajudicial]." He did not bring it up in court, but rather let the two sides present their cases. Ever concerned about the appearance of justice and impartiality, the king wished the rest of the judges to hear the case unprejudiced and to come to their own conclusions.[79] It is perhaps because he had this knowledge that he at one point let slip a comment during the second day of the trial, when the Exeters were laying out their evidence of the impossibility that the countess had written a confession. According to Harwood, James then muttered "he verily believed all was counterfeite."[80]

One cannot but wonder how Lady Roos felt going into Star Chamber, where her parents and brothers were fully invested in proving her right, her father's career hung in the balance, her family's honor and finances depended on the outcome, and yet knowing she had already confessed to the forgeries to the king. It must have been incredibly stressful for the still very young woman, only eighteen at the time of the trial. The Lake lawyers had tried to excuse her father and her brother as much as possible. Perhaps this was at the behest of Lady Roos, who wished to protect them from getting deeper into trouble as a result of her actions. It could also be the result of Lake trying to insulate himself from the actions of his wife and daughter, but it seemed a bit late for that. On the second court day of the main case, Lady Roos's lawyers had pointed out that the Exeter bill did not cite any specific crimes for Sir Arthur Lake, so there was no need to provide answers on his behalf. The lawyers also emphasized that George Gwilliams was the sole witness against Lake, and that since he had malice against him, his testimony should be discounted. Lake had only held and questioned Gwilliams about Roos's illegal flight from England, and that was it. Furthermore, Lake could "not be fond to be the author of the lybell, for that is was brought here by the Lady Roos."

He also did not "publishe the writing till after complaint made thereof to the king."[81] Lake's involvement with the countess's confession was therefore after-the-fact, and even then, minimal. As the king made clear during the verdict and sentencing, it did not matter. Lake had chosen to pursue a matter that dishonored a noblewoman and her powerful husband, and he had to pay the price.

The conclusion of the trial on February 13 occurred almost exactly three years after the marriage of Roos and Anne Lake, a fact not lost on keen observers. After noting the verdicts and sentences in the Lake-Exeter Star Chamber cases in his diary, William Camden also added "It should be noted that this sentence was passed on the 13th of February, while on February 12, 1616, the marriage of Baron Roos with Lake's daughter was celebrated with great joy."[82] The Lakes and the Cecils had been so keen on the match then, Roos outmaneuvering his friend Sir Thomas Puckering to get his bride, and his father moving up the wedding day to make sure that there were no snags. Three years later, all parties probably thoroughly regretted having played a role in the making of that fateful marriage.

12
Fallout

> This business was one of the foullest matters that hath fallen out in our tyme, soe as my Lady Ross was counted a most odious woman.
>
> Anne Clifford's diary, February 1619[1]

After the trial, Sir Thomas Lake immediately set about trying to undo the damage of the legal losses, with little success. The trial did not spell the end of the king's desire to get to the truth: he was especially troubled by rumors that he had favored the earl and countess of Exeter during the trial, and punished Lake excessively. On royal orders, Privy Councilors continued to probe, wanting to establish exactly who was behind the creation of the fraudulent documents. Sara Swarton came under further pressure to confess, as did Lady Roos. Lady Lake and Lady Roos quickly became the public villains in the affair, and rumors and accusations about immoral behavior now focused on them rather than on the countess. For several months after the trials, the pressure on the Lakes, Lady Roos, and their associates was unrelenting. By the summer of 1619, the situation improved slightly for those willing to confess and submit fully. For those who did not, the pressure campaign continued, although it was applied most heavily to female offenders.

A Secretary Replaced, a Family Disgraced

With the conviction and sentencing complete, the king swiftly removed Lake from his post as royal secretary. He had not performed the full duties of his office since the previous summer, but now he lost the position altogether. James sent the Privy Counselor Sir Julius Caesar to fetch the royal seals and official documents from Lake the day after sentencing. The royal seals were both symbols of office and the practical tools of the secretary, affixed to the official royal correspondence.[2]

Several people had been angling and positioning themselves for appointment to secretary if Lake fell, Carleton included. Campaigning from a distance at The Hague was difficult, but Carleton's friends were busy trying to bring it to

Family and Feuding at the Court of James I: The Lake and Cecil Scandals. Johanna Luthman, Oxford University Press.
 DOI: 10.1093/oso/9780192865786.003.0012

pass. Carleton's regular correspondents needed to enlist others in the cause. Sir William Smithe said on February 13 that he would "move my noble Lady and frend the Countesse of Buckingham," Buckingham's mother. He also hoped that Elizabeth Cecil, Lady Hatton (Exeter's daughter) "and your other more powerful frends will also take hold of this opportunity for yor advancement."[3] Encouragingly, Thomas Wynne told Carleton that he had heard "a gentleman of good understanding offered to lay two to one on youre Lordshipp against any man that could be named." Nevertheless, he wished Carleton "weare present heare at this time," as he understood it would be more advantageous.[4] Harwood thought that the place would be up between Endymion Parker (one of Buckingham's men) and Carleton.[5]

Carleton's hopes were not realized at this time either (he did become Secretary of State eventually, but not until 1628, in the reign of King Charles I). The king instead picked Sir George Calvert, Clerk of the Privy Council; a choice no one had really expected. The king made the decision without much discussion with others. Chamberlain had heard that a new patent was drawn up for the new secretary two or three days before the announcement, but the name had been left blank at that time.[6] Harwood had not heard Calvert mentioned at all until after the conclusion of the Star Chamber case. Apparently, not even the friends of the favorite Buckingham, like the countess of Exeter, knew of it until two days after the sentencing. The victorious countess had invited Buckingham to supper, and when she pressed him about the secretaryship (perhaps on Carleton's behalf), Buckingham divulged that the king had already decided it was to be Calvert's.[7]

Calvert himself found out a few days before the announcement. He had neither sought nor expected the promotion: he was unsure if he was the right man for such a lofty and powerful position. The king was very pleased with Calvert's humility, which he found refreshing compared to the fierce ambitions of so many at court. The king also questioned his new secretary-to-be about his wife. The king was tired of troublesome wives, like the countesses Somerset and Suffolk, and Lady Lake. On the third day in the Star Chamber trial, the king had opened the day by admonishing those present that state secretaries, or those who wished to be state secretaries, should "not impart matters of state to theyre wifes."[8] When the king asked, Calvert responded that his wife "was a goode woman and had brought him ten children, and wold assure his Majestie that she was not a wife with a witness." In other words, she behaved in such a way that no one could find any fault with her. Chamberlain believed that this "and some other passages of this kind, seeme to shew that the King is in a greate vaine of taking downe highhanded women."[9]

Historians have often pointed out that King James found assertive women problematic, but it is more appropriate to say that King James did not like women who asserted themselves against him specifically. For example, he liked the Countess of Buckingham, although she was quite forceful in arranging her children's marriages. Likewise, the king enjoyed the company of Lady Hatton when she conformed to his wishes, although he found her more tiresome when she did not.[10]

After the removal of both Suffolk and Lake within a year, the last major vestiges of the Howard faction, it seemed as if Buckingham reigned supreme and controlled the patronage of the court. Indeed, Calvert automatically assumed that it was the powerful Buckingham who had assured his appointment and sent him a jewel as a thank-you gift. However, Buckingham returned the gift, saying that he had nothing to do with Calvert getting the job. James made the choice of Calvert on his own, without Buckingham's input. (Buckingham had pushed to get his own man, John Packer, as the next secretary.) Like Lake, Calvert did not come from a notable family, had served as an administrator in various roles at court for years, having begun his career with Robert Cecil, earl of Salisbury, as his main patron. Unlike Lake, Calvert was a skilled linguist, and had traveled in Europe extensively, the king and Salisbury making use of him for various shorter diplomatic missions. He was from a Catholic family but had converted to Anglicanism in his youth. In Calvert, James found a devoted, hard-working, and competent administrator, who after Salisbury's death did not have any overt ties to any faction at court: he served only the king's interests. A few years later, Calvert's lack of a patron would make it increasingly difficult for him to do his job and he eventually resigned his position in 1625 and reconverted to Catholicism.[11]

On the Monday immediately after sentencing, Sir Thomas Lake, who perhaps refused to realize the severity of his situation, petitioned the king. He asked for mitigation of his fines and damages and requested that he might be placed in house arrest in his own house instead of the Tower. The king thought Lake's requests impertinent. He replied, "for what concerned himself, yt was yet too earlie dayes to make such a motion." By asking the king to change his mind right away, Lake challenged the king's decision only two short days after he made it. The king also emphasized that "for the cost and damages he had nothing to do with them for they belonged to another," that is, the countess of Exeter. Soon thereafter, Lake also wrote to the earl of Exeter and his countess and asked that they "remit and forgeve the costs and damages awarded them" by the court. Like the king, the Exeters were not at all in a forgiving mood and promptly rejected the request.[12]

The king was frustrated that Lake tried to diminish the severity of his actions in his petition and "in a sort justifie himself as not privie to any unlawfull practise." Lake argued that it was true that there had "been set forth many probably reasons to induce his Matie thereunto the justnesse and equity whereof he would not dispute, yet he doubted not but tyme would otherwise resolve his Matie of his innocense."[13] Castle informed Trumbull that Lake had "thereby so extreamely incensed his Maties indignation that he is not like to receave any confort in these demands."[14]

Lake also had supporters who agreed and thought Lake's sentence unjust and overly harsh. Similarly, when the king removed Lake's patron the earl of Suffolk as Treasurer the previous year, some believed that the king had reacted too harshly against the nobleman, thinking that it was mostly the countess of Suffolk who was at fault. The king and council decided on trying the earl and countess of Suffolk in Star Chamber, to publicize the egregiousness of Suffolk's faults and justify the king's actions.[15] Lake had now been publicly tried and found guilty, and yet some still insisted that the king should be more lenient. In response, the king requested that the two chief justices "examine the matter to the bottome," so that no one would be able to say that the king had somehow mistreated or wrongly convicted Lake.[16]

An aspiring Solomon, James was very sensitive to suggestions that he had not been just. In an April 11 sermon at St. Paul's meant to give thanks for the king's recovery after a severe illness previously that spring, the bishop of London "celebrated the king with well-deserved praises," especially for "his justice equitably dispensed to every man." Continuing, the bishop explained that "the King said in the Star Chamber, that even if he suffered from other human frailties, nevertheless he has had a sincere reverence for justice, nor does he have cause to ask forgiveness from God for his injustice."[17] The king wanted to ensure his subjects that he was certain that he had made the correct decision.

The trials had also become infused by religious politics, presenting another reason why the king did not want to have this decision questioned. During the trial, King James had been informed that Lake's cause was favored by English Catholics abroad. Catholic exiles, who perceived Lake as supportive of greater religious toleration, did not want to see him removed from his position. Castle reported "an opinion" that Lake's offenses went deeper than just a plot to dishonor the countess of Exeter, hinting at some issue that "hath a further bottome wch shall in tempor suo be untwisted," and that the discovery of this offense would "strip him of the most he hath." Castle was vague, but clarified by saying that there "was good reason that the Engl. Papists about

Brussels should make their prayers for his good success in his great affairs in Starchamber; for it is believed here that they had not a greater friend in Engl[and]."[18] Thomas Wynne reported that Lake's success was "prayed for att Lovayne," where a convent with Catholic English nuns had been established by 1609.[19] Harwood also mentioned the prayers for Lake at Louvain and Trumbull informed the king that exiled English Catholics in Brussels prayed daily for Lake to win in court.[20]

James was not happy about this news. During sentencing, the king made clear that Catholics should not be looking for favors from him. He told the judges that moving forward in their work, they should "have special care of the papistes and likewise of their wifes for he sayd the women weare the norishers of papistry in this Kingdome and that a papist woman and a whore weare voces convertibles wch oure Catholique ladies take very ill."[21] Harwood argued that the Catholics of England, who initially had "flocked" to support Lake's side, in the end were "ashamed of their cause," once they learned of the fraudulent documents.[22] Castle drily commented that the English Catholic exiles must have been "either without faith, or directed [their prayers] to the wrong Saint."[23]

On the evening of the same day Lake petitioned the king, coaches came to take him, his wife, and his daughter to their imprisonment in the Tower. According to Chamberlain, one of the ladies resisted and "was faine to be carried as yt were by violence into the coach; a thing usual to such insolent natures, that can neither beare prosperity nor adversity."[24] The three were imprisoned separately in the Tower, not allowed to meet or communicate with each other. They were also held as "close prisoners," meaning they were not to have contact with anyone without the king's or the Privy Council's express permission.[25] Lake's friend Sir Nicholas Fortescue, his secretary William Lake, and his solicitor were granted limited access. Even as close prisoners, wealthy people of the elite were not alone: they were allowed to keep servants. Some servants were willing to stay with their employers in prison, but others did not like it. For example, Lettice Williams came to the Tower to continue to serve Lady Lake there. By early May, she wished to "go to her frends and leave her said attendance at the Tower" and asked for permission to do so from the Privy Council. A warrant shows they granted her request, and one assumes that Lady Lake was allowed to replace Williams with another servant.[26]

Now separated from her employers, Sara Swarton was sent to Fleet prison instead of the more prestigious Tower. At the behest of the king, Privy Councilors examined her again and pressured her to provide more details and admit her role in the forgeries. They reminded her that the harsh sentence would be remitted if she only confessed fully. At first, she remained steadfast and silent. When the cart stood ready to bring her to the pillory and the jeering crowds in Westminster, and the whip and branding irons were shown to her, her resolve weakened. She asked to speak to Sir Henry Montagu, Lord Chief Justice. Once he arrived, she began to confess. She said that Lady Roos had bound her to an oath to keep her secrets, and that she had received the sacraments to seal that oath. She admitted that the countess's confession had been forged but refused to say who had written it. She also admitted that she had not been standing behind any hangings in Wimbledon while the countess confessed, but rather that she had been in London at that time.[27]

She still insisted that Hatton's document was real and not fraudulent. The oath she had taken troubled her conscience: she did not know how much she could reveal without completely breaking it. Oaths weighed heavily for most early modern people, especially if sealed with a sacred object or ceremony. Swarton asked to speak to a preacher, who might be able to advise her in her ethical dilemma. She requested to consult with Rev. Nicholas Guy, which the Privy Councilors allowed. After meeting with Guy, Swarton stopped confessing. She would only admit that the forgeries and false accusations were the inventions of Lady Roos, and that Sir Thomas and Lady Lake were not to blame. Annoyed at this turn of events, the Privy Councilors were frustrated to learn that not only was Rev. Guy Swarton's uncle, but that he was also Lake's chaplain, and therefore perhaps not an entirely impartial spiritual adviser in the matter. Moreover, he was probably a "popish priest" or "a papist," which made him even more suspect, Chamberlain and Harwood both surmised.[28] Clearly, the Privy Council would need to continue the pressure on Swarton, as well as her employers.

The Most Odious of Women

Having now lost the trials, the Lakes and Lady Roos became the clear villains in the story. As the coaches drove them from their house in Charing Cross across town to their imprisonment at the Tower, George Gerrard described to Carleton that "she was cursed heavily by the people as she went along," although he did not specify if he was referring to Lady Roos or Lady Lake.[29] This merging of the identities of mother and daughter had begun during the trial and became even more notable in the reactions in the months that followed.

Lady Roos and Lady Lake became the bad women who had led others astray, like the serpent and Eve in the biblical analogy the king had made at sentencing. Accusations of sexual impropriety were now levied against Lady Roos and her mother. The origin of those rumors was Katherine Maynard, the former maid who was angry with Lady Roos, had provided opposing witness testimonies, and had received payments from Sir Thomas Lake the younger and Lady Roos. Harwood said Maynard's stories described Lady Roos as "the most beastly whore that can be" and that it was not "modestlye to write the particulars."[30] Castle informed Trumbull that there "are some great persons that have been in question about their carnall acquaintance" with Lady Roos.[31]

Anne Clifford was more descriptive and recorded in her diary that "there was spoken extraordinarie fowle matter of my Lady Ross, & reports went that among others she lay with her own Brother," Sir Arthur.[32] Chamberlain believed it was Sara Swarton who had turned on her mistress instead, telling tales "so filthy as is not to be named," and that "incest which they would have imposed upon others returns on their own heads, betwixt her brother Sir Arthur and herself."[33] Likewise, Castle told Trumbull that the "incuba" Swarton "delivered likewise strange tales of the private carriage of the Lady Rosse (wch have a fowle sent)."[34] Considering Swarton's reluctant confessions, however, it seems more likely that Harwood was correct: Maynard was the origin of the sexual rumors, and Chamberlain and Castle mixed up the maids.

The rumors about an incestuous relationship between Lady Roos and her brother Arthur did not just affect the two of them. Anne Clifford, who was good friends with Arthur's wife Lettice, noted sadly that "these foul matters did double the miserys of my Lady Lettice Lake, in her unfortunate match."[35] In addition to suffering from the disturbing rumors about her husband, Lettice also fell severely ill. There had been a virulent outbreak of smallpox in London since the previous fall, and many had fallen ill, including Arthur.[36] Rumors circulated that it was not smallpox afflicting Arthur's wife. Chamberlain reported that "Sir Arthur Lake and his wife lie sweating (they say) of another kind, yt beeing yet in question among frends on both sides whether the Lady had them by his guift, or by her owne purchase."[37] Chamberlain was referencing the French pox, the term the English often used for syphilis. Sir Arthur had recovered from his illness, but Lettice did not. On May 3, Clifford noted that around "2 or 3 o'clock in the morning," her dear friend Lettice died, "having been grievously tormented a long time with pains & sores which broke out in Blotches, so that it was reported she died of the French disease."[38] Camden and Chamberlain also concurred that it was the

French pox that killed her, although Lorkin reported that she died in childbed instead, and made no mention of any other diseases.[39] For those observing the Lake and Exeter feud, Lady Lettice's death was interpreted as a continuation of the downfall of the Lakes. Chamberlain noted that her death was "not the least *crève couer* [heartbreak] to the father [Sir Thomas] to see the fruites of so graceless a generation."[40]

Maynard's tales about Lady Roos's sexual immorality found a willing audience: when people found out that Lady Roos was guilty of lying and of imagining the sensational poisoning and subversive sexual crimes, they were also more than willing to entertain that she had committed similar sexual sins herself, even though there had been few such rumors or accusations against her previously. The only mention of any sexual impropriety had been in Lady Roos's second complaint against Sir Peter Chapman in the property case in early 1618. Lady Roos accused Chapman of having spread a rumor that she had become pregnant after her husband left England. Chapman denied it, and no one else seemed to have picked up this rumor: it is never mentioned in the trials by any other witnesses. In his letter to King James written shortly before he died, Lord Roos mentioned that he would reveal information that would prove that Lady Roos "ought not to be my wife," but he did not elaborate on what he meant then and had no time to elaborate later.[41]

Libelous poems also circulated, one portraying Lady Roos as a woman whose vigorous sexual acts with men made her lose her mirkin, or pubic wig, an object usually connected with prostitutes at the time:

A Lybell upon the Ladie Rosse

Waste not a signe that courtly Rosse should fall
When that her Mirkine lost his Coronall
What tricke in dancing could the devil produce
Too fitte her too a haire and make it loose
Twas no Caper for she hath ofte bene boulder
When she advancte her legge on one mans shoulder
Sure some crosse pynte for in open waye
her Mirkine nere was foundered or made straye
who had the harder chance I praye you reade
the Page that founde or she that lost her bearde.[42]

This verse does not specify or name a sexual partner or partners for Lady Roos, but instead provides a more general accusation of sexual promiscuity. After the conclusion of the case, Lady Roos was clearly marked as a bad, immoral woman. Since bad women were more likely to be sexually impure, according to seventeenth-century beliefs, the readers of the verse did not need a specific accusation to believe that Lady Roos was promiscuous.

Lady Lake, who like her daughter had not been accused of any sexual improprieties before or during the proceedings, also became the object of rumors of sexual voracity. A couple of months after her conviction, Chamberlain forwarded reports that Lady Lake was "not doing well in the Tower, because she grows impatient, some say immodest, for want of her husband (as she pretends) or somebody else."[43] Several poems also circulated about Lady Lake, which depicted her as a "woe-to-man," a "staine of weoman kind," a "bitch of court," a "nurse of vice," who loved "Rideing [having sex]," the last punning on Lady Lake's maiden name, Ryder.[44] When the Star Chamber verdict stated that she had lied and perpetuated a forgery, her contemporaries connected her bad speech and her perceived unfeminine, domineering ways with sexual insatiability.

Verse libels also focused on Lady Lake as greedy, unreasonable, immoral, malicious, domineering, prideful, and every other sort of trait that was considered especially bad in women. One verse also emphasized the Lakes' Catholic and Spanish connections, specifically accusing Lady Lake of being a Spanish spy:

Encomium infamissime et infande Cuiusdam Mulieris ignote
Here lyes the breife of badness vices nurse
The badge of usurie the clergies curse,
The staine of weomen kind, tradsmens decay
The patroness of prid, Extortions highway
The forge of slaunder, and each vile action

Frend to Romes whore, Spy to the Spanish faction
A bitch of Court, a comon stincking snake
Worse then all these, Heere Lyes the Ladie Lake.[45]

No doubt the writer of the verse was aware of Lake's support among Catholics abroad, and perhaps also of his friendship with Gondomar and his Spanish annuity. This connection with subversive persons also colored Lady Lake's post-trial reputation.

It is interesting that the rumors or verse libels never mention the actions and connections of the dead person at the center of the feud: Lord Roos. After all, he was the one person who indisputably loved everything Spanish, fled England for Rome, fraternized with English Catholics in exile, spent time with cardinals and other high representatives of the Catholic church, and indeed converted to Catholicism. However, Roos's Catholic connections did not "attach" themselves to his family in general, or to the earl and countess of Exeter more specifically. After Roos's death, his sins were largely forgotten.

Another verse about Lady Lake did not wish to call her a "whore," yet managed to list most other sins:

Heere lyes the breife of badnes vices nurse
Greedie, Envious, malitious proud unstable
Suborner, Plotter, no waies tractable
Forger of Mischeifes, vertues onely Foe
Usurer Mynion Contriver of woe
The nurse of vice, I will not say a whore.

In order to make sure that the reader knew exactly who the author intended, the last verse clarified:

Lyes nowe demancd confin'd with in the tower
A place too good for such a one to take
Who list to knowe her, tis the Ladie Lake.[46]

Another verse, which Alastair Bellany has interpreted as referring to Lady Lake, argued that her character and action was too problematic for ballad writers to even contemplate, as hearers would think it "distastfull."

Say, no man living would vouchsafe a verse
when thou are dead, to hang upon your heirse.
or that the Tyburne poet should refuse
in thy bad cause, to interest his muse.
thinking, thy bawdy story in a Ballet

would be distastfull to ech herbwives pallet.
yet sure on earth, thy fame should longer dwell
then that of scoares of women that live well
now you came you are in that place
I wish for more imbellishing you raise.

According to this poet, Lady Lake's vices had made her even worse than the most infamous of Tower prisoners and female criminals: Overbury's murderer, Frances Howard Carr, the Countess of Somerset. Even though she had had been pardoned and her death sentence commuted, she, her husband, and their little daughter remained in the Tower.

> You match with her, that lyke hath never met
> Till you came there, to find out S. [Somerset]
> Who had the reputation, to be worst
> Ere this came from hells lake where she was nurst.[47]

It is also possible that this last line means that the verse was referring to Lady Roos instead of to her mother. Like Lady Lake, Lady Roos was also in the Tower, and the character was "nurst" or brought up at "hells lake," rather than being the hellish lake itself.

After Lady Roos was found guilty of forgery and false accusations, some commentators began to react to her with alarm and disgust rather than finding the details of the case titillating and sensational, as they had before the trials. Hearing the rumors about alleged incest and other sexual accusations against Lady Roos, Chamberlain told Carleton that "yf but the tenth part of that be true which is commonly reported, I have not heard of so forward an ympe, and yt was more than time that such a cockatrice shold be crushed in the shell."[48] A cockatrice was a mythical beast, a monster, a snake-like dragon with a rooster's head, which could kill both animals and humans by simply staring at them. They hatched out of so-called "cock-eggs," yoke-less eggs, which early modern people believed were laid by roosters. In order to prevent the hatching of such a menacing monster, the eggs needed to be crushed immediately. Chamberlain found the young Lady Roos a dangerous woman, altogether bad. She needed to be stopped before she developed into a full-fledged monster, killing people at will.

Further Confessions

The spring of 1619 became a dark time for the royal court. Queen Anna, who had suffered from intermittent illnesses for years, grew worse. She died on March 2. Although he had visited her earlier, the king was not present at her death bed, nor did he attend her funeral, because he himself fell gravely ill. Many courtiers believed grief over the queen's death and the reminder of his and his loved ones' mortality affected the king. He grew so weak that doctors feared he might not survive. By May, he finally improved somewhat, and in early June, he returned to London in "gallant" garb, a light blue satin suit with silver lace and a blue and white feather in his hat. Chamberlain reported that people were relieved that their king seemed much improved in health, but also noted that he looked "more like a woer than a mourner." They wondered what those ambassadors who had come to bring condolences to the king upon the queen's death would think about the king's lack of mourning dress.[49] Naunton informed Trumbull on June 11 that the king had hunted from four in the morning until seven at night, wearing out both men, horses, and dogs in the process, yet looked as well the day after as "he did any time these seven yeares."[50] The king was past danger.

During the preparations for the queen's funeral and the king's illness and recovery, the Privy Council continued to carry out their orders to get to the bottom of the forged documents, so that further details could bolster the king's justice and sentences. Full confessions and public repentance formed important aspects of early modern justice. An unrepentant criminal who refused to admit fault did not serve as an example to others and did not heal the broken and frayed social bonds. In addition, divine mercy was only available if the sinner recognized the wrong and repented.[51]

In addition to pressuring Sara Swarton, the Privy Council tried to get Lady Roos to reveal more. On February 25, the earl of Exeter invited the Lord Chancellor, the two Chief Justices, and both the Attorney and Solicitor General to a midday meal at Exeter House. After the meal, a group of them went straight to the Tower to press Lady Roos for more details about the forged documents. She refused to say anything, so she remained a close prisoner, unable to speak with her parents.[52] By March, she appeared to have more freedom of movement in the Tower, although her parents were still kept very strictly. Chamberlain guessed that she "growes so impatient of restraint that they say she begins to discover *le pot aux roses* [uncovers a plot], and without respect of father, mother, or other frends, to tell all she knows, and so to purchase her libertie the sooner."[53] Chamberlain was clearly torn about Lady Roos's confessions: on the one hand, she should fully confess her crimes and repent, but on the other hand, her confessions left her parents high and dry and made her a disloyal daughter.

Unable to communicate with their daughter, Lake and his wife were concerned that she might say something that would compromise them further. The concern was warranted, seeing how she had kept them in the dark regarding her pre-trial confession to the king. Chamberlain reported that "indeed I know that both he [Sir Thomas Lake] and other frends complained of her courses and manner of carriage" and "fearing she wold marre all, because she would not conferre and be advised."[54] William Lake, Sir Thomas's secretary, was allowed to visit him in his prison. Around April 20, William Lake tried to smuggle letters from his employer to Lady Roos, but was caught in the act. He was detained and imprisoned in the Gatehouse prison close to Westminster. Curiously, Sir Thomas Lake was allowed more freedom of movement in the Tower but kept away from his wife and daughter. He was also allowed to replace his imprisoned secretary with another servant.[55] William Lake remained in prison for more than a month.[56] Perhaps Lake's greater freedom of movement was due to the assistance from his brother, Arthur Lake, bishop of Bath and Wells, who felt sorry for his incarcerated sibling. The bishop tried to mediate "and doth him all the offices of a kind brother and true frend."[57]

By early May, Lady Roos cracked again. Observers noted that she had been brought to court to see the now recovered king and Privy Council several times and that she had apparently "laid open the whole platforme of theyre villanie" during those visits. She had again tried to clear her father of all wrongdoing, laying more of the blame on her mother and brother Arthur.[58] At one point, the Privy Council also confronted Lady Roos with her mother, whom she had not seen since their imprisonment. The councilors hoped that both would add details or otherwise reveal themselves further, when they had not been able to coordinate their responses in advance. Lady Roos did not play along, simply answering in "Pilates tune *quod scripsi scripsi*: [what is written is written] and that all was true that she had set downe to the Kinge under her hand."[59]

According to rumors circulating seven years later, Buckingham managed to seduce Lady Roos and convince her to confess and speak out against her mother. This story became part of the much broader accusations against Buckingham in 1626, when Parliament attempted to impeach him. Among his political crimes and misdemeanors, the Parliamentary detractors also argued that he was sexually depraved and listed several examples of his "Adulteryes and ye like." Each instance was followed by a mention of witnesses to the crimes. After the note "He lay wth ye Lady Rosse and gate out of her a confession against her mother," the persons listed as witnesses to this action were "Ladye Rosse and Ladye Lake."[60]

It seems strange that Lady Roos would admit to having sex with Buckingham, as it would have added on to her woes and further damaged her reputation. It also seems strange that Lady Lake would admit publicly that her widowed daughter had been unchaste, especially considering that Lady Roos was remarried by the time of Buckingham's troubles. Of course, it could also be a way for Lady Lake to explain what she viewed as her daughter's betrayal. If the young woman had been tricked into doing so, perhaps the betrayal stung less. None of the people commenting on the case in 1619 mentioned Buckingham's supposed seduction.

Whether caused by the pressures of king and Privy Council, or by Buckingham's seduction, or both, Lady Roos's further confessions had dire consequences for her own family members, as well as others connected to the case. Her brother Sir Arthur, who had been free from punishment since Star Chamber judged it did not have enough evidence against him, now found himself imprisoned, with "his own sister [as] his accuser."[61] Sir Thomas Lake's brother the bishop, who had rented a house on Tower Hill to be close at hand, was no longer allowed to see his brother, as king and council worried that he might somehow help Sir Thomas influence Lady Roos and make her change her mind about the confessions.[62]

Henry Parker, the deputy Clerk of the Court of Star Chamber, also found himself in hot water. Lady Roos claimed that he had allowed her to give official testimony to the court without making her take the required oath beforehand. Lady Roos, who had been so reluctant to speak in front of the king and council under oath the year before, had apparently managed to avoid the oath yet again, by paying Parker off, according to her new tale.[63] Parker initially managed to clear himself and was released, only to be rearrested and imprisoned again shortly after. Once the Star Chamber Trinity term began in June, the Privy Council ordered the two Chief Justices to undertake a more thorough investigation into the matter and Parker remained in prison for the duration.[64] He was released in July.

By the end of May, the situation for the Lakes was dire. One report said that Sir Thomas Lake the younger was also imprisoned, and that Lady Roos's younger sister Elizabeth Lake was confined to a house at Tower Hill, but it is not clear if either was true. Perhaps Elizabeth was staying with her uncle the bishop at Tower Hill. Sir Thomas Lake was also trying to come up with the money for his fines, the countess's court costs, and for the various damages he was supposed to pay. He applied to the council to be allowed to sell some land but was denied. At the same time, the council required that he pay promptly, and threatened to confiscate lands if he did not, which some observers found rather unreasonable.[65]

While her family suffered, Lady Roos's situation improved. Her renewed confessions also ignited new marriage rumors. Sir Gerard Herbert reported to Carleton that Lady Roos was to marry Endymion Porter, Master of Horse to the Marquis of Buckingham.[66] Lorkin, who had heard the same rumor a couple of weeks earlier, initially did not believe it, but was not quite as sure by late May. He informed Puckering that:

> I will conclude my letter with a jig, for I think you will esteem it little better, that Endymion Porter, that waits upon my Lord of Buckingham, shall (if general voice deceive not), set my Lady Roos at liberty, and enjoy her for his wife. I heard it above a fortnight since, but gave no credit to it, but now it is confidently assured.[67]

Rumors about Lady Roos marrying someone connected with Buckingham had circulated before. The idea that Buckingham would approve of a match between his own man and Lady Roos pointed to the possibility of her restoration. Granted, Porter was no nobleman, and the marriage would thus be a step down on the social ladder for her. However, Endymion Porter was a man of solid gentry status and made a good career for himself at the courts of James and Charles. He came from a family of substantial landowners, who had also married into a Spanish family. Porter had received his education in Spain and he was fluent in Spanish language and culture, which served him well in his later court career. He had worked as a page in the household of the count-duke Olivares, later a highly influential royal minister in Spain. Most importantly, his employer Buckingham favored him, which served as a powerful career booster. However, the marriage never materialized: Porter instead married Olivia Boteler, Buckingham's niece.[68]

Another, more sinister, rumor appeared in May. In a letter to Sir Thomas Puckering, Lorkin revived reports that the Lakes had ordered Roos's death by poison. According to Lorkin, William Lake was not detained because of trying to smuggle letters to Lady Roos, but rather because of the discovery of a letter of his that had been sent to the king. The letter was "to this effect, impressing upon one that was sent by Sir Thomas Lake to my Lord Roos, that he should be mindful of his errand, advertising him that Sir Thomas's adversaries grew patient, and therefore encouraging him speedily to dispatch that what he had undertook, assuring the performance of whatsoever had been promised." To the uninformed, this letter might seem rather ordinary, since Sir Thomas was at that time already embroiled in the lawsuit with the earl and countess of Exeter, and he had been seeking information about Lord Roos since his flight from England. Lorkin argued that the letter might have a darker meaning, clarifying to Puckering that the "letter brings into men's remembrance the practice upon Sir Thomas Overbury." Lorkin cautioned that "this is not yet public, and therefore I impart it as a secret."[69] No other rumors of Lake ordering Roos poisoned appeared, so Lorkin's information was neither confirmed nor repeated. The Overbury poisoning certainly still shaped how people interpreted fallen courtiers. If the great favorite Somerset and his wife could be guilty of murder, perhaps others at court might be as well.

Submissions and Refusals

When the Trinity term of the Court of Star Chamber began in June, the date was set for Lake, his wife, and his daughter to complete another part of their sentence: to stand in front of Star Chamber and tender their official submission to court, king, and—most humiliating perhaps—to the countess of Exeter. Here, they were supposed to admit their faults, to agree that the court's punishments were just, and to beg for forgiveness from the countess for the wrongs they had committed. This was a form of public penance considered appropriate for men and women of the upper echelons of society. They were to humble themselves in front of their peers, because it would have upset the social order too much if they were forced to do penance in public, as was required of commoners. In the two weeks before the date set for submissions, Lake had permission to spend some time with his wife, who complained she was not well. Perhaps this was an attempt to soften them up a bit before the submission.[70]

Initially, the Lakes and Lady Roos were scheduled to give their submissions on June 18. Lake claimed illness and said he was not able to appear. Lady Roos did not appear either, but Lady Lake arrived, only to find that the court was not quite prepared for the event. She thus returned to the Tower without "doing any thing, but uttering some idle speeches."[71]

The next day, on the king's birthday, the court was ready. A little after eleven o'clock on June 19, Lord Chancellor Sir Francis Bacon spoke, informing the court and audience that this was the day appointed for the Lakes' and Lady Roos's submission. However, Sir Thomas was still ill, and did not appear. Lady Lake also refused to come to court. The court sent word to the king at Greenwich Palace to see what he would have them do considering this development. In the meantime, Bacon explained that Lady Roos would not appear, because the king had given her permission to provide her submission in writing instead of in person. The king had granted her this singular mercy, Bacon explained to the astonished audience, because she had confessed to the forgeries of the countess's and Hatton's writings to the king *before* the February trial. This was the first time the information about Lady Roos's pre-trial

Christmas confession to the king became public, and it caused quite a stir. Bacon commended the king's keen sense of justice, for keeping this quiet so that the other judges in the trial could be unbiased, and to see "how the matter would be carried, and how far impudencie wold go."[72] Chamberlain, who already thought that Lady Roos's May confessions had been a terrible way for her to treat her troubled parents, noted that while "the world" thought the Lakes had acted wrongly, "yet yt doth more detest the Lady Rosse, for so fowlie betrayeng her father and mother more than once."[73]

Spared from appearing at the public humiliation in Star Chamber, Lady Roos's written submission was read out in court. The court had pre-approved the submission and probably in large part written and/or dictated it as well, although it was undersigned "Anna Roos." It closely reflected the crimes of which Lady Roos stood convicted. It specified the forgery of the two documents, as well as making Sara Swarton give false testimony.

> I stand convicted and sentenced for the contriving, forging, and counterfeiting of two several libelous writings; the one in the name of Luke Hatton, thereby charging and accusing the said right hono:ble Countesse of Exeter with an intent and purpose to poison me, and to make away my father Sir Thomas Lake, and to accuse him of some plots against his Ma:tie in the late Queenes tyme; The other writing in the nature of a recognition supposed to be made and written by the said Countesse under her hand, purporting that shee should confesse an attempt to take away my life by poison and confesse a matter of incest to be by her committed w:th the Lo: Roos my late husband deceased, and grand childe to the said righte ho:ble Earl of Exeter, and I stand likewise convicted of the subornacion of Sara Swarton in deposing the matter contained in the said supposed recognition, and of the malicious publication of the said two false writings and other false reports unjustly to slander and defame the said right hono:ble Countesse.[74]

Having thus outlined the crimes of forgery and suborning a witness, Lady Roos continued her submission by stating that she was indeed guilty of these crimes, "sorrowful for the same," and that the sentence and punishment of the king and court was just. This constituted a standard format for submissions. Since she also was supposed to specifically apologize to the countess, she "aske the said right hono:ble Countesse forgiveness for the great wrongs and slanders wch I have done and cast upon her thereby." She ended the submission by requesting the "hono:^{ble} lo:^{pps}" of the court to mediate with the king on her behalf, asking for a pardon of her offenses.[75]

The court then received word back from the king regarding the reluctant Lakes. The king's message said that since Lake was sick, he could also dispense with appearing in person. Like his daughter, he could have his signed submission read in court. The court would even write the submission for him: all he had to do was sign it. Lake responded by arguing that his illness was such that it affected both his body and his mind, and therefore he did not feel comfortable signing something he might not fully comprehend in his weakened state. Lady Lake, apparently given the same opportunity, also refused it, which Thomas Locke thought strange, as he told Carleton that "though she had bin yesterday at the Star Chamber and could then talk yet was she now mute also."[76]

Neither king nor court were amused at the Lakes' stubborn refusal, especially after the full revelation about Lady Roos's earlier confessions as well as her formal submission. Camden noted in his diary that the Lakes's refusal "is adjudged the height of contempt against his Royal Majesty."[77] Sir Thomas and his wife were now committed close prisoners once again and informed that they could only have one servant each "and none to come at them till the Kings further pleasure be knowne."[78] The earl of Pembroke, Lord Chamberlain, noted approvingly in court that "if the punishment had bin greater he should have assented."[79]

Lake's illness was not just tactical stalling, but rather a severe case of scurvy, perhaps a result of a more limited diet while in the Tower. The king eventually softened a bit and allowed Lady Lake to attend to her sick husband until "the extremitie be over."[80] While Lake suffered in the Tower, the earl of Exeter again hosted King James at Wimbledon, further evidence of the stark differences between the situations of the former colleagues and relatives-through-marriage.[81]

The king's grace shone more brightly on Lady Roos. On July 8, the Privy Council signed a warrant to the Lieutenant of the Tower, signifying the king's pleasure to "enlarge and set at liberte the person of the Lady Roos out of that prison of the Tower." Two days later, she was released. Her freedom was not yet absolute: she had to leave a bond to ensure that she would appear in front of the Privy Council "at all times when shee shalbe called for," and she also needed to remain "confined," although she was allowed to choose the place herself.[82] Lady Roos no doubt wished to get out of the London limelight after her ordeals, and perhaps also away from her parents after the revelation of her Christmas confession and her submission. She went to the Isle of Wight, where she remained for a time in the house of Sir Robert Dillington.[83]

Sara Swarton also benefited both from her own confessions, as well as that of Lady Roos. Although her public whipping, branding, and imprisonment for life had been overturned, she had remained imprisoned in the Fleet while the court waited to see how the submissions of Lady Roos and the Lakes played out. After Lady Roos's submission, Sara Swarton was told she could also expect to be set free if she made her own public acknowledgment of fault. Unlike Lady Roos, Swarton was required to do it in person and in a more public setting. She was scheduled to perform public penance at the church of St. Martin in the Field, close to the Lake's townhome in Charing Cross, on July 25. She appeared on the appointed day and performed the penance to everyone's satisfaction. She wore the penitent's simple white tunic, her feet and head bare, while she admitted her "faults and forgeries" to the onlookers. Chamberlain had not himself been present at the penance, but he had been informed about Swarton "in the same place clearing Sir Thomas Lake and his Lady (what she could) and laying all the blame of the Lady Rosse."[84]

King James was clearly in a forgiving mood by this point. Sir Arthur Lake was also released in July, a few days before his sister. Henry (Harry) Parker, the court clerk who Lady Roos had accused of allowing her to testify without oath, was freed in July as well.[85] By July, the king had even relented further regarding Sir Thomas: first, he was allowed the freedom of the Tower in early July, so "that any man may speak to him." By the end of the month, the king allowed Lake to leave the Tower temporarily, so that he could recover his health.

At first, the king had suggested that Lake could go to stay in the custody of his brother the bishop, but Lake argued that it made it more difficult for him to arrange his financial affairs so that he could pay the fines and damages he still owed. He was allowed to put in a bond of £1,000, move more freely, but had to promise to return to the Tower when so ordered.[86] Chamberlain told Carleton that Lake's release "and some other reasons make some that take upon them to know much to geve out that we shall shortly see him in grace again," suggesting a restoration for the former secretary. At the time, Chamberlain did not agree, noting that as far as he was concerned, "*credit Judaeus Apella*," referring to a commonly used quote from Horace, meaning "let credulous people believe it, but I do not."[87] Lake ensured he had a hearty welcome: Chamberlain reported that "against his coming home the bells were ronge, and a noise of trumpets redy to receve and welcome him, and all this by order from himself, yf yt be credible."[88]

After the conclusion of the trials in February, the situation had looked bleak for the Lake family and household, Lady Roos, and Sara Swarton. By the summer of 1619, it already seemed as if the worst may be behind them, as James had shown mercy and released—at least temporarily or conditionally—many of the offenders. There was still one person remaining in the Tower who did not benefit from the king's largesse: the Lady Lake. After having tended to her ill husband, she was returned to her lonely existence as a close prisoner, with her one female attendant.[89] She would stay there for some time to come, because she stubbornly refused to admit fault. The feud between the Lakes and the earl and countess of Exeter did not end with the trials, convictions, and punishments: it continued to simmer for several years.

13
Submissions and Restoration?

> Another result of Spanish influence appears by the presence of the former Secretary Lake in his Majesty's presence on more than one occasion. Some time ago he was forbidden to present himself, but now they think he may shortly return to his office and be employed in the Council, thus overcoming the ill fortune that he suffered for some years in imprisonment and punishment. This matter is considered very significant by every one.
>
> Girolamo Lando, Venetian ambassador in England, to the Venetian Doge and Senate, June 4, 1620[1]

During the fall of 1619, Lady Roos remained out of sight, still residing with Sir Robert Dillington on the Isle of Wight. Lady Lake remained in the Tower, and Sir Thomas—although allowed to live in his own house at Charing Cross—was not out of the woods yet.[2] The king permitted him to visit his wife occasionally. A correspondent of the earl of Doncaster ran into Lake in September and chatted with him briefly. The man congratulated the former secretary on his freedom, but Lake informed him that it was only temporary, a reprieve allowed due to his poor health. He had to return to the Tower by the beginning of Michaelmas term, when he was also supposed to make his formal submission.[3] Lake's submission was delayed, however, and his return to the Tower was put off until All Hallows' Day.[4] The king seemed to relent somewhat toward his disgraced secretary.

The few months after the trial and sentencing were the gravest moments for the Lakes and Lady Roos and the greatest triumph for the countess of Exeter and her husband. The relationship between the families continued to be strained. With the renewed negotiations for a Spanish bride and the return of the Spanish ambassador Gondomar to England, some believed that Lake might be restored to royal favor and to the Privy Council. Lady Lake's stubborn refusal to submit and repent did not help his cause.

Family and Feuding at the Court of James I: The Lake and Cecil Scandals. Johanna Luthman, Oxford University Press.
 DOI: 10.1093/oso/9780192865786.003.0013

Submission and Renewed Refusal

Lake worked diligently to move the king in his favor during the fall of 1619. He was a "frequent resorter" to John Digby, now Lord Digby, Privy Councilor and the person the king relied on for the Spanish marriage negotiations.[5] Lake also cultivated Secretary Calvert to assist him in his cause. The new secretary was generous with his predecessor, as Lake "receaveth all worthie treatment at his access of him."[6] There were other signs that the king might be relenting toward him. In late November, Lake negotiated with the Privy Councilors about the possibility of making his submission in writing instead of in-person, like his daughter had done the previous summer. The councilors formulated a submission statement, which they believed reflected the crimes for which Lake had been convicted and sent it to the king for approval. The king agreed but added the caveat that the countess of Exeter also had to accept the proposal.

The council appointed Lord Digby and Secretary Calvert to go and sound out the countess. The countess politely informed them "that she would in this and in all things be commanded by his Majesty." However, if "his Majesty left it to her liberty and election, she humbly prayed to be excused." In short, she refused. The lords of the council tried to persuade her by pointing out that if Lake had to appear in person, the submission would have to be put off until the next court session. Lady Exeter was not dissuaded: she pointed to "divers wrongs he had done her of late."[7] The countess insisted that Lake appear in person, perform his penance, and humble himself in her presence.

By mentioning the additional "diverse wrongs," the countess might have been alluding to a curious accusation made by one Samuel Peacock, a school master and a minister, who had been abroad during the Lake and Exeter trials. When Peacock returned, he told Lake that he had important information, which might have changed the outcome of the suits. He had become acquainted with "one Atkins a dealer in negromancie and magicke." (This Atkins may or may not have been the same Dr. Atkins who tended to a sick Lady Roos. It is not made clear in the relations of Peacock's account or other sources.) Atkins revealed to Peacock that the countess of Exeter "during the depending of the suite had often resorted to him to know from his skill what might be the success thereof." Atkins said he could not tell this future without seeing both the king's and Sir Thomas Lake's faces in court. After he had attended the court proceedings, Atkins performed some "magicall ceremonies" and then told the countess she "should overcome." Skeptical, Lake asked

Peacock to repeat this information in the presence of Lord Fenton, the king's Groom of the Stool. Peacock also provided the story in writing. Fenton in turn told the king, who ordered Secretary Calvert to investigate. When Calvert questioned Atkins about Peacock's tales, he denied it entirely as a "grosse foule untruth." Peacock was promptly imprisoned and would be further questioned in the following months.[8]

Peacock's accusations mirrored those against that most famous of murderers, Frances Howard, the countess of Somerset. In the Overbury case, Frances Howard had been accused of using the magical services of Dr. Simon Foreman. Howard, at the time married to her first husband, the earl of Essex, had asked Foreman to use magic to prevent Essex from consummating their marriage, so that she would have a chance at getting an annulment. In addition, she had requested Foreman use love magic on Sir Robert Carr (later earl of Somerset), to bind his love to her, so that he would not abandon her. No one made a specific reference to Frances Howard at any time in the letters and sources that mention Peacock, so it is not clear if contemporaries made that connection at the time. Nevertheless, early modern people commonly associated the use of magic with illicit sex.[9]

At the same time as Peacock raised the specter of the countess employing magicians, she was aggressively going after Lake to make sure he paid her the awarded damages. By December, Lake had finally paid all his fines to the king, and part of the damages to the countess. When he was still short eight or nine hundred pounds, she requested and received a royal commission "to fell downe his woods." According to some, it was surely a harsh measure, but "as cruelly doth shee cut upp his trees as he would have done hir honor and good name."[10]

Peacock's accusations did not cause any changes in Lake's scheduled submission. The Star Chamber Court had appointed it for the beginning of Hilary term. The form of the submission, written by the Lord Chancellor, the two Chief Justices, and the Attorney General, circulated well before the date of appearance. Castle and Chamberlain already knew and reported its contents by early to mid-January.[11] On January 28, Lake finally appeared in the court of Star Chamber and read the submission aloud to those present. Since she had insisted so much on this public humiliation earlier, one assumes that the countess of Exeter attended Star Chamber that day, satisfied and vindicated.

Lake's submission admitted to two faults: first, that he had assisted his daughter "in a cause wch is by the judgement of his Matie and this ho:^{ble} Court just censured to be foule and odius to the world and scandalous to the said

Countesse." He had allowed himself to be deceived by his daughter. The court believed it was clear that Lake would "have discerned" Lady Roos's fraud if he had only "used due care and diligence in examynyng the prooffs" rather than be "misled by gross credulity, indulgence and ignorance."[12] Notably, the submission did not state that Lake himself had a hand in creating the fraudulent documents, only that he had stupidly promoted them as true. An officer of state should surely not be so easily fooled. Lake's primary offense consisted of failing in his masculine duties. As a husband and a father, he should have controlled and curbed his wife's and daughter's excesses, but instead he indulged them and made them worse. Having been convinced to do bad deeds by the women of his family, his subordinates, he also lost his ability to serve in a position of power over other men.

Secondly, Lake had to admit to "a greater and high offence in abusing my place trust and [?] as a privy Counsellor by imprisonyng one Luke Hatton and one George Gwilliams for no offence to his Ma^{ty}, but in my owne cause and for my owne private ends." In the king's view, Lake's abuse of his official powers was also an additional betrayal of trust, similar to his revelation of the king's private conversation to the earl and countess of Suffolk. This is why he lost his position as secretary.

As was customary in these sorts of submissions, Lake also had to agree that the sentence against him was just: "I do hereby acknowledge and confesse the said sentence and decree to be in all partes and respectes just and ho^{ble} and that the punishment by his Ma^{tys} Royall judgement inflicted upon me hath bene duely deserved." The submission ended with the portion that must have been especially gratifying to the countess of Exeter. Lake asked her for forgiveness: "I am hartely sorry that I did give any favour or countenance to a cause so foule and hatefull and so fraudulous to the said Countesse, craving pardon of the said Countesse for the wrong I have done her."[13] A year after his sentence, Lake had completed his punishment.

Lake had now finally formally and publicly admitted that his daughter's tales were false, and the documents supposedly written by Hatton and the countess were fraudulent. The still imprisoned Peacock had not changed his tune: he insisted that Atkins had told him about performing magic at the behest of the countess, with the implication that Atkin's had aimed to influence the king's decision in the countess's favor.[14] Peacock's tale did not make the king doubt that his judgment in the case had been sound, but the mention of magic, or potentially witchcraft, concerned him.

Using witchcraft in and of itself was problematic. The period from the 1580s to 1640s constituted the height of early modern witchcraft prosecutions in England, so early Stuart Englishmen and women were especially attuned to the threat. Using witchcraft on the king was not just problematic, but treasonous. King James believed himself to be a victim of witchcraft in the 1590s in Scotland and those accusations had led to a series of witchcraft accusations, trials, and executions. The king also wrote a treatise on witchcraft, *Daemonologie*, published both in Scotland and England. While king of England, James's approach to witchcraft cases generally grew more cautious and skeptical. Although not doubting the reality of witchcraft, the king personally became involved in several cases where it became apparent that those supposedly bewitched were actually faking their symptoms. James, as the wise Solomon, unmasked frauds of all kinds, including fraudulent witchcraft.[15]

Nevertheless, if the countess or anyone else involved in the court cases had employed a witch or magician to influence the king, they might face severe consequences. On February 10, 1620, Francis Bacon wrote to the king to reassure him that all necessary measures were taken in the matter:

> Sir Edward Cook is now on foot, and according to your command, Signified by Mr. Secretary Calvert, we proceed in Peacock's examinations; for although there have been very diligence used, yet certainly we are not at the bottom; and he that would not use the utmost of his line to sound such a business as this, should not have due regard neither to your Majesty's honour nor safety.[16]

As Peacock apparently mostly repeated what he had already told Lake and Lord Fenton, the renewed questioning yielded little of substance. Bacon did not believe him anymore than Calvert had. "A man would think he were in Luke Hatton's case again," Bacon mused, "for as my Lady Roos personateth Luke Hatton, so it seemeth Peacock personateth Atkins."[17]

At length, Bacon recommended using torture to loosen Peacock's tongue and get him to talk. "He deserveth it as well as Peacham did," Bacon argued. He was referring to the 1614 case of Rev. Edmund Peacham, a Puritan minister accused of hatching a treasonable plot against the king. English common law did not allow judicial torture, except in cases of especially heinous crimes, such as witchcraft and treason. Bacon argued that it was only lawful to use torture in order to discover plots and thus prevent further damage, but not solely to extract confessions or produce evidence against an accused person. In the case of Peacock, it was important to ensure that the man was not part of a larger conspiracy against the king.[18]

The council wrote a warrant allowing Peacock's torture with either "the manacles or the racke," so that they could get to be bottom of the business.[19] Peacock was questioned and "hung up by the wrists," but "though he were very impatient of the torture and swooned once or twise," his inquisitors were not able to "wrunge any great matter out of him."[20] In order to ascertain if Lake or his wife had anything to do with Peacock's actions, the Lord Chancellor confronted the prisoner directly with Lake to gauge the reactions of both. After this violent questioning, nothing else came of the matter. Most judged Peacock either a "madman" or an "imposter" and thought his story false.[21]

By early March 1620, Lady Lake had been imprisoned in the Tower for over a year. She had sometimes been close prisoner, and sometimes had more freedom within the complex. Since the previous fall, her husband had been allowed to visit her. Now, she complained of ill health and requested that she be allowed to live at home while she waited for her turn to perform the submission in the court of Star Chamber in the Easter term. She was allowed to do so, if she also put in a bond of £2,000 to ensure that she would either appear at court or return to the Tower.[22]

Lady Lake was scheduled to make her submission in Star Chamber on May 12, 1620. When she arrived, she informed the gathered court and audience that she had no intention of tendering her submission. The wording of it required that she confess herself guilty of the forgeries of Hatton's document and the countess's supposed confession, as well as of suborning Sara Swarton's testimony. Lady Lake argued that she was not guilty of any of those offences and therefore her conscience would not allow her to perform the submission as it was prepared for her. Lady Lake's reprieve from the Tower proved short.[23]

Lake Restored?

Although his wife refused to submit, Lake's prospects were beginning to look decidedly better. The rumor mill had begun directly after Lake's submission in January, with observers guessing that Lake "had new hope to be restored to the Counsell table." At that early juncture, not everyone agreed with the possibility.[24] By mid-May, the situation had improved further. Lake visited the king, who received him and allowed him to kiss the royal hand, a clear mark of favor. Observers believed that it was the work of the Spanish ambassador Gondomar, who had returned to England in March. Gondomar judged that a grateful Lake in the Spaniard's debt could be useful to him if he were restored to his position on the Privy Council "yf not further."[25]

The reasons for Gondomar's return and desire to have especially friendly people at court included the renewal of the negotiations of a Spanish bride for Prince Charles, as well as the increasingly difficult situation in the Holy Roman Empire. King James's son-in-law, Frederick of the Palatinate, had accepted the offer of the Protestant nobles in Bohemia to become their king in 1618. The Protestants in Bohemia were in rebellion against the Catholic Holy Roman Emperor, who argued that the Bohemian crown belonged to the Catholic Habsburgs.

In 1619, Frederick and his English wife Princess Elizabeth arrived in Prague and were crowned king and queen of Bohemia. In 1620, the Holy Roman Empire began its preparations to go to war against Frederick and the Bohemian Protestants. The first major battle of the lengthy and bloody Thirty Years' War began in November 1620. At the Battle of White Mountain, Frederick's forces lost and forced him and his wife to take refuge in The Hague, where they would remain in exile from their domains.

Prince Charles and Buckingham hoped that a Spanish match would lead to Spanish assistance in negotiating with the Holy Roman Empire about at least some partial restoration of Elizabeth and Frederick, although King James remained more skeptical of that goal. In England, the Spanish match was supported by those who wished to see greater freedoms for English Catholics but opposed by a greater majority who viewed Catholicism with great fear and suspicion and equated it with potential sedition and treason. English foreign policy of the early 1620s were dominated by these two issues.[26]

Gondomar approached Buckingham to see if James would consider pardoning Lady Lake without a formal submission to the countess of Exeter. Gondomar made this request at the same time as he was asking James for a more liberal treatment of Catholics within England. James gave a non-committal answer regarding the Catholics in general, but he declined the request regarding Lady Lake outright. Again, the king emphasized the need to remain consistent in order to provide justice for his subjects. He could not pardon Lady Lake with his honor intact, he argued, because pardoning her before she had submitted would make it seem as if he disagreed with his own legal decision. Furthermore, James stated it would force him to "breake my promeis to miladie Exeter in a matter of justice, if I grawnte her [Lady Lake] any ease at this time."[27] James could not put mercy and favor above justice and honor.

Gondomar had also referred to religion somehow in his request for Lady Lake. Perhaps he had suggested that it would be a godly act to have mercy on the long-imprisoned and long-suffering lady. James retorted: "this cause hath no aspect to Religion, excepte the Romishe Religion be composed of the sevin deadlie sinnes; for I dare sweare she is guiltie of thaim all." James concluded by noting that if "Spaine trouble me with suites of this nature both against my justice and honoure, thaire freindshippe will be more burthensome than useful unto me."[28] In James's eyes, Lady Lake was no innocent suffering too harsh a punishment. She was a hardened sinner who needed to repent. Only after she had been brought to heel could Lady Lake hope for mercy from the king.

The king went on progress as usual during the summer of 1620, so Lake did not have as many opportunities to appear at court again. By late September, he had an accident. He was struck by a coach, broke his arm, and was "sore bruisd and brusht." The injuries meant that he was laid up and unable to go to court or do much business at all. As a result, he believed he may have lost his momentum for further advancement. Others agreed: Chamberlain told Carleton that "yt is likewise thought that yf Sir Thomas Lake had not fallen into this late misfortune of breaking his arme," he would have "ben in his old remitter, so potent are the meanes and mediations of the Spanish ambassador."[29] Chamberlain, a staunch Protestant who feared a Spanish match, focused more on his belief in Gondomar's great influence than on Lake's value to the king.

In early 1621, Secretary Naunton managed to anger the king, who promptly told him to absent himself from court. Naunton did not support the Spanish marriage, and made the mistake of talking about a potential French marriage for Charles with the French ambassador. Naunton argued that the discussion was in the abstract only, but since he had no orders to deal with any royal marriage, the king thought he had overstepped his authority. James was jealously guarding any talk of Charles's marriage: decisions regarding royal marriages was strictly the king's prerogative. With Naunton in disfavor, Lake's hopes renewed. Lake was observed having "his traine carried upp after him in Courte [...] like a privie counseller and so he has at other tymes of late." Some even thought that it was Gondomar who had orchestrated Naunton's fall, for Lake's benefit. Others doubted both the plot and Lake's restoration, although rumors of a marriage between Sir Thomas Lake the younger and a relative of the Countess of Buckingham made others more uncertain.[30]

In a poem dated March 1621, which dealt with the fraught and changing Jacobean political situation, one section dealt with the potential restoration of Lake. The section began with a reference to the Spanish match, and the recurring refrain mentioned who would "pay for all." The second stanza referred to the near restoration of the earl and countess of Suffolk, after they had been convicted, fined, and imprisoned in the Tower. Suffolk was quickly released from the Tower, but never returned to a court position.

> When Charles, hath got the Spanish Gearle
> The Puritans will scold & bralle
> But Digbie then shall be made an Earle
> And Spanish gold shall pay for all
>
> When Suffolk getts the king to friend
> & make his wife to cease to brall
> He then may finish Audley end
> & the old accompt shall pay for all.

Obviously, the Puritans (and many others) were vehemently opposed to a Spanish and Catholic bride for the prince. Digby had been James's main negotiator regarding the marriage. The mention of Audley End in the second verse referred to Suffolk's country estate, on which he had spent enormous sums. Another verse referred to Lake's possible rise as a result of Spanish influence:

> When Sackfeild Spinola shall take
> & Wentworth brings Bucquoy to thrall
> then King will then be friends with Lake
> & the Lady Rosse shall pay for all.[31]

According to the editor Bellany, Sackfield (Sackville?) and Wentworth refers to Englishmen who had volunteered to fight for the cause of Frederick of the Palatinate, and the Spaniard Spinola and Bucquoy were generals within the imperial army. The verse refers to the connection between Spanish and Catholic support for Lake's restoration. If Lake was restored, his part in the Lake-Cecil feud would be minimized, and the blame put more squarely on Lady Roos instead, the verse writer implied.

The rumors about Lake's imminent rise soon quieted. Perhaps Lake's injury did indeed cause the king to cool toward him, but more likely the rumors of his restoration had been exaggerated. Naunton lingered on in a sort of limbo until the king finally decided to remove him from the secretary post in 1623. By then, the power at court had shifted more firmly toward Buckingham and Prince Charles, who had taken up the idea of the Spanish match themselves and were increasingly influential and directing policy during the last two years of James's life and reign. Ultimately, it mattered more to Spain to get Buckingham on board than to get Lake restored, as Buckingham was clearly more likely to have great influence with the king.[32]

Sir George Calvert, the remaining secretary, also ensured that Lake's restoration was not viewed as a necessity by the king, because Calvert could do what Lake had done (and more, considering his language skills, which Lake lacked). Calvert had continued to serve the king well, taking over Naunton's tasks when he was no longer allowed to perform his office. Calvert also supported the Spanish match because the king supported it, but not necessarily based on his own interests. (Unlike Lake, he did not receive annuities from the Spanish.) Lake had represented the king in the Commons in the 1614 Addled Parliament, but as the king called Parliament again in 1621 to ask for supply for a potential war in support of the Palatinate, he no longer needed Lake as a manager: he had Calvert. Calvert was elected MP for Yorkshire, serving as a representative of the king's positions in the House of Commons (in the end, Parliament and king clashed over fiscal policies and what the king viewed as unauthorized discussions about Prince Charles's marriage, and James dissolved it). Why would the king need Lake, tainted as he was by scandal and misuse of the powers of his office? Calvert was essentially a Lake without all the negative baggage, and without the tangle of Howard connections so worrisome to Buckingham.[33]

Of course, the Spanish match never happened. Prince Charles and Buckingham, attempting to cut through the slow and uncertain Spanish negotiations, had made the sensational move of traveling to Spain incognito, in order to force the Spanish to conclude the marriage. Once in Spain, it became clear to the two men that the marriage would never happen, and that the Spanish had largely used the marriage negotiations as a means to keep England from going to war in support of Frederick of the Palatine and his English wife. When Charles and Buckingham returned to England in the fall of 1623, they instead supported going to war against what they considered a deceitful Spain. Among the majority Protestants in England, a war with Spain was immensely popular, although King James managed to ensure that England did not go to war at that time. Soon, King James and Charles began negotiating for a French bride instead, which resulted in the marriage to the French king's sister, Henrietta Maria. In this decidedly anti-Spanish, anti-Catholic climate, with the Prince and Buckingham directing so much of the agenda, Lake did not have much to offer the king.[34]

Yet another poem, written in 1623 and titled "Fortune's Wheel," commented on the ups and downs of Jacobean politics, and especially on the rise and fall of so many royal officials. The anonymous author included a verse on Sir Thomas Lake:

> Then comes a Secretarie to the stake
> I neede not name him: yet sir Thomas Lake
> Muste with the rest, the curse of Fortune trye
> For, for his daughter he contriv'de a lye
> But when the reckoninge is up better caste
> All men exclaymer; sayinge, what soe is paste
> Upon thies Lordes, be dangerous woemens sinne
> Whoe still unto the men, their woe being.
> But I doe saie, T'is to resolve this doubte
> that Fortunes wheele is quicklie turned aboute.[35]

The poem suggests it was "woemens sinne" who brought Lake down, and women "still" remained his "woe." Lady Lake's stubbornness probably did not help her husband's drive to be restored at court. She continued her refusal to submit, determined to fight her battle a while longer.

Lady Lake's Delayed Submission

During the Michaelmas term of 1620, the Privy Councilors sitting in the Court of Star Chamber tried in vain to get Lady Lake to tender her submission. Instead, she wrote an extraordinarily defiant letter to the countess of Exeter in the beginning of November. In the letter, she told the countess that she may have won the court cases, but that they both knew she was not innocent. She began:

> Madam, Now after this busines in wch yo^{w} have had so much glorie, cast yor eies upon 139th Psalme, there shall yo^{w} finde what God is. No place nor thoughts are hid from him, he can looke where mens Judgements cannot reach too and his Records must remaine upon the file for ever.[36]

Psalm 139 emphasizes the omniscience and omnipresence of God, and that the believer cannot "flee from [God's] presence" for there "is not a word in my tongue, but, lo, O Lord, though knowest it altogether."[37] Unlike in the flawed human legal system, Lady Lake pointed out that God's "lawyers will not receive bribes, not be corrupted, These exhibitts cannot be stolen in boxes."[38]

Lady Lake suggested that the countess's court victory was the result of decidedly human manipulations, but that God, who knew all, was aware of the countess's faults and sins.

In her letter, Lady Lake also mentioned that she had written to the countess previously, and admonished her to think of the state of her eternal soul:

> To conclude for this time I wish my submission could make yo^{w} an innocent woman, and wash yo^{w} as white as a swan. But it must be yor owne submission to God and many praiers, and teares, and affliccons, wch seeing yo^{w} yet have none outwardlie, examine yor heart and thinke of times past & remember what I have written unto yo^{w} heretofore, the same I do now againe For I that nothing doubt, but that although my Ld: Rosse was sent away and is dead, yet truth lives and Gods glorie will appeare in his good time, and if yo^{w} flatter yourself wth other, it will faile yo^{w}.[39]

The mention of Lord Roos being "sent away" implies that Lady Lake believed the countess and Roos had an illicit relationship, and that Roos left in order to avoid discovery. However, God was aware of the countess's sins, and Lady Lake insisted they would come back and haunt her sooner or later.

Lady Lake also emphasized her intention of staying her course and refusing the submission. She told her rival that:

> this busines will never be well ended till yo^{w} and I may meete in the presence of the Kings Matie, wch have bene often my humble suite, although I cannott yet obtain it, I hope ere yo^{w} and I part this world I shall.

Lady Lake was seeking a direct personal confrontation, in the presence of the king, where she hoped she would prevail. Considering that the king had already investigated the business, and then also decided the case himself as a judge in court, it is highly unlikely that Lady Lake would somehow be able to convince him that she should be allowed to confront the countess of Exeter in his presence. As noted, the king's denial of Gondomar's requests for leniency against Lady Lake also suggested that he had no intention of changing his mind. Lady Lake realized the difficulties and thus ended her letter: "if not I will leave that Testimony as shall make all the world see that I dy Gods servant to whose Justice I comend my selfe."[40]

The countess of Exeter's reactions are not recorded, but neither king nor court welcomed Lady Lake's missive, as it was considered "derogatory to the kingdom's justice," as William Camden put it in his diary.[41] Her letter suggested that the king and his court had been fooled by the trickery of the countess and come to an unjust judgment against Lady Lake. King James was not amenable to such arguments: Solomon was never wrong. On November 15, the Privy Council issued yet another warrant to the lieutenant of the Tower: Lady Lake was to be kept close prisoner again.[42] A month later, she was allowed to stay with her husband at Cannons over the Christmas season but had to supply a bond in order to ensure that she would return to the Star Chamber court for her submission the next term.[43]

Hilary term of 1621 came and went without a submission from Lady Lake. Lady Lake claimed illness on the day appointed for her and did not appear, as she had done before. She was sent back to the Tower. After the close of the term, Lady Lake wrote a letter to the lords of the Privy Council. She explained that after the initial delay, she had been ready to do her submission on the last day of the term, but the court did not meet that day, so it had not been possible. She termed herself their "afflicted sarvant" and thanked them for recently being granted "liberty of the Tower which is some comfort to her."[44]

Now she requested a further favor: she asked if she could put in another bond and stay at home until her submission the next term. She promised she would perform the submission "any day the next Terme that his Mayt^sy shall apoynte." She explained that she was still sick and that her husband was also in poor health. She added that she did "beseech this fafor becaus she is informed that my lady of Exeter is satisfied."[45] Perhaps the countess of Exeter was softening somewhat, or simply tiring of having to deal with the recurrent rescheduling of the submission. The king and council were not tired, but promptly denied her request. The message was clear: Lady Lake would stay in the Tower until she submitted.

At this point, Lady Lake had been in prison on and off for over two years. Her once ironclad resolve was growing weaker. Perhaps her husband was also exerting pressure on her to submit, if he still harbored hope that the king would restore him to office, or at least to the Privy Council. Lady Lake clearly could not wear the king down: he was set on having her submit. He viewed her as the worst of the offenders. Lady Roos had committed crimes but redeemed herself by confessing to the king and council several times. As a result, she was allowed to dispense with appearing in-person for her submission. The king had also been willing to dispense with Lake appearing in person, but since the countess of Exeter insisted, James believed it necessary to enforce it. Lady Lake had proved remarkably resistant to the king's insistence that she admit her faults and repent. Her defiant letter to the countess of Exeter provided further evidence of her sinful perseverance to the king.

April 27 was a Friday and a Star Chamber day. On this day, Lady Lake finally gave in. The words and form of her submission do not survive, so it is not clear exactly to what crimes Lady Lake finally admitted fault. Unlike the year before, she did not argue with the Privy Council's wording, but rather performed it "*modo et forma* as was injoyned her."[46] Consequently, it is likely that it was the same as previous ones, which required her to admit to forging the Hatton document and the countess's confession, and of having suborned Sara Swarton. Finally, Lady Lake was released from the Tower for the last time.[47]

Although Lake continued to hope that he would be able to return to court politics, it never happened: the royal court and events moved on without him. Lake had courted Buckingham since the beginning of his rise, but was never able to receive the favorite's consistent patronage, despite his many offers of sizeable payments. With the Howard faction brought down, new officials at court, and the Spanish match no longer a possibility, Lake could not get any traction. After King James's death in 1625, Lake was elected MP to the 1626 Parliament. At that time, the public view of Buckingham had shifted: from being hailed as a Protestant hero after his turn away from Spain and desire to restore the Palatinate, he turned into the object of people's disaffections instead. The failed attacks against Spain coupled with Buckingham's ostentatious spending, his monopoly on the king's affections and courtly patronage, charges of sexual improprieties, and suspicions that he may have hastened King James's death ensured that the Commons assembled in 1626 turned on the favorite. Lake, who just a few years earlier had so assiduously sought Buckingham's assistance, now participated in the Common's prolonged attack against Buckingham instead. The Commons was not able to unseat Buckingham, who had the new King Charles's full and firm support. Buckingham remained the king's powerful favorite until his assassination in 1628, and Lake did not sit in any further Parliaments, vanishing into obscurity.[48]

14
Aftermath

> I heare of a new fire kindling twixt [the countess of Exeter] and the Lady Lake, but there is much labour to kepe yt from blasing.
>
> John Chamberlain to Sir Dudley Carleton, December 7, 1622[1]

The Lake-Cecil feud did not even end with the Lakes' delayed submissions. It just entered a colder period. At times, it threatened to flare up again, requiring interventions to "kepe yt from blasing," as Chamberlain put it. Lingering issues regarding Roos's estate and property caused renewed ire. Sir Thomas Lake and Lady Roos appeared the most willing to forget their past mistakes and move forward. They had the most to gain from forgetting the past: Lake had hoped for a return to politics and Lady Roos wished to rebuild her life and be done with the vestiges of her disastrous first marriage. By contrast, Lady Lake and the earl and countess of Exeter were more stubbornly holding on to their grievances.

The Earl and Countess of Exeter

The victories in the Star Chamber slander case and the submissions of Lady Roos, Lake, and—after a long delay—Lady Lake ensured that the countess of Exeter had managed to clear her reputation. Once Lady Roos and the Lakes had been branded as liars, all their accusations against Lady Exeter were rejected and the countess considered innocent. Except for Lady Lake's insistence that the countess had crimes she should repent, rumors of sexual misconduct or about the paternity of the countess's youngest daughter did not resurface. Either others were fully convinced of the countess's innocence, or they dared not impugn her character with any suggestions of impropriety after the hullabaloo of the scandal and the decisive outcomes in court. The fact that the king himself had judged the case also made it difficult for anyone to openly disagree with his decision. Court cases do not allow for gray areas, they have clear winners and losers. Thus, after the trials, the feud between the Lakes, Lady Roos, and the earl and countess of Exeter quickly became

Family and Feuding at the Court of James I: The Lake and Cecil Scandals. Johanna Luthman, Oxford University Press.
 DOI: 10.1093/oso/9780192865786.003.0014

"remade" as a clear-cut slander case. Nonetheless, the family disputes continued to simmer.

The earl and countess of Exeter were welcomed at courtly affairs in the years following the trials. In August 1621, the countess was present at Burleigh on the Hill during the king's visit. Buckingham had recently purchased the country estate and fêted his royal guest and the rest of the company in predictably splendid fashion. As part of the entertainments, Buckingham had commissioned Ben Johnson to write and put together a masque entitled *Gypsies Metamorphosed.* It contained the requisite poetry, dances, audience-interactive elements, and rich costumes of the court masques.

Characters dressed as gypsies were at the center of the plot. Interspersed with the dancing, the gypsies provided complimentary "fortunes" to the king, Prince Charles, and the notable ladies in attendance. Between Queen Anna's death in 1619 and Prince Charles's marriage in 1625, there were no royal women at court. Instead, the women connected to Buckingham made up the leading ladies of court society. The ladies honored with fortunes by Ben Johnson's gypsies included Buckingham's new wife Katherine Manners, his mother-in-law the countess of Rutland, his sister-in-law Frances Coke Villiers, Viscountess Purbeck, and his sister-in-law's mother, the formidable Lady Hatton (the countess of Exeter's step-daughter). While the Buckingham women's versified fortunes were longer and more complex, the countess of Exeter also received a few lines. By the first couple of lines, it appears that the players (and Jonson) did not find out that she was coming until shortly before the performance, so they may have had to put together the verse rather hastily:

> Madam wee knew of yor coming so late,
> Wee could not well fitt you a nobler fate,
> Then what you have readie made,
> An old mans wife,
> Is the light of his life,
> A younge one is but his shade,
> You will not importune,
> The change of yor fortune;
> For if you dare trust to my forecasting,
> Tis presentlie good and it wilbe lasting.[2]

Even though this verse is complimentary, calling the countess the "light" of the earl's life, it nevertheless points out the age difference between the couple.

Everyone present during the performance of the masque would be aware of the previous scandals and trials, but Johnson did not allude to the matter other than the rather opaque reference to the countess's "good" and "lasting" fortune. The masque was performed two more times, although the ladies' fortunes were exchanged for fortunes for the attending men during the last performance. The countess of Exeter appeared to have defended her position in court society.

Despite the positive "forecasting" at the royal entertainment, soon after tragedy befell the countess and her husband. Georgi-Anna (or Sophia-Anne) Cecil, the daughter whose birth had caused wagging tongues in 1616, fell ill and died in early September 1621. Doctors may have bled the little girl in a desperate attempt to cure her in her last illness. At least one person suggested that it was the phlebotomy that ultimately killed her.[3] Some doctors believed that one should avoid bleeding very young and very old patients, as it might cause further harm. Georgi-Anna was only five at the time, so bleeding would probably have been considered a treatment of last resort. She was buried in Westminster Abbey.[4]

The earl of Exeter did not give up on trying to recoup as much of Roos's property as possible. The state of Roos's finances had always been a mess, but when he left suddenly and then died abroad, it became even more difficult to untangle what had been sold, pawned, given away, abandoned, and so forth. Roos had also left goods in the care of others, probably with the intention of requesting it be sent to him later or sold and the money sent instead. The earl of Exeter and Sir Thomas Lake had already tried to deal with this issue in the lawsuits they started in the fall of 1617. The fight then had focused mostly on the Walthamstow estate, but that had been a lost cause for Exeter. In the early 1620s, the earl tried again, focusing more on goods than real estate, making use of the equity Court of Chancery.

After the victory in the slander trials, Exeter requested to receive the rights of administration of Roos's goods once more, although the king had granted that authority to Lady Roos in the fall of 1618. Exeter argued that Roos had declared his will in front of witnesses on his deathbed: all his goods still in England should go to his grandfather. However, Roos had not specified who should be executor, so therefore Exeter sought to receive legal administration. Roos had left no written will, so his stated desires were not necessarily legally binding. Probably swayed by the outcomes of the trials, Chancery granted Exeter administration by June 7, 1621.[5] The earl now set about gathering more information about who held Roos's various goods, leases, and rents, and how they had come to be in control of it. He argued that Roos had been in possession of goods to the value of £6,000, a substantial sum. Only Exeter's original complaint and the answers of the named defendants survive in the Chancery suit he filed, so we cannot know whether Exeter was successful in getting some, all, or any of the items and money back. The Chancery documents can tell us about the continued bad blood between the families, as well as how Roos's previous actions reverberated for years after his flight and death.

Exeter's January 1622 suit named several defendants. Lady Roos, her new husband, and Sir Thomas and Lady Lake were prime among them, along with more peripheral people who had dealt with Roos's goods. The suit highlights the privileged position of English married men, as the English law of coverture ensured that husbands legally owned and controlled all the goods in the marital household, including even the very clothes a wife might wear, or gifts he had given her during their marriage.[6] Exeter could legally claim that any item of Roos's in his wife's hands should belong to him as the heir, based on common law. In the complaint, as well as the answers, one can clearly see that the wounds from the feud and scandals continued to fester, more for some than for others.

By the time of the Chancery suit, Lady Roos had remarried (more on her second marriage later in this chapter). She and her new husband seemed relatively uninterested in giving any detailed answers to Exeter's complaints. Lady Roos likely desired to move on from her troubled past, and her new husband may not have wished to get involved in her old feud. Lady Roos and her husband provided brief joint answers, informing the court that they had nothing of Lord Roos's, no one else held anything of Lord Roos's on their behalf, and that they knew nothing about any unpaid rents, pawned jewelry, or other financial agreements mentioned in the complaint.[7]

Lake and his wife were more detailed in their answers, provided separately (it is the only suit in which they respond separately rather than jointly). They answered Exeter's specific questions, but they also made sure to point out Roos's faults and weaknesses. For example, Lake reminded Exeter and the court that he had supported his married daughter both before and after Roos left England, as she had been living in his household. Lake wished to justify Lady Roos's actions regarding the few items of Roos's property. In other words, Roos had not been a good husband by not providing for his wife, and therefore the few scraps he left behind rightfully belonged to her. The only Roos property Lake had any knowledge of consisted of the furnishings that Lady Roos used for her chamber in Lake's house. He believed that Roos had gifted those furnishings to his wife before he left for the Spanish embassy. Therefore, Lake implied, Lady Roos ought to be able to control them by the principles of equity, albeit perhaps not according to common law. It made sense to appeal to equity in the Court of Chancery, since that was the court's guiding legal principle.

Exeter had also asked about Roos's jewelry. Gold, silver, pearls, and precious stones could make up a substantial portion of a person's movable goods and were therefore no trivial matter. Lake stated that he was aware that Roos had given his wife a cross of diamonds and that she had sold this to pay off both her own and some of her husband's debts after Roos left England. Furthermore, he believed this cross of diamonds was rightfully Lady Roos's to do with as she wished, as Roos had given it in recompense for the jewels he had taken from his wife to pay for his embassy to Spain. Again, Lake appealed to equity.

To make sure he was providing full disclosure, Lake added that he had received a small cabinet as a gift from Lady Roos, presumably a piece that had been part of Lady Roos's furnishings. Lake argued that his daughter had given him this cabinet at the time when she had letters of administration of Roos's goods, so she was in her full legal right to do so. Lake also admitted that he had received forty pounds from the Exchequer while Suffolk was still treasurer. These forty pounds were part of an unpaid sum due to Roos as recompense for some of his expenses for the Spanish embassy. Lake argued that he had only used this money to "ymploy uppon a messenger senten expressly for the sayd Lord Roos into Italy and aboute other charges concerning the seeking and sending for of the sayd Lord Roos."[8] If Roos had not fled England illegally, Lake would not have had to use some of his money to try to find him, he explained.

Lady Lake provided even more details in her answer, making sure to point out every item that could possibly be in question. Even considering the legal language and other requirements, the document reads like a passive-aggressive missive toward the earl and countess of Exeter. She was providing an exhaustive answer to Exeter's complaint, while also making a point about what she perceived as Exeter's pettiness and greed, especially in the face of Roos's financial mismanagements. Like her husband, she highlighted how they had supported Roos's wife for most of the marriage, and that Roos had taken his wife's jewels for his own ends, even those which had been hers before their marriage. Lady Lake pointed out that Lady Roos had given her bedroom furnishings to her sister-in-law Lettice Lake (her brother Arthur's wife), right before she went to the Tower, thus getting rid of most of the furnishings Roos had gifted her before. The only Roos furnishings that remained at Cannons consisted of "Twoe oulde leather chayres and fower small peaces of the ould hangings."[9]

Lady Lake mentioned further goods and chattel. When Roos left, he owed ten pounds to his butler and Lady Roos asked her mother to help her pay the servant. In exchange, Lady Roos, who then had administration of her dead husband's goods, gave Lady Lake some of Roos's bedlinens still in the butler's hands. Lady Lake claimed it was a poor bargain, considering "some of yt beinge ould & much usyt since that tyme ytterly worn out." Furthermore, Lady Roos brought a mare with her when she stayed at Wimbledon during the summer of 1616. The horse, Lady Roos's since before her marriage, had become pregnant while there. The mare was sent to Cannons, where she had the foal, presumably fathered by one of Exeter's horses or more likely donkeys, as the foal was described as a mule. The mare and the foal had stayed at Cannons ever since, at Lake's expense. In effect, Lady Lake wondered if Exeter really wanted to make all this trouble over some worn furniture, scraps of linen, and half a mule.

The final missive in Lady Lake's answers was directed toward the countess of Exeter. Lady Lake informed the court that she "hath hearde that the Complt^{s} wife the Lady of Exeter Rob[ert] Dixon and Roberte Hooke in the complt^{s} bill menconed & one George Gwilliams can discover or make knowne to the complt^{s} what is become of many of the goods and personal estate of the sayd Lord Roos."[10] Lady Lake, still carrying a grudge, told the earl of Exeter to look closer to home. He should ask his wife and Roos's and da Silva's former servants if he wanted to know more about Lord Roos's doings and belongings, rather than keep accusing the Lakes.[11]

When Chamberlain reported the "new fire kindling twixt" the countess of Exeter and Lady Lake late in 1622, it might have been caused by this renewed ire regarding Roos's property. An immediate intervention kept the fire between the two women "from blasing," ensuring that the hard feelings were at least kept from escalating further.[12] Considering Lady Lake's letter to the countess of Exeter two years prior, along with the new Chancery suit, it does not seem likely that she had changed her mind about the countess, regardless of her submission.

If Exeter did manage to get control of any of Roos's goods, he was not able to enjoy that victory for long. In December 1622, the elderly earl of Exeter fell very ill, potentially developing gangrene in a foot. He lingered for a few weeks. At one point, it looked like he might pull through, but his old body eventually gave up. He died on February 7, 1623, at the advanced age of eighty.[13]

Exeter was generous to his "wellbeloved wife" in his will, which suggests a good relationship between the spouses. The will also demonstrates the complete control of property husbands enjoyed under the rules of coverture. Except for dower or separate jointure agreements, nothing automatically belonged to the widow unless specified in a will. Exeter made his wife executrix and ensured that she received her personal affects, like the jewelry he had given her throughout their marriage, the bedroom silver toiletry items engraved with both of their names "wch shee useth daily," two dozen pieces of silver plate and dishes, Exeter's best coach and four of his best "coachmares," and £500 in cash. In addition, she also received household goods in Parsons Green, the estate her first husband had given to her children, but in which she held a lifetime interest. Exeter now gave his wife "all my household stuffe wch I used at Parsons Greene house att the tyme I lay there."[14] Any dower or jointure agreements were separate from the will, so the dowager countess probably received a lifetime interest in some part of the Cecil property. Those agreements are unclear, but they did not include Exeter House in London or the grand Wimbledon estate: those went to Exeter's son and heir, Lord Burghley, now the second earl Exeter.

Thomas Cecil, earl of Exeter, joined his first wife and little Georgi-Anna in the St. John the Baptist chapel in Westminster Abbey. In the center of the chapel stands a large monument, upon which rests the marble effigies of Thomas Cecil and his first wife Dorothy Neville to his right. Next to Exeter's left side is an empty space. The inscription on the monument implies that the space was reserved for a similar effigy of Cecil's second wife:

> Thomas Cecil, Earl of Exeter, Baron of Burleigh, Knight of the Garter, Privy Counsellor to King James, with his two dearly beloved wives, Dorothy Neville, daughter and co-heir to the noble Lord Latimer, his first wife, and Frances Brydges of the noble family of the Chandos, his second wife. They rest under this monument in firm hope of a Resurrection.[15]

But the dowager countess of Exeter, aged forty-three when her second husband died, had much living left to do. When she finally died forty years later, she chose to be buried in Winchester Cathedral instead, leaving the left-hand side of Exeter's tomb permanently empty.

Although she had lost Georgi-Anna, the new dowager countess of Exeter still had a son and a daughter from her first marriage, Robert and Margaret, for whom to care. The two children had been too young to be involved in the feud with the Lakes. The only time either of them get mentioned in the court records occurs in Lake's suit against Hatton, when Hatton said that he left Exeter's service for a few months, but then returned to serve young Robert Smith as he went to school. A year after the trials had ended, a fifteen-year-old Robert matriculated at Oxford to start his university education. His health was not robust. At the young age of twenty, he realized he may not last long and consequently wrote his will in 1625. He died the following year. He left the Parson's Green estate in Fulham, inherited from his father, to his "beloved" mother and sister. He also made the usual bequests of small sums and objects to friends, kin, and servants. Luke Hatton was not mentioned in Robert's will, although other servants were named specifically. Hatton may have left his service, died, or remained with the countess instead.[16]

In the early 1620s, the countess of Exeter set about arranging a good marriage for her daughter Margaret. At one point in 1623, a Frenchman in the French ambassador's entourage had wooed a teenage Margaret, but he was not successful in securing a match.[17] In 1624, the dowager countess negotiated for a match between Margaret and Sir David Cecil, her step-grandson. After the death of Lord Roos, the second earl of Exeter had only daughters. Therefore, Sir Richard Cecil, the second earl's brother, was heir presumptive. David Cecil was Richard Cecil's eldest son, second in the line of succession to the Exeter earldom. Marrying her daughter to the potential next earl of Exeter certainly would have been a way for the dowager countess to stay more closely connected to the large and wealthy Cecil family after the death of her husband. Lady Hatton, the dowager's stepdaughter, did not agree. Consequently, Chamberlain reported "that match was marred by the Lady Hatton at the very upshot."[18] David Cecil married Elizabeth Egerton instead, became the third earl of Exeter in 1640, and died in 1643. Margaret Smith married Sir Thomas Carey in 1627. Carey served as King Charles's Groom of the Bedchamber, and thus ensured that his wife had entry to the royal court. After Carey's death, Margaret married Sir Edward Herbert.[19]

The countess of Exeter was not connected to any further public scandals, but a curious note in a letter to Lady Hatton in 1627 suggests a possible intrigue. The note is difficult to interpret. John Holles, earl of Clare, wrote a letter with the London news to his friend and close associate, Lady Hatton. At the time, she was away in the country. Among the news at court, Holles included:

> Your famous stepmother of Exeter is married to Sergeant Hichman, and the potticary defeated: this mads Tom Cary, and neer hands kills his wife, who is sayd farr advanced in a consumption: in the mean time the mother hath sport, peradventure ill sauced, for the speech is the lawyer hath the pox, the worst fee his client could have conferred upon him.[20]

To call a woman "famous" could be two-edged. A woman might be well known as a result of her lofty position, beauty, or other traits considered positive. However, a truly virtuous woman should ideally not be the topic of anyone's conversation. The countess of Exeter, even though she had been victorious in her trials, had still become famous as a result of the accusations of poisoning and adultery, which had required her and her family to air the details of their lives in public in a troubling way. The "Sargeant Hitchman" Holles mentioned was likely Sir Robert Hitcham, a lawyer and an MP who never married and held a position as the king's sergeant from 1616 onwards.[21]

Holles suggests a rivalry between Hitcham and an unnamed apothecary, or at least someone nicknamed as an apothecary. His tone suggests that Lady Hatton would know these men. The "Tom Cary" must be Margaret's new husband, who one assumes would be troubled if his mother-in-law was involved in sexual scandals or a marriage below her station.[22] "Pox" probably refers to syphilis. It is not clear if the "client" to which Holles alluded was supposed to be the countess of Exeter, but if that was the case, he was also suggesting that the countess had given Hitcham syphilis. No other mentions of this episode exist to shed any further light on it: there is no record of a remarriage for the countess of Exeter. The note could also be part of a private joke between Holles and Lady Hatton, perhaps, but it is nonetheless interesting that it is placed in the middle of other news in London and the court. The message is not prefaced with any words or statements labeling it as a joke or amusement.

Publicly at least, the countess of Exeter chose to remain a widow. For a time, she lived at Parsons Green in Fulham, her first husband's estate. The countess of Exeter may have given up her claim on the estate by 1632, as her daughter and her husband eventually took over control of Parsons Green.[23]

The countess's primary concern in her widowhood consisted of staying involved in her daughter's life through her two marriages and multiple children. Mother and daughter experiences and survived the turbulence of the civil war, interregnum, and restoration of the monarchy. In the 1630s, the dowager countess of Exeter had her portrait painted by the popular court painter Anthony van Dyck, in which the viewer sees a somber and staid woman in widow's black, a mature matriarch (see Fig. 14.1).

Lady Roos Remade

After the end of her ordeals of 1619—the trials and sentencing, the pressure campaign to confess further, being cast as a sinful and immoral woman, the imprisonment in the Tower, and, finally, the pardon and release and move to the Isle of Wight—Lady Roos was ready to move forward with her life. She was mostly successful in doing so.

Fig. 14.1 Frances Cecil (née Brydges), countess of Exeter. Published by William Faithorne, after Anthony van Dyck, 1630s. © National Portrait Gallery, London.

Lady Roos slowly returned to society after her stint on the Isle of Wight. By early February 1620, the king remitted her fine of 10,000 marks. Buckingham had managed to intercede on Lady Roos's behalf, although it is not clear what prompted this generosity.[24] By April, she was back in London for the first time since her release from the Tower the previous summer. She did not stay at the Lake residence in Charing Cross, but rather in a house at Holborn, suggesting a less-than-cordial relationship with her parents.[25]

Chamberlain related how "the eagles resort" to Lady Roos in Holborn. He may have been referring to the biblical quote from Matthew 24:28, which reads "For wheresoever the carcase is, there will the eagles be gathered together," in a section which discusses Jesus's prediction that the temple in Jerusalem would fall. Chamberlain likened Lady Roos to a carcass, and people hungry for fresh rumors and scandals flocking to see her. Chamberlain clearly continued to have a very low opinion of Lady Roos. He also related how "on Goode Friday night the earle of Oxford and Sir Harry Parker (the Lord Monteagles sonne) for some yll rule thereabout were well beaten and battered by the watch, specially the earl that is scant well yet."[26] The Harry Parker that Chamberlain mentioned may well be the same clerk of the Star Chamber court who spent weeks in jail after Lady Roos accused him of not tendering her oath before her testimony. It is not clear what the earl of Oxford and Parker were doing outside of Lady Roos's house, but it seems the presence of Lady Roos was still stirring up hot feelings.

Despite her damaged reputation, Lady Roos was able to make another marriage. It was not as grand as her first one. Before, during, and after the slander court cases, marriage rumors for Lady Roos had abounded. For the most part, those rumors included a potential groom connected to Buckingham. In the end, Lady Roos did not marry a relative or client of Buckingham's, or anyone else particularly influential. Instead, she married George Rodney, the second son of Sir John Rodney, from a gentry-family in Somerset, in November 1621. Chamberlain described him as "a yong gentleman of small meanes as being a younger brother."[27]

George's elder brother Sir Edward Rodney had some connections to the royal courts. He had angered the king by assisting Thomas Seymour's secret marriage to the king's cousin Arabella Stuart in 1610, but after a stint in the Tower followed by a year abroad in exile with Seymour, Rodney was forgiven and returned to England. In 1614, he married Frances Southwell, one of Queen Anna's maids of honor. The queen paid for the wedding feast, as well as for the bride's gown and rich wedding presents of plate. Rodney was knighted shortly before the wedding. He served in the Parliaments in the 1620s, but his younger brother George, Lady Roos's new husband, was neither at court nor in Parliament.[28]

During her second marriage, Lady Roos kept her name and title rather than changing to plain Mistress Rodney. Considering that she had been a baroness in her first marriage, it is possible that she was allowed to keep using the title even after her marriage to Rodney. It is also possible that she insisted on it herself, in order to emphasize her status. Her husband appears to have obliged her. In legal documents initiated by George Rodney and Lady Roos after 1621, the couple is usually described as "George Rodney Esq and dame Ann the Lady Roose his wife," or some version thereof.[29] In his 1622 Chancery complaint, the earl of Exeter named her "Dame Anne now [Rodney's] wife late the wife of the said Lord Roos," insisting on further distance between their families instead.[30] There are other instances when women used titles from their first marriages even after remarrying. Most notably, Exeter's daughter Elizabeth Cecil, Lady Hatton, called herself by her first married title (as did others) throughout the rest of her life, including during her long, contentious and unhappy marriage to the lawyer Sir Edward Coke. King James also gave Buckingham's mother the title countess of Buckingham in her own right, even though she was married at the time and her husband did not receive a corresponding title.[31]

While the earl of Exeter was trying to recover some of Roos's goods in the Court of Chancery, Lady Roos and her new husband began a long journey to claim the estate of Walthamstow, the manor and lands which had been the focus of the family feud for so long. After the Star Chamber trials in 1619, the Exeters had taken over the income from Walthamstow as part of the payment of the damages Lady Roos owed the countess. They later transferred their interest in the profits of the estate to Thomas, Lord Wentworth (who also served as a witness for the countess in the court case) and others. In 1623, George Rodney paid off his wife's remaining debts encumbered on the estate and tried to take direct control of it. The Lakes had created a trust for Lady Roos, which held Walthamstow for her after they wrested it from Lord Roos. The trust included Lady Roos's uncle Arthur Lake, bishop of Bath and Wells, as well as her brother Sir Arthur, and they were not willing to let George Rodney have it. They wished to protect and preserve the estate for any potential future children Lady Roos may have. As a result, the Rodneys sued the trustees in Chancery.[32]

The suit took over three years, but the court decision gave Lady Roos and her husband control of the estate for life, and then to Lady Roos's children. If she died childless, she could dispose of it as she wished. A year later, Lady Roos "settled the reversion of the manor on her husband in fee." The couple were thus able to get full control as well as ownership of Walthamstow. Lady Roos may have lost the slander suit, but she received Walthamstow after much ado. When she died, her elder brother Thomas argued that he should receive Walthamstow as her heir, but the courts disagreed: Rodney kept it. Nine years after the death of his wife, Rodney sold it to Charles Maynard. The manor exited the grasp of both the Cecils and the Lakes for good.[33]

At the time of the earl of Exeter's funeral in 1623, a rumor circulated that Roos might still be alive. His father, now the second earl of Exeter, "best acquainted with his humors and tricks" seemed convinced it was true for some time.[34] Considering Roos's illegal flight, his keen ability to stay out of sight, and complex plans to have money and goods moved about to assist him in his exile, it is perhaps not so strange that Roos's father may have thought that Roos had faked his own death in order to be free of his troubles. If true, Lady Roos's second marriage would have been invalid. However, Lord Roos did not reappear and stayed dead and gone.

Lady Roos had no children in her second marriage. Other than the battle to take control of Walthamstow, we know very little about this part of her life. It appears that she mostly lived a quiet and simple life in the country. In the early 1620s, the Rodneys lived in the small village of Pilton in Somerset. By 1626, the couple had moved to the coastal village of Netley, just outside of Southampton.[35] These places were a long cry from the vast and luxurious Wimbledon House, but hopefully filled with more happiness and contentment.

Lady Roos was not fated to live long: she died in 1630, aged only thirty. We do not know the cause of her death. She was buried in the Rodney Chapel in St. Leonard church in the small village of Rodney Stoke, Somerset, the site of other Rodney family burials. Her grave monument is quite elaborate, situated beneath a window, with a stone canopy arching over it (see Fig. 14.2 and Fig. 14.3). The canopy is studded with both small stars and little clouds. On top of the stone coffin rests an intricately carved effigy crafted of Somerset alabaster. This is the only known likeness of Lady Roos. As is common with effigies, the figure is lying down, with palms pressed together in pious prayer. The head rests on a pillow decorated with tassels, with her hair fashionably short and tightly curled. She is wearing a dress decorated with pearls, a well-detailed lace collar, sleeves trimmed with ribbons and more lace, and a sash tied around her waist. A two-row pearl collar encircles her neck, along with what looks like a string that disappears within the bodice of the dress. Memorial pieces and other treasured objects were sometimes secured with black string, so perhaps that is what we see here as well. The black string was also meant to contrast with, and emphasize, the whiteness of the skin.[36] The feet peek out under the voluminous skirt of the dress, clad in high-heeled shoes. Underneath the platform, the stone masons carved a skull and two

Fig. 14.2 Tomb of Anne Lake. St. Leonard's Church, Rodney Stoke, Somerset. Photo: Michael Statham.

Fig. 14.3 Effigy of Anne Lake. St. Leonard's Church, Rodney Stoke, Somerset. Photo: Michael Statham.

hourglasses, to remind the viewers of their pending mortality. The inscription on the monument reads:

> Here rests in the Peace of God the Body of the Right Hon:ble Anna Lakes Daughter of Sir Thomas Lakes of Channons in Middlesex sometime Principal Secretary & Councellor to King James ye 1st. Married to William Cecil Lord Ross, Eldest son of the 2nd Earle of Exeter of that family. Since wife to GEORGE RODNEY, Esq.; son of Sir John Rodney Knight, by the space of ten years, who by this Stone doth acknowledge her deserts toward him, & desireth to perpetuate the Memory of a Good Wife & a most Penitent Christian. She dyed in the year of Grace 1630, of her own age ye 30th. & now hopes for a Joyfull Resurrection.
>
> Come Lord Jesus, come quickly. Revel. 22nd, 20th.[37]

Although grave inscriptions generally tend to laud the deceased, naturally, it seems at least as if Lady Roos had striven to make up for past mistakes and had more success in her second marriage than in her first.

Endings

Several others in the Lake family also died around the same time as Lady Roos. Sir Thomas Lake died on September 17, 1630, and was buried in Little Stanmore Church, the parish church connected to the Lake country home Cannons. Lady Roos's brother Sir Arthur Lake died in December 1633.

Mary Lake outlived her husband by twelve years. She came to the attention of the Privy Council yet again as a result of her youngest daughter's marriage in the mid-1630s. Bridget Lake was the child born in the summer of 1616, when the countess of Exeter and Lady Lake had "both bought daughters." Perhaps wary after the difficulties of Lady Roos's marriage, Lady Lake intervened in Bridget's marriage, prompting her new son-in-law to ask for assistance from the Privy Council.

Bridget married William Domville in April 1636. Seven months after the wedding, Domville petitioned the Privy Council, complaining that Lady Lake had detained his wife after she had gone back home for a visit. Lady Lake kept her as a "recluse," Domville said, and would not allow her to return to her husband or for her husband to come and fetch her or learn the cause of this troubling behavior. The Privy Council ordered Lady Lake to appear at court with her daughter, so that they could investigate the matter. There is no note about any further action, so perhaps this family dispute was settled quickly. Lady Roos's bad experiences in her first marriage might have made Lady Lake overly cautious, or perhaps, if one chose to believe her detractors, she was up to her old tricks again. In any case, Bridget Lake remained married to William Domville.[38] Mary Lake died in 1642.

In 1653, Sir Thomas Lake the younger also died, which meant that every principal person in the Lake-Cecil feud was dead and gone, except for the dowager countess of Exeter. She died in 1663 at the respectable age of eighty-three. In her will, she was generous to her sole surviving child Margaret, as well as her grandchildren and other relatives.[39] By then, the Lake-Cecil feud and the scandals that developed from it had become part of the history of the court of King James, already debated in the biographies of King James produced by Anthony Weldon, William Sanderson, and Geoffrey Goodman in the mid-1600s.

Epilogue

> The particulars [of the Lake-Exeter trials] I leave to Mr. Whitwick's relation, at his return into the country, because they require a book, rather than a letter.
>
> Thomas Lorkin to Sir Thomas Puckering, February 9, 1619[1]

Remarks like Lorkin's are common in letters describing the twists and turns in the Lake-Cecil feud and its scandals. Many details are lost, as letter-writers felt it was too much to include in their missives, or they hesitated to put sensitive details in writing. The case has attracted comments across the centuries, with historians attempting to retell the events succinctly, but rarely venturing beyond a few pages at most. Those abbreviated attempts included skipping over contradictory details and establishing clear villains and heroes, even though they did not always agree on who fits in which category. The interpretations of the Lake-Cecil feud have shifted over time, as the paradigms and lenses through which people understood the actions changed.

Seventeenth-century writers focusing on the reign of King James sometimes included brief overviews of the Lake-Cecil feud, primarily elaborating on the trials in order to explain the fall of Secretary Lake. In the 1640s and 1650s, England was going through its wrenching civil wars, the trial and execution of James's son Charles I, and the experiment in rule as a Commonwealth during the Interregnum of the 1650s. Pro-Parliamentarian and radical writers like Anthony Weldon (1543–1648) in his *Court and Character of King James* presented the king and the Jacobean court's failures as foundations for the degradations of the Stuart line as a whole, which also justified the overthrow of Charles I. Weldon died in 1648, and thus did not live to see the execution of King Charles in early 1649. However, his book, popular among Parliamentarians, was published in several editions shortly after the king's death.[2] Weldon, a one-time Jacobean courtier who was fired when he wrote a tract denouncing the king's Scottish courtiers in the 1610s, had a famously low opinion of the king, believing him sexually immoral because of his attachments to male favorites, physically deformed, and politically weak.

Weldon's account includes a retelling of the Overbury scandal, serving to illustrate how the Jacobean court was wholly morally corrupt.[3]

Weldon's ire against King James also included a negative opinion of Sir Thomas Lake. Weldon believed Lake was a lowborn, grasping fellow, who ingratiated himself at court by enriching the Scots around the king to the detriment of deserving Englishmen. Unlike the more detailed coverage of the Overbury scandal, Weldon did not discuss the Lake-Cecil feud or the trials at length. He merely remarked that Lake's wife "overawed" him and eventually caused his overthrow.[4] Clearly, Weldon viewed the Overbury scandal as more scandalous and damaging to the Jacobean court than the Lake-Exeter feud.[5] Weldon did imply that the feud and the trials were all Lady Lake's fault, and therefore that part of the problem with King James's rule was that his court was disrupted by out-of-control women, further emasculating the already weak king.

King James and the Stuarts also had supporters and defenders during the tumultuous Interregnum in the 1650s, and they had more to say about the Lake-Exeter fights than Weldon. The royalists William Sanderson (1586–1676) and Godfrey Goodman, bishop of Gloucester (ca. 1582–1656) both wrote books about James and his reign in direct response to Weldon's missive. Sanderson defended James as a peace-loving and just ruler, who punished misdeeds appropriately but was also merciful to penitent sinners. Similarly, Goodman believed that Weldon had slandered James, who fundamentally had been a good king dealing with challenging events. Where Sanderson tended to be overwhelmingly positive, Goodman, while vehemently disagreeing with Weldon's account, was more cautious in ascribing only positive motives to James's actions.[6]

Like Weldon, Sanderson and Goodman had lived through the Jacobean period and knew many of the people involved in the Lake-Exeter feud personally. The fact that even Goodman and Sanderson had slightly different versions of the feud and scandals reveals the complexity of the case. Later historians often quote or follow Sanderson and Goodman, making the duo "foundational" in the interpretation of events. Both Goodman's and Sanderson's accounts contain many of the main elements of the story, but sometimes get the chronology or the specific accusations wrong. Those mistakes in turn have been perpetuated by others.

Sanderson had worked as a secretary on Roos's 1616–17 embassy to Spain and at court during James's reign. Unlike Weldon, Sanderson thought Lake a competent administrator and generally a good man. However, he agreed with Weldon that Lake's wife and daughter's quarrels were the "chief and only cause of his cause of his ruine." Therefore, "malice and revenge, two violent passions overruling the weaker sex," ended the otherwise honest and capable Lake's career.[7]

Sanderson believed that the "deadly feud" between Lady Lake and the countess began in 1616–17, while Roos was in his embassy in Spain, although he refused to give a specific reason, claiming "tis no matter for what" at that time.[8] According to Sanderson, Roos neglected his wife when he returned from Spain and refused to complete a jointure agreement about Walthamstow, and then he fled to Italy. In his absence, Lady Lake and Lady Roos began to accuse the countess of adultery with Roos, and of trying to poison Lady Roos and her mother. They argued that Roos fled the country when Lady Roos discovered his adultery.

The countess went to the king to profess her innocence. At this point Lady Lake and Lady Roos counterfeited a confession from the countess. Sanderson falsely states that Lady Lake was present at the countess's Wimbledon confession as well, mirroring the common melding of Lady Lake and Lady Roos's roles in the feud at the time. The king sent Dendy to Italy, where Roos and da Silva swore on the Eucharist that they were innocent. It is not entirely clear where Sanderson received that information, because it did not appear in surviving letters or other contemporary comments. The abstracts of proofs from the trial only says that Roos denied the accusations "before an altar" and that da Silva denied the same "with many deep oaths."[9]

In Sanderson's telling, the king found that the confession did not match the countess's handwriting. Lady Lake and Lady Roos needed to provide other witnesses and that is when they suborned Sara Swarton. The king then visited Wimbledon to check out the site of the supposed confession, finding that the hangings did not go all the way to the floor, and that Swarton could not have heard a conversation at the other end of the room.

Next Lady Lake and Lady Roos claimed that Luke Hatton had produced a writing, stating that the countess offered to pay him £40 to poison the two of them. (Sanderson is wrong about this, of course.) At that point, the king sent for Lake and advised him not to get involved in the business. Lake insisted he had to be a father and a husband and assist the women of his family. The king kept some private confessions of Lady Roos and Swarton in secret. In the end, he declared the countess innocent and punished the Lakes and Lady Roos. Lady Roos confessed, and was pardoned faster. Sanderson specifically remembered that the king made the Adam, Eve, and serpent comparison, and that Lake told him the sentence had cost him £30,000 pounds and his honor and office. Many felt sorry for him, considering him an honest man. According to

Sanderson, the king, a wise investigator, was able to get to the bottom of the deceptions and find the truth.[10]

Godfrey Goodman served as chaplain to Queen Anna and later became bishop of Gloucester. In *The Court of King James I*, he argued that Weldon's charge that Lake was overawed and beaten by his wife was not true. Goodman liked the people on both sides in the feud, making it difficult for him to choose a particular side to blame. He did not think that Lady Exeter was guilty of the accusations against her, but rather thought the feud was the result of a misunderstanding. This misconception resulted from the vast age difference between the earl and his new wife, since such marriages often caused factions and jealousy in a household. To please her husband, the young countess wanted to demonstrate how much she cared for all the earl's children and grandchildren. She was therefore especially friendly toward Roos and did him many favors, because she knew the earl was fond of him. According to Goodman, the Lakes and Lady Roos misconstrued the countess's friendliness.[11]

Providing further detail, Goodman argued that the misunderstanding began when the marriage between Lord and Lady Roos faltered, Roos neglected his wife, and left for Italy. (Goodman has the chronology wrong, stating that the Rooses married after his return from his embassy to Spain in 1616–17.) According to Goodman, Lady Roos found some letters which suggested that her husband's "love was carried another way," and this ensured that Lady Roos "easily believed that she was to be poisoned." The distraught young woman told her mother, who "took it to heart." Lady Lake "breaks into very rash and inconsiderate words" which "did touch very much upon the honour of the Countess of Exeter."[12] While the countess was innocent, Ladies Lake and Roos were truly convinced of her guilt: this is what made the matter so complex and the two sides so insistent, Goodman thought. The countess then decided to clear herself and sued the Lakes and Lady Roos in Star Chamber. Lake filed a crossbill, and this was how the Star Chamber cases began. Goodman never mentioned the property disputes between the two families.

Unlike Sanderson, Goodman believed that King James clearly favored the Exeters in the trials, exemplified by the king's leniency toward the countess. James allowed some of the countess's private letters to be burnt rather than entered into evidence. The countess argued the letters had nothing to do with the cause, but Lake thought that was prejudiced against him.[13] In addition, Goodman also seemed a bit skeptical about some of the testimony for the countess. "Truely, things were very strangely discovered for the quitting of the countess; that an ordinary man keeping no memorials of his business yet should make good proof by others, where he was at such time two or three years agone, with many such difficult passages hard to be proved." Goodman speculated that maybe the king did that to "gratify the Cecils, who were several ways joined with the Howards and other great families of the kingdom." He added that the king was very fond of Exeter, and rightfully so, because he was "an honest and goodnatured man." In the end, Goodman claims, King James found for the countess and against Lady Roos and the Lakes, but also said that Lake was "free and innocent in that business." (Here Goodman is just plain wrong: at the sentencing, King James specifically emphasized that Lake also must be found guilty along with the rest.)

If the king believed that Lake was innocent, why did he remove him from his position? Goodman commented that many were puzzled about that decision. Goodman presented two reasons, both completely unrelated to the slander cases. First, Lake had unwittingly been responsible for the death of a Spaniard who served as a spy for the English at the Spanish court. Lake had revealed the identity of the spy to his son-in-law Roos, and Roos in turn told Gondomar about it. Once Gondomar revealed it to the Spanish king and council, the spy was quickly caught and executed. Having caused the English king to lose such an important asset, James turned on Lake. Secondly, Lake "had applied [the king] with bills and reversions" so much that the king began to "mislike him" for all the press of suits and requests. Goodman thought that Lake rightfully should have been restored, but the king, somewhat capriciously, simply decided not to do it out of personal preference. Goodman also suggested that Lake paid £2,000 to someone for assistance with restoration to royal favor. The person receiving the money—presumably Buckingham, although Goodman provides no name—did not actually help him, so Lake was tricked out of his money.[14]

Throughout the 1800s, the story of the Lake-Cecil feud was repeated very briefly in the various genealogical works produced by John Burke and Sir Bernard Burke, quoting and following Sanderson's account. In their works, like the *Dictionary of the Peerage and Baronetage* and *Anecdotes of the Aristocracy, and Patricians*, the Burkes wrongly named Lady Roos Elizabeth, rather than Anne.[15] Other historians using these sources also followed suit in using the wrong name.

In 1854, the writer William Harrison Ainsworth published a novel titled *The Star-Chamber: An Historical Romance* in two volumes. Ainsworth had become a popular author in England during the 1830s and 1840s, when he produced several books of historical fiction in the romantic and gothic style.

At the height of his fame, many viewed him as the successor to Sir Walter Scott. Ainsworth break-through novel *Rookwood* was set in the 1700s, but many of the books that followed focused on the Tudor and Stuart periods, in "merry old England," as Ainsworth termed it. Ainsworth's historical work also often centered on a place, or an institution, and he wove his narratives around the people who inhabited or engaged with it, like in *The Tower of London* (1840), *Old Saint Paul's* (1840), and *Windsor Castle* (1842). He also published at least two other books that specifically dealt with the Jacobean period: *The Lancashire Witches* (1848), which centered on the 1612 witch trials of several women from the Pendle Hill area, and *Guy Fawkes* (1841), focusing on the events around the Gunpowder Plot of 1605. While his works were fictionalized, Ainsworth often based them on his reading of archival sources. By the time Ainsworth wrote *The Star Chamber* in the 1850s, his literary star had begun to wane, as readers had moved on to the social realism of Charles Dickens and others. As a result, the novel made little impact, and Ainsworth works have mostly been ignored.[16]

The main villain in Ainsworth's story was the arbitrary and oppressive court of Star Chamber itself, especially how it was abused by monopolists such as Sir Giles Montpessom. The novel weaves together several narratives that are connected to the Star Chamber, with the Lake and Cecil fights forming one of those tales. One scholar argues that the tale of Lord Roos's conflicts with his wife and in-laws seemed to be "thrust irrelevantly into the midst of action involving other principals" without being integrated very well.[17] It perhaps also suggests that Ainsworth, like so many others, found pieces of evidence of the feud in his research, became fascinated, but could not shape the complex story into a more comprehensive narrative.

In Ainsworth's romance, the men are the main villains, and the women make valiant attempts to maintain moral order, even if their emotions sometimes get the better of them. The dashing but immoral Lord Roos plans to poison his wife and mother-in-law when they threaten to reveal his affair with the youthful countess of Exeter. As revenge against the adulterous countess, Lady Lake also planned to falsely accuse her of practicing witchcraft, by bewitching Roos to love her. The countess tries to dissuade Roos from his poisonous plot, arguing that murder is too great a sin to add to their crime of adultery. Lady Roos, hopelessly in love with her husband and blind to his faults, only wishes him to leave the countess and return to her. Lady Lake schemes and produces a fraudulent confession in order to catch the countess in a trick.

Luke Hatton appears as an apothecary, skilled in mixing poisons and mimicking anyone's handwriting. At the behest of Roos and the reluctant countess,

Hatton attempts to murder Lady Roos and Lady Lake by poison. Sara Swarton discovers his plot and manages, with the assistance of Lake and his wife, to force Hatton to make an antidote. The two women survive. The countess, now disgusted by the depth of Roos's depravity, falls out with her lover. Cowardly Roos flees the country, whereas the braver countess decides to stay, fight, and simply deny her crimes. The Lakes were outmaneuvered in Star Chamber by the crafty Luke Hatton and the countess, and by the fact that the weak Lady Roos admitted to having forged the countess's confession and refused to charge her husband with adultery. The king promptly found the Lakes guilty in Star Chamber, and the countess, having managed to convince her husband the earl of her innocence, triumphs. Ainsworth called Lady Roos Elizabeth, which suggests he had mostly used Sanderson and Burke as his sources.

A few decades after Ainsworth's publication, Samuel Rawson Gardiner (1829–1902) also recounted the Lake and Cecil scandals. Gardiner, one of the most prolific historians focusing on the seventeenth century, was also at the forefront of the new professionalization of history as an academic field in the nineteenth century. As a result, his interpretations of Stuart political history have heavily influenced later historians.

Gardiner's account of the Lake-Cecil fights takes up six pages of Volume 3 in the massive ten-volume *History of England from the Accession of James I to the Outbreak of the Civil War, 1603–1642* published in the mid-1880s.[18] Gardiner predominantly relied on correspondence in the State Papers collections, which also included the abstracts of the witness testimonies, the sentence in the court, and the submissions, but not the court records. As a result, Gardiner's account is more accurate and detailed than both Goodman's and Sanderson's. Unlike the two seventeenth-century writers, he recognized that the disputes between the families started with the fight over Walthamstow.

Considering that Gardiner was just providing a brief account of the downfall of Lake, it is not surprising that he did not dig into the lengthy and complex court case records. But that also means that he got some parts of the story wrong. For example, he claimed that Lord and Lady Roos's stay at Wimbledon took place after the Cannon's incident, right before Roos fled to Italy, rather than the year before. He also argued that Exeter, at the behest of his wife, had put a stop to the conveyance of Walthamstow to Lady Roos. Because Lady Roos hated the countess of Exeter, Lady Roos began to make up accusations against her. Once she had started, she seemed incapable of stopping.

Gardiner initially judged that the persons most at fault for the feud were Roos, "a dissolute and heartless youth," and Lady Roos and Lady Lake, both "artful and unprincipled women." After having recounted the sentencing, Gardiner concluded that of "the guilt of the Lady Roos and her maid, there could be no doubt whatsoever." Lake also held some blame, in Gardiner's view, because he had assisted his daughter in circulating the libels against the countess. However, Gardiner was more uncertain about Lady Lake's guilt in the end, because she was so stubbornly refusing to admit that she had anything to do with the fraudulent documents. "Whatever evidence has reached us," Gardiner concluded, "favours the theory that she was herself deceived by her artful daughter." Trying to understand what might lead Lady Roos to make such specific false accusations, and convince her parents they were true, Gardiner suggested that "Lady Roos's prurient imagination brought before her mind the chief incidents of the Essex divorce."[19] Gardiner guessed that the specter of the sinful and murderous Frances Howard served as the impressionable Lady Roos's inspiration, but did not provide any evidence for this supposition.

In an 1885 book about Sir Edward Cecil, son of the earl of Exeter, Charles Dalton mostly followed Sanderson when telling the story of the Lake-Cecil feud but also filled it out with more detail from State Paper letters.[20] Dalton argued that the person most to blame was Lady Lake. He saw Lady Roos as "a lady of sweet seventeen" who was "stirred up by her Mother Jezebel." Mother and daughter came to believe that the countess had an affair with Roos, and then set their plans of revenge in action. The two women were able to come up with the elaborate lies and forgeries, because, according to Dalton, when "jealousy and hatred once take possession of women's hearts they become utterly bereft of reason, and are hardly accountable for their actions." Hysterical, uncontrollable women were thus behind "one of the most scandalous libels of a scandalous age." Dalton also wrongly claimed that Lake was restored to the king's favor, "which he never really lost."[21]

In his book about the Cecil family published in 1914, George Ravenscroft Dennis similarly stated that the countess of Exeter was entirely innocent, and that the fault for the feud lay with Lady Lake and Lady Roos, although he was not quite as judgmental in his language. Dennis primarily used Gardiner's account.[22] More recent books about the Cecils tend to focus on William Cecil, first Lord Burghley, or Sir Robert Cecil, earl of Salisbury, neither of which was involved in the disputes with the Lakes, and so they therefore include no account of the story.

Some modern biographies of King James mention the Lake-Cecil scandals. D. Harris Willson's 1956 biography of King James includes an account a page and a half long of Lake's fall, "dragged down by his wife and by his venomous daughter," primarily following Goodman's version and the letters of John Chamberlain.[23] In his *Great Britain's Solomon* (1990), Maurice Lee mentioned that Buckingham "cleared out" the Howards from court, including "their chief client, Lake, from the secretaryship, thanks chiefly to the incredible behavior of his awful daughter."[24]

Late twentieth- and twenty-first-century biographies of King James either do not mention the scandal at all or only mention it very briefly. For example, Alan Stewart's *The Cradle King* (2003), Pauline Croft's *King James I* (2002), and Thomas Cogswell's *James I* (2019) are silent on the matter. In *Dynastic Politics and the British Reformations, 1558–1630* (2019), Michael Questier mentions the downfall of Secretary Lake as the result of him being "mired in the Lake-Exeter case" and that the king judged against him in February 1619, but provides no further explanation.[25]

The scandals at the Jacobean court have also garnered attention as cause behind an increasing distaste for the royal court and its inhabitants among the influential gentry in the decades leading up to the civil war. In *The Crisis of the Aristocracy, 1558–1641* (1965), Lawrence Stone argued that the series of sexual scandals at the court of King James caused the Puritan gentry to associate the court and the aristocracy with sexual license and immorality, which resulted in "undermining the moral authority of both the peerage and the Court" and then, by extension, led to a breakdown between court and country in the 1640s civil wars.[26] Among these scandals, Stone emphasizes the annulment and remarriage of Frances Howard to Robert Carr, earl of Somerset, and the connected murder of Overbury. In a brief two sentences, Stone also mentions Lady Roos's accusations of attempted poisoning and incest against the countess of Exeter, but mistakenly writes that in "the end Lady Roos's accusations were exposed as lies, and she herself convicted of incest with her brother."[27]

Stone's work, although impressive in scope, has been criticized by historians for the practice of drawing sweeping general conclusions from evidence that in some cases remain anecdotal. In a significantly more nuanced way, Alastair Bellany has investigated the many meanings and consequences of the Overbury murder, arguing that the heady brew of poison, murder, witchcraft, illicit sex, and rumors of a popish plot "could horrify in a number of ways." Rather than simply casting the court as an immoral place in the eyes of a more Puritan country gentry, the scandals surrounding the Overbury case:

> subverted images of court virtue; they crystallized and energized traditional and Tacitean stereotypes of court corruptions, which cast court scandals as

> part of a larger trend of political decay; they embodied unnerving social and gender disorder; they suggested that true honour and worth had been banished, and that the court had rejected good counsel (Overbury) for bad (Carr); and, most dangerously of all, the sins of the Overbury murderers linked court scandal to popery, the master sin of religious decay.[28]

In Bellany's exhaustive account, courtly scandals resonated with all levels of society in a multitude of ways and cast long shadows, ultimately contributing to the erosion of trust in the early Stuart monarchy. Bellany briefly discusses the Lake-Cecil fights in this book, but largely explained the narratives in the case—the accusations of adultery and poisoning—as an echo of elements of the Overbury case, potentially following in Gardiner's footsteps.

After the rise of women's history and gender studies in the late twentieth century, historians have been less hostile to Lady Lake and Lady Roos. Instead, they have been more sensitive to sexual double standards and gendered ideas and patriarchal strictures in the early seventeenth century when interpreting their actions, and how others reacted to them. In addition, the focus has been less on assigning guilt, and more on understanding the context of the accusations and reactions. For example, in his book on the Overbury murder, Bellany described how Lady Lake especially became a focus for libels after the sentencing, because she transgressed the feminine norms, like Frances Howard before her.[29]

Bellany also edited and published five libelous verses produced against Lady Lake and Lady Roos after they lost their court cases and included an introduction explaining the main accusations and events.[30] He has written the *Oxford Dictionary of National Biography* (2004 ed.) entries for Roos, Lady Roos, and the countess of Exeter, which outline the scandals as well. Yet, each of these contributions is short, and does not include the court records, leaving Bellany to conclude that "the exact origins in the trouble [between the families] are now impossible to discover."[31] Indeed, Bellany has pointed out that the Lake-Cecil feud "has not been systematically investigated."[32] Likewise, legal scholar R. W. Hoyle, in a 2019 essay which briefly mentions the case, notes that "there seems to be no definite account of this suit [in Star Chamber]."[33]

I have also looked at the case before. In *Love, Lust and License in Early Modern England: Illicit Sex and the Nobility* (2008), I included the Lake and Exeter trials as an example of cases of illicit sex (and accusations of illicit sex) that became scandalous in James's reign because it included other, more serious offenses. I argued that James rarely punished illicit sex on its own, unless it was accompanied by other crimes. Comparing it with other Jacobean court scandals, like the Overbury murder and the illegal flight and bigamy of Robert Dudley and the maid of honor Elizabeth Southwell, the women in these cases had their reputations sullied, but they were yet able to function in early modern society after a time in the cold.[34] I also briefly discussed the case in a 2017 biography of Frances Coke Villiers, Viscountess Purbeck (*Love, Madness, and Scandal: The Life of Frances Coke Villiers, Viscountess Purbeck*). Lady Purbeck and Lord Roos were first cousins.[35] As mentioned in Chapter 3 here, shortly before Roos fled to Italy, he temporarily became involved in the epic fights between Lady Purbeck's parents, Lady Hatton and Sir Edward Coke, over the issue of her marriage.

In 2021, Carole Levin published a chapter using Lady Lake as an example of the sort of "unruly women" and "shrews" that King James disliked and tried to tame.[36] Levin interprets Lady Lake as "a strong woman who supported her family, though in some unethical ways," but argues that Lady Roos had a "bad reputation" even before her marriage as a "very pert lady" who domineered her mother.[37] Levin makes a good case for King James's dislike of assertive women, but her coverage of the Lake and Cecil feud is limited and includes some mistakes and omissions. For example, she claims Lady Lake never submitted to Star Chamber.[38] This is largely a result of the sources: Levin uses a limited set of printed sources and does not include the Star Chamber and Chancery court cases or other archival sources. Most of the details of the accusations are in the court documents and in the fuller versions of letters and other sources in the State Papers archives.

Other accounts have largely focused on the main slander court case, and on the women, Lake, and the earl of Exeter. By contrast, I have taken a longer approach in this book, focusing on the slow development and escalation of the feud, as well as the continuation of it after the court cases were concluded. It is also crucial to understand the role of Lord Roos better. Although his life was short, and he removed himself from the fighting between his families, he was indeed "the cause of it all," as one letter writer understood it in the spring of 1618. Roos's character, motivations, and actions are as important for understanding the feud as those of the other family members. This account is also more detailed because I have dug into the records of the court cases the feud engendered for the first time. I also look at the totality of court cases, and not just the main slander case. Since the disputes began over property, it is crucial for the historian to include those complex and protracted legal battles.

Even so, because we do not have all the required information to make a final judgment in the Lake and Cecil feud, it is more fruitful to use the feud to learn about the mental world of early Stuart people by analyzing the meaning of the accusations, crimes, and the reactions to them. This is what I have attempted to do throughout this book. Nevertheless, the desire to know "what actually happened" is strong and hard to suppress, as is the wish to produce a more cohesive and understandable narrative. Having spent so much time with the Lakes and Cecils, I will venture to do what earlier historians have, and draw some conclusions about the actions of the feuding families.

The feud between the families was more complex than the outcome of the trials suggest. Clearly, neither side was free of guilt in such a lengthy fight, which involved so many different disputes and layers of accusations. It is clear that Lady Roos, with some assistance, produced fraudulent evidence in the form of the countess's confession and Hatton's document. The fact that Lady Roos admitted to these forgeries led her contemporaries, and historians, to believe that all the accusations against the countess were made up. However, Lady Roos and Lady Lake were convinced that the countess was not innocent.

Lady Roos believed that the countess was guilty of something, if not outright adultery, then at the very least being a rival for her husband's affections. She also appeared to be convinced that others were out to destroy her marriage, evidenced by her insistence that Exeter and Roos servants were trying to sow distrust between the spouses and their families. She insisted on this again and again, even before her more detailed revelations about the summer of 1616. The fact that she went to the lengths of forging evidence suggests that she was fully aware that others would not take her accusations seriously unless she provided solid proof. Confessions were often viewed as the best way to ensure the guilt of a criminal.

The story of the poisoning is less clear. Obviously, Lady Roos was not able to produce sufficient evidence of being poisoned to satisfy the court. Since she admitted to forging the two documents, the only tangible proofs, she had to forfeit the notion of being poisoned altogether. As the doctors testified in court, Lady Roos's symptoms did not match those produced by roseacre, the purported poison. Any number of scenarios are possible: Lady Roos might have made it up entirely, she might have become ill and interpreted it as a poison attempt after the fact, or she might have simply consumed too large a dose of the conserve and/or syrup of roses, making the medicines have a stronger effect than planned.

Lady Lake also believed the countess was not innocent. She suggested that letters had passed between her and the countess as early as during the summer of 1617, when Lady Lake told the countess to stop spreading rumors of Roos's impotence. Lady Lake then construed it as the countess was trying to cover her "own faults," referencing the earlier reports that the earl was not the father of the countess's youngest daughter. Lady Lake also seemed to have been convinced that the countess might have already tried to poison her daughter before, and perhaps might try again. Many of Lady Lake's contemporaries (and others since) interpreted her long resistance to the submission as further evidence of her stubborn, contrarian, and sinful nature, but it could of course be due to her conviction that she was, in fact, right, and unlike her daughter, not guilty of forging any documents.

Out of the many servants who testified on behalf of Lady Roos and the Lakes, only Sara Swarton was found guilty of perjury. She was also the only servant specifically named as a defendant in the Exeters' slander suit against the Lakes and Lady Roos. Swarton lied about having been hidden in the chamber at Wimbledon while the countess wrote her confession and cooperated with Lady Roos when producing the accusations of adultery against the countess. She suffered greatly because she performed what her employer asked of her.

However, Swarton was not the only one in court who claimed to have heard about the "unlawful love" between Roos and the countess: many other servants, and family and friends of servants, reportedly heard rumors of the same, and were willing to restate it under oath. Unless the Lakes were able to pay, coerce, and produce a whole slew of witnesses, it is fair to state that—at minimum—rumors about a possible affair must have been circulating among the people who served the Lakes, Cecils, and Rooses. No other witnesses were accused of, or punished for, deposing falsely in the case. Since the countess of Exeter's victory in Star Chamber was so complete, it would not have been necessary for her to proceed against anyone else, unless they persisted in telling their stories. The first Lord Burghley had also argued that it was not right for nobility and gentry to sue poor people, since they did not have the same means to defend themselves. Like in a duel, legal battles should take place between equals, Burghley contended.[39] Not everyone followed that advice, of course.

Lake was put in a difficult bind, in a "labyrinth" as Chamberlain expressed it. He had nothing to gain from a direct confrontation with the earl and countess of Exeter, and everything to lose. He always tried the private route in disputes first. He blamed bad servants and avoided ever suing the earl and countess of Exeter directly. Lake must have sincerely believed that he was supporting and protecting his daughter and defending his wife's reputation. He did not do it for financial gain: the Lakes had already managed to get control of Walthamstow for Lady Roos. The fact that Lake was never a driving force against the countess and earl of Exeter was not lost on his contemporaries, who believed that his guilt was lesser than that of his wife and daughter. While Lake did everything he could to protect his daughter, she, in turn, betrayed him.

It must be concluded that Lady Roos treated her parents rather horribly. She forged the evidence and did not tell her parents what she had done. She did not even tell her parents about the countess's forged confession, surprising everyone by bringing it to the king. Again, Lake and his wife had to react to it after the fact. Her parents were put in the position of choosing to believe their daughter, or to dismiss what she was saying altogether. They chose to support her. And yet, Lady Roos confessed the forgeries to the king before the trials, again without telling her parents about it, letting them go through the entire trial with the outsized public scrutiny, fighting what the king had already predetermined was a losing battle.

Other historians have vilified Lady Roos for her betrayal and her forgeries, but a modern reader might be more forgiving toward the young woman's poor decision-making. Her marriage, which had held so much promise, failed miserably. Her husband abandoned her, leaving her entirely dependent on her parents. He did not just separate from her, but left her in a spectacular and humiliating manner, fleeing the country and never sending a single word to her after that. King James certainly relented toward her rather quickly, largely because of her willingness to confess and repent her faults. A repentant sinner could be forgiven more easily.

Lord Roos certainly strikes one as a remarkably irresponsible person, whose decisions and actions made every contentious moment worse rather than better. His contemporaries were divided in their judgments. Some of those who knew him personally found him charming company, a cosmopolitan traveler who enjoyed art, religious discussions, drink, and carousing. Others judged him not very bright, too debauched, too immature, and too drawn to Catholicism. Most agreed that he was irresponsible with his finances, but in that he was hardly alone among his contemporaries.

His flight and refusal to return made his actions seem particularly suspicious. Before the public accusations against the countess, Roos's flight appeared more of a mystery to his contemporaries, potentially seditious and religiously motivated. After the accusations, Roos's flight made more sense: he had left what he felt was an untenable family situation, where his wife and mother-in-law were accusing him of adultery and had, according to what he believed, tricked him out of Walthamstow. The flight also does not appear to be the actions of an innocent man. Whether he was guilty of having a relationship with his step-grandmother, or whether he simply feared his wife and in-laws would accuse him of such a crime, he certainly did not solve his dilemma by fleeing. By fleeing, and by refusing to return, he dumped all his problems on his wife, family, and in-laws. As we now know, they were not very good at solving them.

APPENDIX

Family Trees

What follows are simplified family trees for the Cecil and Lake families. Not all family members are included, since the family trees focus on the individuals that were involved in the feud. I use the abbreviation "m" to denote a marriage, followed by a number if the person married multiple times.

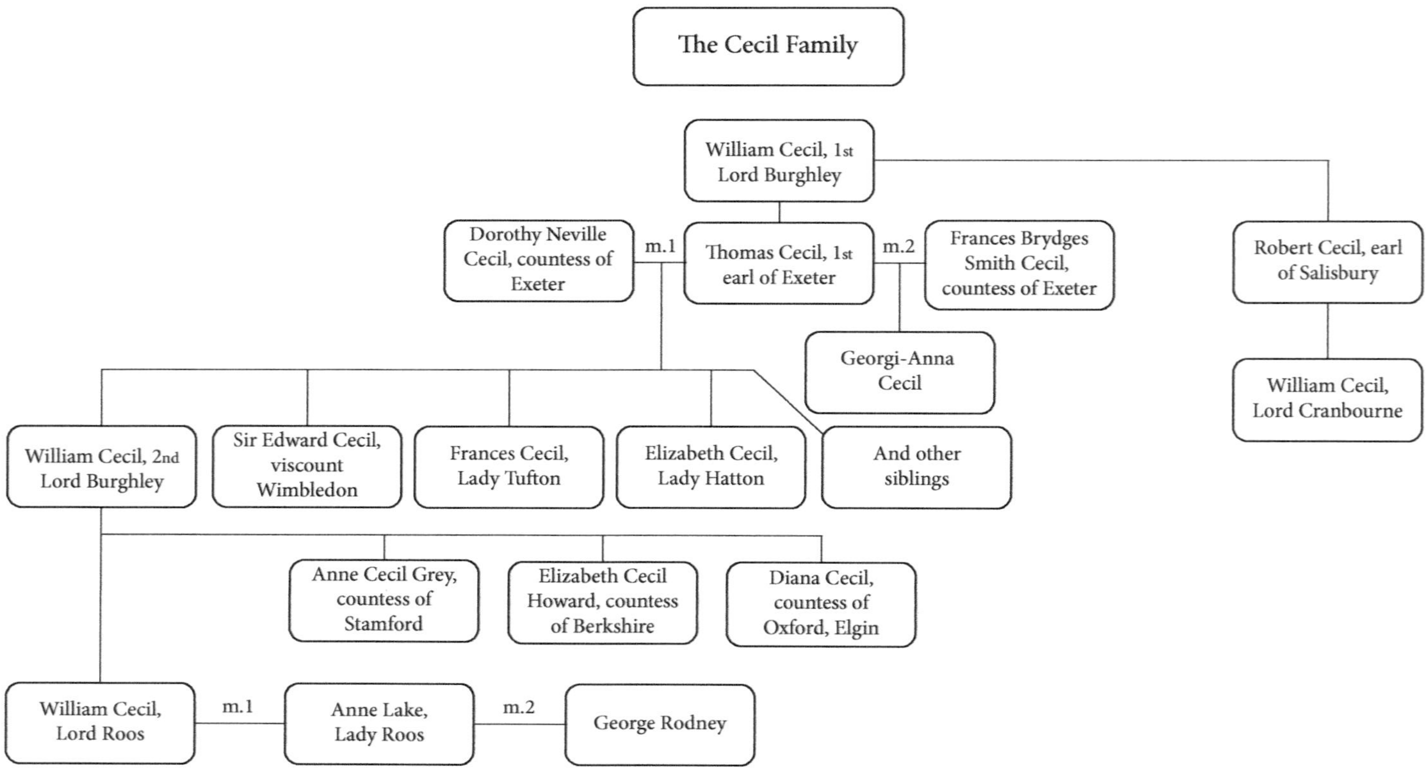
The Cecil Family
William Cecil, 1st Lord Burghley
Dorothy Neville Cecil, countess of Exeter
m.1
Thomas Cecil, 1st earl of Exeter
m.2
Frances Brydges Smith Cecil, countess of Exeter
Robert Cecil, earl of Salisbury
Georgi-Anna Cecil
William Cecil, Lord Cranbourne
William Cecil, 2nd Lord Burghley
Sir Edward Cecil, viscount Wimbledon
Frances Cecil, Lady Tufton
Elizabeth Cecil, Lady Hatton
And other siblings
Anne Cecil Grey, countess of Stamford
Elizabeth Cecil Howard, countess of Berkshire
Diana Cecil, countess of Oxford, Elgin
William Cecil, Lord Roos
m.1
Anne Lake, Lady Roos
m.2
George Rodney

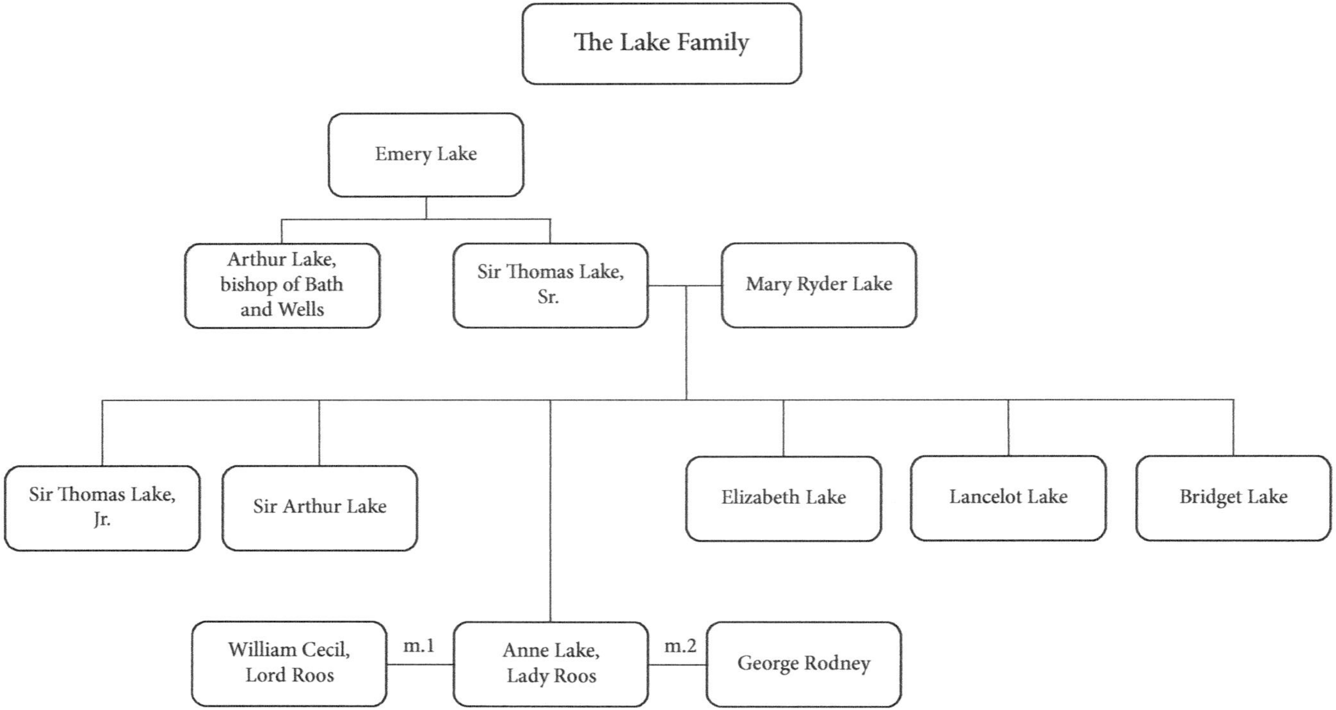

The Lake Family
Emery Lake
Arthur Lake, bishop of Bath and Wells
Sir Thomas Lake, Sr.
Mary Ryder Lake
Sir Thomas Lake, Jr.
Sir Arthur Lake
Elizabeth Lake
Lancelot Lake
Bridget Lake
William Cecil, Lord Roos
m.1
Anne Lake, Lady Roos
m.2
George Rodney

Endnotes

Prologue

1. John Chamberlain to Sir Dudley Carleton, February 28, 1618, Norman Egbert McClure, ed., *The Letters of John Chamberlain* (Philadelphia: The American Philosophical Society, 1939), vol. 2, 145.
2. Adam Newton to Sir Thomas Puckering, February 26, 1628, Thomas Birch, ed., *The Court and Times of James the First; Illustrated by Authentic and Confidential Letters, from Various Public and Private Collections* (London: Henry Colburn, 1849), vol. 2, 68.
3. On Robert Cecil's role in the early reign of James, see Pauline Croft, *King James* (London: Palgrave Macmillan, 2003), 48–49, 69–86.
4. For two opposing views on female rule, see John Knox, *The First Blast of the Trumpet against the Monstrous Regiment of Women* (London: 1558); and John Aylmer, *An Harborow for Faithful and Trewe Subiects* (London: 1559).
5. For an overview of Lake's early career, see "Lake, Sir Thomas (bap. 1561, d. 1630)," *ODNB*; and "Lake, Sir Thomas [1561–1630]," accessed at *HPO*, https://www.historyofparliamentonline.org.
6. For a recent overview of reformation politics in England, see Michael Questier, *Dynastic Politics & the British Reformations, 1558–1630* (Oxford: Oxford University Press, 2019).
7. For an overview of the Spanish match, see Glyn Redworth, *The Prince and the Infanta: The Cultural Politics of the Spanish Match* (New Haven: Yale University Press, 2003).
8. Albert Loomie, *Spain and the Jacobean Catholics*, Vol. II: *1613–1624* (London: Catholic Record Society, 1978), xvii–xix; Charles H. Carter, "Gondomar: Ambassador to James I," *Historical Journal* 7.2 (1964): 193–97.
9. On Anna of Denmark, see J. Leeds Barroll, *Anna of Denmark, Queen of England: A Cultural Biography* (Philadelphia: University of Philadelphia, 2001).
10. SP 14/109/59, quoted in Roger Lockyer, *Buckingham: The Life and Political Career of George Villiers, First Duke of Buckingham 1592–1628* (New York: Longman, 1981), 43.
11. The libelous publication *Corona Regia* was a notable exception. The book was published in Latin in the Spanish Netherlands in 1615, and charged King James with many faults, among them being ruled by his appetites, including his sexual desires for his beautiful male favorites. King James fought hard for several years to find out the authors, printers, and distributers of the book, in order to be able to suppress it. By the early 1620s, a few copies had clearly been read by a troubled English commentator, who worried about the reputation the king and the concerning implications. Alastair Bellany and Thomas Cogswell, *The Murder of King James* (New Haven: Yale University Press, 2015), 146–47.
12. The most convincing argument has been presented by Michael Young, who believes that the king's relationships with his favorites were sexual. Michael Young, *James VI*

and I and the History of Homosexuality (Basingstroke: Macmillan, 2000), ch. 2. Alan Bray has argued that the language and behavior displayed by James instead fits into a longer tradition of friendship. Alan Bray, *The Friend* (Chicago: University of Chicago Press, 2003), see esp. ch. 4, "The Body of the Friend." Croft, *King James*, ch. 4; Alan Stewart, *The Cradle King: A Life of James VI and I* (London: Pimlico, 2004), 257–59, 280–82; Thomas Cogswell, *James I: The Phoenix King* (London: Penguin Books, 2019), 7; Lockyer, 22–23, 33.

13. For James's letters to Buckingham, see G. P. V. Akrigg, ed., *Letters of King James VI and I* (Berkeley: University of California Press), 372–74, 376, 385–426, 431, 436–42.
14. In 1618, a faction led by the earl of Suffolk tried to introduce William Monson at court, as a rival for the king's affections for Buckingham. The project failed. Lockyer, *Buckingham*, 35–36.
15. Chamberlain to Carleton, November 20, 1619, McClure, vol. 2, 274. The Treasurer was recently imprisoned Thomas Howard, earl of Suffolk; the Chamberlain was Robert Carr, earl of Somerset; the captain of the pensioners was Theofilus Howard, Lord Walden and Suffolk eldest son; and the secretary was Sir Thomas Lake.
16. "Fortune's Wheel" K-K2, in Alastair Bellany and Andrew McRae, eds., "Early Stuart Libels: An Edition of Poetry from Manuscript Sources," Early Modern Literary Studies Text Series I (2005), http://purl.oclc.org/emls/texts/libels/.
17. Alastair Bellany, *The Politics of Court Scandal in Early Modern England: News Culture and the Overbury Affair, 1603–1660* (Cambridge: Cambridge University Press, 2002).
18. I have written about Frances Coke and her contentious marriage previously, Johanna Luthman, *Love, Madness, and Scandal: The Life of Frances Coke Villiers, Viscountess Purbeck* (Oxford: Oxford University Press, 2017), esp. ch. 2.
19. For books on the scandal, see Bellany, *The Politics of Court Scandal*; David Lindley, *The Trials of Frances Howard: Fact and Fiction at the Court of King James* (New York: Routledge, 1993); Anne Somerset, *Unnatural Murder: Poison at the Court of King James* (London: Weidenfeld & Nicolson, 1997).
20. For the fall of the Suffolks, see for example Luthman, *Love, Madness, and Scandal*, 68–69; Lockyer, *Buckingham*, 36–37, 64–65, and Andrew Thrush, "The Fall of Thomas Howard, 1st Earl of Suffolk and the Revival of the Impeachment in the Parliament of 1621," *Parliamentary History* 37.2 (2018): 197–211.
21. James sat in Star Chamber in person in only one other case during his reign, as far as I can tell. That was a case of two men charged with dueling in 1617. Chamberlain to Carleton, February 22, 1617, McClure, vol. 2, 54–55; John Throckmorton to Sir Dudley Carleton, February 12, 1617, SP 84/76/61; Edward Sherburn to Carleton, February 23, 1617, SP 14/90/155.
22. On James as Solomon, see for example Alastair Bellany and Thomas Cogswell, *The Murder of King James* (New Haven: Yale University Press, 2015), 51–53; Cogswell, *James I*, 54–55. On James's penchant for exposing frauds, see James Sharpe, *The Bewitching of Anne Gunter: A Horrible and True Story of Deception, Witchcraft, Murder, and the King of England* (New York: Routledge, 2000), 178–96; D. H. Willson, *King James VI and I* (London: Jonathan Cape, 1956), 309–11.
23. Barbara Shapiro, "Law and the Evidentiary Environment," in Lorna Hutson, ed., *The Oxford Handbook of English Law and Literature, 1500–1700* (Oxford: Oxford University Press, 2017), 257.

24. I am using a similar approach to Cynthia Herrup in her study of the earl of Castlehaven's sodomy and rape case in the 1630s. Herrup argues that it is difficult to establish objective truth, but the most useful part of studying the Castlehaven trial is understanding what the actions, words, and interpretations of those involved and of those commenting on the case can tell us about early Stuart society and culture. Cynthia Herrup, *A House in Gross Disorder: Sex, Law, and the Second Earl of Castlehaven* (New York: Oxford University Press, 1999).

Chapter 1

1. M. S. Giuseppi, ed., *Calendar of the Cecil Papers in Hatfield House* (Cecil papers) (London: H. M. Stationery Office, 1940), vol. 18, 155–67.
2. David Lloyd (1635–92), *State-worthies, or, The states-men and favourites of England since the Reformation* (London, 1670), 777. Similar description in Thomas Fuller's *The History of the Worthies of England*, quoted by John Brewer, ed., in Godfrey Goodman, *The Court of James I* (London: Richard Bentley, 1839), vol. 1, 192.
3. For William Cecil, see Stephen Alford, *Burghley: William Cecil at the Court of Elizabeth I* (New Haven: Yale University Press, 2008); David Loades, *The Cecils: Privilege and Power behind the Throne* (Kew: The National Archives, 2007).
4. Edward Chaney and Timothy Wilks, *The Jacobean Grand Tour: Early Stuart Travellers in Europe* (London: I. B. Taurus, 2014), 15–24; John Gallagher, *Learning Languages in Early Modern England* (Oxford: Oxford University Press, 2019), 158–60; William Cecil, Lord Burghley's instructions to his ward the earl of Rutland in 1571, printed in Sara Warneke, *Images of the Educational Traveller in Early Modern England* (Leiden: Brill, 1995), 295–98.
5. Cecil to Windebank, quoted in Alford, *Burghley*, 116.
6. Cecil to Windebank, November 4, 1561, *Calendar of State Papers Domestic: Edward VI, Mary, and Elizabeth, 1547–80 (CSP Edward, Mary, and Elizabeth)*, ed. Robert Lemon (London: H. M. Stationary Office, 1856), *British History online*, accessed April 2, 1618, https://www.british-history.ac.uk/cal-state-papers/domestic/edw-eliz/1547-80, 188–89; Loades, *Cecils*, 174–79; Alford, *Burghley*, 113, 116–17.
7. Quoted in Loades, *Cecils*, 176.
8. Quoted in Alford, *Burghley*, 116–17.
9. Windebank to Cecil, November 18, 1562, *CSP Edward, Mary, and Elizabeth*, 210–12.
10. Windebank to Cecil, January 11, 1562, *CSP Edward, Mary, and Elizabeth*, 215–18. The correspondence regarding Thomas's travels and behavior stretches from August 1561 to early 1563.
11. Loades, *Cecils*, 177–79.
12. Thomas Cecil, Lord Burghley to Sir Robert Cecil, June 13, 1603, *Cecil Papers*, vol. 15, 118–36.
13. Loades, *Cecils*, chs. 9–10; Alan Haynes, *Robert Cecil Earl of Salisbury, 1563–1612: Servant of Two Sovereigns* (London: Peter Owen, 1989), 102, 123.
14. "Cecil, Thomas, first earl of Exeter (1542–1623)," *ODNB*.
15. Sir Edward Stafford to Lord Burghley, July 5, 1585; same to same July 29, 1586, *Calendar of State Papers Domestic: Elizabeth, Addenda 1580–1625*, ed. Mary Anne

Everett Green (London: H. M. Stationery Office 1872), *British History Online*, accessed April 2, 2018, http://www.british-history.ac.uk/cal-state-papers/domestic/edw-eliz/addenda/1580-1625, 146–47, 180–83.

16. Oswald Barron, ed., *Northamptonshire Families* (London: Archibald Constable & Co., 1906), 29.
17. Elizabeth and Elizabeth's mother, the widowed countess of Rutland, had preferred to name him Edward, after the dead earl of Rutland. The elder William Cecil, 1st Lord Burghley, was upset at this potential breach of decorum—he was the child's godfather, after all. The new father had to write to his grandfather and pray he excuse the willful notion of his young wife and mother-in-law: the child was to be named William after all. Alford, *Burghley*, 311–12.
18. Barron, 29.
19. On the disputes over the Roos title, see Barron, 29–30; William Camden. *Diary (1603–1623)*, ed. Dana Sutton, Philological Museum, accessed March 9, 2018 http://www.philological.bham.ac.uk/diary/), entries for January 3 and February 1, 1616; Chamberlain to Carleton, July 13, 1615, McClure, 607; Letters Patent, July 12, 1616, *Calendar of State Papers Domestic: James I, 1611–18*, ed. Mary Anne Everett Green (London: H. M. Stationery Office, 1858), 430–38. *British History Online*, accessed April 16, 2021, http://www.british-history.ac.uk/cal-state-papers/domestic/jas1/1611-18/, pp. 378–89.
20. The three daughters, and Roos's half-sisters, all married earls. Anne Cecil married Henry Grey, 1st earl of Stamford, Elizabeth Cecil married Thomas Howard, 1st earl of Berkshire, and Diana Cecil married Henry de Vere, 18th earl of Oxford. Barron, 29–30.
21. It is not clear exactly where Roos was educated: he is not listed as having matriculated at either Cambridge or Oxford.
22. Travel licenses were usually granted for three years at a time, so Roos must have received multiple licenses to travel. Unfortunately, the *APC*, which usually records the granting of such licenses, do not survive for the years 1605–12. Roos's license dated April 24, 1612, is noted in the *Cecil Papers*, vol. 21, 352–62.
23. Chaney and Wilks, 49, 66, 148–9. Thomas Windebank, the long-suffering tutor of Thomas Cecil (Exeter), could certainly attest to the fact that young Thomas did not listen much to what he had to say. Burghley's (Roos's father) tutor had a similar experience, as did Thomas Lorkin, tutor to Sir Puckering.
24. Count de Harley to Salisbury, April 22/May 2, 1606, *Cecil Papers*, vol. 18, 112–27.
25. Roos to Salisbury, June 3, 1606, *Cecil Papers*, vol. 18, 155–67. Chamberlain to Carleton, October 6, 1606, McClure, vol. 1, 233. "We heare that the Lord Ros shall marry a younge widow in Fraunce, that was sometime of Tremouille or Mouy or one of those of the religion."
26. Chaney and Wilks, 49–50, Chamberlain to Carleton, July 7, 1608, McClure, vol. 1, 259.
27. Logan Persall Smith, ed., *Life and Letters of Sir Henry Wotton* (Oxford: Clarendon Press, 1907), 70–71; Sir Henry Wotton to Lord Roos, May 17, 1608, Smith, *Wotton*, 428–29; Wotton to Salisbury, December 5, 1608, Smith, *Wotton*, 442–43; Wotton to Salisbury, June 18, 1609, Smith, *Wotton*, 456–76; Francesco Contarini, Venetian ambassador in Rome, to the Doge and Senate, September 6, 1608, *Calendar of State Papers Relating to English Affairs in the Archives of Venice* (*CSP Venice*), ed. Horatio Brown and Allen B. Hinds (London: H. M. Stationery Office, 1904–10) *British History*

Online, accessed February 21, 2018, http://www.british-history.ac.uk/cal-state-papers/venice/vol11/pp164-174, vol. 11, 164–74. Sir Henry Wotton to Salisbury, undated, in "Appendix," in *Calendar of State Papers, Ireland, 1606–1608*, ed. C. W. Russell and John P. Prendergast (London: Longman and Co., 1874), 623–70, *British History Online*, accessed November 11, 2022, http://www.british-history.ac.uk/cal-state-papers/ireland/1606-8/pp623-670.

28. Chamberlain to Carleton, October 21, 1608, McClure, vol. 1, 264–65; Chamberlain to Carleton, October 22, 1612, McClure, vol. 1, 283; Chamberlain to Sir Ralph Winwood, November 3, 1612, McClure, vol. 1, 385; John Pory to Carleton, January 3, 1610, *CSP James (1603–1610)*, 579–90; Chamberlain to Carleton, January 10, 1618, McClure, vol. 2, 128.
29. Collegio Secreta, Esposizioni Principi, Venetian Archives, December 16, 1608, *CSP Venice (1607–1610)*, vol. 11.
30. Collegio Secreta, March 30, 1609, *CSP Venice (1607–1610)*, vol. 11.
31. Chaney and Wilks, 89–90.
32. Carew to Salisbury, 15 June 1609, William Becher to Thomas Wilson, July 25, 1609, quoted in Chaney and Wilks, 74, 89–90.
33. "It is certayne the Lord Roos—as he is called—is gon into Spayne." Thomas Screven to the earl of Rutland, November 9, 1609; same to same again on November 16, "For the Lord Roos—as he is called—there is not anything more than a certenty that he is gon into Spayne, but he writes not hither at all, and his Tutor Mole contynues in the Inquisition." Historical Manuscript Commission, *The Manuscripts of His Grace the Duke of Rutland, Preserved at Belvoir Castle* (*Rutland*) (London: Printed for H. M. Stationery Office, by Eyre and Spottiswoode, 1888–1905), vol. 1, 418–19.
34. Francis Cottington to William Trumbull, November 11, 1610, *Downshire*, vol. 2, 394.
35. According to Francis Cottington, English ambassador in Spain, Roos first planned to stay six months to a year. Francis Cottington to William Trumbull, March 7, 1610, *Downshire*, vol. 2, 257. "My Lord Roos is still here, and means to remain here yet a Year to learn the Language." Sir Francis Cottington to Sir William Trumbull (from Madrid), January 7, 1609 (should be 1610), Edmund Sawyer, ed., *Memorials of Affairs of State in the Reign of Q. Elizabeth and K. James I* (London: T. Ward, 1725), vol. 3, 104. Cottington reported that with the exception of Lord Roos, he had "never seen one honest man of them come to see and learn the language as in other parts." Cottington to Trumbull, 11 November 1610, *Downshire*, vol. 2, 394.
36. Correspondence from Roos to Salisbury, March through May 1610: SP 14/54/142; SP 14/54/166; SP 14/62/119.
37. Roos to Salisbury, July 1610, SP 94/17/119.
38. John Beaulieu to Trumbull, November 27, 1610, *Downshire*, vol. 2, 399–400.
39. Lorkin's letter is listed as 1612 in BL Harleian, but it is not dated. Letters from Roos to Salisbury in spring of 1611 refer to this same trip, making it clear that it took place in 1611. SP 61/201; SP 14/63/107. Sir Thomas Edmondes to William Trumbull, March 9, 1611, *Downshire*, vol. 3, 33–34.
40. Roos to Salisbury, February 26, 1611, SP 14/61/201. Roos also hoped to see Lord Cranbourne, his cousin and Salisbury's son, who was traveling through Germany at the time.

41. Roos had forwarded a letter from Puckering to Sir Adam Newton in 1610 or 1611, so they knew each other by then. Roos to Sir Adam Newton, February 10, 1610/1611, BL Landsdowne vol. 92, f. 2. On Puckering being in Paris at the time: John Beaulieu to Trumbull, November 27, 1610, *Downshire*, vol. 2, 399–400.
42. Lorkin to Sir Adam Newton, [May 1611], BL Harleian 7002, f. 199. All the quotes in the following paragraphs describing this journey are from this letter.
43. Sir Thomas Edmondes to William Trumbull, March 9, 1611, *Downshire*, vol. 3, 33–34; Roos also informed Salisbury that his honorable reception at the court at Brussels was no doubt due to the fame of Salisbury and his own relation to the powerful man. Roos to Salisbury, May 4, 1611, SP 14/63, f. 107.
44. Jean Beaulieu to William Trumbull, April 6, 1611, *Downshire*, vol. 3, 53–54.
45. Lyonell Wake to William Trumbull, April 22, 1611, *Downshire*, vol. 3, 57.
46. See John Thory and John Monger's letters to Trumbull on October 8, 10, 17, 24, and 26 and November 8 and 13, 1611, *Downshire*, vol. 3, 155, 158, 165, 169, 170, 178, 181.
47. Roos to Prince Henry, October 11, 1611, Thomas Birch, ed., *Life of Prince Henry Prince of Wales, Eldest Son of King James I* (London: A Millar, 1760), 212–13; Thomas Screven to earl of Rutland, January 21, 1612, *HMC Rutland*, vol. 1, 433.
48. Roos's license dated April 24, 1612, is noted in the *Cecil Papers*, vol. 21, 352–62; Thomas Screven to earl of Rutland, April 17, 1612, *HMC Rutland*, vol. 1, 436. Roos was still in London on April 29. John Thorys to William Trumbull, April 29, 1612, *Downshire*, vol. 3, 287.
49. Chamberlain informed Carleton that "those instructions [to congratulate the new emperor] sent to the Lord Rosse (who is in the Low Countries) to do that office." June 17, 1612, McClure, vol. 1, 360; Roos to Lake, July 3, 1612, SP 14/70/3.
50. Salisbury's death also set off the creation of a flurry of libels against him, illustrating a reaction against the Cecil power and public distaste for the Jacobean court. See Pauline Croft, "The Reputation of Robert Cecil: Libels, Political Opinion and Popular Awareness in the Early Seventeenth Century," *Transactions of the Royal Historical Society* 1 (1991): 43–69.
51. By August 7, 1612, Roos had arrived in Venice, via Augusta, in the company of Mr. Cranfield. Tobie Mathews arrived in Venice at the same time, but via a different route. Carleton to Trumbull, August 7, 1612, Edmund Sawyer, ed., *Memorials of Affairs of State in the Reign of Q. Elizabeth and K. James I* (London: T. Ward, 1725), vol. 3, 384; Carleton to Chamberlain, August 14, 1612, Maurice Lee, ed., *Dudley Carleton to John Chamberlain 1603–1624* (New Brunswick: Rutgers University Press, 1972) 132.
52. Roos to Sir David Murray, November 25, 1612, Birch, *The Life of Henry*, 320–22, 371.
53. December 10/20, 1613, Carleton to Chamberlain; same to same December 24, 1613 / January 3, 1614, Lee, *Letters of Carleton*, 153–55.
54. Chaney and Wilkes, 89, 183.
55. On art, art collections, and diplomacy, see R. Malcolm Smuts and Luc Duerloo, "Occasio's Lock of Hair: The Artist and the Ruler in Pursuit of Opportunity," in R. M. Smuts and L. Duerloo, eds., *The Age of Rubens: Diplomacy, Dynastic Politics, and the Visual Arts in Early Seventeenth-Century Europe* (Turnhout: Brepols Publishers, 2016), 6–8; Christine Hille, *Visions of the Courtly Body: The Patronage of George Villiers, Duke of Buckingham, and the Triumph of Painting at the Stuart Court* (Berlin: Akademie Verlag, 2012), 24–26.

56. October 3, 1614, *APC* (London: H. M. Stationery Office 1929), vol. 33, 665.
57. December 23, 1614, *APC*, vol. 33, 665.
58. Chamberlain to Carleton, December 22, 1614, McClure, vol. I, 565. "Don Diego" could refer to Don Diego de Sarmiento, the Spanish ambassador in England, but it seems from the context of these letters that it is referring to Diego da Silva instead.
59. January 5, 1615, Chamberlain to Carleton, McClure, vol. 1, 568–69.
60. Carleton to Chamberlain, from Turin, 1615, April 13, Lee, *Letters of Carleton*, 180. "My lord Roos is gone safe through the Grisons and Swiss towards the Low Countries, so for England. He purposed to have returned from hence to Milan, but an affront offered him at Novara by searching his chamber with an officer and 40 soldiers at three hours at night for his Spanish servant Diego (who, upon an item I gave him of some danger [whereof I had news] left him at Vercelli) made him forbear going any further into that state."
61. Sir John Throckmorton to William Trumbull, February 23, 1615, *Downshire*, vol. 5, 144; Andre Paul to Trumbull, April 21, 1615, *Downshire*, vol. 5, 199; same to same, May 11, 1615, *Downshire*, vol. 5, 213.
62. Her funeral was held on April 20, 1609. Carleton to Chamberlain, April 21, 1609; Lee, *Letters of Carleton*, 110.
63. Thomas Screven to earl of Rutland, December 3, 1610, *HMC Rutland*, vol. 4, 211. Others also reported the marriage: John More to William Trumbull, December 13, 1610, *Downshire*, vol. 2, 406; John Sanford to William Trumbull, December 13, 1610, *Downshire*, vol. 2, 407. Sanford noted that Exeter had given his new bride "1,000 marks jointure by the year."
64. *ODNB*, "Cecil, [née Brydges, other married name Smith] Frances, Countess of Exeter (1588–1663)."
65. Sir Thomas Edmondes to William Trumbull, September 14, 1609, *Downshire*, vol. 2, 128. Same to same October 19, 1609, *Downshire*, vol. 2, 162; same to same, November 13, 1609, *Downshire*, vol. 2, 185. "To appease his pains he hath taken some stupefying pills to procure sleep, which by all men's opinion will shorten his end." Same to same, November 24, 1609, *Downshire*, vol. 2, 191; same to same, November 30, 1609, *Downshire*, vol. 2, 194; same to same, December 14, 1609, *Downshire*, vol. 2, 199.
66. Charles James Feret, *Fulham Old and New* (London: Leadenhall Press, 1900), vol. 2, 136–37 (although Feret gets the year of the marriage of the earl of Exeter and Frances Brydges Smith wrong).
67. Sir Thomas Smith's will copied in Feret, 136.
68. Andrew Thrush and John P. Ferris, "Lake, Sir Thomas I"; *ODNB*, "Lake, Sir Thomas (bap. 1561, d. 1630)," *The History of Parliament: The House of Commons (1604–1629)* (Cambridge University Press, 2010), accessed at *HPO*, https://www.historyofparliamentonline.org.
69. Thrush and Ferris, *The History of Parliament*, "Lake, Sir Thomas I"; *ODNB*, "Lake, Sir Thomas (bap. 1561, d. 1630)."
70. Levinus Muncke to Ralph Winwood, 14 May, 1605. Sawyer, *Memorials of State*, 59.
71. Lake's early career is well summarized by *HPO*, as well as in *ODNB*.
72. Sir Thomas Lake, b. around 1595, "Lake, Sir Thomas II (c. 1595–1653)," *HPO*; Sir Arthur Lake, bap. November 26, 1598; Lancelot Lake, bap. February 10, 1608/9; Anne Lake, bap. November 14, 1599; Elizabeth Lake, probably bap. March 12, 1601; Bridget

Lake, bap. 9 July, 1616, all at St. Martin in the Fields, *Westminster, London, England, Church of England Baptisms, Marriages and Burials, 1558–1812* (database on-line), Lehi, UT: Ancestry.com Operations, Inc., 2020.

73. Carole Levin, "James I and Unruly Women," in Amy Leonard and David Whitford, eds., *Embodiment, Identity, and Gender in the Early Modern Age* (London: Rutledge, 2021), 70–72, 78.
74. Chamberlain to Carleton, July 9, 1612, McClure, vol. 1, 368.
75. Goodman, 181–82.
76. Chamberlain to Carleton, January 28, 1613, McClure, vol. 1, 409. In a note, McClure says Lady Caesar refers to Alice, wife of Sir Julius Caesar, Chancellor of the Exchequer, but that cannot be right. Lady Lake's sister Susan was married to Thomas Caesar, Julius's brother.
77. Thomas Sayer to Sir Thomas Lake, November 20, 1613, SP 14/75/43.
78. Thomas and Arthur Lake were both at Middle Temple in 1609, and then at Oxford 1610–1613. "Arthur Lake," "Thomas Lake," in Joseph Foster, ed., *Alumni Oxonienses 1500–1714* (Oxford: University of Oxford, 1891), 868–92.
79. Thomas and Arthur traveled to Heidelberg with the newlywed Princess Elizabeth and Frederick of the Palatine in 1613 and came home via the Low Countries, "to see the court and some towns in passing." Sir Thomas Lake to Trumbull, June 10, 1613, *Downshire*, vol. 4, 132. Thomas Lake received the standard license to travel for educational purposes on April 30, 1615, *APC*, vol. 34, 131. It is not clear if he did travel, or if he did, it was only for a shorter period, as he was in England in June 1616 and forward. Arthur Lake received license to travel on November 30, 1615, *APC*, vol. 34, 340. He returned from France in February 1617. Mr. Castle to James Miller, February 1617, Thomas Birch, ed., *The Court and Times of James the First: Illustrated by Authentic and Confidential Letters from Various Public and Private Collections* (London: Henry Colburn, 1848), vol. 1, 460.
80. Chamberlain to Carleton, December 31, 1612, McClure, vol. 1, 399.
81. Anne Lake was baptized in St. Martin in the Fields, Westminster, November 14, 1599. "Anna Lake," in *Westminster, London, England, Church of England Baptisms, Marriage, and Burials 1558–1812*, retrieved from Ancestry.com. Her burial monument noted her age as in the thirtieth year when she died in 1630.

Chapter 2

1. Acheson, Katherine, ed., *The Diary of Anne Clifford 1616–1619: A Critical Edition* (London: Garland Publishing, 1995), 40.
2. Throckmorton to Trumbull, February 23, 1615, *Downshire*, vol. 5, 144; Andre Paul to Trumbull, April 21, 1615, *Downshire*, vol. 5, 199; Andre Paul to Trumbull, May 11, 1615, *Downshire*, vol. 5, 213; Ranier Zen, Venetian ambassador in Savoy, to the Doge and Senate, April 24, 1615, *CSP Venice (1613–1615)*, vol. 13; Antonio Antelmi, Venetian Resident at Milan, to the Doge and Senate, April 8, 1615, *CSP Venice (1613–1615)*, vol. 13.
3. This action caused some dispute. One of Roos's relatives, the earl of Rutland, had challenged the claim to the Roos title, arguing that it should not have devolved through

the maternal line. Rutland sued, and the matter was still undecided in the courts by the time Roos carried the king's sword. A decision in Roos's favor was announced soon thereafter. Chamberlain to Carleton, July 13, 1615, McClure, vol. 1, 607; Letters patent declaring William Cecil Lord Roos with rights to sit in House of Lords, July 22, 1616, SP 14/88/45.

4. Elizabeth Foyster, *Manhood in Early Modern England: Honour, Sex, Marriage* (London: Longman, 1999), 29–30, 65–67, 87–89.
5. Courtney Erin Thomas, *If I Lose Mine Honour, I Lose Myself: Honour among the Early Modern English Elite* (Toronto: University of Toronto Press, 2017), 106. The "heir" to Exeter Thomas mentions here must be Roos, rather than Exeter's son Burghley, who had already re-married.
6. Sir John Throckmorton to Trumbull, September 9, 1615, *Downshire*, vol. 5, 334. Lake had initially relied on the Howards, and specifically the earl of Suffolk and his son-in-law Somerset, for assistance in getting appointments at court. When Suffolk failed to secure him an office, Lake temporarily switched allegiances to the earl of Pembroke. After finally being appointed secretary, and after it was clear that the Suffolks would survive the fall of their son-in-law and daughter in the spring of 1616, Lake switched back to the Suffolks. Chamberlain told Carleton that the bearer of his letter can tell him "the course of the cards here and how we shuffle and cut." Chamberlain to Carleton, May 25, 1615, McClure, vol. 1, 599; Thrush and Ferris, "Lake, Sir Thomas (1561–1630)," *HPO*.
7. For rumors and information about the appointment, see letters to Trumbull throughout September 1615 to January 1616, *Downshire*, vol. 5, 383, 388, 400, 403, 404, 411, 413–14; George Lord Carew to Sir John Roe, January 25, 1616, SP 14/86/27.
8. For discussion on age of marriage, see E. A. Wrigley, R. S. Davies, J. E. Oeppen, and R. S. Schofield, *English Population History from Family Reconstitution 1580–1837* (New York: Cambridge University Press, 1997), 122–26. Peter Laslett, *The World We Have Lost, Further Explored*, 3rd ed. (London: Routledge, 2000), 81–121; Alan Macfarlane, *Marriage and Love in England: Modes of Reproduction 1300–1840* (Cambridge: Blackwell, 1986), 119–47; Mary Abbott, *Family Ties: English Families 1540–1920* (New York: Routledge, 1993), 6–10; Johanna Rickman, "'He Would Never Consent in His Heart': Child Marriages in Early Modern England," *Journal of the History of Children and Youth* 6 (2013): 295.
9. Another connection between the Cecils and Howards occurred later but was perhaps not as helpful: Roos's cousin Frances Coke had an affair with another of Suffolk's sons, Robert Howard, in the 1620s, resulting in an illegitimate son. See Luthman, *Love, Madness, and Scandal*, chs. 4–8.
10. Carter, 193–97; Albert Loomie, *Spain and the Jacobean Catholics*, Vol. II: *1613–1624* (London: Catholic Record Society, 1978), xvii–xix.
11. John Holles to his son, January 22, 1616, P. R. Seddon, ed., *Letters of John Holles, 1587–1632* (Nottingham: Thoroton Society, 1975), vol. 1, 108; Thomas Locke to Trumbull, January 24, 1616, *Downshire*, vol. 5, 413–14.
12. John Holles informed his son in Paris that Roos and Anne Lake were married on "Shrovemunday," with "the good lyking of my Lord Burley, and the rest interessed, whereof I am glad, for this Secretary is my frend, and I love him well." John Holles to his son, February 23, 1616, Seddon, vol. 1, 117.

13. John Holles to Sir Thomas Lake, January 28, 1616, Seddon, vol. 1, 110.
14. Anne Clifford noted that Roos married Anne Lake in February, Acheson, *Diary of Anne Clifford*, 40; William Camden noted that the two married on February 12, William Camden, *Diary (1603–1623)*, ed. Dana Sutton, Philological Museum, accessed March 9, 2018, http://www.philological.bham.ac.uk/diary/; George Lord Carew to Sir John Roe, January 25, 1616, SP 14/86/27; John Holles to his son, February 23, 1616, Seddon, vol. 1, 117.
15. February 26, 1618, Adam Newton to Sir Thomas Puckering, Birch, *James*, vol. 2, 68–69.
16. Puckering married a daughter of Sir John Morley. Chamberlain to Carleton, July 6, 1616, McClure, vol. 2, 15.
17. February 26, 1618, Adam Newton to Sir Thomas Puckering, Birch, *James*, vol. 2, 68–69.
18. Chamberlain to Carleton, March 27, 1616, McClure, vol. 1, 616–17.
19. Edward Sherburn to Dudley Carlton, March 23, 1616, SP 14/86/167.
20. Acheson, *Diary of Anne Clifford*, 57.
21. Camden, *Diary (1603–1623)*, July 1616.
22. George Gerrard to Carleton, March 1, 1618, SP 14/96/83.
23. Chamberlain to Carleton, July 20, 1616, *Chamberlain*, vol. 2, 16; Clifford, 57; Camden, *Diary*, July 1616. The joy of the birth was also tinged with sadness, as Lady Exeter lost her sister, Lady Turberville, to smallpox around the same time. (Chamberlain, same letter as birth announcement July 20.)
24. Parish records are quoted in John Nichols, *The Progresses, Processions, and Magnificent Festivities of King James the First* (London: J. B. Nichols, 1828), vol. 4, 1098; also in Daniel Lysons, "Wimbledon," in *The Environs of London*, Vol. 1: *County of Surrey* (London: T. Cadell and W. Davies, 1792), 519–40. *British History Online*, accessed March 9, 2021, http://www.british-history.ac.uk/london-environs/vol1/pp519-540; Elizabeth Gresham's answers in Sir Thomas Lake, Jr. v. earl and countess of Exeter, George Gwilliams, and Elizabeth Gresham, STAC 8/196/24. For Sophia Ann Cecil's burial in Westminster Abbey, see Westminster Abbey, "Thomas and William Cecil, 1st and 2nd earls of Exeter," accessed March 20, 2020, https://www.westminster-abbey.org/abbey-commemorations/commemorations/thomas-william-cecil-earls-of-exeter.
25. Chamberlain to Carleton, July 20, 1616, McClure, vol. 2, 16. For the ceremony of churching, see Patricia Crawford, *Blood, Bodies, and Families in Early Modern England* (New York: Routledge, 2014), 98.
26. Richard Burns, *Ecclesiastical Law* (London: Stahan and Woodfall, 1788), vol. 1, 110, Crawford, 117–19.
27. Crawford, 212–13; Martin Ingram, *Carnal Knowledge: Regulating Sex in England, 1470–1600* (Cambridge: Cambridge University Press, 2017), 89–91.
28. Sir John Throckmorton (Throgmorton) to Sir Dudley Carleton, February 24, 1618, SP 84/82/235.
29. William Sanderson, *A Compleat History of the Lives and Reigns of Mary Queen of Scotland, and of Her Son and Successor, James the Sixth, King of Scotland; and (After Queen Elizabeth) King of Great Britain, France, and Ireland, The First (Of ever Blessed Memory)* (London: Printed for Humphrey Moseley, Richard Tomlins, and George Sawbridge, 1656), 447.

30. Sarah Toulalan, "'Elderly yeares cause a Total dispaire of Conception': Old Age, Sex and Infertility in Early Modern England," *Social History of Medicine* 29.2 (2015): 333–59.
31. On notions of the cuckold, see Ingram, *Carnal Knowledge*, 70–71, 75, 185; Sara F. Matthews-Grieco, "Picart's Browbeaten Husband in 17th-Century France: Cuckoldry in Context," in Sara Matthews-Grieco, ed., *Cuckoldry, Impotence and Adultery in Europe (15th–17th century)* (Aldershot: Ashgate, 2014), 249–89; Philip D. Collington, "Sans Wife: Sexual Anxiety and the Old Man in Shakespeare," in Erin Campbell, ed., *Growing Old in Early Modern Europe* (Aldershot: Ashgate, 2006), 185–207; Susan Amussen, "Cuckold's Haven: Gender and Inversion in Popular Culture," in Malcolm Smuts, ed., *The Oxford Handbook of the Age of Shakespeare* (Oxford: Oxford University Press, 2016), 528–42; Foyster, *Manhood in Early Modern England*, 104–15.
32. Lack of sex in virgins was believed to cause a disease called "greensickness." Lack of sex for women who were not virgins could also be problematic and contribute to other health problems. See Jennifer Evans and Sara Read in *Maladies & Medicine: Exploring Health & Healing, 1540–1740* (Barnsley: Pen and Sword, 2017), chs. 19 and 20.
33. Theodore de Mayerne, *Opera Medica*, ed. Joseph Browne (London: 1703), 171–76. Big thanks to my colleague Thomas Greene, who helped me with the Latin translations.
34. Chamberlain to Carleton, December 6, 1616, McClure, vol. 2, 43.
35. Acheson, *Diary of Anne Clifford*, 78.
36. Edward Waldegrave to Trumbull, April 25, 1616, *Downshire*, vol. 5, 487.
37. Lando to Doge and Senate, October 21, 1616, *CSP Venice (1615–1617)*, vol. 14.
38. Gregorio Barbarigo to the Doge and Senate, May 13 and May 28, 1616, *CSP Venice (1615–1617)*, vol. 14.
39. Chamberlain to Carleton, April 30, 1616, McClure, vol. 1, 626.
40. Chamberlain to Carleton, October 12, 1616, McClure, vol. 2, 24–25; Castle to Trumbull, September 26, 1616, *Downshire*, vol. 6, 17; Castle to Trumbull, October 1, 1616, *Downshire*, vol. 6, 26.
41. Cottington to Trumbull, July 3, 1616, *Downshire*, vol. 5, 542.
42. Archbishop of Canterbury to Trumbull, July 10, 1616, *Downshire*, vol. 5, 547.
43. Edward Valdegrave to Trumbull, August 28, 1616, *Trumbull*, vol. 5, 585.
44. Cottington to Trumbull, June 6, 1616, *Downshire*, vol. 5, 525.
45. Cottington to Trumbull, September 6, 1616, *Downshire*, vol. 6, 4.
46. Throckmorton to Trumbull, May 23, 1616, *Downshire*, vol. 5, 507.
47. Sir Francis Bacon reported the finances of the state to King James in 1617, and the list of extraordinary expenses for the previous year included "Lord Roos into Spain," as well as "Lord Hay's imployment into France." Francis Bacon, "A Memorial for your Majesty" in Robert Stevens, ed., *Letters of Sir Francis Bacon, Baron Verulam, Viscount St. Alban, and Lord High Chancellor of England. Written during the Reign of King James the First* (London: Benjamin Tooke, 1702).
48. "I know not whether I be more sorry or ashamed to consider how much it was my ill fortune to persuade you to engage yourself for my L. Roos." Tobie Matthew to Trumbull, August 11, 1611, *Downshire*, vol. 3, 118.

49. John Holles to his son, calling Roos "unworthy" and that he "useth the noble Lord his father so ill, that he can not respect any of his frends," June 2, 1616, Seddon, vol. 2, 129–30; Carleton to Chamberlain October 24, 1616, Lee, 222.
50. Nathaniel Brent to Carleton December 1, 1616, SP 14/89/112. "I heare that in my Ld Rosse his marriage there is no great contentment on eyther side. He hath taken fen his al her jewels, and suffered his father in law to pay 6000 li for him." Lake and Lady Lake's answer in Exeter suit C 8/31/33.
51. These accounts are based on what the two sides had to say in later lawsuits in the Court of Star Chamber, STAC 8/24/20 and STAC 8/111/27.
52. Stephen Barns, *Calendar of Deeds Relating to Walthamstow 1595–1890* (Walthamstow Antiquarian Society No. 11, 1923), 7.
53. Chamberlain to Carleton, April 30, 1616, McClure, vol. 1, 626.
54. Chamberlain to Carleton, October 12, 1616, McClure, vol. 2, 26–27.
55. Carleton to Chamberlain, 1616, October 24, Lee, 222.
56. Roos to King James, June 1, 1618, SP 14/97/231.
57. Chamberlain to Carleton, October 12 and November 14, 1616, McClure, vol. 2, 26–27, 36.
58. Edward Sherburn to Carleton, July 13, 1616, SP 14/88/28. "I omitted in my last, to let yo. L knowe, that my L: Rosse hath spoiled yor sale of the statues, [?] after all his paines and charges bestowed, in collecting and gathering together such antiquities of this kind as he could get in his travails, he has nowe in a humor (and I may say an ill one), giuen them all to my Lord of Arundell, wch has exceedinglie beautified his L: gallerie."
59. Chamberlain to Carleton, October 12, 1616, McClure, vol. 2, 26–27.
60. William Beecher to Carleton, November 9, 1616, SP 14/89/41. "My Lo Roos is now at length parted from Portsmouth 4 dayes since, and it is coniectured by the faire windes that hee is by this time arrived: and alredy I hear some wellwishers of Sr. Jhon Digbie say, that he shall shortlie follow him wth the charge of some businesse wch was thought to heavy for my Lord."
61. Lionelli to Doge and Senate, November 17, 1616, *CSP Venice (1615–1617)*, vol. 14.
62. Chamberlain to Carleton, October 12, 1616, McClure, vol. 2, 26–27.
63. Giovanni Battista Lionello, Venetian secretary in England, to the Doge and Senate, September 23, 1616, *CSP Venice (1615–1617)*, vol. 14.
64. Answer of Robert Hooke in earl of Exeter's suit, C 8/31/33.
65. Chamberlain to Carleton, November 14, 1616, McClure, vol. 2, 35–36.
66. Roos to earl of Arundel, January 22, 1617, Edmund Lodge, ed., *Illustrations of British History, Biography, and Manners, in the Reigns of Henry VIII, Edward VI, Mary, Elizabeth, & James I* (London: John Chidley, 1838), vol. 3, 286–90.
67. Chamberlain to Carleton, February 8, 1617, McClure, vol. 2, 52; Cottington to Trumbull, December 10, 1616, *Downshire*, vol. 6, 65.
68. Cottington to Trumbull, December 10, 1616, *Downshire*, vol. 6, 65; Roos to earl of Arundel, January 22, 1617, Lodge, *Illustrations of British History*, vol. 3, 286–90.
69. Chamberlain to Carleton, March 29, 1617, *McClure*, vol. 2, 66; Roos to earl of Arundel, January 22, 1617, Lodge, *Illustrations of British History*, vol. 3, 286–90.
70. See Jonathan Brown, "Enemies of Flattery: Valzequez' Portraits of Philip IV," in Robert I. Rotberg and Theodore K. Rabb, eds., *Art and History: Images and Their Meaning* (Cambridge: Cambridge University Press, 1988), 137–54.

71. Roos to earl of Arundel, January 22, 1617, Lodge, *Illustrations of British History*, vol. 3, 286–90.
72. Roos to earl of Arundel, January 22, 1617, Lodge, *Illustrations of British History*, vol. 3, 286–90.
73. January 19, 1617, Cottington to Trumbull, *Downshire*, vol. 6, 97; C 8/31/33. No source explains if there was supposed to be any meaning behind the letter A, or if this was simply deemed a jewel available as a gift.
74. In November, Carleton was getting reports that the prince was cheerful because of the intended Spanish marriage, and that James intended to send Digby to Spain for the purpose (so, not to have Roos do it). William Beecher to Carleton, November 9, 1616, and Sherburn to Carleton, November 9, 1616, *CSP James (1611–1618)*, 404–10; Lionello to Doge and Senate, November 17, 1616, *CSP Venice (1615–1617)*, vol. 14.
75. Lionello to Doge and Senate, December 22, 1616, *CSP Venice (1615–1617)*, vol. 14.
76. Sanderson, 447. Sanderson does give the wrong year for the embassy, however. He says it occurred in 1611, when in fact, it was 1617 (or 1616, based on Old Style).
77. Cottington to Trumbull, February 16, 1617, *Downshire*, vol. 6, 113. Roos himself mentioned to Arundel that he planned to go through France, and that Arundel could address any letters he wished to send him to Paris. Roos to Arundel, January 22, 1617, in Mary Hervey, *Life, Correspondence and Collections of Thomas Howard, Earl of Arundel* (Cambridge: Cambridge University Press, 1921), 108–9.
78. Chaney and Wilks, 89–90.
79. Dudley Carleton to William Trumbull, March 7, 1617, *Downshire*, vol. 6, 133: "I am of the opinion that Tobie Matthew's purpose in going to Paris is to meet either Lord Roos or Griffin Markham." John Woodford to Trumbull, March 20, 1617, *Downshire*, vol. 6, 146: "Lord Roos passed through Paris last week with a number of gentlemen of his retinue. He lodged one night at St. Denye, where he was visited by Mr. Toby Mathew. If I am not deceaved, the latter hopes that by his Lordship's intervention, he will be permitted to return to England."
80. Giovanni Battista Lionello to the Doge and Senate, March 9, 1617, *CSP Venice (1615–1617)*, vol. 14.
81. Jean Beaulieu to Trumbull, April 3, 1617, *Downshire*, vol. 6, 156.
82. Giovanni Battista Lionello, Venetian secretary in England, to the Doge and Senate, October 21, 1616; same to same, March 9, 1617, *CSP Venice (1615–1617)*, vol. 14.
83. Chamberlain to Carleton, March 29, 1617, McClure, vol. 2, 66.
84. Edward Sherburn to Carleton, April 6, 1617, SP 14/91/35.

Chapter 3

1. Chamberlain to Carleton, February 28, 1618, McClure, vol. 2, 80.
2. Natalie Zemon Davis, *The Return of Martin Guerre* (Cambridge, MA: Harvard University Press, 1984); Cynthia Herrup, *A House in Gross Disorder: Sex, Law, and the Second Earl of Castlehaven* (Oxford: Oxford University Press, 1999). For more recent example of a similar approach, see Clare Egan, "Jacobean Star Chamber Records and the Performance of Provincial Libel," in Kesselring and Mear, eds., *Star Chamber Matters*, 136.

3. Complaints and answers in earl of Exeter v. Sir Thomas Lake, Mary Lake, Sir Arthur Lake, Sir Nicholas Fortescue, Mathew Patteson, Thomas Sayer, William Sanford, and John Falconer, STAC 8/111/27.
4. On the problems of eliciting women's (and men's) voices in court records, see Tim Stretton, "Women, Legal Records, and the Problem of the Lawyer's Hand," *Journal of British Studies* 58 (2019): 684–700. Stretton concludes that "in interpreting legal materials, and determining whether particular women played instrumental or marginal roles in legal cases, researchers need to analyze each document on its merits, corroborating and comparing it with other available materials," because "context is everything." I have attempted to follow that maxim while analyzing the Lake and Cecil court cases.
5. Earl of Exeter v. Sir Thomas Lake, Mary Lake, Sir Arthur Lake, Sir Nicholas Fortescue, Mathew Patteson, Thomas Sayer, William Sanford, and John Falconer, STAC 8/111/27; Roos to the King James, June 1, 1618, SP 14/97/231.
6. STAC 8/111/27 and Roos to King James, June 1, 1618, SP 14/97/231.
7. STAC 8/24/20 and STAC 8/24/19.
8. Exeter's complaint, STAC 8/111/27.
9. The quote is from Roos's letter to the king, rather than from the Star Chamber complaint.
10. According to Exeter's complaint, based on Roos's written account, Roos had told his wife he was preparing Charter House Yard for them, and she had agreed to come and live with him there. When he came to Cannons, he told Anne that the house was ready for them, and he had come to take her there, "whereunto she seemed willing and made herself ready to goe wth him." In his letter to the king, Roos added the story of Anne and her brother Arthur being in cahoots to trap him, and Anne sending the message to come and get her. Roos to King James, June 1, 1618, SP 14/97/231.
11. This description of Lady Lake's renewed threats when Roos contemplated Star Chamber actions is also only in Roos's later letter, not in the written description to his grandfather and not in the Star Chamber complaint.
12. As mentioned, the Lake's stories come from the answers of Sir Thomas Lake, Lady Mary Lake, Arthur Lake, the Lake's butler William Sanford, and the Lake's bailiff John Falconer, STAC 8/111/27.
13. Roos sent along letters to his father-in-law via Winwood on May 2. He may have also informed Lake about the incident at that time. Winwood to Lake, May 2, 1617, *CSP Domestic, James (1611–1618)*, 462–63.
14. Arthur Lake received the standard license to travel for three years on November 30, 1615, *APC*, vol. 34, 340. He returned from France in February 1617. Mr. Castle to James Miller, February 1617, Birch, *James*, vol. 1, 460.
15. STAC 8/111/27.
16. STAC 8/111/27.
17. For interpretations of ideals of early modern English manhood, see Patricia Crawford, *Blood, Bodies, and Family in Early Modern England* (Harlow: Pearson, 2004), esp. chs. 4 and 6; Foyster, *Manhood in Early Modern England*; Alexandra Shepard, *Meanings of Manhood in Early Modern England* (New York: Oxford University Press, 2003).
18. Jennifer Evans, "'They Are Called Imperfect Men': Male Infertility and Sexual Health in Early Modern England," *Social History of Medicine* 29.2 (2014): 311–13;

Helen Berry and Elizabeth Foyster, "Childless Men in Early Modern England," in Berry and Foyster, eds., *The Family in Early Modern England* (Cambridge: Cambridge University Press, 2007), 165–69; Collington, 186–88.

19. Susan Amussen, "Failing at Patriarchy," in Naomi Pullin and Kathryn Woods, eds., *Negotiating Exclusion in Early Modern England, 1550–1800* (New York: Routledge, 2021), 181.
20. Sir Edward Coke, *Third Part of the Institutes of the Laws of England* (London: E. and R. Brooke, 1748), 175; William Blackstone, *Commentaries on the Laws of England* (Oxford: Clarendon Press, 1770), vol. 4, 30.
21. Chamberlain to Carleton, 4 June, 1617, McClure, vol. 2, 80.
22. STAC 8/111/27.
23. Alexandra Shepard, "Brokering Fatherhood: Illegitimacy and Paternal Rights and Responsibilities in Early Modern England," in Steve Hindle, Alexandra Shepard, and John Walter, eds., *Remaking English Society: Social Relation and Social Change in Early Modern England* (Woodbridge: The Boydell Press, 2013), 47.
24. Chamberlain says that Roos initially excused his wife's actions, because her parents were leading her. Chamberlain to Carleton, April 1, 1618, McClure, vol. 2, 154.
25. Roos to King James, June 1, 1618, SP 14/97/231.
26. Roos to King James, June 1, 1618, SP 14/97/231.
27. On parents making similar arguments when exerting control over their married daughters, see Elizabeth Foyster, "Parenting Was for Life, Not Just for Childhood: The Role of Parents in the Married Lives of Their Children in Early Modern England," *History* 86 (2001): 313–27.
28. Abstracts of proof in case of earl and countess of Exeter v. Lake. February 5, 1619, SP 14/105/82; SP 14/105/81.
29. STAC 8/111/27.
30. Lake says in the fall 1617 case against Chapman that Chapman's tale caused months of dissent between Lake and Roos. King's attorney Yelverton against Sir Peter Chapman, Diego da Silva, Francis Featherstonehowe, Henry Russell, STAC 8/24/20.
31. Chapman argues he came to Lake well before March but does not specify when. Chapman's answer, STAC 8/24/20.
32. STAC 8/24/20.
33. Blackstone, *Commentaries*, vol. 4, 30.
34. STAC 8/111/27.
35. For a classic study on charivaris, see Martin Ingram, "Ridings, Rough Music and Mocking Rhymes in Early Modern England," in Barry Reay, ed., *Popular Culture in Seventeenth-Century England* (London: St. Martin's Press, 1985), 166–97. See also Susan Amussen, "Cuckold's Haven: Gender and Inversion in Popular Culture," in Malcolm Smuts, ed., *The Oxford Handbook of the Age of Shakespeare* (Oxford: Oxford University Press, 2016), 528–42.
36. STAC 8/111/27.
37. John Holles discussed Roos problems with both his father and grandfather. Holles to his son, John Holles, June 2, 1616, Seddon, vol. 1, 129–30 (thinks Roos has mistreated his father, but doesn't say why); Holles to Sir Thomas Lake, May 30, 1617, vol. 1, 161–62 (says Roos is penitent for errors past, specifically for a lease which he had

"unnaturally" taken "over his fathers head"). William Sanderson, Roos's secretary on the Spanish embassy, argued that he learned of a "deadly feud" between Lady Lake and the countess of Exeter while in Spain, but did not mention the reason for it. Sanderson, 447.

38. On intergenerational patriarchal conflicts, as well as competing notions of manhood, see for example Alexandra Shepard, "From Anxious Patriarchs to Refined Gentlemen? Manhood in Britain, c. 1500–1700," *Journal of British Studies* 44.2 (2005): 289–94; Collington, 186–88, 189–90. On the worries of a younger man to not be as successful in the role as patriarch as their fathers, see Jared van Duinen, "The Obligations of Governing Masculinity in the Early Stuart Gentry Family: The Barringtons of Hatfield Broad Oak," in Susan Broomhall and Jacqueline van Gent, eds., *Governing Masculinities in the Early Modern Period* (Burlington: Ashgate, 2011), 113–30.
39. STAC 8/111/27.
40. See for example Angus McClaren, *Impotence: A Cultural History* (Chicago: University of Chicago Press, 2007), esp. ch. 3; Crawford, 113; Meredith K. Rey, "Impotence and Corruption: Sexual Function and Dysfunction in Early Modern Italian Books of Secrets," in Sara F. Matthews-Grieco, ed., *Cuckoldry, Impotence, and Adultery in Europe (15th–17th century)* (Aldershot: Ashgate, 2014), 128, 131–36.
41. Sir George Gerrard to Sir Dudley Carleton, 4 June 1617, SP 14/92/162.
42. Chamberlain to Carleton, 4 June, 1617, McClure, vol. 2, 80. One of Roos's men, Carleton's old servant named Duppa, now served Roos and was one of the men hurt in the Cannons melee. Chamberlain said Duppa was the "chief man about my Lord in his chamber, and some say his bedfellow." Two others of Roos's servants were people that Chamberlain knew. Chamberlain's old servant Christopher was now Lord Roos's steward, and John Cooke was clerk of the kitchen. Cooke had married one of Carleton's maids.
43. See letters from Chamberlain to Carleton, McClure, vol. 1, 469, 474–75, 478, 495; BL Add. MS. 4129, f. 18; T. B. Howell, ed., *A Complete Collection of State Trials and Proceedings for High Treason and Other Crimes and Misdemeanors from the Earliest Period to the Year 1785* (London: T. C. Hansard, 1816), vol. 2, 785–87.
44. In the abstracts of proofs from the Star Chamber trial, February 5, 1619, SP 14/105/82. (In this case, the Exeters were suing the Lakes for slander, since at that point, Lady Roos had accused Lady Exeter of having an incestuous affair with her step-grandson Lord Roos, and of having attempted to poison her twice. The Exeters introduced the note about Roos's impotence as evidence against even the possibility of the alleged adultery and incest between Lord Roos and the countess of Exeter.)
45. STAC 8/111/26, 004.
46. Holles to Sir Thomas Lake, May 30, 1617, Seddon, vol. 2, 162.
47. Holles to Sir Thomas Lake, May 30, 1617, Seddon, vol. 2, 162.
48. Chapman was described as "Sir Peter Chapman that belongs to the Lord of Exeter" when he was knighted during a party at Lady Hatton's house, which the king attended. Chamberlain to Carleton, November 15, 1617, McClure, vol. 2, 117. Francis Featherstonehowe (also spelled Featherstonehaugh in sources) is described as Exeter's servant by 1604. Thrush and Ferris, "Fetherstonhaugh, Francis, 1574/5–1638)," *HPO*.
49. STAC 8/24/20.

50. STAC 8/24/20.
51. Holles to Lake, June 25, 1617, Seddon, vol. 3, 170.
52. Holles to Lake, June 25, 1617, Seddon, vol. 3, 170.
53. I have written about these disputes in a previous book; see Luthman, chs. 2 and 3.
54. Holles to Lake, July 26, 1617, Seddon, vol. 3, 180–81.

Chapter 4

1. *CSP Venice (1615–1617)*, vol. 14.
2. Chamberlain to Carleton, August 9, 1617, McClure, vol. 2, 92–3; George Gerrard to Carleton, August 18, 1617, SP 14/93/41; Lake to Sir Ralph Winwood, August 16, 1617, SP 14/93/36; Holles to Lake, August 15, 1617, Seddon, vol. 2, 193.
3. Chamberlain gives the impression that Winwood had shown him Roos's letter. Chamberlain to Carleton, August 9, 1617, *Chamberlain*, vol. 2, 92–93; Thomas Locke to William Trumbull, August 20, 1617, *Downshire*, vol. 6, 258; Clifford, *Diary*, 60; George Gerrard to Carleton, August 18, 1617, SP 14/93/41.
4. Holles to Lake, August 15, 1617, Seddon, vol. 2, 193.
5. For a good overview on the politics of Catholicism during the reign of James, see Questier, *Dynastic Politics*, esp. chs. 5 and 6; and Katy Gibbons for the reign of Elizabeth, in "English Catholics and the Continent," in Malcolm Smuts, ed., *The Oxford Handbook of the Age of Shakespeare* (Oxford: Oxford University Press, 2016), 367–80.
6. Rickman, *Love, Lust, and License*, 77–84, 89–90.
7. Lionelli noted: "All are surprised, indeed the more so because at present he enjoys an income of 20,000 crowns and certainly expects more than 100,000 crowns in addition on the death of his father and grandfather." Lionelli to Venetian Doge and Senate, August 25, 1617, *CSP Venice (1615–1617)*, vol. 14.
8. See Jennifer Low, *Manhood and the Duel: Masculinity in Early Modern Drama and Culture* (New York: Palgrave Macmillan, 2003), esp. ch. 3, "Sexual Status and the Combat."
9. For a good overview of dueling in sixteenth- and seventeenth-century England, see Markku Peltonen, *The Duel in Early Modern England: Civility, Politeness and Honour* (New York: Cambridge University Press, 2003), chs. 1–2.
10. Peltonen, chs. 1–2.
11. Peltonen, 87–91; Chamberlain to Carleton, February 22, 1617, McClure, vol. 2, 54–55; John Throckmorton to Sir Dudley Carleton, February 12, 1617, SP 84/76/61; Edward Sherburn to Carleton, February 23, 1617, SP 14/90/155.
12. Robert Branthwait to William Trumbull, August 28, 1617, *Downshire*, vol. 6, 268–69; Winwood to Lake, August 14, 1617, SP 14/93/f. 34; John Castle to William Trumbull, September 18, 1617, *Downshire*, vol. 6, 292.
13. Lake to Winwood, August 16, 1617, SP 14/93/36.
14. Robert Branthwait also argued that Roos knew that Arthur Lake was not in London when he sent his challenge, but had gone to meet the king coming from Scotland to William Trumbull, August 28, 1617, *Downshire*, vol. 6, 268–69.

15. Lake to Carleton, August 28, 1617, SP 84/78/232.
16. Nathaniel Brent to Carleton, October 11, 1617, SP 14/93/217.
17. Lake to Winwood, August 16, 1617, SP 14/93/36.
18. Chamberlain to Carleton, October 11, 1617, McClure, vol. 2, 101.
19. Nathaniel Brent to Carleton, October 11, 1617, SP 14/93/217. Herbert Croft had left for France by early May 1617 (Lake to Carleton, May 6, 1617, SP 84/97/98).
20. Chamberlain to Carleton, October 25, 1617, McClure, vol. 2, 107–8.
21. Chamberlain to Carleton, April 1, 1618, McClure, vol. 2. 154.
22. Lake to Winwood, August 16, 1617, SP 14/93/36; Lake to Buckingham, November 27, 1617, Samuel Rawson Gardiner, ed., *Fortescue Papers* (Camden Society, 1871), vol. 1, 35–36; Lake to Carleton, October 20, 1617, Philip Yorke, earl of Harwicke, *Letters to and from Sir Dudley Carleton during His Embassy in Holland* (London: 1775), 198.
23. Chamberlain to Carleton, January 3, 1618, McClure, vol. 2, 124.
24. Chamberlain to Carleton, January 10, 1618, McClure, vol. 2, 128.
25. "Trumbull, William 1576*80?–1635," *ODNB*. While the king was peeved at Roos's irresponsible behavior, his flight did not constitute the king's primary foreign policy concern during the fall of 1617. Trumbull's main engagement at the time consisted of finding out more about the publication of a satirical book, entitled *Corona Regia*, which made King James out to be a ridiculous figure. The book was produced by an anonymous writer in the Spanish Netherlands. James was furious and felt that the archduke was not doing enough to catch and punish the person. James even sent a special ambassador to Brussels to demand further action and was not happy with how the archduke treated the person or the issue. The king even contemplated having the suspected author kidnapped and brought back to England for punishment. Trumbull seems to have been actively engaged in making the practical arrangements for the kidnapping, but in the end the king decided to abandon the scheme.
26. Trumbull to Winwood, September 3/13, 1617, *Downshire*, vol. 6, 275; Trumbull to Winwood, September 10/20, 1617, *Downshire*, vol. 6, 281.
27. Winwood to Carleton, August 27, 1617, Yorke, 169; Chamberlain to Carleton, October 11, 1617, McClure, vol. 2, 101.
28. Lake to Buckingham, November 27, 1617, *Fortescue Papers*, vol. 1, 34–35; Lake to Carleton, October 20, 1617, SP 84/79/189; Trumbull to Lake, SP 77/12/427.
29. Trumbull to Carleton, December 16/26, 1617, SP 77/12/438.
30. Lake to Trumbull, November 28, 1617, *Downshire*, vol. 6, 333; Trumbull to Buckingham, November 29, 1617, *Downshire*, vol. 6, 335; Francis Cottington to Trumbull, January 11, 1618, *Downshire*, vol. 6, 367.
31. August 24, *ACP*, vol. 35, 327. As early as August, Winwood told Lake "yf we could learne what ys become of my L. Roos he should be sent for." Winwood to Lake, August 23, 1617, SP 14/93/73. By September, it had been sent, according to the Venetian envoy's report: "An intimation has been sent in the king's name to Lord Roos, who had withdrawn to France, to return immediately upon the penalty to which nobles who leave the kingdom without permission are subject." Lionelli to Doge and Senate. September 23, 1617, *CSP Venice (1617–19)*, vol. 15, 1–14.
32. John Castle to Trumbull, September 18, 1617, *Downshire*, vol. 6, 292. Chamberlain told Carleton in October that the "Lord Rosse is sent for by order of the counsaile

but the questions is where he may be found, for he playes least in sight and stayes not long in a place." Chamberlain to Carleton, October 11, 1617, McClure, vol. 2, 101.

33. Chamberlain to Carleton, November 29, 1617, McClure, vol. 2, 120. By late November, Lake knew that Roos was in Rome and asked the king, via Buckingham, if he should send a royal order for him to return. Lake to Buckingham, November 27, 1617, *Fortescue Papers*, vol. 1, 34–35. At that point, Roos withdrew to Naples.
34. Archbishop of Canterbury to Trumbull, December 19, 1617, *Downshire*, vol. 6, 350.
35. December 4, 1617, *APC*, vol. 35, 400–401.
36. Carleton to Chamberlain, August 14, 1612, December 10/20, 1613, December 24, 1613/January 3, 1614, Lee, 132–33, 152–53, 154–55.
37. Winwood to Carleton, September 16, 1617, Yorke, 169.
38. Chamberlain to Carleton, August 9, 1617, McClure, vol. 2, 93.
39. Carleton to Lake, October 13/12, 1617, SP 84/79/164.
40. Lake to Trumbull, October 30, 1617, *Downshire*, vol. 6, 317.
41. Lake to Trumbull, November 28, 1617, *Downshire*, vol. 6, 333.
42. The Latin phrase comes from Horace, and means that both barbers and bleary-eyed people know it.
43. Trumbull to Lake, December 18/28, 1617, SP 77/12/443–44.
44. Trumbull to Lake, December 18/28, 1617, SP 77/12/443–44.
45. Lake to Buckingham, November 27, 1617, *Fortescue Papers*, vol. 1, 35–36.
46. Lake's answers in STAC 8/111/26. In his answers to Sir Thomas Lake, Jr.'s suit the following year, Gwilliams argued that he had not known anything about Roos's plan to leave England, and that he had not coordinated his flight with the countess of Exeter. In fact, he had only spoken to the countess of Exeter once before Roos left, and that was when da Silva sent him to see Mistress Maddock, one of the countess's servants, to see about borrowing some linens for Frances da Silva's childbed. The countess of Exeter happened to come through the room and told Gwilliams to make sure that "the sayd lynnen should after yt was used bee washed out of starche and sent home again." Gwilliams answer, STAC 8/196/24.
47. "Diegos man (called Gwilliams) was he that passed this way towards Paris." Trumbull to Lake, January 1, 1618, SP 77/13/1.
48. Lake's answers to Exeter's complaints in STAC 8/111/26.
49. Lake's answers to Exeter's complaints in STAC 8/111/26.
50. Chaney and Wilks suggests that he commissioned it at the time of his marriage, but if so, he must have done it via letters. His usual contact, Sir Henry Wotton was not in Venice 1616–19. Roos also commissioned a portrait of himself by Tintoretto. Chaney and Wilkes, 183, 191.
51. Laura Walters, "Oduardo Fialetti (1573–c.1638): The Interrelation of Venetian Art and Anatomy, and His Importance in England" (unpublished PhD dissertation, 2 vols, University of St. Andrews, 2009), 96–101, 170–72.
52. Chaney and Wilkes, 74, 155–58. The worries about nefarious influence of Catholicism and Catholics were ubiquitous when the Protestant English discussed travel.
53. Wolrad de Plessen to Trumbull, September 3, 1617, *Downshire*, vol. 6, 275.
54. Castle to Trumbull, September 18, 1617, *Downshire*, vol. 6, 292.

Chapter 5

1. SP 84/79/189.
2. Winwood to Lake, August 20, 1617, SP 14/93/51; same to same, August 23, 1617, SP 14/93/73.
3. Chamberlain to Carleton, October 25, 1617, McClure, vol. 2, 106–7.
4. Chamberlain to Carleton, October 31, 1617, McClure, vol. 2, 108–9.
5. Chamberlain to Carleton, December 20, 1617, McClure, vol. 2, 123.
6. "Sir Thomas Lake and his Lady have put in a bill into the Star Chamber against certain that have had heretofore dealings with him [Roos], and another bill into the chauncerie, which upon the aunswer of the parties is dismissed the court and now the earle of Exeter prefers a crosse bill in the chauncerie against Sir Thomas and his Lady in the Lord Rosses behalf: who is thought will soone return yf he find that his grandfather and father mean to sticke to him." Chamberlain to Carleton, November 29, 1617, McClure, vol. 2, 120. The records that survive are for two Star Chamber cases, against Peter Chapman and others. In the later May 1618 slander suit, Exeter's complaint mentions "in a Cause depending in the honourable Court of Star Chamber between yo:r Ma:ties Attorney general ptl and Sir Peter Chapman and other defendants." That must be referring to the second, February 1618 suit, STAC 8/24/19.
7. STAC 8/25/20.
8. STAC 8/24/20.
9. Yelverton's complaint, STAC 8/24/20.
10. Abstract of proofs, February 5, 1619, SP 14/105/82.
11. Yelverton's complaint, STAC 8/24/20.
12. Yelverton's complaint, STAC 8/24/20.
13. Yelverton's complaint, STAC 8/24/20.
14. Chamberlain to Carleton, November 29, 1617, McClure, vol. 2, 120.
15. J. H. Baker, *An Introduction to English Legal History*, 4th ed. (London: Butterworts Tolley, 2002), 97–115.
16. C 8/32/151/001.
17. C 8/32/151/001.
18. The description of Lady Roos's bedroom furniture comes from Lady Lake's answers in another of Exeter's lawsuits in 1621–22. This well was after the big scandal and the main slander suits of 1618–19, when the Lakes and Lady Roos lost against the Exeters and were publicly discredited. At this juncture, Exeter was again trying to recover some of Roos's property. It was in Mary Lake's interest at the time to downplay the value of any goods, of course. C 8/31/33.
19. C 8/32/151/001.
20. C 8/32/151/001.
21. C 8/32/151/001.
22. C 8/32/151/001. Dunscombe's brother-in-law, Robert Dixon, later received some of the goods in return payments for money that Dunscombe owed him. Dixon had to justify his ownership and sale of Roos's goods in a later suit of the earl of Exeter in 1622, and he then detailed the legal procedure Dunscombe had gone through in 1617. Dixon claimed that Roos had owed about £100 to Dunscombe when he left, but Dunscombe himself had only argued for about £30. C 8/31/33.

23. Chamberlain to Carleton, November 29, 1617, McClure, vol. 2, 120.
24. Answers of Sir Ingilby Daniell, C 8/31/33.
25. Roos to Trumbull, June 9, 1611, *Downshire*, vol. 3, 87.
26. John Thorys and James Monger to Trumbull, October 8, 10, 17, 24, and 26 and November 8 and 13, 1611, *Downshire*, vol. 3, 155, 158, 165, 169, 170, 178, 181.
27. Tobie Mathews to Trumbull, August 9, 1611, *Downshire*, vol. 3, 118.
28. James Monger to Trumbull, October 17, 1611; same to same, October 24, 1611; same to same, October 26, 1611; November 8; same to same, 1611; same to same, November 13, 1611, *Downshire*, vol. 3, 165, 170, 178, 181.
29. Answers of Robert Hooke to earl of Exeter's suit in 1622, C 8/31/33.
30. Answers of Edward Webster to earl of Exeter's suit in 1622, C 8/31/33.
31. Lady Lake's and Sir Thomas Lake's answers to earl of Exeter's suit in 1622, C 8/31/33.
32. Lady Roos's answers to suit of earl and countess of Exeter, May 1618, STAC 8/111/26.
33. Lady Roos's answers to suit of earl and countess of Exeter, May 1618, STAC 8/111/26.
34. Lady Roos's answers to suit of earl and countess of Exeter, May 1618, STAC 8/111/26.

Chapter 6

1. Sir Thomas Lake, Jr.'s bill of complaint, STAC 8/196/24.
2. Lady Roos's answer, STAC 8/111/26.
3. The most thorough descriptions of the house are in C. S. S. Higham, *Wimbledon Manor House under the Cecils* (London: Longmans, 1962). In 1597 and in August 1599, Queen Elizabeth visited. John Nichols, *The Progresses and Public Processions of Queen Elizabeth* (London: J. B. Nichols, 1823), vol. 3, 413–14, 439–40. James visited in June 1616, June 1619. Nichols, *James*, vol. 3, 173–74, 177, 554; Caroline Knight, "The Cecils at Wimbledon," in Pauline Croft, ed., *Patronage, Culture and Power: The Early Cecils* (New Haven: Yale University Press, 2002), 47–63.
4. Paula Henderson, "A Shared Passion: The Cecils and Their Gardens," in Pauline Croft, ed., *Patronage, Culture and Power: The Early Cecils* (New Haven: Yale University Press, 2002), 105–9; Higham, 46.
5. From a 1649 inventory, partially printed in Daniel Lyson, *The Environs of London*, Vol. 1: *County of Surrey* (London: T. Cadell and W. Davies, 1792), *British History Online*, accessed April 4, 2020, http://www.british-history.ac.uk/london-environs/vol1, 519–40.
6. John Fenitt, *Finetti Philoxenis: Some Choice Observations of Sir John Fenitt, Knight, and Master of Ceremonies of the Two Last Kings, Touching the Reception and Precedence, and Treatment and Audience, the Punctillos and Contrasts, of Forren Ambassadors in England* (London: 1656), 35; Nichols, *James*, vol. 3, 173–74, 187–88.
7. Nichols, *James*, vol. 4, 1098.
8. The earl and countess of Exeter v. Sir Thomas Lake, Mary Lake, Lady Roos, Sara Swarton, and Sir Arthur Lake, 1618, STAC 8/111/26; Sir Thomas Lake the younger vs. earl and countess of Exeter, George Gwilliams, and Elizabeth Gresham, 1618, STAC 8/196/24; abstract of proofs, February 5, 1619, SP 14/105/82.
9. Sir Thomas Lake, Jr.'s suit, 1618 STAC 8/196/24.
10. See esp. chs. 4 and 11 in Susan North, *Sweet and Clean: Bodies and Clothes in Early Modern England* (Oxford: Oxford University Press, 2020).

11. Evans and Read, *Maladies and Medicine*, ch. 6.
12. Alice Butler's and Robert Marsh's deposition were also part of the later slander case. Abstracts of proofs on both sides, principally taken from the examination of witnesses, in the case of the earl and countess of Exeter v. Sir Thomas Lake and others. February 5, 1619, SP 14/105/82.
13. Sir Edward Harwood to Carleton, February 6, 1619, SP 14/105/135.
14. It was Swarton who added the details about her employer's anger and physical violence against her servant. Swarton's answer, STAC 8/111/26.
15. The complaint of Sir Thomas Lake, Jr., STAC 8/196/24.
16. Sir Thomas Lake, Jr.'s complaint. STAC 8/196/24.
17. Evans and Read, *Maladies and Medicine*, ch. 6.
18. The English royals had a tradition of visiting the homes of their nobility and wealthy gentry during the late summer months, which was called the royal "progress."
19. Nichols, *James*, vol. 3, 180. On August 5 (anniversary of the Gowry conspiracy), "Bishop Andrews preached before the king at Burleigh neere Okeham: on the topic of Esther," ii, 21. Nichols, *James*, vol. 3, 185.
20. Abstracts of proofs in Exeter v. Lakes trial, February 5, 1619, SP 14/105/82.
21. Evans and Read, *Maladies and Medicine*, ch. 6. Dr. Henry Atkins was one of the king's physicians, who also had a private practice. He attended Prince Henry in his last illness, along with Mayerne. He also testifies in later slander trial. "Atkins, Henry (1554/5–1635)," *ODNB*.
22. The answers of earl and countess of Exeter to Sir Thomas, Jr.'s suit, STAC 8/196/24.
23. The complaint of earl and countess of Exeter, STAC 8/111/26.
24. Countess of Exeter's answer to Sir Thomas, Jr.'s suit, STAC 8/196/24.
25. Nichols, *James*, vol. 3, 174.
26. Abstracts of proofs, February 5, 1619, SP14/105/82.
27. The answers of the countess of Exeter to Sir Thomas, Jr.'s suit, STAC 8/196/24.
28. The answers of the countess of Exeter to Sir Thomas, Jr.'s suit, STAC 8/196/24.
29. The answers of the countess of Exeter and Elizabeth Gresham to Sir Thomas, Jr.'s suit, STAC 8/196/24.
30. Abstracts of proofs, SP 14/105/82.
31. Abstracts of proofs, SP 14/105/82.
32. Abstracts of proofs, SP 14/105/82.
33. Thomas, Jr., suit, complaint STAC 8/196/24.
34. Coke and Montagu quoted in Miranda Wilson, *Poison's Dark Works in Renaissance England* (Lanham, MD: Bucknell University Press, 2014), 54.
35. Una McIlvenna, "Poison, Pregnancy, and Protestants: Gossip and Scandal at the Early Modern French Court," in Heather Kerr and Claire Walker, eds., *Fama and Her Sisters: Gossip and Rumor in Early Modern Europe* (Turnhout: Brepols Publishers, 2015), 48; Bellany, *Politics of Court Scandal*, 144–48; Lindley, 163–67; Wilson, ch. 3; Frances Dolan, *Dangerous Familiars: Representation of Domestic Crime in England 1550–1700* (Ithaca: Cornell University Press, 1994), 29–31.
36. Bellany, *The Politics of Court Scandal*; Lindley; Somerset.
37. "The Proceedings which Happened Touching the Divorcement between the Lady Frances Howard and Robert, Earl of Essex (c. 1615)," BL Add. 11600, ff. 10–21, at

"Manuscript Pamphleteering in Early Modern England," accessed June 21, 2022, https://mpese.ac.uk/t/ProceedingsDivorceHowardEssex.html.

38. He only gives one mention of it in a letter between Lorkin and Puckering in 1619 as a source for it. Mostly, he argues it based on the similarities between the two cases. Bellany, *The Politics of Court Scandal*, 252–54.
39. Lorkin to Puckering, May 24, 1619, Birch, *James*, vol. 2, 166.
40. Swarton's answer, Exeter's slander suit. STAC 8/111/26. I have been unable to find the specific case Swarton was referring to here, but Chamberlain noted a case of a wife poisoning a husband in Aldgate London in the summer of 1616. "The same day [the previous Monday] likewise another woman poisoned her husband about Aldgate." Chamberlain to Carleton, July 6, 1616, McClure, vol. 2, 15.
41. Abstracts of proofs, SP 14/105/82.
42. Wolley to Trumbull, February 12/22, 1618, *Downshire*, vol. 6, 383.
43. Bellany, *Murder of King James*, 83–91.
44. See Johanna Rickman, *Love, Lust, and License in Early Modern England: Illicit Sex and the Nobility* (Aldershot: Ashgate, 2008), 81, 84–87; Lindley, 168–73; Bellany, *Politics of Court Scandal*, 153–56, 164–65; Susan Staub, *Nature's Cruel Stepdames: Murderous Women in the Street Literature of Seventeenth Century England* (Pittsburg: Duquesne University Press, 2005), 13, 27, 30–32.
45. Lady Roos's complaint (via Yelverton), STAC 8/24/20; Lady Roos's answer in STAC 8/111/26; Sir Thomas Lake, Jr.'s complaint, STAC 8/196/24.
46. Bellany, *Politics of Court Scandal*, 148–56; Alastair Bellany, "Thinking with Poison," in Malcolm Smuts, ed., *The Oxford Handbook of the Age of Shakespeare* (Oxford: Oxford University Press, 2016), 578; Luthman, *Love, Madness, and Scandal*, 85–87.
47. Gervase Markham, *Country Contentments, Or The English Housewife* (London: 1623), dedication. On women's roles as medical experts within the household, see Elaine Leong, "'Herbals she peruseth': Reading Medicine in Early Modern England," *Renaissance Studies* 28.4 (2016): 556–78; Anne Stobart, *Household Medicine in Seventeenth Century England* (New York: Bloomsbury Publishing, 2016). On the same practice in Italy, see Sharon Strocchia, *Forgotten Healers: Women and the Pursuit of Health in Late Renaissance Italy* (Cambridge, MA: Harvard University Press, 2019), ch. 1.
48. Goodman, 194.
49. Chamberlain to Carleton, October 25, 1617, McClure, vol. 2, 107.
50. Markham, 4–5.
51. On households' purchases of medicines or medical ingredients, see Stobart, 60; North, 267.
52. John Gerard, *The Herbal or Generall Historie of Plantes* (1630s), 1259–70; W. M., *The Queens Closet Opened Incomparable Secrets in Physick, Chyrurgery, Preserving, and Candying &c. which were Presented unto the Queen* (1659); Nicholas Culpeper, *The English Physitian Enlarged. Or an Astrologo-Physical Discourse of the Vulgar Herbs of this Nation* (London: Thomas Kelly, 1850, org. 1650), 152–55. Medical recipe books were very popular in the 1500s and 1600s. Mary Fissell, "Popular Medical Writing," in Joad Raymond, ed., *The Oxford History of Popular Print Culture* (Oxford: Oxford University Press, 2011), 420–22.

53. Stobart, 90–91.
54. Gerard, 1259–70; Hannah Newton, in *The Sick Child in Early Modern England, 1580–1720* (Oxford: Oxford University Press, 2012), 68, mentions that "clysters often contained syrup of roses, oil of violets, sugar, and egg whites."
55. Swarton's answer in Exeter's slander suit, STAC 8/111/26.
56. North, *Sweet and Clean*, 35, 93–94.
57. Answer of Lady Lake, STAC 8/111/26.
58. Answer of Sara Swarton, STAC 8/111/26.
59. Answer of Sara Swarton, STAC 8/111/26.
60. Answer of Sara Swarton, STAC 8/111/26.
61. Answer of Sara Swarton, STAC 8/111/26.
62. Earl and countess of Exeter's complaint, STAC 8/111/26.
63. Earl and countess of Exeter's complaint, STAC 8/111/26.

Chapter 7

1. Birch, *James*, vol. 2, 68.
2. Lake's complaint in suit against Hatton, STAC 8/196/23.
3. It is not clear why they would have met at Durham House. It was in the Strand, at some point inhabited by Thomas Coventry, made Solicitor General in 1617. It also served as the seat for bishop of Durham, although the bishops did not use it. French and Savoyard ambassadors had been housed there as well. The main implication here is that the meeting took place safely away from Exeter House, and thus conducted without Exeter's knowledge.
4. Lake's complaint in suit against Hatton, STAC 8/196/23.
5. This story is part of the answer Lady Roos gives in the later slander trial. STAC 8/111/26.
6. Luke Hatton's alleged document, copied in Lake suit against Hatton, STAC 8/196/23, as well as in Exeter's complaint in Exeter v. Lakes and Lady Roos, STAC 8/111/26. I have modernized some of the spelling and added punctuation and paragraph divisions in this text for greater clarity.
7. Answers of Sir Peter Chapman, STAC 8/24/19.
8. Mary Lake's reply in STAC 8/111/26.
9. Lake's complaint in STAC 8/196/23.
10. A year later, John Castle argued that Lake's main defense consisted of the fact that he had believed his daughter when she told him about Hatton's story, and he believed that Hatton's written account was true. Castle to Trumbull, March 3, 1619, BL Add. MS 72275, ff. 46–47.
11. The Exeters' complaint, STAC 8/111/26.
12. Answers of Sir Thomas Lake in STAC 8/111/26.
13. The Exeters' complaint, STAC 8/111/26.
14. "Honor is now described (much as it was in early modern period) as both an interior and exterior quality, as a deeply personal value that had a role in understandings of self-identity and as a communal asset, and as something self-generated by birth whilst concomitantly bestowed through service and behavior." Thomas, 4.

15. See especially Lindley on Frances Howard's annulment trial, in which she had to discuss the intimate details of her failed sex life with her first husband, the earl of Essex. In later pamphlets and retellings of the Overbury murder, the annulment case was used as an explanation for the beginning of Howard's sexual immorality, and therefore fall into sin. Lindley, ch. 3. Similarly, the countess of Castlehaven ran into the same problem when she had to testify about her rape in the trial against her husband in the 1630s. Herrup, 45.
16. The classic study on this topic is Laura Gowing's *Domestic Dangers: Women, Words, and Sex in Early Modern London* (Oxford: Clarendon Press, 1998). Gowing found that most cases women brought to the London church courts during the years 1570–1640s were sexual slander, although the details of the cases often revealed other, non-sexual, aspects of the disputes; see esp. ch. 4 and pp. 270–73.
17. On Penelope Rich's separation and contested remarriage, see Rickman, *Love, Lust, and License*, 127–39.
18. See Gowing; Martin Ingram, *Church Courts, Sex, and Marriage in England 1570–1640* (Cambridge: Cambridge University Press, 1987); Martin Ingram, "Law, Litigants and the Construction of 'Honour': Slander Suits in Early Modern England," in Peter Coss, ed., *The Moral World of the Law* (New York: Cambridge University Press, 2000).
19. Krista Kesselring and Tim Stretton, *Marriage, Separation, and Divorce in England, 1500–1700* (Oxford: Oxford University Press, 2022), 55.
20. Nathaniel Brent to Carleton, January 12, 1618, SP 14/95/23; John Chamberlain to Carleton, January 17, 1618, *McClure*, vol. 2, 132.
21. Nathaniel Brent to Carleton, January 17, 1618, SP 14/95/34; John Chamberlain to Carleton, January 17, 1618, *McClure*, vol. 2, 132.
22. Earl of Exeter's complaint, STAC 8/111/26.
23. Exeter's complaint, STAC 8/111/26.
24. George Gwilliam's answers in Sir Thomas Lake, Jr.'s suit, STAC 8/196/24.
25. Exeter's complaint, STAC 8/111/26.
26. Trumbull to Lake, January 1, 1618, SP 77/13/1.
27. Exeter's complaint, STAC 8/111/26.
28. R. C. Richardson, *Household Servants in Early Modern England* (Manchester: Manchester University Press, 2010), ch. 9.
29. Lake sued Hatton for slander in the court of Star Chamber in the spring of 1618, STAC 8/196/23.
30. Hatton's answer, STAC 8/196/23.
31. Hatton's reply, STAC 8/196/23.
32. Exeter's complaint, STAC 8/111/26.
33. Hatton's reply, STAC 8/196/23.
34. Hatton's reply, STAC 8/196/23.
35. Hatton's reply, STAC 8/196/23.
36. Lake to Buckingham, January 21 and 24, 1618, Gardiner, *Fortescue Papers*, vol. 1, 43–44.
37. Nathaniel Brent to Carleton, February 7, 1618, SP 14/96/20; Chamberlain to Carleton, January 31, 1618, and February 7, 1618, *McClure*, vol. 2, 134, 136.
38. John Levington described Sir Frances Crane as a man "whoe was her husbands man at that tyme." Levington to Carleton, February 28, 1618, SP 14/96/66.

39. George Gerrard to Carleton, March 6, 1618, SP 14/96/83; John Levingston to Carleton, February 28, 1618, SP 14/96/66. Francis Crane was knighted on September 4, 1617, but did not have that title in 1610 when the widow Lady Smith married the earl of Exeter. "Crane, Sir Francis (c. 1579–1636)," *ODNB*.
40. Ingram, *Carnal Knowledge*, 57–65, 324–26.
41. Levington to Carleton, February 28, 1618, SP 14/96/66.
42. George Gerrard to Carleton, March 6, 1618, SP 14/96/83.
43. Gerard Herbert to Dudley Carleton, February 23, 1618, SP 14/96/53.
44. Chamberlain to Carleton, February 28, 1618, *McClure*, vol. 2, 144–45.
45. *APC*, vol. 36, 49.
46. *APC*, vol. 36, 46–49; Camden, *Diary*, February 22, 1618; Sir Gerard Herbert to Carleton, February 23, 1618, SP 14/105/53; Sherburn to Carleton, February 23, 1618, SP 14/96/55; Harwood to Carleton, February 23, 1618, SP 14/96/57; Gerrard to Carleton, Mach 6, 1618, SP 14/96/83.
47. Chamberlain to Carleton, February 28, 1618, McClure, vol. 2, 145.
48. Lake v. Hatton, STAC 8/26/111.
49. Chamberlain reported that "We have hitherto had a very untoward spring, and such as the oldest men alive say that they have not seen the like, specially for this moneth of Aprill wherin yt is observed that there hath not a day past but that within the compasse of twelve howres there hath ben either raine, haile, snow or frost." Chamberlain to Carleton, April 29, 1618, McClure, vol. 2, 159.
50. *APC*, vol. 36, 53.
51. Brent to Carleton, January 12 and 17 and February 7, SP 14/95/23, SP 14/95/34, SP 14/96/20.
52. George Gerrard to Carleton, March 6, 1618, SP 14/96/83.
53. Sir John Throckmorton to Carleton, February 24, 1618, SP 84/82/235. Unfortunately, the correspondence of William Trumbull, usually containing such a wealth of information about the goings-on at the English court as well as abroad, is not very helpful for events during the early months of 1618. After a long wait to get permission to return home temporarily to attend to his private business, William Trumbull was in England during the spring of 1618, not returning to Brussels until later that summer. Therefore, the English correspondents who normally kept him informed about events at the English court had no need to write to him about the developing Lake and Exeter scandal. During that spring, Trumbull could get the information directly from his court contacts instead, thus depriving historians of an excellent source of information.
54. Chamberlain to Carleton, February 28, 1618, *McClure*, vol. 2, 145.
55. Adam Newton to Sir Thomas Puckering, February 26, 1618, Birch, *James*, vol. 2, 68–69.
56. Levington to Carleton, February 28, 1618, SP 14/96/66.
57. Sir Edward Conway to Carleton, March 29, 1618, SP 14/96/154.
58. February 17, 1618, Viscount Fenton to Earl of Mar, *Historical Manuscript Commission, Report on the Manuscripts of the Earl of Mar and Kellie (Mar and Kellie)* (London: H. M. Stationary Office, 1904), vol. 2, 82.
59. See Joy Wiltenburg, "Soundings of Laughter in Early Modern England: Women, Men, and Everyday Uses of Humor," *Early Modern Women: An Interdisciplinary Journal* 10.2 (2016): 28–31; Amussen, "Failing at Patriarchy," 188–89.

60. Chamberlain to Carleton, February 28, 1618, McClure, vol. 2, 145.
61. George Gerrard to Carleton, March 6, 1618, SP 14/96/83.
62. Nathaniel Brent to Carleton, Mach 7, 1618, SP 14/96/89.
63. Lockyer, *Buckingham*, 32–33.
64. Chamberlain to Carleton, January 10, 1618, McClure, vol. 2, 127; same to same, January 17, 1618; McClure, vol. 2, 132; Harwood to Carleton, January 12, 1618 SP 14/95/23.
65. Lake to Buckingham, January 24, 1618, *Fortescue Papers*, vol. 1, 44.
66. Camden, *Diary*, March 5, 1618; Chamberlain to Carleton, March 7, 1618, McClure, vol. 2, 147–48; Gerard Herbert to Carleton, March 1618, SP 14/96/116.
67. Chamberlain to Carleton, March 27, 1618, McClure, vol. 2, 152.
68. Chamberlain to Carleton, April 1, 1618, McClure, vol. 2, 153.
69. Chamberlain to Carleton, February 28, 1618, McClure, vol. 2, 145.

Chapter 8

1. Nathaniel Brent to Carleton, March 7, 1618, SP 14/96/89.
2. John Wolley to Trumbull, May 13/23, 1618, *Downshire*, vol. 6, 419. The kinsman may have been Sir Giles Brydges.
3. Chamberlain to Carleton, March 27, 1618, McClure, vol. 2, 152; Nathaniel Brent to Carleton, March 30, 1618, SP 14/96/156.
4. Chamberlain to Carleton, April 1, 1618, McClure, vol. 2, 154.
5. Chamberlain to Carleton, April 1, 1618, McClure, vol. 2, 153–54.
6. Nathaniel Brent to Carleton, March 30, 1618, SP 14/96/156.
7. John Wolley to Trumbull, April 2/12, April 9/19, May 13/23, 1618, *Downshire*, vol. 6, 405, 408, 419.
8. Chamberlain to Carleton, April 1, 1618, McClure, vol. 2, 154.
9. Roos to King James, June 1, 1618, SP 14/97/231.
10. Nathaniel Brent also reported that Roos had requested permission to remain abroad for several more years. Brent to Carleton, March 30, 1618, SP 14/96/156.
11. Bernard Capp, "'Jesus Wept' but Did the Englishman? Masculinity and Emotion in Early Modern England," *Past and Present* 224 (2014): 79.
12. Krista Kesselring, "No Greater Provocation? Adultery and the Mitigation of Murder in English Law," *Law and History Review* 34.1 (2016): 199–225; Foyster, *Manhood*, ch. 5.
13. Edward Norgate to Trumbull, July 28, 1618, *Downshire*, vol. 6, 460.
14. Rev. Thomas Larkin to Sir Thomas Puckering, July 14, 1618, Birch, *James*, vol. 2, 81.
15. Sir Henry Wotton to Sir Thomas Lake, June 1, 1618, Smith, *Wotton*, vol. 2, 141.
16. Ranier Zen to the Doge and Senate, June 12, 1618, *CSP Venice (1617–1619)*, vol. 15, 224–36.
17. Trumbull to Secretary of State, July 30, 1618, SP 77/13/26. Camden noted in his diary that Roos died on June 27, 1618. Trumbull's information is probably the more reliable of the two here.
18. Lorkin to Puckering, July 28, 1618, Birch, *James*, vol. 2, 83; William Jones to Trumbull, July 31, 1618, *Downshire*, vol. 6, 464.

19. Lake to Trumbull, July 27, 1618, *Downshire*, vol. 6, 460.
20. Lake to Trumbull, July 27, 1618, *Downshire*, vol. 6, 460.
21. Jones to Trumbull, July 31, 1618, *Downshire*, vol. 6, 464; Lake to Trumbull, September 4, 1618, *Downshire*, vol. 6, 497.
22. Camden, *Diary*, July 27, 1618. "News is reported of the death of Baron Roos at Naples, not without suspicion of poison."
23. Sir Edward Cecil to Carleton, August 22, 1618, SP 84/85/208.
24. William Jones to Trumbull, July 31, 1618, *Downshire*, vol. 6, 464.
25. Archbishop of Canterbury to Trumbull, October 27, 1618, *Downshire*, vol. 6, 559–60.
26. Archbishop of Canterbury to Trumbull, October 27, 1618, *Downshire*, vol. 6, 559–60; William Jones to Trumbull, July 31, 1618, *Downshire*, vol. 6, 464; Camden, *Diary*, Jun 27, 1618. For the view on problematic Jesuits, see Michael Questier, *Catholicism and Community in Early Modern England: Politics, Aristocratic Patronage and Religion, c. 1550–1640* (Cambridge: Cambridge University Press, 2006), 289–92.
27. Sir Edward Harwood to Carleton, October 3, 1618, SP 14/103/16; archbishop of Canterbury to Trumbull, October 27, 1618, *Downshire*, vol. 6, 559–60.

Chapter 9

1. *Downshire*, vol. 6, 596.
2. Commentators also focused on the various participants when describing the case, sometimes emphasizing the women, and sometimes the men, or a combination of the two. For example, Captain Thomas Brett called it the "famous womens cause" (Brett to Trumbull, October 2, 1618, *Downshire*, vol. 6, 530). Wolley "the busines between the Earle of Exeter and Sir Thomas Lake (Wolley to Trumbull, October 5, 1618, *Downshire*, vol. 6, 535); but another time he called it "Lady Rooses busines." October 9, 1618, 539.
3. On the Star Chamber, see Krista Kesselring with Natalie Mears, "Introduction: Star Chamber Matters," in K. J. Kesselring and Natalie Mears, eds., *Star Chamber Matters: An Early Modern Court and Its Records* (London: University of London Press, IHR, 2021), 1–18; William Hudson, *A Treatise of the Court of Star Chamber*, ed. Francis Hargrave and intro. by Thomas Barnes (Birmingham: Legal Classics Library reprint, 1986); G. R. Elton, *Star Chamber Stories* (New York: Barnes and Nobles, 1958), 9–17; John Guy, *The Court of Star Chamber and Its Records to the Reign of Elizabeth I* (London: H. M. Stationary Office, 1985), 1–17; Krista Kesselring, *Star Chamber Reports: BL Harley MS 2143*, List and Index Society, Special Series 57 (2018), v–x; Cora Louise Scofield, *A Study of the Court of Star Chamber* (Chicago: University of Chicago Press, 1990 reprint).
4. On the processes in Star Chamber, see for example Deborah Youngs, "'A Besy Woman… and Full of Lawe': Female Litigants in Early Tudor Star Chamber," *Journal of British Studies* 58 (2019): 737.
5. On the history on suits for defamation in early modern England, see Lindsay Kaplan, *The Culture of Slander in Early Modern England* (Cambridge: Cambridge University Press, 1997), 12–33; Ingram, "Law, Litigants," 140–41, 147; Clare Egan, "Jacobean Star Chamber Records and the Performance of Provincial Libel," in Kesselring and Mears, eds., *Star Chamber Matters*, 135–53.

6. Hudson, 100.
7. Ingram, "Laws, Litigants," 158; David Cressy, *Dangerous Talk: Scandalous, Seditious, and Treasonable Speech in Pre-Modern England* (Oxford: Oxford University Press, 2010), 35; Richard Cust, "Honour and Politics in Early Modern England: The Case of Beaumont v. Hastings," *Past and Present* 149 (1995): 75–76; Diane Strange, "From Private Sin to Public Shame: Sir John Digby and the Use of Star Chamber in Northamptonshire and Bedfordshire, 1610," *Midland History* 44 (2019): 39–40, 51–52; Alastair Bellany, "Libel," in Joad Raymond, ed., *The Oxford History of Popular Print Culture* (Oxford: Oxford University Press, 2011), 149–51.
8. Exeter's complaint, STAC 8/111/26.
9. Chamberlain commented on rumors that Lake might face further hardships after the Lakes had lost their case in 1619 as follows: "I thincke there need no other torture then to let the Lady of Exceter loose to sue them upon *scandalum magnatum*, which would quite undo them." Chamberlain to Carleton, March 19, 1619, McClure, vol. 2, 222.
10. For literature on the legal consequences of illicit sex, see Richard Adair, *Courtship, Illegitimacy and Marriage in Early Modern England* (Manchester: Manchester University Press, 1996); Ingram, *Carnal Knowledge*; Ingram, *Church Courts*; Luthman, 82, 192; Rickman, *Love, Lust, and License*, 22–24.
11. See Rickman, *Love, Lust, and License*, Intro. and chs. 1 and 2; and Luthman, 82–84.
12. Luthman, chs. 5 and 6.
13. Lake v. Hatton, STAC 8/196/23.
14. Lake's complaint, STAC 8/196/23.
15. Young, "A Besy Woman," 741–50; Tim Stretton, *Women Waging Law in Elizabethan England* (Cambridge: Cambridge University Press), 199, ch. 6; Kesselring and Stretton, 216–19.
16. Hudson, 9. Castle and Locke both called it the "case between Sir Thomas Lake and the countess of Exeter." October 15 and December 1, 1618, *Downshire*, vol. 6, 546, 596. Sir Edward Harwood called it the "Lady Rosse & my Lad. Exeter's cause," September 23, 1618, SP 14/99/154. At another time he called it "My Lad. Exeter hir cause," November 13, 1618, SP 14/103/142. Chamberlain called it "the suit twixt the countesse of Excester and Secretarie Lake." Chamberlain to Carleton, October 14, 1618, McClure, vol. 2, 171.
17. Egan, "Jacobean Star Chamber Records," 144–48.
18. Wolley probably meant the Star Chamber rather than the Chancery. Wolley to Trumbull, October 9, 1618, *Downshire*, vol. 6, 539–40. Witnesses were required to give testimony under oath. Barbara Shapiro, "Law and the Evidentiary Environment," in Lorna Hudson, ed., *English Law and Literature, 1500–1700* (Oxford: Oxford University Press, 2017), 259–61.
19. Thomas Locke to William Trumbull, December 1, 1618, *Downshire*, vol. 6, 596; Smith to Carleton, December 2, 1618, SP 14/104/4.
20. Chamberlain to Carleton, November 14, 1618, McClure, vol. 2, 183.
21. Abraham Williams to Trumbull, October 9, 1618, *Downshire*, vol. 6, 539.
22. Buckingham to Secretary Naunton, October 10, 1618, *Fortescue Papers*, 55.
23. Abstract of proofs on both sides, SP 14/105/82.

24. Abstract of proofs on both sides, SP 14/105/82.
25. Abstract of proofs on both sides, SP 14/105/82.
26. Abstract of proofs on both sides, SP 14/105/82.
27. Sir Thomas Lake to earl of Buckingham, November 4, 1618, *Fortescue Papers*, 59–60.
28. Hillary Taylor, "The Price of the Poor's Words: Social Relations and the Economics of Deposing for Ones 'Betters' in Early Modern England," *Economic History Review* 72.3 (2019): 833–34.
29. Constance, Lady Lucy to Sir Thomas Lake, October 10, 1618, SP 14/103/38.

Chapter 10

1. *Downshire*, vol. 6, 546.
2. Chamberlain to Carleton, February 28, 1618, McClure, vol. 2, 144.
3. Chamberlain to Carleton, March 27 and April 10, 1618, McClure, vol. 2, 151, 156; Maurice, Lee, *Great Britain's Solomon: James VI and I in His Three Kingdoms* (Urbana: University of Illinois Press, 1990), 250–51; Lockyer, *Buckingham*, 35–37, Andrew Thrush, "The Fall of Tomas Howard, 1st Earl of Suffolk and the Revival of Impeachment in the Parliament of 1621," *Parliamentary History* 32.2 (2018): 197–211.
4. Chamberlain to Carleton, July 9, 1612, McClure, vol. 1, 367–68.
5. Camden, *Diary*, May 23, 1618; Stephen Gardiner, *History of England from the Accession of James I to the Outbreak of the Civil War, 1603–1642*, vol. 3, 185–88, based on Gondomar's account to the king of Spain. Contarini to the Doge and Senate of Venice, June 14, 1618, *CSP Venice (1617–1619)*, vol. 15. "The ambassador will remain here until able to obtain the arrears of his salary, not without some hope of replacing the Secretary Lake, whose power has declined, and who is out of favour with the king and in great danger of losing his post." Carleton's arrival in England also meant that there was no need for Chamberlain to write letters to him about news at court and in England over the summer, so Chamberlain cannot serve as a source during that time.
6. Chamberlain to Carleton, May 5, 1618, McClure, vol. 2, 161.
7. Lorkin to Puckering, June 16, 1618, Birch, *James*, vol. 2, 76.
8. Gardiner, vol. 3, 187–88, based on Gondomar's account.
9. Trumbull received several letters about Suffolk's removal from office. Thomas Locke, July 19, Abraham William, July 19, Robert Branthwaith, July 21, Philip Burlamacchi, July 22, William Jones, July 22, 1618, *Downshire*, vol. 6, 451–55.
10. Lord Fenton to earl of Mar, July 1, 1618, *Mar and Kellie*, vol. 2, 85.
11. Abraham Williams to Trumbull, July 19, 1618, *Downshire*, vol. 6, 452.
12. William Jones to Trumbull, July 22, 1618, *Downshire*, vol. 6, 455.
13. Abraham Williams to Trumbull, July 23, 1618, *Downshire*, vol. 6, 457–58. "Mr. Secretary Lake was in good forwardness to have ben restored on Saterday last but was then crossed by the then Lord Treasurer. He hath fayre promises and good hopes yet left him to wayte his progresse, to which ende he hath sente his stuffe and diette along."
14. Edward Norgate to Trumbull, July 28, 1618, *Downshire*, vol. 6, 460: "the delay and expectation of my Lord Roos his answeare to certaine interrogatories intended to be propounded unto him by Sir Giles Bridges lately sent to him for that purpose." Frances Brydges Smith had a younger brother named Giles, and a first cousin by the same name.

15. Edward Norgate to Trumbull, July 28, 1618, *Downshire*, vol. 6, 460.
16. Abraham Williams to Trumbull, July 31, 1618, *Downshire*, vol. 6, 464; same to same, August 6, 1618; *Downshire*, vol. 6, 467. "Sir Thomas Lake is not yet restored."
17. David Coast, *News and Rumour in Jacobean England: Information, Court Politics and Diplomacy, 1618–25* (Manchester: University of Manchester Press, 2014), ch. 3.
18. August 22, 1618, Lord Fenton to earl of Mar, *Mar and Kellie*, vol. 2, 86; Thomas Locke to Trumbull, August 28, 1618, *Downshire*, vol. 6, 487. "Sir Thomas Lake has not yet been at the court." John Wolley to Trumbull, September 4/14, 1618, *Downshire*, vol. 6, 497–98. "I cannot understand but that he is in the same estate as he was at your departure, neither see I any likelihood but that he will yet awhile so continue."
19. Trumbull to Sir Robert Naunton, August 28, 1618, SP 77/13/59–60.
20. John Wolley to Trumbull, September 4/14, 1618, 497–98. Lord Fenton had not lost hope for Lake's restoration, but thought "a lytell tyme will cleer things," and that the king would deal with the issue once he returned to Hampton Court from his progress. Fenton to Mar, September 7, 1618, *Mar and Kellie*, vol. 2, 86.
21. John Wolley to Trumbull, September 11, 1618, *Downshire*, vol. 6, 505. King is on progress, neither of the secretaries are with him, Naunton because he did not have any need to go on the short trip, and Lake because "for wante of leave to come thither, he being, as I understand, so fare of as he was at the firste and rather farther, for the other hath now all the imployment in the busineses at home and all forrayn letters are addressed unto him, and what will become of him hereafter God knoweth, for it is thought of many he will never (unlesse the marriage goeth forwards of the which there is now no speech) be in so great a favor with the King as he was before."
22. Fenton to Mar, October 14, 1618, *Mar and Kellie*, vol. 2, 88.
23. John Castle to William Trumbull, September 17, 1618, *Downshire*, vol. 6, 513. "It is thought here Mr Secretary Lake will not be restored to his office before the hearing of the case, which the Countess hopes will take place next term."
24. Philip Burlamacchi to William Trumbull, July 22, 1618, *Trumbull*, vol. 6, 454–55.
25. On Raleigh, see the biography by Mark Nichols and Penry Williams, *Sir Walter Raleigh in Life and Legend* (New York: Continuum, 2011). On the failed expedition, Raleigh's return, and eventual execution, see esp. chs. 12 and 13.
26. Nicholls and Williams, 309–31; Lorkin to Puckering, July 14, 1618, Birch, *James*, vol. 2, 81–82; Chamberlain to Carleton, August 8, 1618, McClure, vol. 2, 163–64; same to same, August 13, 1618, McClure, vol. 2, 165; Robert Branthwaith to Trumbull, July 21, 1618, *Downshire*, vol. 6, 454.
27. Loomie, xvii–xix; Carter, 193.
28. Sir Thomas Lake to William Trumbull, July 16, 1618, *Downshire*, vol. 6, 447.
29. Chamberlain to Carleton, December 12, 1618, McClure, vol. 2, 192–93.
30. Castle to Trumbull, October 15, 1618, *Downshire*, vol. 6, 546.
31. Wolley to Trumbull, October 16, 1618, *Downshire*, vol. 6, 549; John Castle to Trumbull, October 23, 1618, *Downshire*, vol. 6, 556; Jean Beaulieu to Trumbull, October 23, 1618, *Downshire*, vol. 6, 537.
32. Locke to Trumbull, December 1, 1618, *Downshire*, vol. 6, 596.
33. Kesselring and Mears, *Star Chamber Matters*, 10–11.
34. Wolley to Trumbull, October 21, *Downshire*, vol. 6, 552; Wolley to Trumbull, November 13, 1618, *Downshire*, vol. 6, 580–81; Harwood to Carleton, November 13,

1618, SP 14/103/142; William Smith to Carleton, December 2, 1618, SP 14/104/4; Chamberlain to Carleton, November 14, 1618, McClure, vol. 2, 183; Sir John Chamberlain to Dudley Carleton, November 14, 1618, McClure, vol. 2, 183. John Wolley says it was Exeter's wish to move it.

35. See the letters to Carleton from Ben Rudyard, October 28, Richard Harrison, October 29, Nathaniel Brent, October 30, Chamberlain, October 31, Abraham Williams, October 31, Thomas Murray, November 2, Chamberlain again on November 3, 8, and 9, Matthew Carey, November 10, all in *CSP James I (1611–1618)*, 486–501.
36. Countess of Bedford to Carleton, October 18, 1618, SP 14/103/50.
37. Rudyard to Carleton, November 30, 1618, SP 14/103/183; Sir Arthur Tyringham to Carleton, December 7, 1618. SP 14/104/25.
38. Harwood to Carleton, September 23, 1618, SP 14/99/154.
39. Harwood to Carleton, November 13, SP 14/103/142.
40. Smith to Carleton, December 2, 1618, SP 14/104/4.
41. Harwood to Carleton, December 20, 1618, SP 14/104/63. Shortly before, Carleton had learned from Sir Horace Vere that Lake "comes not to the court," presumably because he was not welcome there. Sir Horace Vere to Carleton, December 4, 1618, SP 14/104/10.
42. Castle to Trumbull, September 17, 1618, *Downshire*, vol. 6, 513.
43. Lorkin to Puckering, Birch, *James*, vol. 2, 93.
44. Archbishop of Canterbury to Trumbull, October 27, 1618, *Downshire*, vol. 6, 559–60.
45. John Wolley to Trumbull, October 5, 1618, *Downshire*, vol. 6, 535.
46. John More to Trumbull, December 28, 1618, *Downshire*, vol. 6, 627.
47. Archbishop of Canterbury to Trumbull, December 28, 1618, *Downshire*, vol. 6, 625–26.
48. Abraham Williams to Trumbull, September 25, 1618, *Downshire*, vol. 6, 522–23.
49. Thomas Locke to Carleton, November 14, 1618, SP 14/103/150.
50. Wolley to Trumbull, October 2, 1618, *Downshire*, vol. 6, 531.
51. Abraham Williams to Trumbull, September 25, 1618, *Downshire*, vol. 6, 522–23.
52. Brett to Trumbull, October 2, 1618, *Downshire*, vol. 6, 530–31.
53. Wolley to Trumbull, October 2, 1618, *Downshire*, vol. 6, 531.
54. Harwood to Carleton, October 3, 1618, SP 14/103/16.
55. Harwood to Carleton, October 3, 1618, SP 14/103/16.
56. Chamberlain to Carleton, December 12, 1618, McClure, V. 2, 192–93; Thomas Wynne tells the same to Carleton, but with less detail (although he argued that it was Lady Exeter, rather than Exeter, who sent for de Silva), December 9, 1618, SP 14/104/27.
57. Harwood to Carleton, November 18, 1618, SP 14/163/166.
58. Archbishop of Canterbury to Trumbull, December 28, 1618, *Downshire*, vol. 6, 625–26.
59. Harwood to Carleton, December 20, 1618, SP 14/104/63.
60. Countess of Exeter to Trumbull, November 20, 1618, *Downshire*, vol. 6, 587.
61. Sir Thomas Lake to William Trumbull, November 17, 1618, *Downshire*, vol. 6, 584.
62. Sir Thomas Leedes to William Trumbull, November 24 / December 4 and November 29 / December 9, 1618, *Downshire*, vol. 6, 590, 595.
63. Sir Thomas Lake to Trumbull, December 9, 1618, *Downshire*, vol. 6, 607.
64. Sir Thomas Lake to Trumbull, December 9, 1618, *Downshire*, vol. 6, 607.

65. Chamberlain described Duppa as Roos's servant and "some say his bedfellow" after the incident at Cannons. Chamberlain to Carleton, June 4, 1617, McClure, vol. 2, 80.
66. The countess of Exeter to Trumbull, December 12, 1618, *Downshire*, vol. 6, 611.
67. Exeter to Trumbull, December 12, 1618, *Downshire*, vol. 6, 611.
68. Duppa had served Carleton before he became Roos's servant. Carleton to Trumbull, October 1619, BL Add. MS 72271–73, f. 39.
69. In the trial, Exeter claimed he had spent £200 on trying to get Roos and da Silva to return to England, presumably to be witnesses in his cause. Abstracts of proofs, February 5, 1616, SP 14/105/82.
70. Lake to Buckingham, January 11, 1619, *Fortescue Papers*, vol. 1, 80–81.
71. Cottington to Trumbull, January 1619, BL Add. MS 72281.
72. Trumbull to Lake, January 31, 1619, SP 77/13/161.
73. Trumbull to Carleton, February 2/12, 1619, SP 77/13/165.
74. *Calendar of Privy Seals*, Signed Bills (Chancery), 2 Charles I, March 31 and April 2, 1626. "Confirmation of a grant of the king's interest in a lease made for a 100 years made by Lord Roos, to Diego de Silva, of London, of the manor of Morton Grange, co York, which Trumbull bought of Diego de Silva, who is liable to forfeiture of his estate, being a fugitive. P. S."
75. Cottington to Trumbull, January 1619, BL Add. MS 72281.
76. Sir Thomas Leeds to Trumbull, December 30, 1618, *Downshire*, vol. 6, 628.
77. John More to Trumbull, December 28, 1618, *Downshire*, vol. 6, 627.

Chapter 11

1. Harwood to Carleton, February 16, 1619, SP 14/105/174.
2. Lorkin to Sir Thomas Puckering, January 5, 1619, Birch, *James*, vol. 2, 120.
3. Lorkin to Puckering, January 19, 1619, Birch, *James*, vol. 2, 126.
4. Bellany, *The Politics of Court Scandal*, 218–19; quoted in Cogswell, *James I*, 55; Stewart, 146–47, 298.
5. Bellany and Cogswell, *The Murder of King James I*, 52–54.
6. Edward Wakeman, *Report of a Speech of King James the First in the Court of Star Chamber* (London: Bentley, Wilson, and Fley, 1848), 6–7.
7. Peltonen, 87–91; Chamberlain to Carleton, February 22, 1617, McClure, vol. 2, 54–55; John Throckmorton to Sir Dudley Carleton, February 12, 1617, SP 84/76/61; abstract of the king's speech, SP 14/90/117; Edward Sherburn to Carleton, February 23, 1617, SP 14/90/155.
8. 1 Kings 3:16–28. In this story, two women who lived together had a dispute over a baby. The women each had a child, but one died, having been smothered in bed during the night. Both women claimed that the surviving child was theirs. They went to Solomon for judgment. Solomon ordered that the baby should be cut in half, so that each woman could have a share. One of the women asks him to stop, save the child, and promises that she will end her claim to it. Solomon then gives her the baby, having determined that only the true mother would want to save the child's life at all cost.
9. Chamberlain to Carleton, February 6, 1619, McClure, vol. 2, 211.

10. Chamberlain to Carleton, February 28, 1618, McClure, vol. 2, 145.
11. Hudson, 8–9.
12. Hudson, 9.
13. STAC 8/196/124 and STAC 8/111/27.
14. Bellany, *Politics of Court Scandal*, ch. 5. See also Kevin Sharpe, *Image Wars: Promoting Kings and Commonwealths in England, 1603–1660* (New Haven: Yale University Press, 2010), 127–33.
15. Edward P. Cheyney, "The Court of Star Chamber," *American Historical Review* 18.4 (1913): 727–50; Cora L. Scofield, "Accounts of Star Chamber Dinners, 1593–94," *American Historical Review* 88 (1899): 83–95.
16. In office 1616–21, created earl of Manchester in 1626.
17. Chamberlain to Carleton, February 13, 1619, McClure, vol. 2, 213–14.
18. Other members of the Privy Council, who may have been in Star Chamber, but who are not directly mentioned in letters: Lord Privy Seal (Edward Somerset, earl of Worcester); earl of Arundel, Lord Viscount Wallingford, Lord Bishop of Winchester (Lancelot Andrewes), Edward, Lord Zouch, George Lord Carew, Master of the Rolls (Sir Julius Caesar), Lord Steward (Ludovico Stewart, Duke of Lennox), Lord Chamberlain (William Herbert, 3rd earl of Pembroke), Mr. Treasurer, archbishop of Canterbury (George Abbott), earl of Southampton, Mr. Comptroller (Henry Carey, later Viscount Falkland).
19. Hudson, 9.
20. Hudson, 8–9.
21. Abstract of the king's speech in Star Chamber, February 13, 1617, SP 14/90/117; R. W. Hoyle, "Fountains of Justice: James I, Charles I, and Equity," in Michael Lobban, Joanne Begiato, and Adrian Green, eds., *Law, Lawyers, and Litigants in Early Modern England: Essays in Memory of Christopher W. Brooks* (Cambridge: Cambridge University Press, 2019), 79, 94–96.
22. In the State Papers collection, there are three abstracts from the trial. Two are dated February 5, 1618(19), which was on the second day of the trial, and the third on February 8, which was the third day of the trial. No author is listed, so we do not know who produced them. The first, SP 14/105/82, has abstracts of the proofs on both sides and is the most extensive and detailed. It is organized into the main arguments and points of contention on both sides, includes names of witnesses, and a brief description of the main points of the witness depositions. First, the plaintiffs' arguments, and the supporting witnesses. Then, the defendants responded to those arguments, with witnesses of their own. The plaintiffs replied to defendants, questioned their counter-argument, and also presented exceptions to defendants' witnesses who they believed not to be trustworthy. The State Papers 14/105/81 document provides an overview of the main Exeter accusations of slander and forgery against Lady Roos and a shorter list of the plaintiff's proofs (but not with the same detailed description of witness names and depositions). The SP 14/105/143 (dated February 8), has a summary of Lady Roos's answers to the plaintiffs' accusations, and also includes brief abstracts of witness depositions. State Papers also has an abstract of the king's sentencing, as well as a document that lists the fines due (SP 14/105/156 and SP14/105/157).
23. Harwood to Carleton, January 30, 1619, SP 84/88/126; Harwood to Carleton, February 6, 1619, SP 14/105/135; Harwood to Carleton, February 16, 1619,

SP 14/105/174; Lorkin to Puckering, February 2, 1619, Birch, *James*, vol. 2, 131; Lorkin to Puckering, February 9, 1619, Birch, *James*, vol. 2, 134; Lorkin to Puckering, February 16, 1619, Birch, *James*, vol. 2, 139; Chamberlain to Carleton, January 23 and 30, February 6 and 13, 1619, McClure, vol. 2, 204, 207, 211, 214; Sir Robert Naunton to Carleton, February 4, 1619, SP 84/88/144, Sir William Smith to Carleton, February 13, 1619, SP 14/105/158; Alexander Williams to Carleton, February 15, 1619, SP 14/105/173; Sir Thomas Wynne to Carleton, February 14, 1619, SP 14/105/165.

24. Chamberlain, January 30, 1619, McClure, vol. 2, 207.
25. Philip Mainwaring to earl of Arundel, November 22, 1622, Lodge, *Illustration of British History*, vol. 3, 293.
26. Harwood to Carleton, January 30, 1619, SP 84/88/126.
27. Lake to Buckingham, January 23, 1619, *Fortescue Papers*, 81–82.
28. Lorkin to Puckering, February 2, 1619, Birch, *James*, vol. 2, 131; Harwood to Carleton, January 30, 1619, SP 84/88/126.
29. Harwood to Carleton, February 6, 1619, SP 14/105/135.
30. Harwood to Carleton, February 6, 1619, SP 14/105/135. Camden also noted the king's presence at Star Chamber this day. Camden, *Diary*, February 3, 1619.
31. Chamberlain to Carleton, January 30, 1619, McClure, vol. 2, 209. Camden says almost two; Camden, *Diary*, February 5, 1619.
32. Harwood to Carleton, February 6, 1619, SP 14/105/135.
33. Sir Thomas Holcroft was a relative of Roos's young mother, and within the Cecil sphere. He went to Rome to see Roos, sent by Exeter. He served as an MP for Cheshire and Chester.
34. Lady Roos's answer, STAC 8/111/26.
35. See James Sharp, *Witchcraft in Early Modern England* (London: Routledge, 2019), chs. 3 and 4.
36. Abstracts of proofs, February 5, 1616, SP 14/105/82.
37. Abstracts of proofs, February 5, 1616, SP 14/105/82.
38. Abstracts of proofs, February 5, 1616, SP 14/105/82, Harwood to Carleton, February 6, 1619, SP 14/105/135. This episode was also recounted by Sanderson, 448–49.
39. Abstracts of proofs, February 5, 1616, SP 14/105/82.
40. Abstracts of proofs, February 5, 1616, SP 14/105/82.
41. Chamberlain to Carleton, February 13, 1619, McClure, vol. 2, 213–14.
42. Abstracts of proofs, February 5, 1616, SP 14/105/82; answers of Lady Roos on behalf of Sir Thomas Lake and herself, February 8, SP 14/105/143.
43. Harwood to Carleton, February 6, 1619, SP 14/105/135.
44. Abstracts of proofs, February 5, 1616, SP 14/105/82.
45. Judith Brown claimed to have seen the letter in Dunscombe's trunk. Lady Constance also testified that she had heard Brown talk about the letter. Abstracts of proofs, February 5, 1616, SP 14/105/82. In one of Exeter's later suits regarding Roos's property, Dunscombe's brother-in-law Robert Dixon stated that Dunscombe had "travalyed into Spaine onto the said Lord Roos wth wome he continued until the death of the said Lord Roos." Dixon must have mistaken the country, as Roos was in Italy, and not in Spain. C 8/31/33.
46. Lorkin to Puckering, February 9, 1619, Birch, *James*, vol. 2, 134.

47. Harwood to Carleton, February 6, 1619, SP 14/105/135; Chamberlain to Carleton, February 6, 1619, McClure, vol. 2, 211.
48. Chamberlain to Carleton, February 13, 1619, McClure, vol. 2, 213.
49. Taylor, 829; Alexandra Shepard, *Accounting for Oneself: Worth, Status, and the Social Order in Early Modern England* (Oxford: Oxford University Press, 2018), 133–45.
50. Exeter's complaint, STAC 8/111/26.
51. Abstracts of proofs, February 5, 1616, SP 14/105/82.
52. Taylor, 842–43.
53. Abstracts of proofs, February 5, 1616, SP 14/105/82.
54. Philip Watson to Lake, February 1619, SP 14/105/223.
55. Abstract of proofs, February 5, 1616, SP 14/105/82; Harwood to Carleton, February 6, 1619, SP 14/105/135.
56. Abstracts of proofs, February 5, 1616, SP 14/105/82.
57. Abstracts of proofs, February 5, 1616, SP 14/105/82.
58. It was under heavy debate in the negotiations for a Spanish match. King James was sometimes willing to allow less strict enforcement of recusancy laws, but he did not wish to have them repealed or significantly changed. Questier, 384–85; Redworth, 17.
59. Sir Nicholas Tufton married Frances Cecil, the earl of Exeter's daughter.
60. Sir William Paddy was accused of being the lover of Elizabeth Brydges, the countess of Exeter's first cousin. Brydges was maid of honor to Queen Elizabeth, and married Sir John Kennedy, a Scotsman who moved south with King James. It turned out that Kennedy already had a wife, however, so the couple became estranged. Kennedy believed Paddy to be having an affair with his estranged wife, and attacked her house, with Paddy in it, although the two were able to escape unharmed.
61. Abstracts of proofs, February 5, 1616, SP 14/105/82; SP 14/105/143.
62. Chamberlain to Carleton, February 13, 1619, McClure, vol. 2, 213–14.
63. "Fortune's Wheel," K1v, in Bellany and McRae, "Early Stuart Libels."
64. February 13, 1619, SP 14/105/156.
65. Sir Thomas Wynne to Carleton, February 14, 1619, SP 14/105/165; Lorkin to Puckering, Birch, *James*, vol. 2, 140.
66. Chamberlain to Carleton, February 13, 1619, McClure, vol. 2, 214.
67. Chamberlain, February 13, 1619, McClure, vol. 2, 214; Lorkin to Puckering, February 16, 1619, Birch, *James*, vol. 2, 139; Sir Thomas Wynne to Carleton, February 14, 1619, SP 14/105/165; Abstracts of proofs, February 13, 1619, SP 14/105/156.
68. Lorkin to Puckering, Birch, *James*, vol. 2, 139–40; Sanderson, 448.
69. John Castle to William Trumbull, September 17, 1618, *Downshire*, vol. 6, 513.
70. A mark was not a currency, but an accounting-term. One mark was worth roughly two-thirds of a pound.
71. Lorkin to Puckering, February 16, 1619, Birch, *James*, vol. 2, 139, Sir William Smith to Carleton, February 13, 1619, SP 14/105/158 Sir Thomas Wynne to Carleton, February 14, 1619, SP 14/105/165, Sir William Smith to Carleton, February 13, 1619, SP 14/105/158, Harwood to Carleton, February 16, 1619, SP 14/105/174, abstract of proofs, SP 14/105/82; Chamberlain to Carleton, February 13 and 20, 1619, McClure, vol. 2, 213–15.
72. Sanderson, 449.

73. £6.3 million. I used the converter at https://www.bankofengland.co.uk/monetary-policy/inflation/inflation-calculator.
74. "Sir Arthur Lake was reputed generally, in the conscience of the court, guilty; but for want of direct proof, not censured." Lorkin to Puckering, February 16, Birch, *James*, vol. 2, 139.
75. For similar punishments of other poorer persons convicted of perjury, see Taylor, 833–34.
76. King's sentence, SP 14/105/157; Chamberlain, February 20, 1619, McClure, vol. 2, 215–16.
77. Chamberlain, February 20, 1619, McClure, vol. 2, 215–16.
78. See King James revealing the false witchcraft accusations of Brian and Anne Gunter in Sharpe, *The Bewitching of Anne Gunter*, chs. 8–9; Gaskill, *Witchfinders*, 31–32. James's biographer Willson noted that the Lake-Exeter trials was "a case that fascinated the King, for it roused the spirit of the detective and offered scope for the prurient." Willson, 396.
79. Thomas Locke to Dudley Carleton, June 19, 1619, SP 14/109/180. This revelation took place when Lady Roos offered her submission in Star Chamber. While Lake and Lady Lake were supposed to appear personally to offer their submission to Star Chamber, Lady Roos was spared "the publicke shame and disgrace of appearing in person" by the king, "by cause she had discovered to his Ma:tie in the Christmas holidays both the forgerie of the ltr supposed to be written by Luke Hatton and of the [hole] -tion charged upon the Countess of Exeter wch was done in the presence of his Ma:tie, the Prince, the Marquis Buck: and Mr. Secret. Naunton was also called this the king kept in secrinio pectecis and made no use of it at their hearing of the cause, bycause it was extrajudiciall, though it were before the cause was begin to be hard a great while."
80. Harwood to Carleton, February 6, 1619, SP 14/105/135.
81. Answers of Lady Roos, February 8, 1619, SP 14/105/143.
82. Camden, *Diary*, February 13, 1616.

Chapter 12

1. Acheson, *Diary of Anne Clifford*, 100.
2. Chamberlain to Carleton, February 20, 1619, McClure, vol. 2, 215. Camden said this happened on February 15, one day later. Camden, *Diary*, February 15, 1619.
3. William Smith to Carleton, February 14, 1619, SP 14/105/158.
4. Thomas Wynne to Carleton, February 14, 1619, SP 14/105/165.
5. Harwood to Carleton, February 16, 1619, SP 14/105/174.
6. Chamberlain to Carleton, February 20, 1619, McClure, vol. 2, 216.
7. Harwood to Carleton, February 16, 1619, SP 14/105/174; Camden, *Diary*, February 16, 1619. Antonio Donato to Doge and Senate, February 28, 1619, *CSP Venice (1617–1619)*, vol. 15. "His Majesty has deposed the Secretary Lake and condemned him with his wife and a daughter to perpetual imprisonment upon a question of honour. He has substituted in Lake's place a young man of approved virtue." Castle told Trumbull about Calvert's new post as secretary on February 25. Castle to Trumbull, February 25, 1619, BL Add. MS 72275, ff. 44–45.

8. Chamberlain to Carleton, February 13, 1619, McClure, vol. 2, 214.
9. Chamberlain, February 20, 1619, McClure, vol. 2, 217; George Gerrard to Carleton. February 20, 1619, SP 14/105/120.
10. Levin, 71–73. For example, the countess of Buckingham pushed to have her son John Villiers marry Frances Coke, despite Lady Hatton's protests. The countess also participated in the coup to get the wealthy heiress Katherine Manner's father to agree to a marriage with her son the Marquis of Buckingham, without protests from James. Furthermore, once Lady Hatton had agreed to her daughter's marriage to John Villiers, the king showed many signs of goodwill toward her. Luthman, 45–48; Lockyer, 55–61.
11. Sir George Calvert was ennobled, becoming Lord Baltimore. Later, he and his descendants were involved in the colonization of North America, specifically the establishment of the colony Maryland. Austin Nuttall, ed., *The History of the Worthies of England, by Thomas Fuller* (London: T. Tegg, 1840), vol. 3, 417–18; Lockyer, 69. On Calvert's court career in the 1600–1610s, see John D. Krugler, *English and Catholic: The Lords Baltimore in the Seventeenth Century* (Baltimore: Johns Hopkins University Press, 2004), 30–45.
12. Chamberlain, February 27, 1619, McClure, vol. 2, 218.
13. Castle to Trumbull, February 25, 1619, BL Add. MS 72275, ff. 44–45.
14. Castle to Trumbull, February 25, 1619, BL Add. MS 72275, ff. 44–45; same to same, March 3, 1619, BL Add. MS 72275, ff. 46–47.
15. Thrush, "The Fall of Thomas Howard," part 3.
16. Chamberlain, February 20, 1619, McClure, vol. 2, 215.
17. Camden, *Diary*, April 11, 1619.
18. Castle to Trumbull, February 25, 1619, BL Add. MS 72275, ff. 44–45.
19. Thomas Wynne to Carleton, February 14, 1619, SP 14/105/165.
20. Harwood to Carleton, February 16, 1619, SP 14/105/174; Chamberlain, February 13, 1619, McClure, vol. 2, 213–14.
21. Thomas Wynne to Carleton, February 14, 1619, SP 14/105/165.
22. Harwood to Carleton, February 16, 1619, SP 14/105/174.
23. Castle to Trumbull, February 25, 1619, BL Add. MS 72275, ff. 44–45.
24. Chamberlain to Carleton, February 20, 1619, McClure, vol. 2, 215. Chamberlain only says "she," but does not clarify if it was Lady Roos or Lady Lake. Given that Lady Roos had confessed to the forgeries, she may have been more compliant than her mother, who was still processing the loss in the court cases. Other sources that say they were brought to Tower on February 15: Acheson, *Diary of Anne Clifford*, 100; Camden, *Diary*, February 15, 1619.
25. George Gerrard to Carleton, February 20, 1619, SP 14/105/120; Castle to Trumbull, February 25, 1619, BL Add. MS 72275, ff. 44–45.
26. May 9, 1619, *APC*, vol. 36, 445.
27. Chamberlain, February 27, 1619, McClure, vol. 2, 217–18.
28. Chamberlain, February 27, 1619, McClure, vol. 2, 217–18; Harwood to Carleton, March 6, 1619, SP 14/107/9; Castle to Trumbull, February 25, 1619, BL Add. MS 72275, ff. 44–45; same to same, March 3, 1619, BL Add. MS 72275, ff. 46–47.
29. George Gerrard to Carleton, February 20, 1619, SP 14/105/120.

30. Harwood to Carleton, March 6, 1619, SP14/107/9.
31. Castle to Trumbull, March 3, 1619, BL Add. MS 72275, ff. 46–47.
32. Acheson, *Diary of Anne Clifford*, 100.
33. Chamberlain to Carleton, February 27, 1619, McClure, vol. 2, 217–18.
34. Castle to Trumbull, February 25, 1619, BL Add. MS 72275, ff. 44–45.
35. Acheson, *Diary of Anne Clifford*, 100.
36. Chamberlain to Carleton, October 24, December 2 and 12, 1618, *McClure*, vol. 2, 174, 189, 193.
37. Chamberlain to Carleton, March 6, 1619, McClure, vol. 2, 220.
38. Acheson, *Diary of Anne Clifford*, 109.
39. Chamberlain, May 8, 1619, 235; Camden, *Diary*, May 4, 1619. "Letitia, wife of Arthur, said to be the natural daughter of Charles Blunt earl of Devonshire and Penelope Lady Rich, dies of the French pox"; Lorkin to Puckering, May 4, 1619, Birch, *James*, vol. 2, 157–58.
40. Chamberlain to Carleton, May 8 and June 19, 1619, McClure, vol. 2, 235, 247. "Since the death of Sir Arthur Lake's Lady there is a daughter of hers come to light (thought to be Dick Martins, or rather a great mans) that by the help of goode frends layes the claime to Sir George Caries [Lettice's previous husband, before Arthur] land because she was born in wedlock: yt were a strange case yf she should recover yt, and yet for-soth in strictness of law they say yt must be so, and though there could be any law (saving God's without exception. But to salve the matter I heare that the heyre in possession having a young sonne of fit yeares fore her meanes to compound the matter with marriage."
41. Roos to King James, June 1, 1618, SP 14/97/231.
42. "The Lake-Roos Affair 1617–1620," J1, Bellany and McRae, "Early Stuart Libels."
43. Chamberlain to Carleton, April 10, 1619, McClure, vol. 2, 227.
44. "The Lake-Roos Affair 1617–1620," J2, J3, J4, Bellany and McRae, "Early Stuart Libels."
45. "The Lake-Roos Affair 1617–1620," J3, Bellany and McRae, "Early Stuart Libels."
46. "The Lake-Roos Affair 1617–1620," J4, Bellany and McRae, "Early Stuart Libels."
47. "The Lake-Roos Affair 1617–1620," J5, Bellany and McRae, "Early Stuart Libels."
48. Chamberlain to Carleton, March 6, 1619, McClure, vol. 2, 220.
49. Stewart, 300–302; Lockyer, 55–56; Chamberlain to Carleton, March 6, April 17 and 24, May 14, June 5, 1619, McClure, vol. 2, 219–20, 229–30, 232, 237–38, 242.
50. Naunton to Trumbull, June 11, 1619, BL Add. MS 72304, f. 29.
51. For a brief overview of the importance of repentance, see Bellany, *The Politics of Court Scandal*, 220–29.
52. Chamberlain, February 27, 1619, 218; Castle to Trumbull, March 3, 1619, BL Add. MS 72275, ff. 46–47.
53. March 6, 1619. Harwood to Carleton, SP 14/107/9; Chamberlain, March 19, 1619, McClure, vol. 2, 221–22.
54. Chamberlain to Carleton, May 8, 1619, McClure, vol. 2, 235.
55. Camden, *Diary*, April 21, 1619; Chamberlain to Carleton, April 24, 1619, McClure, vol. 2, 233–34; April 24 and May 7, 1619, *APC*, vol. 36, 427, 444; Thomas Locke to Carleton, SP 14/109/8.

56. May 25, 1619, *APC*, vol. 36, 459. Warrant to release William Lake from the Gatehouse.
57. Chamberlain to Carleton, April 24, 1619, McClure, vol. 2, 233; May 1, 1619, Thomas Locke to Carleton, SP 14/109/8.
58. Chamberlain to Carleton, May 8, 1619, McClure, vol. 2, 235; Harwood to Carleton, May 14, 1619, SP 14/109/76; Nathaniel Brent to Carleton, May 15, 1619, SP 14/109/77.
59. Chamberlain to Carleton, May 14, 1619, McClure, vol. 2, 238.
60. BL Add. MS 4155, f. 143r; Bellany and Cogswell, *Murder of King James*, 243.
61. Lorkin to Puckering, May 24, 1619, Birch, *James*, vol. 2, 165–66; Chamberlain to Carleton, May 14, 1619, McClure, vol. 2, 238; Harwood to Carleton, May 14, 1619, SP 14/109/76; Nathaniel Brent to Carleton, May 15, 1619, SP 14/109/77; Camden, *Diary*, May 26 and 27, 1619.
62. Chamberlain to Carleton, May 8, 1619, McClure, vol. 2, 235.
63. Lorkin to Puckering, May 11, 1619, Birch, *James*, vol. 2, 162; Chamberlain to Carleton, May 14, 1619, McClure, vol. 2, 238; Camden, *Diary*, June 3, 1619.
64. June 14, 1619, *APC*, vol. 36, 473.
65. Chamberlain to Carleton, March 19, 1619, McClure, vol. 2, 221–22; May 14, 1619, Harwood to Carleton SP 14/109/76.
66. Sir Gerard Herbert to Carleton, May 24, 1619, SP 14/109/100.
67. Lorkin to Puckering, May 24, 1619, Birch, *James*, vol. 2, 165–66.
68. Dorothea Towshend, *Life and Letters of Endymion Porter: Sometime Gentleman of the Bedchamber to King Charles the First* (London: T. Fischer Unwin, 1897), 2–14.
69. Lorkin to Puckering, May 24, 1619, Birch, *James*, vol. 2, 165–66.
70. "Sir Thomas Lake had leave now a fortnight to converse with his Lady, to coole her kidneys, which was the griefe she complained of." Chamberlain to Carleton, June 19, 1619, McClure, vol. 2, 246–47.
71. Thomas Locke to Carleton, June 19, 1619, SP 14/109/180.
72. Thomas Locke to Carleton, June 19, 1619, SP 14/109/180; Chamberlain to Carleton, June 19, 1619, McClure, vol. 2, 246–47; Sanderson, 449.
73. Chamberlain to Carleton, June 26, 1619, McClure, vol. 2, 249.
74. The submission of Lady Roos, SP 14/109/250.
75. The submission of Lady Roos, SP 14/109/250.
76. Thomas Locke to Carleton, June 19, 1619, SP 14/109/180.
77. Camden, *Diary*, June 22, 1619.
78. Chamberlain to Carleton, June 19, 1619, McClure, vol. 2, 246–47.
79. Thomas Locke to Carleton, June 19, 1619, SP 14/109/180.
80. Chamberlain to Carleton, June 26, 1619, McClure, vol. 2, 249; letter to Trumbull in Brussels (unknown writer) June 28, 1619, Birch, *James*, vol. 2, 177.
81. Camden, *Diary*, June 28, 1619.
82. July 8, 1619, *APC*, vol. 37, 9; Chamberlain to Carleton, July 15, 1619, vol. 2, 251–52; Abraham Williams to Lord Viscount Doncaster, July 9, 1619, Birch, *James*, vol. 2, 179; Camden, *Diary*, July 15, 1619.
83. Camden, *Diary*, September 3, 1619.
84. June 17, 1619, *APC*, vol. 36, 485. A warrant to the warden of the Fleete. A warrant for the release of Sara Swarton. "This warrant was delivered the 25 of July, after shee made her submission in St. Martin Church." Chamberlain to Carleton, July 31, 1619,

McClure, vol. 2, 255; Ralph Cox to Christopher Keighley, July 24, 1619, *Cecil Papers*, vol. 22, 87.

85. July 9, 1619, Abraham Williams to Lord Viscount Doncaster, Birch, *James*, vol. 2, 179; Chamberlain to Carleton, July 15, 1619, McClure, vol. 2, 251–52.
86. Camden, *Diary*, July 15, 1619; Chamberlain to Carleton, July 31, McClure, vol. 2, 255.
87. Chamberlain to Carleton, July 31, 1619, McClure, vol. 2, 255.
88. Chamberlain to Carleton, July 31, 1619, McClure, vol. 2, 255.
89. Abraham Williams to Lord Viscount Doncaster, July 9, 1619, Birch, *James*, vol. 2, 179; Chamberlain to Carleton, July 31, 1619, McClure, vol. 2, 255.

Chapter 13

1. *CSP Venice (1619–1620)*, vol. 16.
2. "Sr. Tho Lake is not yet gone back to the tower; there is hope that he shall obtayne his absolute liberty, for which his friends are infinitely diligent to worke his Maties favor & [?]. His wife continueth still in the tower; and his virtuous daughter Rosse lieth confined to the house of one Mr. Dillington in the Isle of Wight." Castle to Trumbull, October 2, 1619, BL Add. MS 72275, f. 88.
3. Probably Thomas Murray to earl of Doncaster, September 16, 1619, Birch, *James*, vol. 2, 190.
4. Castle to Trumbull, October 15, 1619, BL Add. MS 72275, ff. 89–90.
5. Castle to Trumbull, September 22, 1619, BL Add. MS 72275, f. 86.
6. Castle to Trumbull, October 22, 1619, BL Add. MS 72275, f. 78.
7. November 28, 1619. Francis Bacon (Lord Chancellor) to Buckingham; same to same November 29, 1619; same to same, James Spedding, ed., *Letters and the Life of Francis Bacon* (London: Longman, Green, Reader, and Dyer, 1874), vol. 7, 65–66; Chamberlain to Carleton, December 4, 1619, vol. 2, 277.
8. Castle to Trumbull, November 18, 1619, BL Add. MS 72275, f. 80. In his letter to Trumbull on December 8, Castle reported that the "matter of Peacock is fallen ashen, no more spoken of it, save that Peacock remaineth still in prison." Castle to Trumbull, December 8, 1619, BL Add. MS 72275, ff. 93–94.
9. The Viscountess Purbeck, Roos's cousin, *did* make visits to a Dr. Lambe, who had been convicted of witchcraft. Lady Purbeck did so in the company of her lover. She was later convicted of adultery, but the accusations of using witchcraft against her husband and/or Buckingham were later dropped. Luthman, 72–73, 86–87.
10. Castle to Trumbull, December 8, 1619, BL Add. MS 72275, ff. 93–94.
11. Castle to Trumbull, January 9, 1619, BL Add. MS 72275, f. 95; Chamberlain to Carleton, January 22, 1620, McClure, vol. 2, 284.
12. Lake's submission, 1620, January 28, SP 14/112/75; Camden, *Diary*, January 28, 1620.
13. Lake's submission, 1620, January 28, SP 14/112/75; Camden, *Diary*, January 28, 1620.
14. Chamberlain also reported this rumor, although he thought it was Peacock who was guilty of "practicing to infatuate the Kings judgement by sorcerie (they say) in the business of Sir Thomas Lake and the Lady of Exceter." Chamberlain to Carleton, February 26, 1620, McClure, vol. 2, 291.

15. For brief overviews on witchcraft in England and Scotland, see Bengt Ankarloo, "Witch Trials in Northern Europe, 1450–1700," in Bengt Ankarloo and Stuart Clark, eds., *Witchcraft and Magic in Europe: The Period of the Witch Trials* (Philadelphia: University of Pennsylvania Press, 2002), 55–80; Malcolm Gaskell, *Witchfinders: A Seventeenth-Century English Tragedy* (Cambridge, MA: Harvard University Press, 2005), 27–33; James Sharpe, *The Bewitching of Anne Gunter: A Horrible and True Story of Deception, Witchcraft, Murder, and the King of England* (New York: Routledge, 2000), 175–79.
16. Sir Frances Bacon to the king, February 10, 1620, Spedding, vol. 7, 77–78.
17. Sir Frances Bacon to the king, February 10, 1620, Spedding, vol. 7, 77–78.
18. For an overview of the law and practice of torture in early Stuart England, see Alastair Bellany, "The Torture of John Felton, 1628," in Lorna Hutson, ed., *The Oxford Handbook of English Law and Literature, 1500–1700* (Oxford: Oxford University Press, 2017), 549–60.
19. *APC*, February 19, 1620, vol. 37, 137.
20. February 26, 1620. Chamberlain, vol. 2, 291; Camden, *Diary*, February 22, 1620.
21. Chamberlain to Carleton, February 26, 1620, McClure, vol. 2, 291; Camden, *Diary*, February 22, 1620.
22. Chamberlain to Carleton, March 20, 1620, vol. 2, 296; Camden, *Diary*, March 10, 1620.
23. Rowland Woodward to Francis Windebank[?], May 12, 1620, SP 14/115/29; Camden, *Diary*, May 15, 1620; Chamberlain to Dudley Carleton, May 20, 1620, McClure, vol. 2, 303.
24. Castle told Trumbull that the matter of Lake's restoration "may be, but I thincke it impossible," quoting the "wise Mayor of Cambridge." Castle to Trumbull, February 11, 1619, BL Add. MS 72275, f. 96.
25. Camden, *Diary*, May 15, 1620; Chamberlain to Carleton, May 20 and 27, 1620, McClure, vol. 2, 303–4; 1620, Rowland Woodward to Francis Windebank[?], SP 14/115/73; Lando to Doge and Senate, June 4, 1620. *CSP Venice (1619–1621)*, vol. 16.
26. Questier, *Dynastic Politics*, ch. 7; Redworth, 1–51.
27. James I to Buckingham, undated (probably between 1620–21), Henry Ellis, ed., *Original letters, Illustrative of English History; Including Numerous Royal Letters; from Autographs in the British Museum, and One or Two Other Collections* (London: Harding, Triphook, and Lepard, 1824), vol. 3, 119–20.
28. James I to Buckingham, undated (probably between 1620 and 1621), Ellis, vol. 3, 119–20.
29. Chamberlain to Carleton, October 14, 1620, McClure, vol. 2, 322; Camden, *Diary*, September 27, 1620.
30. Thomas Locke to Carleton, February 5, 2021, SP 14/119/114; Chamberlain to Carleton, January 20 and February 3, 1621, McClure, vol. 2, 336–38; Thrush and Ferris, "Lake, Sir Thomas," *HPO*.
31. "Monopolies and Corruption, The 1621 Parliament," Miii2, Bellany and McRae, "Early Stuart Libels."
32. Lockyer, 133–37; Redworth, 40–60; Questier, 410–14.
33. Krugler, ch. 3.

34. Questier, 415–20; Redworth, 138–40; Lockyer, 168–80, 192–93; Croft, *King James*, 120–26, Bellany and Cogswell, *The Murder of King James*, 4–6.
35. "Fortune's Wheel," K-K2, in Bellany and McRae, "Early Stuart Libels."
36. November 9, 1620. Mary Lake to Countess of Exeter, copy in Wellcome Library, Miscellanea XII, MS 805, ff. 91–92.
37. King James's Bible, Psalm 139. When Goodman copied this letter, he claimed that Lady Lake referred to Psalm 136. The copy of the letter in the Wellcome Library says it was 139, which makes more sense.
38. November 9, 1620. Mary Lake to Countess of Exeter, copy in Wellcome Library, Miscellanea XII, MS 805, ff. 91–92.
39. November 9, 1620. Mary Lake to Countess of Exeter, copy in Wellcome Library, Miscellanea XII, MS 805, ff. 91–92.
40. November 9, 1620. Mary Lake to Countess of Exeter, copy in Wellcome Library, Miscellanea XII, MS 805, ff. 91–92.
41. Camden, *Diary*, November 16, 1620.
42. November 15, *APC*, 1620, vol. 37, 300; Camden, *Diary*, November 16, 1620; Thomas Locke to Carleton, November 18, 1620, SP 14/117/147.
43. Camden, *Diary*, December 14, 1620; Chamberlain to Carleton, December 22, 1620, McClure, vol. 2, 331; Locke to Carleton, December 27, 1620, SP 14/118/75.
44. Mary Lady Lake to the Privy Council, February(?) 1621, SP 14/119/268.
45. Mary Lady Lake to the Privy Council. February(?) 1621, SP 14/119/268.
46. Chamberlain to Carleton, May 2, 1621, McClure, vol. 2, 370.
47. Thomas Locke to Carleton, May 5, 1621, SP 14/121/30.
48. Thrush and Ferris, "Lake, Sir Thomas," *HPO*; Bellany and Cogswell, *The Murder of King James*, 203–7, 235–44.

Chapter 14

1. McClure, vol. 2, 466.
2. George Watson Cole, ed., *The Gypsies Metamorphosed by Ben Johnson* (New York: Century Co., for Language Association, 1939), 137.
3. In 1622, a woman named Margaret Russell argued that the mysteriously ill thirteen-year-old Elizabeth Jennings should not be bled as "the doctors would kill [Elizabeth] thereby as they had Exeter's child." Margaret Russell was later accused of having bewitched Elizabeth. Orig. in BL 36674, quoted in Kirsten C. Uszkalo, *Being Bewitched: A True Tale of Madness, Witchcraft, and Property Development Gone Wrong* (Kirksville, MO: Truman University Press, 2017), 50, 188–89. Uszkalo wrongly suggests that the comment elicited associations of witchcraft, as Georgi-Anna's mother the countess of Exeter had been accused of witchcraft by Lady Roos. Uszkalo also says that Roos married Elizabeth Lake, getting the name wrong. The name mix-up is clearly a result of the sources used (Burke and Dalton). Uszkalo may have been referring to Peacock's discredited tale, but that was well after the trials were over, and the sources she cites do not reflect it. In a nineteenth-century novel, W. H. Ainsworth makes a fictionalized Lady Lake plan to accuse the countess of using magic to bewitch Roos (which smacks of Frances Howard, perhaps), but Uszkalo does not cite that book either.

4. Westminster Abbey, "Thomas and William Cecil, Earls of Exeter."
5. Exeter's complaint, C 8/31/33, 1622. Exeter says that it was the Court of Chancery, as well as members of the Privy Council, who gave him letters of administration.
6. On the continuity and flexibility of the law of coverture, see Krista Kesselring and Tim Stretton, *Married Women and the Law: Coverture in England and the Common Law World* (Montreal: McGill-Queen's University Press, 2013), 3–23.
7. Answers of George Rodney and his wife, Anne, formerly Lady Roos, C 8/31/33.
8. Answers of Sir Thomas Lake, C 8/31/33.
9. Lady Lettice Lake must not have enjoyed these furnishings very long, as she died less than two months after Lady Roos's imprisonment in the Tower. Perhaps her husband, Lady Roos's brother Arthur, continued to use them.
10. Lady Lake's answer, C 8/31/33.
11. Robert Dixon was Roos's servant Giles Dunscombe's brother-in-law. Dunscombe had died by 1622, and Dixon held some of Roos's goods, which Dunscombe had received in lieu of his outstanding wages. Robert Hooke had helped Roos raise money by pawning jewels, and George Gwilliams was of course Diego da Silva's servant, whom the Lakes had accused of helping Roos flee abroad and of stealing some of Roos's goods. Robert Dixon and Robert Hooke both provided answers in Exeter's suit as well, but Gwilliams did not.
12. Chamberlain to Carleton, December 7, 1622, McClure, vol. 2, 466.
13. Chamberlain to Carleton, December 7, 1622, February 10, 1623, McClure, vol. 2, 466, 477; Camden, *Diary*, February 1623.
14. Thomas Cecil, earl of Exeter's will, PROB 11/141/276.
15. Westminster Abbey, "Thomas and William Cecil, Earls of Exeter."
16. Will of Robert Smith, PROB 11/149/454. 11/149/454.
17. Chamberlain to Carleton, February 10, 1623, McClure, vol. 2, 477.
18. Chamberlain to Carleton, February 21 and March 20, 1624, McClure, vol. 2, 550, 546. David Cecil instead married Lady Elizabeth Egerton, daughter of John Egerton, earl of Bridgewater.
19. Thrush and Ferris, "Cecil, Frances, countess of Exeter," *ODNB*; Feret, 136–37.
20. Holles to Lady Hatton, February 12, 1627, Seddon, vol. 2, 345. Lady Hatton was probably in Wickersley, outside of Sheffield (Wickelsey, Holles says).
21. Thrush and Ferris, "Hitcham, Sir Robert (1573–1636)," *HPO*.
22. Holles to Lady Hatton, February 12, 1627, Seddon, vol. 2, 345.
23. Feret, 136–37.
24. Castle to Trumbull, February 11, 1620, BL Add. MS. 72275, f. 96.
25. Chamberlain to Carleton, April 29, 1620, McClure, vol. 2, 302.
26. Chamberlain to Carleton, April 29, 1620, McClure, vol. 2, 302.
27. Chamberlain to Carleton, November 17, 1621, McClure, V. 2, 409.
28. Thrush and Ferris, "Rodney, Sir Edward (1590–1657)," *HPO*.
29. C 8/31/33; C 2/JasI/R1/57; Barns, *Calendar of Deeds Relating to Walthamstow*, 8–11.
30. Exeter's complaint, C 8/31/33.
31. Lockyer, 34; Chamberlain to Carleton, August 8, 1618, McClure, vol. 2, 163.
32. Barns, *Calendar of Deeds Relating to Walthamstow*, 9–10; Rodney v. Arthur Lake, bishop of Bath and Wells, Sir Arthur Lake, Sir Nicholas Fortescue, 1622, C2/JasI/R1/57.

33. C2/JasI/R1/57; Barns, *Calendar of Deeds Relating to Walthamstow*, 8–13; W. R. Powell, ed., "Walthamstow: Manors," in *A History of the County of Essex* (London: Victoria County History, 1973), vol. 6, 253–63. On p. 8, Barns must have the year of Lady Roos's declaration wrong. He has it listed as 1617, but she is called Lady Rodney and is described as being married to George Rodney, so that cannot be correct. It mentions the fifth year of King Charles's reign, so it must be in 1629 or 1630.
34. Chamberlain to Carleton, March 8, McClure, vol. 2, 483.
35. In suits and deeds regarding the Walthamstow property, George Rodney is described as "of Pilton in Somerset" in 1622 and 1623. By 1626, he is "of Netley in Southampton," and again so described in 1627, and 1629 or 1630. Barns, 8–11. Rodney remarried, and he may have lived at Walthamstow with his new wife Sara before he sold it. He is listed as "of Walthamstow" in 1636 and 1639. Barns, 12–13.
36. Diane Scarisbrick, *Tudor and Jacobean Jewellry* (London: Tate Publishing, 1995), 45, 94–95.
37. John LeNeve, ed., *Monumenta Anglicana, 1600–1649* (London, 1719), vol. 1, 128.
38. Petition of William Domvill to the Privy Council, November 13, 1636, SP 16/335/97.
39. Will of Frances, countess of Exeter, PRO 11/311/498.

Epilogue

1. Birch, *James*, vol. 2, 134.
2. Anthony Weldon, *The court and character of King James* (London, 1649).
3. Bellany, *The Politics of Court Scandal*, 266–69; Bellany and Cogswell, *The Murder of King James*, 469–73.
4. Weldon, 49–53.
5. Arthur Wilson, another writer critical of King James's reign in the 1650s, mentions the Overbury-Somerset scandal at length, but the Lake and Cecil scandal not at all. In fact, he does not even mention Lake as secretary, but rather says that at the death of Winwood, James appointed Sir Robert Naunton and Sir George Calvert as new secretaries. In addition, while he described Lord Hay's embassy to France in 1616 at length, he does not mention Roos's twin embassy to Spain at all. Arthur Wilson, *The History of Great Britain, being the Life and Reign of James the First* (London: Richard Lownds, 1653), 97.
6. William Sanderson, *A Complete History of the Lives and Reigns of Mary Queen of Scotland and Her Son and Successor, James the Sixth, King of Scotland, and (after Queen Elizabeth), King of Great Britain, France, and Ireland, the First (of Ever Blessed Memory)* (London: Printed for Humphrey Moseley, Richard Tomlins, and George Sawbridge, 1656); Godfrey Goodman, *The Court of James I*, ed. John Brewer (London: Richard Bentley, 1839); Bellany, *The Politics of Court Scandal*, 271–73; Bellany and Cogswell, *The Murder of King James*, 495–96, 498–502.
7. Sanderson's account is on pp. 446–49.
8. Sanderson served as Roos's secretary during his Spanish embassy and claimed that he received a letter that described the fighting between Lady Lake and the countess. He showed this to Roos at that time. Sanderson gets the year of the embassy wrong: he

says it took place in 1611. This may be a typo or printer's mistake, because the account is placed among other events that took place in 1616–17. Sanderson, 447.

9. Abstract of proofs, SP 14/105/82.
10. Here, Sanderson echoed the same sentiments that the eulogies of James had declared after his death: James as "an abstract of knowledge, an oracle to resolve questions and mysteries," in the words of royal chaplain Phineas Hodson. Quoted in Sharpe, *Image Wars*, 131.
11. Goodman knew the earl of Exeter. He was once at dinner at Wimbledon with Exeter when Gondomar sent a complimentary gift of a meat pie to the earl. Goodman, clearly a man influenced by his stomach, specifically remembered the various delicacies in the "Spanish olio, a pie consisting of many ingredients, out of which pie I did eat bacon, pheasant, partridge, chestnuts, pease, and many other things there were." Goodman, 194.
12. Goodman, 193.
13. Goodman may have been referring to the restrictions placed on the prosecution in Lake's suit against Hatton: no other source mentions burning of letters, specifically, other than Dunscombe using one of the countess's letters to Roos to light his pipe.
14. Weldon mentions that Lake had paid £2,000 for his restoration also, but that it failed, and that it made others think he was a fool.
15. Bernard Burke, *A Genealogical History of the Dormant, Abeyant, and Extinct Peerages of the English Empire* (London: Harrison, 1866), 381; Bernard Burke, *Anecdotes of the Aristocracy, and Patricians* (London: H. Colburn, 1850), 204–8.
16. Stephen James Carver, *The Life and Works of the Lancashire Novelist William Harrison Ainsworth, 1805–1882* (Lewiston: The Edwin Mellen Press, 2003), chs. 2, 4–6; George Worth, *William Harrison Ainsworth* (New York: Twayne Publishers, 1972), 15–45, 62–65; S. M. Ellis, *William Harrison Ainsworth and His Friends* (London: John Lane, 1911), vol. 2, ch. 20, 189–91. It is interesting that none of the scholars who focus on Ainsworth have much to say about *The Star Chamber* novel specifically, although they spend much more time expounding on analyzing some of the author's other books.
17. Worth, 59–60.
18. Samuel R. Gardiner, *History of England from the Accession of James I to the Civil War 1603–1644* (London: Longman, Green, and Co., 1883), vol. 3, 189–95.
19. Gardiner, 193.
20. Charles Dalton, *The Life and Times of General Sir Edward Cecil, Viscount Wimbledon, Colonel of an English Regiment in the Dutch Service, 1605–1631 and One of His Majesty's Most Honourable Privy Council, 1628–1638* (London: Sampson Low, Marston, Searle, and Rivington, 1885). Dalton also calls Lady Roos Elizabeth.
21. Dalton, 274–75, 283.
22. George Ravenscroft Dennis, *The Cecil Family* (New York: Houghton Mifflin Co., 1914), 127–30. Dennis also calls Lady Roos Elizabeth.
23. Willson, 395–97.
24. Lee, *Great Britain's Solomon*, 251.
25. Questier, *Dynastic Politics*, 387.
26. Lawrence Stone, *The Crisis of the Aristocracy, 1558–1641* (Oxford: Clarendon Press, 1965), 668.
27. Stone, 667. Stone cites Gardiner and quotes one of Chamberlain's letters to Carleton. Stone also mistakenly says that "scandalous stories" about homosexual behavior

"circulated about Francis Bacon, Sir Anthony Ashley, Philip Lord Stanhope, Lord Roos, and the 4th Earl of Bath." None of the sources he cites actually allude to William Cecil, Lord Roos, however.

28. Bellany, *The Politics of Court Scandal*, 179.
29. Bellany, *Politics of Court Scandal*, 252–54. The only evidence Bellany provides is the 1619 letter from Lorkin, which had reminded people of "the practice upon Sir Thomas Overbury," but this is the only time that Overbury is ever explicitly mentioned in surviving letters about the feud.
30. "Early Stuart Libels," J0–J5, Bellany and McRae.
31. "Cecil, Anne, née Lake, Lady Roos," "Cecil, Frances, countess of Exeter," "Cecil, William, sixteenth Baron Ros," *ODNB*. Roger Lockyer has written the *ODNB* article on Lake, which includes three and a half paragraphs on the scandal. Lockyer blames Lady Lake and Lady Roos entirely, also believing Roos entirely blameless. He used Weldon and Goodman as sources.
32. "Early Stuart Libels," J0, Bellany and McRae.
33. Hoyle, 95–97. Hoyle follows Bellany's *ODNB* accounts.
34. Rickman, *Love, Lust, and License*, 81–83, 86–88, 90.
35. Luthman, 48–49.
36. "James I and Unruly Women," in Amy Leonard and David Whitford, eds., *Embodiment, Identity, and Gender in the Early Modern Age* (London: Routledge, 2021), 70–81.
37. However, the quote about Lady Roos being a pert lady came from Chamberlain and was written *after* the scandals and Lady Roos's accusations had already become public. No one made any comments about Lady Roos's character before her marriage. Levin, 73.
38. She gets the year of the Wimbledon summer wrong, perhaps following Gardiner's account, although it is not listed in the notes. She claims Chamberlain mentioned a scandal about Lord Roos "as early as April 1616" but that he did not mention of what the scandal consisted. However, in that particular letter, Chamberlain discussed some slanderous matter that Lord Roos and his "mother" (specified as Lady Burghley) had said about Secretary Winwood. Levin, 75–76; Chamberlain to Carleton, April 30, 1616, McClure, vol. 1, 626.
39. Taylor, "Price of the Poor's Words," 828.

Bibliography

Archival Sources

British Library
   Additional Manuscripts (Add.)
   Harleian Manuscripts (Harl.)
The National Archives, Kew
   Court of Chancery (C)
   Probate records (PROB)
   State Papers (SP)
   Court of Star Chamber (STAC)
Wellcome Library Collection, London

Printed Primary Sources

Acheson, Katherine, ed. *The Diary of Anne Clifford 1616–1619: A Critical Edition*. London: Garland Publishing, 1995.

Akrigg, G. P. V., ed. *The Letters of King James VI and I*. Berkeley: University of California Press, 1984.

Aylmer, John. *An Harborow for Faithful and Trewe Subiects*. London, 1559.

Barns, Stephen. *Calendar of Deeds Relating to Walthamstow*. Walthamstow: Walthamstow Antiquarian Society 11, 1923.

Bellany, Alastair, and Andrew McRae, eds. "Early Stuart Libels: An Edition of Poetry from Manuscript Sources." *Early Modern Literary Studies Text Series* I (2005), http://purl.oclc.org/emls/texts/libels/.

Birch, Thomas, ed. *Life of Prince Henry Prince of Wales, Eldest Son of King James I*. London: A. Millar, 1760.

Birch, Thomas, ed. *The Court and Times of James the First: Illustrated by Authentic and Confidential Letters from Various Public and Private Collections*. 2 vols. London: Henry Colburn, 1848.

Calendar of State Papers Domestic: Edward VI, Mary and Elizabeth, 1547–80 (*CSP Edward, Mary, Elizabeth*). Ed. Robert Lemon. London: H. M. Stationery Office, 1856. *British History Online*, accessed April 2, 2018, http://www.british-history.ac.uk/cal-state-papers/domestic/edw-eliz/1547-80.

Calendar of State Papers Domestic: Elizabeth, Addenda 1580–1625 (*CSP Elizabeth, Add.*). Ed. Mary Anne Everett Green. London: H. M. Stationery Office, 1872. *British History Online*, accessed April 2, 2018, http://www.british-history.ac.uk/cal-state-papers/domestic/edw-eliz/addenda/1580-1625.

Calendar of State Papers Domestic: James I, 1611–18 (*CSP James*). Ed. Mary Anne Everett Green. London: H. M. Stationery Office, 1858. *British History Online*, accessed April 16, 2021, http://www.british-history.ac.uk/cal-state-papers/domestic/jas1/1611-18/pp430-438.

Calendar of State Papers, Ireland, 1606–1608 (*CSP Ireland*). Ed. C. W. Russell and John P. Prendergast. London: Longman and Co., 1874, 623–70. *British History Online*, accessed April 3, 2020, http://www.british-history.ac.uk/cal-state-papers/ireland/1606-8/pp623-670.

Calendar of State Papers Relating to English Affairs in the Archives of Venice (*CSP Venice*). Ed. Horatio Brown and Allen B. Hinds. London: H. M. Stationery Office, 1904–10. Vols. 11–16. *British History Online*, accessed February 21, 2018, http://www.british-history.ac.uk/cal-state-papers/venice/vol11/pp164-174.

Camden, William. *Diary (1603–1623)*. Ed. Dana Sutton. Philological Museum. Accessed March 9, 2018, http://www.philological.bham.ac.uk/diary/.

Coke, Edward. *Third Part of the Institutes of the Laws of England*. London: E. and R. Brooke, 1748.

Cole, George Watson, ed. *The Gypsies Metamorphosed by Ben Johnson*. New York: Century Co. for Language Association, 1939 (facsimile of contemporary manuscript).

Culpeper, Nicholas. *The English Physitian Enlarged. Or an Astrologo-Physical Discourse of the Vulgar Herbs of this Nation*. London: Thomas Kelly, 1850, org. 1650.

Ellis, Henry, ed. *Original Letters, Illustrative of English History; Including Numerous Royal Letters; from Autographs in the British Museum, and One or Two Other Collections*. 3 vols. London: Harding, Triphook, and Lepard, 1824.

Fenitt, John. *Finetti Philoxenis: Some Choice Observations of Sir John Fenitt, Knight, and Master of Ceremonies of the Two Last Kings, Touching the Reception and Precedence, and Treatment and Audience, the Punctillos and Contrasts, of Forren Ambassadors in England*. London, 1656.

Gardiner, Samuel Rawson, ed. *The Fortescue Papers: Consisting Chiefly of Letters Relating to State Affairs, Collected by Samuel Packer, Secretary to George Villiers, Duke of Buckingham*. Vol. 1. London: Camden Society, 1871.

Gerard, John. *The Herball or Generall Historie of Plantes*. London, 1630s.

Goodman, Godfrey. *The Court of James I*. 2 vols. Ed. John Brewer. London: Richard Bentley, 1839.

Guiseppi, M. S., ed. *Calendar of the Cecil Papers in Hatfield House*. Cecil Papers. 24 vols. London: H. M. Stationery Office, 1940.

Hargrave, Francis, ed. *A Treatise of the Court of Star Chamber by William Hudson as Taken from Collectanea Juridica*. Intro. by Thomas G. Barnes. Birmingham: The Legal Classics Library, 1986.

Historical Manuscript Commission. *Report on the Manuscripts of the Marquess of Downshire* (*Downshire*), vols. 2–6. London: H. M. Stationary Office, 1924–96.

Historical Manuscript Commission. *The Manuscripts of His Grace the Duke of Rutland, preserved at Belvoir Castle* (*Rutland*). 4 vols. London: Printed for H. M. Stationery Office by Eyre and Spottiswoode, 1888–1905.

Historical Manuscript Commission. *Report on the Manuscripts of the Earl of Mar and Kellie* (*Mar and Kellie*). 3 vols. London: H. M. Stationary Office, 1904–30.

Howell, T. B., ed. *A Complete Collection of State Trials and Proceedings for High Treason and Other Crimes and Misdemeanors from the Earliest Period to the Year 1785*. London: T. C. Hansard, 1816.

Knox, John. *The First Blast of the Trumpet against the Monstrous Regiment of Women*. London, 1558.

Lee, Maurice, ed. *Dudley Carleton to John Chamberlain 1603–1624: Jacobean Letters*. New Brunswick: Rutgers University Press, 1972.

Lloyd, David. *State-worthies, or, The States-men and Favourites of England since the Reformation*. London, 1670.
Lodge, Edmund. *Illustrations of British History, Biography, and Manners, in the Reigns of Henry VIII, Edward VI, Mary, Elizabeth, & James I*. 3 vols. London: John Chidley, 1838.
Lyle, J. V., ed. *Acts of the Privy Council of England*. London: H. M. Stationery Office, 1929. *British History Online*, accessed July 5, 2018, http://www.british-history.ac.uk/acts-privy-council/vol36.
Markham, Gervase. *Country Contentments, Or The English Housewife*. London, 1623.
de Mayerne, Theodore. *Opera Medica*, ed. Joseph Browne. London, 1703.
McClure, Norman Egbert, ed. *The Letters of John Chamberlain*. 2 vols. Philadelphia: American Philosophical Society, 1939.
"The Proceedings which Happened Touching the Divorcement between the Lady Frances Howard and Robert, Earl of Essex (c. 1615)." BL Add. 11600, ff. 10–21, at "Manuscript Pamphleteering in Early Modern England," accessed June 21, 2022, https://mpese.ac.uk/t/ProceedingsDivorceHowardEssex.html.
Nuttall, Austin, ed., *The History of the Worthies of England, by Thomas Fuller*. 3 vols. London: T. Tegg, 1840.
Sanderson, William. *A Complete History of the Lives and Reigns of Mary Queen of Scotland and of Her Son and Successor, James the Sixth, King of Scotland, and (after Queen Elizabeth), King of Great Britain, France, and Ireland, the First (Of ever Blessed Memory)*. London: Printed for Humphrey Moseley, Richard Tomlins, and George Sawbridge, 1656.
Sawyer, Edmund, ed. *Memorials of Affairs of State in the reign of Q. Elizabeth and K. James I*. Vol. 3. London: T. Ward, 1725.
Seddon, P. R., ed. *Letters of John Holles, 1587–1632*. 3 vols. Nottingham: Thoroton Society, 1975.
Smith, Logan Persall, ed. *Life and Letters of Sir Henry Wotton*. Oxford: Clarendon Press, 1907.
Spedding, James, ed. *Letters and the Life of Francis Bacon*. Vol. 7. London: Longman, Green, Reader, and Dyer, 1874.
Stevens, Robert, ed. *Letters of Sir Francis Bacon, Baron Verulam, Viscount St. Alban, and Lord High Chancellor of England. Written during the Reign of King James the First*. London: Benjamin Tooke, 1702.
T. E. *Lawes Resolution of Womens Rights*, 1632.
W. M. *The Queens Closet Opened Incomparable Secrets in Physick, Chyrurgery, Preserving, and Candying &c. which were Presented unto the Queen*. London, 1659.
Wakeman, Edward. *Report of a Speech of King James the First in the Court of Star Chamber*. London: Bentley, Wilson, and Fley, 1848.
Weldon, Anthony. *The Court and Character of King James whereunto is now added The Court of King Charles*. London, 1649.
Westminster Abbey. "Thomas and William Cecil, Earls of Exeter." Accessed April 20, 2020. https://www.westminster-abbey.org/abbey-commemorations/commemorations/thomas-william-cecil-earls-of-exeter.
Westminster, London, England, Church of England Baptisms, Marriage, and Burials 1558–1812 (database online). Lehi, UT: Ancestry.com Operations, Inc., 2020.
Wilson, Arthur. *The History of Great Britain, being the Life and Reign of James the First*. London: Richard Lownds, 1653.
Yorke, Philip, earl of Harwicke. *Letters to and from Sir Dudley Carleton during His Embassy in Holland*. London, 1775.

Secondary Sources

Abbott, Mary. *Family Ties: English Families 1540–1920*. New York: Routledge, 1993.

Adair, Richard. *Courtship, Illegitimacy and Marriage in Early Modern England*. Manchester: Manchester University Press, 1996.

Ainsworth, William Harrison. *The Star Camber: An Historical Romance*. 2 vols. Leipzig: Bernard Tauchnitz, 1854.

Alford, Stephen. *Burghley: William Cecil at the Court of Elizabeth I*. New Haven: Yale University Press, 2008.

Amussen, Susan. "Cuckold's Haven: Gender and Inversion in Popular Culture." In Malcolm Smuts, ed., *The Oxford Handbook of the Age of Shakespeare*. Oxford: Oxford University Press, 2016: 528–42.

Amussen, Susan. "Failing at Patriarchy." In Naomi Pullin and Kathryn Woods, eds., *Negotiating Exclusion in Early Modern England, 1550–1800*. New York: Routledge, 2021: 181–199.

Ankarloo, Bengt. "Witch Trials in Northern Europe, 1450–1700." In B. Ankarloo and Stuart Clark, eds., *Witchcraft and Magic in Europe: The Period of the Witch Trials*. Philadelphia: University of Pennsylvania Press, 2002: 55–95.

Baker, J. H. *An Introduction to English Legal History*. London: Butterworts Tolley, 2002.

Barron, Oswald. ed. *Northamptonshire Families*. London: Archibald Constable & Co., 1906.

Bellany, Alastair. "Libel." In Joad Raymond, ed., *The Oxford History of Popular Print Culture*. Oxford: Oxford University Press, 2011: 141–63.

Bellany, Alastair. *The Politics of Court Scandal in Early Modern England: News Culture and the Overbury Affair, 1603–1660*. New York: Cambridge University Press, 2002.

Bellany, Alastair. "The Torture of John Felton, 1628." In Lorna Hutson, ed., *The Oxford Handbook of English Law and Literature, 1500–1700*. Oxford: Oxford University Press, 2017: 549–65.

Bellany, Alastair. "Thinking with Poison." In Malcolm Smuts, ed., *The Oxford Handbook of the Age of Shakespeare*. Oxford: Oxford University Press, 2016: 559–79.

Bellany, Alastair, and Thomas Cogswell. *The Murder of King James*. New Haven: Yale University Press, 2015.

Berry, Helen, and Elizabeth Foyster. "Childless Men in Early Modern England." In Berry and Foyster, eds., *The Family in Early Modern England*. Cambridge: Cambridge University Press, 2007: 158–83.

Blackstone, William. *Commentaries on the Laws of England*. 4 vols. Oxford: Clarendon Press, 1770.

Bray, Alan. *The Friend*. Chicago: University of Chicago Press, 2003.

Brown, Jonathan. "Enemies of Flattery: Velázquez' Portraits of Philip IV." In Robert I. Rotberg and Theodore K. Rabb, eds., *Art and History: Images and Their Meaning*. Cambridge: Cambridge University Press, 1988: 137–54.

Burke, Bernard. *Anecdotes of the Aristocracy, and Patricians*. London: H. Colburn, 1850.

Burke, Bernard. *A Genealogical History of the Dormant, Abeyant, and Extinct Peerages of the English Empire*. London: Harrison, 1866.

Burns, Richard. *Ecclesiastical Law*. London: Stahan and Woodfall, 1788.

Capp, Bernard. "'Jesus Wept' but Did the Englishman? Masculinity and Emotion in Early Modern England." *Past and Present* 224 (2014): 75–108.

Carter, Charles H. "Gondomar: Ambassador to James I." *Historical Journal* 7.2 (1964): 189–208.

Carver, Stephen James. *The Life and Works of the Lancashire Novelist William Harrison Ainsworth, 1805–1882*. Lewiston: The Edwin Mellen Press, 2003.

Chaney, Edward, and Timothy Wilks. *The Jacobean Grand Tour: Early Stuart Travellers in Europe*. New York: I. B. Tauris, 2014.

Cheyney, Edward P. "The Court of Star Chamber." *American Historical Review* 18.4 (1913): 727–50.

Coast, David. *News and Rumour in Jacobean England, 1618–1625*. Manchester: Manchester University Press, 2014.

Cogswell, Thomas. *James I: The Phoenix King*. London: Penguin, 2019.

Collington, Philip D. "Sans Wife: Sexual Anxiety and the Old Man in Shakespeare." In Erin Campbell, ed., *Growing Old in Early Modern Europe*. Aldershot: Ashgate, 2006: 185–207.

Crawford, Patricia. *Blood, Bodies, and Families in Early Modern England*. New York: Routledge, 2014.

Cressy, David. *Dangerous Talk: Scandalous, Seditious, and Treasonable Speech in Pre-Modern England*. Oxford: Oxford University Press, 2010.

Croft, Pauline. *King James I*. London: Palgrave Macmillan, 2002.

Croft, Pauline, ed. *Patronage, Culture and Power: The Early Cecils*. New Haven: Yale University Press, 2002.

Croft, Pauline. "The Reputation of Robert Cecil: Libels, Political Opinion and Popular Awareness in the Early Seventeenth Century." *Transactions of the Royal Historical Society* 1 (1991): 43–69.

Cust, Richard. "Honour and Politics in Early Modern England: The Case of Beaumont v. Hastings." *Past and Present* 149 (1995): 57–94.

Dalton, Charles. *The Life and Times of General Sir Edward Cecil, Viscount Wimbledon, Colone of an English Regiment in the Dutch Service, 1605–1631. and One of His Majesty's Most Honourable Privy Council, 1628–1638*. 2 vols. London: Sampson Low, Marston, Searle, and Rivington, 1885.

Davis, Natalie Zemon. *The Return of Martin Guerre*. Cambridge, MA: Harvard University Press, 1984.

Dennis, George Ravenscroft. *The Cecil Family*. New York: Houghton Mifflin Co., 1914.

Dolan, Frances. *Dangerous Familiars: Representation of Domestic Crime in England 1550–1700*. Ithaca: Cornell University Press, 1994.

van Duinen, Jared. "The Obligations of Governing Masculinity in the Early Stuart Gentry Family: The Barringtons of Hatfield Broad Oak." In Susan Broomhall and Jacqueline Van Gent, eds., *Governing Masculinity in the Early Modern Period: Regulating Self and Others*. Burlington: Ashgate, 2011: 113–30.

Egan, Clare. "Jacobean Star Chamber Records and the Performance of Provincial Libel." In K. J. Kesselring and Natalie Mears, eds., *Star Chamber Matter: An Early Modern Court and Its Records*. London: University of London Press, IHR, 2021: 135–53.

Ellis, S. M. *William Harrison Ainsworth and His Friends*. 2 vols. London: John Lane, 1911.

Elton, G. R. *Star Chamber Stories*. New York: Barnes and Nobles, 1958.

Evans, Jennifer. "'They Are Called Imperfect Men': Male Infertility and Sexual Health in Early Modern England." *Social History of Medicine* 29.2 (2014): 311–32.

Evans, Jennifer, and Sara Read, eds. *Maladies & Medicine: Exploring Health & Healing, 1540–1740*. Barnsley: Pen and Sword, 2017.

Feret, Charles James. *Fulham Old and New*. London: Leadenhall Press, 1900. 3 vols.

Fissell, Mary. "Popular Medical Writing." In Joad Raymond, ed., *The Oxford History of Popular Print Culture*. Oxford: Oxford University Press, 2011: 417–30.

Foster, Joseph, ed. *Alumni Oxonienses 1500–1714*. Oxford: University of Oxford, 1891.

Foyster, Elizabeth. *Manhood in Early Modern: Honour, Sex, and Marriage*. New York: Longman, 1999.

Foyster, Elizabeth. "Parenting Was for Life, Not Just for Childhood: The Role of Parents in the Married Lives of Their Children in Early Modern England." *History* 86 (2001): 313–37.

Gallagher, John. *Learning Languages in Early Modern England*. Oxford: Oxford University Press, 2019.

Gardiner, Samuel R. *History of England from the Accession of James I to the Civil War 1603–1642*, Vol. 3: *1616–1621*. London: Longman, Green, and Co., 1883.

Gaskill, Malcolm. *Witchfinders: A Seventeenth-Century English Tragedy*. Cambridge, MA: Harvard University Press, 2005.

Gibbons, Katy. "English Catholics and the Continent." In Malcolm Smuts, ed., *The Oxford Handbook of the Age of Shakespeare*. Oxford: Oxford University Press, 2016: 367–83.

Gowing, Laura. *Domestic Dangers: Women, Words, and Sex in Early Modern London*. Oxford: Clarendon Press, 1998.

Guy, J. A. *The Court of Star Chamber and Its Records to the Reign of Elizabeth I*. London: H. M. Stationary Office, 1984.

Haynes, Alan. *Robert Cecil Earl of Salisbury, 1563–1612: Servant of Two Sovereigns*. London: Peter Owen, 1989.

Herrup, Cynthia. *A House in Gross Disorder. Sex, Law and the Second Earl of Castlehaven*. Oxford: Oxford University Press, 1999.

Henderson, Paula. "A Shared Passion: The Cecils and Their Gardens." In Pauline Croft, ed., *Patronage, Culture and Power: The Early Cecils*. New Haven: Yale University Press, 2002: 99–120.

Hervey, Mary F. S. *The Life Correspondence and Collections of Thomas Howard Earl of Arundel*. Cambridge: Cambridge University Press, 1921.

Higham, C. S. S. *Wimbledon Manor House under the Cecils*. London: Longmans, 1962.

Hille, Christine. *Visions of the Courtly Body: The Patronage of George Villiers, Duke of Buckingham, and the Triumph of Painting at the Stuart Court*. Berlin: Akademie Verlag, 2012.

Hoyle, R. W. "Fountains of Justice: James I, Charles I, and Equity." In Michael Lobban, Joanne Begiato, and Adrian Green, eds., *Law, Lawyers, and Litigants in Early Modern England: Essays in Memory of Christopher W. Brooks*. Cambridge: Cambridge University Press, 2019: 79–113.

Ibbetson, David. *Edward Coke, Roman Law, and the Law of Libel*. In Lorna Hutson, ed., *The Oxford Handbook of English Law and Literature, 1500–1700*. Oxford: Oxford University Press, 2017: 487–506.

Ingram, Martin. *Carnal Knowledge: Regulating Sex in England, 1470–1600*. Cambridge: Cambridge University Press, 2017.

Ingram, Martin. *Church Courts, Sex, and Marriage in England 1570–1640*. Cambridge: Cambridge University Press, 1987.

Ingram, Martin. "Law, Litigants and the Construction of 'Honour': Slander Suits in Early Modern England." In Peter Coss, ed., *The Moral World of the Law*. New York: Cambridge University Press, 2000: 134–160.

Ingram, Martin. "Ridings, Rough Music and Mocking Rhymes in Early Modern England." In Barry Reay, ed., *Popular Culture in Seventeenth-Century England*. London: St. Martin's Press, 1985: 166–97.

Kaplan, Lindsay M. *The Culture of Slander in Early Modern England*. Cambridge: Cambridge University Press, 1997.

Kesselring, Krista. "No Greater Provocation? Adultery and the Mitigation of Murder in English Law." *Law and History Review* 34.1 (2016): 199–225.

Kesselring, Krista. *Star Chamber Reports: BL Harley MS 2143*. List and Index Society, Special Series 57, 2018.

Kesselring, K. J., and Natalie Mears. *Star Chamber Matter: An Early Modern Court and Its Records*. London: University of London Press, IHR, 2021.
Kesselring, Krista, and Tim Stretton. *Marriage, Separation, and Divorce in England, 1500–1700*. Oxford: Oxford University Press, 2022.
Kesselring, Krista, and Tim Stretton. *Married Women and the Law: Coverture in England and the Common Law World*. Montreal: McGill-Queen's University Press, 2013.
Knight, Caroline. "The Cecils at Wimbledon." In Pauline Croft, ed., *Patronage, Culture and Power: The Early Cecils*. New Haven: Yale University Press, 2002: 47–66.
Krugler, John D. *English and Catholic: The Lords Baltimore in the Seventeenth Century*. Baltimore: Johns Hopkins University Press, 2004.
Laslett, Peter. *The World We Have Lost, Further Explored*. London: Routledge, 2000.
Lee, Maurice. *Great Britain's Solomon: James VI and I in His Three Kingdoms*. Urbana: University of Illinois Press, 1990.
Leeds, Barroll J. *Anna of Denmark, Queen of England: A Cultural Biography*. Philadelphia: University of Philadelphia, 2001.
LeNeve, John, ed. *Monumenta Anglicana, 1600–1649*. London, 1719.
Leong, Elaine. "'Herbals she peruseth': Reading Medicine in Early Modern England." *Renaissance Studies* 28.4 (2016): 556–78.
Levin, Carole. "James I and Unruly Women." In Amy Leonard and David Whitford, eds., *Embodiment, Identity, and Gender in the Early Modern Age*. London: Routledge, 2021: 70–81.
Lindley, David. *The Trials of Frances Howard: Fact and Fiction at the Court of King James*. London: Routledge, 1993.
Loades, David. *The Cecils: Privilege and Power Behind the Throne*. Kew: The National Archives, 2007.
Lockyer, Roger. *Buckingham: The Life and Political Career of George Villiers, First Duke of Buckingham, 1592–1628*. Harlow: Longman, 1981.
Loomie, Albert. *Spain and the Jacobean Catholics*, Vol. II: *1613–1624*. London: Catholic Record Society, 1978.
Low, Jennifer. *Manhood and the Duel: Masculinity in Early Modern Drama and Culture*. New York: Palgrave Macmillan, 2003.
Luthman, Johanna. *Love, Madness, and Scandal: The Life of Frances Coke Villiers, Viscountess Purbeck*. Oxford: Oxford University Press, 2017.
Lysons, Daniel. *The Environs of London*, Vol. 1: *County of Surrey*. London: T. Cadell and W. Davies, 1792. *British History Online*, accessed March 9, 2021, http://www.british-history.ac.uk/london-environs/vol1/pp519-540.
Macfarlane, Alan. *Marriage and Love in England: Modes of Reproduction 1300–1840*. Cambridge: Blackwell, 1986.
Matthews-Grieco, Sara. "Picart's Browbeaten Husband in 17th-Century France: Cuckoldry in Context." In Sara Matthews-Grieco, ed., *Cuckoldry, Impotence and Adultery in Europe (15th–17th century)*. Aldershot: Ashgate, 2014: 249–89.
McIlvenna, Una. "Poison, Pregnancy, and Protestants: Gossip and Scandal at the Early Modern French Court." In Heather Kerr and Claire Walker, eds., *Fama and Her Sisters: Gossip and Rumor in Early Modern Europe*. Turnhout: Brepols Publishers, 2015: 137–60.
Newton, Hannah. *The Sick Child in Early Modern England, 1580–1720*. Oxford: Oxford University Press, 2012.
Nichols, John. *The Progresses, Processions, and Magnificent Festivities of King James the First*. 4 vols. London: J. B. Nichols, 1828.
Nichols, John. *The Progresses and Public Processions of Queen Elizabeth*. 3 vols. London: J. B. Nichols, 1823.

Nicholls, Mark, and Penry Williams. *Sir Walter Raleigh in Life and Legend.* New York: Continuum, 2011.

North, Susan. *Sweet and Clean: Bodies and Clothes in Early Modern England.* Oxford: Oxford University Press, 2020.

Oxford Dictionary of National Biography (*ODNB*). Online version at https://www.oxforddnb.com/.

Peltonen, Markku. *The Duel in Early Modern England: Civility, Politeness and Honour.* New York: Cambridge University Press, 2003.

Powell, W. R., ed. *A History of the County of Essex*, Vol. 6. London: Victoria County History, 1973.

Questier, Michael. *Catholicism and Community in Early Modern England: Politics, Aristocratic Patronage and Religion, c. 1550–1640.* Cambridge: Cambridge University Press, 2006.

Questier, Michael. *Dynastic Politics & the British Reformations, 1558–1630.* Oxford: Oxford University Press, 2019.

Redworth, Glyn. *The Prince and the Infanta: The Cultural Politics of the Spanish Match.* New Haven: Yale University Press, 2003.

Richardson, R. C. *Household Servants in Early Modern England.* Manchester: Manchester University Press, 2010.

Rickman, Johanna. *Love, Lust, and License in Early Modern England: Illicit Sex and the Nobility.* Burlington: Ashgate, 2008.

Rickman, Johanna. "'He Would Never Consent in His Heart': Child Marriages in Early Modern England." *Journal of the History of Children and Youth* 6 (2013): 293–313.

Scarisbrick, Diane. *Tudor and Jacobean Jewellry.* London: Tate Publishing, 1995.

Scofield, Cora. "Accounts of Star Chamber Dinners, 1593–94." *American Historical Review* 88 (1899): 83–95.

Scofield, Cora. *A Study of the Court of Star Chamber.* Chicago: University of Chicago Press, 1900).

Shapiro, Barbara. "Law and the Evidentiary Environment." In Lorna Hutson, ed., *The Oxford Handbook of English Law and Literature, 1500–1700.* Oxford: Oxford University Press, 2017: 257–76.

Sharpe, James. *The Bewitching of Anne Gunter: A Horrible and True Story of Deception, Witchcraft, Murder, and the King of England.* New York: Routledge, 2000.

Sharpe, James. *Witchcraft in Early Modern England.* London: Routledge, 2019.

Sharpe, Kevin. *Image Wars: Promoting Kings and Commonwealths in England, 1603–1660.* New Haven: Yale University Press, 2010.

Shepard, Alexandra. *Accounting for Oneself: Worth, Status, and the Social Order in Early Modern England.* Oxford: Oxford University Press, 2018.

Shepard, Alexandra. "Brokering Fatherhood: Illegitimacy and Paternal Rights and Responsibilities in Early Modern England." In Steve Hindle, Alexandra Shepard, and John Walter, eds., *Remaking English Society: Social Relation and Social Change in Early Modern England.* Woodbridge: The Boydell Press, 2013: 41–63.

Shepard, Alexandra. *Meanings of Manhood in Early Modern England.* New York: Oxford University Press, 2003.

Shepard, Alexandra. "From Anxious Patriarchs to Refined Gentlemen? Manhood in Britain, c. 1500–1700." *Journal of British Studies* 44.2 (2005): 281–93.

Somerset, Anne. *Unnatural Murder: Poison at the Court of James I.* London: Weidenfeld & Nicolson, 1997.

Smuts, R. Malcolm, and Luc Duerloo. "Occasio's Lock of Hair: The Artist and the Ruler in Pursuit of Opportunity." In Smuts and Duerloo, eds., *The Age of Rubens: Diplomacy,*

Dynastic Politics, and the Visual Arts in Early Seventeenth-Century Europe. Turnhout, Belgium: Brepols Publishers, 2016: 5–17.

Staub, Susan. *Nature's Cruel Stepdames: Murderous Women in the Street Literature of Seventeenth Century England.* Pittsburg: Duquesne University Press, 2005.

Stewart, Alan. *The Cradle King: A Life of James VI and I.* London: Chatto and Windus, 2003.

Stobart, Anne. *Household Medicine in Seventeenth-Century England.* London: Bloomsbury Academic, 2016.

Stone, Lawrence. *The Crisis of the Aristocracy, 1558–1641.* Oxford: Clarendon Press, 1965.

Strange, Diane. "From Private Sin to Public Shame: Sir John Digby and the Use of Star Chamber in Northamptonshire and Bedfordshire, 1610." *Midland History* 44 (2019): 39–55.

Stretton, Tim. "Women, Legal Records, and the Problem of the Lawyer's Hand." *Journal of British Studies* 58.4 (2019): 684–700.

Stretton, Tim. *Women Waging Law in Elizabethan England.* Cambridge: Cambridge University Press, 1998.

Strocchia, Sharon. *Forgotten Healers: Women and the Pursuit of Health in Late Renaissance Italy.* Cambridge, MA: Harvard University Press, 2019.

Taylor, Hillary. "The Price of the Poor's Words: Social Relations and the Economics of Deposing for Ones 'Betters' in Early Modern England." *Economic History Review* 72.3 (2019): 828–47.

Thomas, Courtney Erin. *If I Lose Mine Honour, I Lose Myself: Honour among the Early Modern English Elite.* Toronto: University of Toronto Press, 2017.

Thrush, Andrew. "The Fall of Tomas Howard, 1st Earl of Suffolk and the Revival of Impeachment in the Parliament of 1621." *Parliamentary History* 32.2 (2018): 197–211.

Thrush, Andrew. "The Personal Rule of James I, 1611–1620." In Thomas Cogswell, Richard Cust, and Peter Lake, eds., *Politics, Religion and Popularity in Early Stuart England.* Cambridge: Cambridge University Press, 2002: 84–102.

Thrush, Andrew, and John P. Ferris. *The History of Parliament: The House of Commons 1604–1629* (*HPO*). Cambridge: Cambridge University Press, 2010. Accessed at History of Parliament, https://www.historyofparliamentonline.org.

Toulalan, Sarah. "'Elderly yeares cause a Total dispaire of Conception': Old Age, Sex and Infertility in Early Modern England." *Social History of Medicine* 29.2 (2015): 333–59.

Towshend, Dorothea. *Life and Letters of Endymion Porter: Sometime Gentleman of the Bedchamber to King Charles the First.* London: T. Fischer Unwin, 1897.

Uszkalo, Kristen. *Being Bewitched: A True Tale of Madness, Witchcraft, and Property Development Gone Wrong.* Kirksville, MO: Truman State University Press, 2017.

Walters, Laura. "Oduardo Fialetti (1573–c.1638): The Interrelation of Venetian Art and Anatomy, and His Importance in England." Unpublished PhD dissertation. 2 vols. University of St. Andrews, 2009.

Warneke, Sara. *Images of the Educational Traveller in Early Modern England.* New York: E. J. Brill, 1995.

Westminster Abbey at https://www.westminster-abbey.org/abbey-commemorations/commemorations/thomas-william-cecil-earls-of-exeter, accessed April 10, 2021.

Willson, D. Harris. *King James VI and I.* London: Jonathan Cape, 1956.

Wilson, Miranda. *Poison's Dark Works in Renaissance England.* Lanham, MD: Bucknell University Press, 2014.

Wiltenburg, Joy. "Soundings of Laughter in Early Modern England: Women, Men, and Everyday Uses of Humor." *Early Modern Women: An Interdisciplinary Journal* 10.2 (2016): 22–41.

Wrigley, E. A., R. S. Davies, J. E. Oeppen, and R. S. Schofield. *English Population History from Family Reconstitution 1580–1837.* New York: Cambridge University Press, 1997.

Worth, George. *William Harrison Ainsworth.* New York: Twayne Publishers, 1972.

Young, Michael. *James VI and I and the History of Homosexuality.* Basingstroke: Macmillan, 2000.

Youngs, Deborah. "'A Besy Woman…and Full of Lawe': Female Litigants in Early Tudor Star Chamber." *Journal of British Studies* 58 (2019): 735–50.

Picture Credits

1. Thomas Cecil, earl of Exeter. Unknown artist. © National Portrait Gallery, London.

2.1. A portrait of a child, said to be Georgianna Cecil. Cornelius Janssens van Ceulen, 1617. The Burghley House Collection. In the top right corner, it says "Aetatis 1 ¼ An. 1617." Georgi-Anna would have been a little over a year old in the fall of 1617.

2.2. Sir Ralph Winwood. Michiel van Miereveldt. © National Portrait Gallery, London. Winwood, King James's Secretary of State tasked with the foreign correspondence, was Sir Thomas Lake's colleague and rival. To Lake's chagrin, Winwood befriended Roos.

6.1. View of Wimbledon House, 1678. Etching by Henry Winstansley. The Trustees of the British Museum. The Tudor period ornate decorations on the roof had been removed by the later 1600s.

6.2. Plan of Wimbledon House and the grounds, Wimbledon. Drawing by Robert Smythson, 1609. RIBA Collections.

11. King James VI of Scotland and I of England. Daniel Mytens, 1621. © National Portrait Gallery, London.

14.1. Frances Cecil (née Brydges), countess of Exeter. Published by William Faithorne, after Anthony van Dyck, 1630s. © National Portrait Gallery, London.

14.2. Tomb of Anne Lake. St. Leonard's Church, Rodney Stoke, Somerset. Photo: Michael Statham.

14.3. Effigy of Anne Lake. St. Leonard's Church, Rodney Stoke, Somerset. Photo: Michael Statham.

Index

Note: Figures are indicated by an italic "*f*", following the page number.

For the benefit of digital users, indexed terms that span two pages (e.g., 52–53) may, on occasion, appear on only one of those pages.